THE JOURNALS

OF

MAJOR-GEN. C. G. GORDON, C.B.,

AT KARTOUM.

THE JOURNALS

OF

MAJOR-GEN. C. G. GORDON, C.B.,

AT KARTOUM.

PRINTED FROM THE ORIGINAL MSS.

INTRODUCTION AND NOTES

BY

A. EGMONT HAKE.

WITH PORTRAIT, TWO MAPS, AND THIRTY ILLUSTRATIONS AFTER SKETCHES
BY GENERAL GORDON.

LONDON:
DARF PUBLISHERS LIMITED
1984

First published 1885

Reprinted 1984

ISBN 1 85077 0387

Printed by A. Wheaton & Co. Ltd
Exeter

PREFACE.

THE work of editing these Journals is at an end; it only remains now for me to thank one of my oldest and most valued friends, whose assistance in every way I wish most thoroughly to acknowledge: this is Mr. Godfrey Thrupp. When it became obvious that the public demand for the work made its completion in so short a time impossible—as the conscientious achievement of one man—he generously came forward. His knowledge of the East and his deep interest in the subject made him an invaluable colleague.

A. EGMONT HAKE.

June 11, 1885.

TABLE OF CONTENTS.

Book IV.

Book V.

Book VI.

INTRODUCTION.

"Friends, Romans, countrymen, lend me your ears;
I come to bury Cæsar, not to praise him.
The evil that men do lives after them;
The good is oft interred with their bones.
*   *   *   *   *
Good friends, sweet friends, let me not stir you up
To such a sudden flood of mutiny.
They that have done this deed are honourable;
What private griefs they had, alas! I know not,
That made them do it; they are wise and honourable
And will, no doubt, with reasons answer you.
*   *   *   *   *
But were I Brutus,
And Brutus Antony, there were an Antony
Would ruffle up your spirits, and put a tongue
In every wound of Cæsar, that should move
The stones of Rome to rise and mutiny."

THESE grand lines force themselves upon me, though maybe their analogy is incomplete. Mark Antony was a casuist, and pleaded the cause of revenge; I am only earnest in the cause of justice. Yet I trust in my pleading to enable Englishmen to realise how great and how sad is the loss of Charles Gordon, not only to those who loved him, but to the cause of suffering humanity. Gordon is dead. We cannot bring him back to life. Yet from his death we may learn at least how fit he was to teach us while he lived, how fit to hold his country's honour in his hand, how fit to judge of what was right and what was wrong. His journals are his last words to the world as much as they are instruction and information to his Government, and Englishmen who value England's honour may well read them with a heavy heart—with eyes dimmed by tears. I say Gordon is dead, and we cannot bring him back to life, but we can do much he would have done for us *had he been allowed to live.*

His journals tell us how we can best repair mischief already done (and I understand his words to apply rather to the English people than to the Government which represents them), and they tell us what is best for the Soudan. In the interest of this unhappy land he devoted much of his life; in its interest he died. Let us then compare the opposite conditions under which the people existed during Gordon's presence and absence, and in doing this let us mark well what Gordon said during his life, and what his journals say for him now that he is dead.

*
* *

Gordon used to tell the story of how, when Said Pasha, Viceroy of Egypt before Ismail, went up to the Soudan, so discouraged and horrified was he at the misery of the people, that at Berber he threw his guns into the river, declaring he would be no party to such oppression. In this spirit Gordon went there as Governor of the Equator in 1874, and in this spirit he expressed his views on the duties of foreigners in the service of Oriental States. His ardent and unstudied words are worthy of the deepest study. They breathe the kindliest wisdom, the most prudent philanthropy; and it would be well if those whose lot is thrown in barbarous lands would take them for a constant guide. To accept government, only if by so doing you benefit the race you rule; to lead, not drive the people to a higher civilisation; to establish only such reforms as represent the spontaneous desire of the mass; to abandon relations with your native land; to resist other governments, and keep intact the sovereignty of the State whose bread you eat; to represent the native when advising Ameer, Sultan or Khedive, on any question which your own or any foreign government may wish solved; and in this to have for prop and guide that which is universally right throughout the world, that which is best for the people of the State you serve.

Such were Gordon's sentiments when he first entered upon his task; well would it have been for Egypt, England, and the world, had his successors taken them to heart and made them their ideal. In such a case the peace, the happiness he brought to the Soudan might still have been preserved.

Never perhaps in the histories of barbarous rule were the ideals of justice and truth more needed than at this date (1874). Seven-eighths of the population were slaves; the country swarmed with slave-hunters and slave-dealers; and district governors, greedy for pelf, aided and abetted them in their raids. So crushed were the remaining population that they regarded all comers as their foes; so destitute that they were ready and willing to exchange their own kin for cattle or for grain. Their flocks and herds, like their kindred, had been robbed. To sow they were afraid, for governors and slave-hunters never let them reap; and if perchance they cultivated ground, it was a mere patch hidden in some distant nook out of the enemy's way. The maxims of their rulers, prior to Gordon's advent, had been that if the natives—poor unenlightened blacks—did not act in the most civilised fashion, then must they be punished; and when these rulers for their own acts were brought to book, they cited the native custom of "plunder no offence" in their own excuse. How the governors, in league with dealers and hunters, had acted up to these precepts, was apparent enough in the desolation which reigned around, for amid the jungle of stunted trees and tall grasses not a soul was to be seen—all driven away by the slavers in past years. With the Egyptian Government such was the estimate of this waste, that it did service as a colony for misdemeanants among Arab troops; and hundreds of these died from the damp and the dulness of the scene. In other parts less than 100 men dared not move from one station to another, in fear of the retaliating tribes, and so far were these stations apart that it took six weeks to communicate one with the other. In addition to this certain chieftains who inhabited the borders of the great lakes were engaged in wars in which the capture of slaves was the main motive.

Such, in brief, was the state of affairs between Kartoum and the Lakes when Gordon made his journey thither; yet it afforded in no way the only instance of oppression, anarchy or misrule in these lands. In Kordofan and Darfour[1] the slave-traffic was even more formidable than here. In the latter

[1] Land of Fors; *Hill*, 62.

province a war between the slave-dealers and the Sultan's troops was just concluded, and the two vast lands, with Dar Fertit,[2] had been made into a Hukumdircat, or Governor-General's district responsible to Cairo, and separated from the Soudan. But Gordon's work was for the present confined to laying down a chain of posts between Gondokoro and the Lakes, and by this and other means contributing to the welfare of the tribes and the confusion of the slavers. To gain the confidence of the natives was his first care; and to this end he ventured alone and unarmed into those isolated spots, whither not less than a hundred men had dared to go. Then he showed the people how they might sow their grain without fear, supplying them with enough to live on until their wants were met; he also taught them the use of money, and gave them task-work. It was infinitely little, he said, among such a mass, but it was at any rate something, and might perhaps enable him to solve the question whether the negroes would work sufficiently to keep themselves if life and property were secured. To give them this protection, he seized all convoys of slaves, and ivory and cattle coming from the south, punished the slave-dealers, or converted them into troops, for they were hard, active fellows, the remnant of an ancient race; and designing and despotic governors he despatched to Cairo or Kartoum. The slaves themselves, until he could deliver them over to their kinsfolk, he kept; the cattle and the ivory he confiscated, and with the proceeds swelled the Government treasury.

It would seem the fate of those who devote their lives to the cause of humanity to be foiled instead of aided in their aim. In all his efforts for the good of these blacks Gordon met with every form of interference whence he might at least expect support. Ismail Pasha Yacoub, the Governor-General of the Soudan, jealous of the new Governor of the Equator and fearful of exposure from so conscientious a servant of the State, put every obstacle in Gordon's way; and the Khedive himself was not always mindful of the many difficulties to be encountered. But Gordon said, to blame the Khedive for

[2] Land of Fertits: *Hill*, 242.

his actions you must blame his people, and blame their Creator; they act after their kind, and in the fashion they were made. So that he took little heed of all this. He was content to let it be widely known that the motto of his province would henceforth be Hurryat (liberty); and this meant that no man should interfere with another, that there should be an end to kidnapping and all plunder, an end to despotic Pashas; and those who objected were told that the motto included *their* liberty to quit. Moreover, he was of opinion that those who annexed the province needed as much civilisation as those they attempted to civilise; and, whenever it was necessary, in the interests of his people, he never hesitated to show them that this was his view.

Still, though he succeeded in giving peace and happiness to the people, in reforming the cruelties of Mudirs and Pashas, in settling the disputes of warring chiefs, and in laying down the chain of posts between Gondokoro and the Lakes: in making all these beneficent reforms, his heart was ever burdened with the thought of how this new and unaccustomed good would affect the people and their lands when, as time went on, himself and his influence were removed, and his successors, who understood his high intent as little as they understood the people themselves, ruled in his stead. "I think, what right have I to coax the natives to be quiet for them to fall into the hands of rapacious Pashas? I think sometimes that through my influence I am seducing the natives into a position where they will be a prey to my Arab successor. They would never do for an Arab what they do for me. I make friends with the tribes right and left."

But, apart from these feelings, he was not satisfied; his success in his own province had been complete, but, instead of meeting with co-operation from the adjoining Soudan, he had encountered nothing but interference from its then Governor-General, Ismail Pasha Yacoub, to whose interests it was to let slavery go on. For this reason, therefore, Gordon, after three years' labour, resigned his post as Governor of the Equator. But the step was taken in a wavering spirit; and these are among his last words ere he left: "By retiring I do not aid anything; by staying I keep my province safe from injustice and cruelty in some degree. Why should I fear? Is man stronger than God? Things have come to such a pass in these Mussulman countries that a crisis must come about soon."

These significant words, so terribly confirmed less than ten years later, were uttered in September of 1876.

Gordon's resignation soon led to his reinstatement on terms more fitted to his views. In the new position he felt strongly that, great as was the trust and the almost superhuman work expected of him, if he did not entirely succeed at least he would not be hampered. He was not only appointed Governor-General of the Soudan in Ismail Pasha Yacoub's stead; he was given authority such as none had previously enjoyed—complete power, civil and military, with the life or death of his subjects in his hand; and no man dare enter his dominions without special leave. He had stipulated that this supreme command should be independent of Cairo, for he knew the Egyptian authorities to be in favour of the slave-trade. The undefined territory now his had hitherto been subject to several governments—Arab, Egyptian, Turkish. Henceforth Soudan was to mean the vast territory limited on the north by Upper Egypt, on the south by the Lakes, on the south-east by Abyssinia, on the east by the Red Sea, and on the west to extend beyond Kordofan and the newly acquired sultanate of Darfour—the whole roughly estimated at more than 1600 miles in length, and 700 miles in width. There were to be three Vakeels or Sub-Governors: one for the original Soudan, another for Darfour, and a third for the Red Sea, or Eastern Soudan.

The suppression of slavery, in which he had been so far successful in his own province, and the improvement of communications, which he had long declared to be the one means by which that traffic could be effectually checked, were the two objects to which Gordon was to specially direct his aim.

Remembering his recent experiences, he was fully prepared for the condition of his new subjects. In his predecessor, Ismail Pasha Yacoub, he had already recognised the quintessence of Egyptian cupidity and Turkish misrule—the main cause of the people's ruin. The experiences of the first months of his administration only served to confirm his worst fears; whithersoever he looked he saw an enlarged picture of native misery and destitution, of alien cruelty and oppression he had before witnessed. He saw that the Circassian Pashas, the Bashi-Bazouks, the Arab soldiery, the slave-hunters in Darfour and in the Bahr Gazelle, were by their acts fast goading the people to revolt; that tribes which without their interference would have been at peace were now at war; and that towns which under proper rule would have flourished were starving or besieged. On every hand he found caravans of packed slaves hungering and parching in the sun, far from their homes and far from their goal, unless that goal were death; deserts strewn with innumerable bones; armed bands of slave-hunters, dogged by the vulture-like dealers, waiting and watching for further prey; and over all these reigned the miscreant spirit of Zubair, the slave-king, now ostensibly a prisoner at Cairo for past deeds, but actually aiding and abetting this cruel war against man through his son Suleiman, the chief of his deserted band. To remove Zubair's influence was as impossible of achievement as to cut off the demand for slaves at Cairo, Constantinople, or Stamboul; but to break up Suleiman and his band lay within Gordon's grasp, and, as one of the main causes of trouble, he made it his foremost aim. How he did this by the simple power of his presence, and how Suleiman and his six thousand, after signal submission, again broke out into open revolt so soon as Gordon's presence was required elsewhere, affords one of the most striking examples of the personal influence he had acquired. Alone and himself unarmed he had temporarily succeeded in disarming these rebels; but, this failing in permanent use, he effectually quelled them in battle; then, to show his people, his Government, and the world how great a wrong this slavery was, he ordered the summary execution of the ringleaders. "With the death of Zubair's son," he said, "there is an end of the slave-trade." Never had the Government such a chance of preventing its renewal. He had disbanded the Bashi-Bazouks, he had dismissed the peculating

Mudirs and Pashas; and when he left the country, after a three years' reign, the people blessed him, and begged him to return.

Had he been allowed to act according to the letter and the spirit of the Firman he received, it is most probable that he would never this second time have resigned; but the overthrow of Ismail at Cairo and the dissolution of the Dual Control had with other changes brought new law-makers for the Soudan. Ismail, though in many respects an imprudent ruler, had at least the merit of believing in his English Governor-General, and of supporting him whenever it lay in his power. Gordon's lonely ride into the slavers' camp at Shaka had fired the ex-Khedive's imagination, and it was observed that, whenever the Court Pashas attempted to criticise Gordon's methods of rule, the Khedive referred them to this deed. Moreover, he openly acknowledged him as his superior, and fought his battles as those of one who was above the murmur of men. Gordon has, indeed, himself recorded how the Khedive sent him a congratulatory letter on the suppression of Suleiman, adding that during the time of his rule the ex-Khedive supported him through thick and thin against his own Pashas and his own people; and certain it is that to the files of petitions sent to him against Gordon he would never listen. But when Towfik was set up it was a different affair. Never was he heard to mention Zubair's name. As for the slave-trade, it was equally ignored. Nay, worse than this, the Cairo Pashas, powerless in Ismail's time, had now full sway, and it being in their interests that the slave-trade should revive, the choice of Gordon's successor was settled among themselves. It fell to Raouf Pasha, a man whom Sir Samuel Baker had already exposed as a murderer, and whom Gordon had in 1877 turned out of Harrar for acts of oppression. The appointment, therefore, meant nothing more nor less than a declaration in favour of the slavers; and it was because Gordon feared this result that he had said six months before, viz., in April 1879, that "If the liberation of slaves takes place in 1884, and *if the present system of government goes on, there cannot fail to be a revolt of the whole country.*" And again he said in 1878, "There is no doubt that if the Government of France and England pay more attention to the Soudan and see that justice is done, the disruption of the Soudan from Cairo is only a matter of time. This disruption, moreover, will not end the troubles for the Soudanese, though their allies in Lower Egypt will carry on their efforts in Cairo itself." [3]

How prophetic these words have since proved to be it is needless to say. In April 1880, just a year later, Gordon wrote, as he left for India:—

> I have learned with equal pain and indignation that the Khedive and his subordinate officers have permitted the resuscitation of the slave-trade in Darfour and the other provinces of central and equatorial Africa, and that fresh parties of slave-hunters are forming at Obeyed in Kordofan, and that every order which I gave concerning the suppression of this abomination has been cancelled.
>
> The two missionaries—Wilson and Felkin—who have lately come down from Uganda, passed through these districts, and they tell me that the slave-hunters are all ready to start once more upon their detestable trade, and that there is a very strong feeling abroad that all the Europeans, including of course Gessi and the other officers who acted under me, are about to be turned out of the country. This report, even if it be untrue, will largely serve to lower the authority of the European officers, and to render their work more difficult.
>
> This news is very disheartening, especially when one realises the immense misery which will ensue to the remains of these poor tribes of helpless negroes.

The events which followed on these first examples of a wholesale perversion of Gordon's methods have proved over and over again the value of his warning words; it is worthy of special remark that among the causes of the great rebellion which ensued, as interpreted by the English Government in their history of the insurrection of the False Prophet,[4] not the religious fanaticism of the native tribes has a foremost place, but the venality and oppression by Egyptian officials, the unjust manner of collecting the taxes, and, *above all, the suppression of the slave-trade, which Gordon had repeatedly said must lead to future troubles, unless* ***accompanied*** *by* ***a*** *proper system of government.*

Thus the condition into which the Soudan drifted during

[3] Hill's 'Colonel Gordon in Central Africa,' p. 373.
[4] See Appendix to Book IV.

Gordon's absence was due to deliberate neglect of the precautions he had urged. Had the Egyptian Government watched and warded off the regeneration of the slavers after Gordon dealt his final blow in Suleiman's death; had they set their face against the oppression and cupidity of their own officials, the Soudan might still have been at peace, as Gordon left it in 1879. But the new rulers were in favour of slavery, in favour of oppression, in favour of *backsheesh;* and "a revolt of the whole country" was their reward.

* * *

It is needless to do more than briefly recall the events preceding those related by Gordon himself in these Journals. Every one remembers his going, and the triumph of his journey and reception in the Soudan; the wide welcome which his first Proclamation received, and the fortunes of the peace policy he at first endeavoured to pursue. Every one remembers how, before he had been in Kartoum a week, he issued a further Proclamation, warning the rebellious against forcing him to severe measures. The Sheikhs and people were anxious to be loyal; without Government protection they would be forced, in self-defence, to join the Mahdi. This view Colonel Stewart subsequently confirmed during his journey up the White Nile. Zubair had been asked for, because he was the only man of enough prestige to hold the country together. A Pasha among the Shaggyeh irregulars, a tribe wavering between loyalty and revolt, and blockaded at Halfeyeh, outside the city,—to him were open sources of information closed to the English Governor-General. Zubair would prove stronger than the Mahdi, and the Mahdi must be "smashed up;" otherwise, not only would peace and the evacuation of Kartoum be impossible, but Egypt itself would be in danger. This state of affairs and the measures necessary for a new departure being alike unacceptable to Her Majesty's Government, Gordon thereupon used, as he had every right to do, the resources to his hand. His predictions as to what would result if Zubair were not sent up were soon realised. The rebels gradually gathered round the city, besieged its outlying suburbs, and cut the communications. His suffering subjects, unable to hold out, were either killed or, escaping, went over to the enemy. In some cases he managed to drive the rebels from the trenches of Kartoum, and even to relieve the beleaguered villages, and return loaded with ammunition and stores; in others, his army of defence, composed largely of Egyptians and Bashi-Bazouks, encountered miserable defeat. These expeditions were made in small steamers, armoured with boiler plates and carrying mountain guns, with wooden mantlets of his own contriving. On one occasion the rebels so harassed the city that Gordon resolved on a sortie; but no sooner had the rebels retired to a place of safety than five of his own commanders charged back on their men and aided the rebels, who suddenly leaped from their hiding-place, driving the affrighted army back to Kartoum. In this treacherous and cowardly affair the loss on both sides was great; but the disgrace was the besieged, and of it they showed their sense by crying out for justice on the traitors. Two of them were tried and found guilty, and were shot by the men they had outraged. Henceforth the city was exposed to the attacks of the Mahdi's troops; the streets, the Mission House, the Palace were hourly shelled; citizens died as they passed from end to end; but the Governor-General, always exposed as in old days, though daily inspecting the lines or pacing the Palace roof, escaped unhurt.

Meantime the strength of the rebellion grew with every day; the Mahdi, still at El Obeyed, had despatched his emissaries in all directions; around Suakin, Berber, Shendy, Kassala, the rebels rapidly recruited their ranks. The would-be loyal fell from sheer collapse; they were unable to help themselves. All chance of relief was gone, and the rebel leaders re-echoed in jeering tones the Governor-General's reiterated words, "The English are coming." Then Berber, the main link between Kartoum and Cairo, cried out for help, but, like those at Tokar and those at Sinkat, it cried out in vain. To do as he pleased was the answer sent to its hitherto loyal Governor; and, to save his people and himself, he joined the Mahdi's hordes. In his triumph, the False Prophet despatched two dervishes to Kartoum, to ask if Gordon would himself become a follower of the Imam, the Expected One; but they were told that no terms would be made while Kartoum held its ground.

All hope of a peace, all hope of aid from his own Government or country, at an end, Gordon forthwith provisioned the town, and took such steps as would ensure a safe means of defence and attack. Money was scarce, so a paper currency was established, and those of the wealthier citizens were called upon to advance sums on the Governor-General's security. Arrears due to the troops were paid, the poor were succoured, and rations issued. All possible precautions were taken for the safety of the people. Mines were contrived by means of shells, broken glass and wire entanglements arranged, and watchers posted everywhere. The blacks quartered in the poorer district of the town were made to serve, and all men ordered to bear arms; the staple food of officers was biscuit, and dhoora was given the men. Having made all his arrangements on land, he now turned his attention to the Nile; and, as in the campaign against the Taipings, so in this desperate struggle with the Arabs, he organised his fleet in such a way as the rebels could not withstand it. Thus he avenged defeat, drew in stores and guns, and held the enemy at bay. So that for eleven long months, spite of mutiny, cowardice and treachery within, and the constant attacks from the enemy without, he held his own; and spared, out of the navy, a steamer for the conveyance of his comrades, Stewart, Power, Herbin, and the Greeks. Moreover, when at last the news of the English Expedition reached him, he was able to send down five other boats to Metemma, fully manned and provisioned, with a force of 400 men for their aid.[5] It is at this point, when vainly watching day and night for English help, that the Journals begin. How his time was passed till we should come, how he viewed our chances of success, and how he proposed to act if we at last did arrive —this is a story which the Journals tell themselves.

***

I have endeavoured to show the conditions under which the people of the Soudan existed during Gordon's absence and during his presence. The contrast is sufficient to enable the world to believe that if any man were capable of restoring

[5] This left General Gordon with only two steamers, which much crippled him, for he considered each steamer as equal to 2000 men.

order to the country, that man was Gordon. But when he left England for the Soudan as the Envoy of Her Majesty's Government, he had no authority to *act*, for his mission was only to advise. He was to report to Her Majesty's Government on the military situation in the Soudan, and on the measures which it might be deemed advisable to take for the security of the Egyptian garrisons still holding positions in that country, and for the safety of the European population in Kartoum; and, further, upon the manner in which the safety and good administration of the Egyptian Government of the ports on the sea-coast could best be secured. So far then all *action* lay in the hands of the Government to which Gordon was to make his report: the administrators were to be Her Majesty's Ministers and their representative at Cairo, while Gordon was to be their informant, and perhaps subsequently their agent, to carry out such measures as they might think fit to adopt. With this arrangement in view, all who knew Gordon's character and antecedents felt that the only chance for the Soudan lay in Her Majesty's Government first accepting such suggestions as he might append to his report, and, second, in their giving him *carte blanche* to carry out those suggestions in his own way. Little heed was paid to the clause which said, "You will consider yourself authorised and instructed to perform such other duties as the Egyptian Government may desire to entrust to you," for its possible value seemed upset by the concluding sentence, "and as may be communicated to you by Sir E. Baring." Yet this clause, strangely enough, enabled Gordon to hold a position over which even Her Majesty's Government could have no control, unless they openly declared the annexation of Egypt and the Soudan. The Egyptian Government, that is the Khedive and his ministers, elected again to appoint Gordon Governor-General of the Soudan; Gordon elected to accept that appointment; and Her Majesty's Government elected to sanction the acceptance, in an official communication forwarded to him through their representative, Sir E. Baring. From this moment Gordon's position was entirely altered. Her Majesty's Government and the Egyptian Government agreed that his mission was no longer to be one of mere reporting. He was to "*evacuate the Soudan, and the Egyptian Government had the fullest confidence in his judgment and knowledge of the country, and of his comprehension of the general line of policy to be pursued; and no effort was to be wanting on the part of the Cairo authorities, whether English or Egyptian, to afford him all the co-operation and support in their power.*"

When it became an established fact that General Gordon, Governor-General of the Soudan, had been sent up to evacuate the garrisons of the country, it also became an established fact that the method of conducting that evacuation had passed out of the hands of Her Majesty's Government; and one may also say it had virtually passed out of the hands of the Egyptian Government while Gordon held the Firman of the Khedive. Therefore, as this Firman was never cancelled from the day of Gordon's departure from Cairo to the day of his death at Kartoum, and as it said, amongst other things, "We do hereby appoint you Governor-General of the Soudan, and we trust that you will carry out our good intentions for the establishment of justice and order, and that you will assure the peace and prosperity of the people of Soudan by maintaining the security of the roads open, &c.," it is as unfair as it is illogical to talk about "*General Gordon having exceeded the instructions conveyed to him by Her Majesty's Government.*" These instructions were neither more nor less than those conveyed to him by the Khedive of Egypt, who actually delegated his own power to his Governor-General. To exceed his instructions was an impossibility; to fulfil or to disappoint all the hopes expressed in them was a possibility dependent solely on the good or bad faith of the Governments who employed him.

***

The fact that Gordon held his commission in Her Majesty's service and the Governor-Generalship of the Soudan at the same time, in no way compromised him with Her Majesty's Government in regard to their wishes as to how this or that should be done, or as to how this or that should be left undone: yet he tried earnestly to identify himself with their wishes as far as in doing so he could keep faith with the people he was endeavouring to assist, and with whom he began to compromise himself. That he was justified in so doing there should be no shadow of doubt even in the minds of Mr. Gladstone's ministry. The wishes of the Khedive were accepted by Gordon as the wishes of Her Majesty's Government, and he had begun to act, *i.e.* to compromise himself with the Soudanese and the beleaguered garrisons before he reached Kartoum.

These are the Khedive's wishes as expressed in a letter to Gordon, dated January 26th, 1884:—

EXCELLENCY,

You are aware that the object of your arrival here and of your mission to the Soudan is to carry into execution the evacuation of those territories, and to withdraw our troops, civil officials, and such of the inhabitants, together with their belongings, as may wish to leave for Egypt. We trust that your Excellency will adopt the most effective measures for the accomplishment of your mission in this respect, and that, after completing the evacuation, you will take the necessary steps for establishing an organised Government in the different provinces of the Soudan, for the maintenance of order, and the cessation of all disasters and incitement to revolt.

We have full confidence in your tried abilities and tact, and are convinced that you will accomplish your mission according to our desire.

The Khedive could hardly have written this letter had he imagined Lord Granville would telegraph three months later to Gordon, saying that "undertaking military expeditions was beyond the scope of the commission he held, and at variance with the pacific policy which was the purpose of his mission to the Soudan."

Effective measures for the accomplishment of General Gordon's mission included the possibility and great probability of serious fighting in the interest of a pacific policy, and it is strange if Lord Granville were unable to grasp that fact when he endorsed the Khedive's Firman.

So far I have advanced only a few of the innumerable proofs of Gordon's authority to act as he thought fit; as to his capabilities and his judgment it is unnecessary to speak. Of those who subsequently would not accept his judgment, one, Mr. Gladstone, said, "It was our duty, whatever we might feel, to beware of interfering with Gordon's plans, and before we adopted any scheme that should bear that aspect (*i.e.* the aspect of interference), to ask whether *in his judgment* there would or would not be such an interference." The other, Sir Charles Dilke, said, "He is better able to *form a judgment* than anybody. He will have, I make no doubt, every support he can need in the prosecution of his mission."

Personally I do not believe that a single Cabinet Minister doubted Gordon's authority to act as he thought fit, nor do I believe a single Cabinet Minister doubted either his capabilities or his judgment. It was only when the Government realised how strong that authority was; how significantly Gordon proposed to wield it, and how he meant to call upon his country to support him in what was right, irrespective of party feeling and of prejudiced public opinion, that references were made to "*General Gordon's peculiar views*" and to "*his disobedience of orders.*" I would let the latter remark pass as unworthy of further comment, were it not for the fact that it has become a common phrase among the working classes in the North of England, when they are either speaking of or are spoken to about General Gordon. Now I sincerely trust and believe that the Journals will be read eagerly by the working classes; they cannot occupy their leisure time better than in reading them, and, indeed, in learning much of them by heart. I would say then, to these people, *Do not believe that General Gordon was disobedient to his Government.* His Government permitted him to accept the Khedive's Firman, appointing him Governor-General of the Soudan, with full powers, civil and military, and the Khedive desired him to "evacuate the garrisons of the country, and to restore order;" and the way in which this was to be done was left to the discretion of the man who had to do it. I would also ask these people to note particularly that the Khedive did not tell him to evacuate the garrisons of Kartoum and leave the other garrisons in the lurch; did not tell him to sacrifice everything rather than engage in military operations against the Mahdi; did not tell him to identify his interests with those of the people and then to get away as best he could, and to leave the people to their fate. Had the Khedive told him to do this, he would never have accepted the Governor-Generalship of the Soudan; and, when his own Government suggested this method as a way out of difficulties, the substance of his numerous replies was, "Our relative positions do not justify you in giving me such orders. I can only accept them as your wishes; and the duty I owe to myself, as a God-fearing and an honourable man, prevents me being able to comply with them."

When Gordon telegraphed to Sir E. Baring, "You must see that you could not recall me nor could I possibly obey until the Cairo *employés* get out from all the places. I have named men to different places, thus involving them with the Mahdi; how could I look the world in the face if I abandoned them and fled? As a gentleman could you advise this course?" he really telegraphed a bitter rebuke to the English Government; and when he added, "It may have been a mistake to send me up, but, having been done, I have no option but to see evacuation through," he merely pointed out what the Government already knew, namely, that the position they had allowed him to accept was one over which they had no legal control, unless they announced the annexation of Egypt. I, therefore, again most emphatically repeat, that Gordon in no instance disobeyed his Government, though he frequently had to tell them how utterly unable he was to execute their wishes. The Governor-General of the Soudan had definite orders from the Khedive, whose servant he was, and these orders could not be capsized by the English Government, unless the Khedive were deposed or Egypt were annexed.

I cannot conclude this portion of my subject in a better way than by quoting what the Khedive said to Baron Malortie, after he had appointed Gordon Governor-General of the Soudan. Speaking of his mission, he remarked:—

I could not give a better proof of my intention than by accepting Gordon as Governor-General with full powers to take whatever steps he may judge best for obtaining the end my Government and Her Majesty's Government have in view. I could not do more than delegate to Gordon my own power and make him irresponsible arbiter of the situation. Whatever he does will be well done, whatever arrangements he will make are accepted in advance, whatever combination he may decide upon will be binding for us; and in thus placing unlimited trust in the Pasha's judgment I have only made one condition: *that he should provide for the safety of the*

Europeans and the Egyptian civilian element. He is now the supreme master, and my best wishes accompany him on a mission of such gravity and importance, for *my heart aches at the thought of the thousands of loyal adherents whom a false step may doom to destruction.* I have no doubt that Gordon Pasha will do his best to sacrifice as few as possible ; and, should he succeed, with God's help, in accomplishing the evacuation of Kartoum and the chief ports in the Eastern Soudan, he will be entitled to the everlasting gratitude of my people, who at present tremble that help may come too late. To tell you that he will succeed is more than I or any mortal could prognosticate, for there are tremendous odds against him. But let us hope for the best, and, as far as I and my Government are concerned, he shall find the most loyal and energetic support.[6]

* * *

The points I have already dwelt upon are all-important for the correct interpretation of what Gordon says in his Journals. There are now two other questions, with which I must deal. The first of these is " To what extent were H.M. Government morally bound to support Gordon? The answer is to be found in the conditions laid down in the Khedive's Firman, which H.M. Government endorsed. Mr. Gladstone admitted as much in the House of Commons on Feb. 14th, when he said : " The direct actions and direct functions in which General Gordon is immediately connected with this Government are, I think, pretty much absorbed in the greater duties of the large mission he has undertaken under the immediate authority of the Egyptian Government, *with the full moral and political responsibility of the British Government.*" Therefore we owed the same kind of responsibility to Gordon as it owed to Egypt, moral and political. Gordon shows in his Journals what brought about our responsibility to Egypt. First, we were morally to blame for General Hicks's defeat, for had we prevented the Fellaheen conscripts being dragged in chains from their homes, and sent up to recruit Hicks's army, Hicks would not have left Kartoum, and his troops would not have been annihilated. Through this disaster we became morally responsible for the extended influence of the Mahdi, who, previous to crushing a huge army, had merely defeated small detachments of troops far inferior to his own. It was the crushing of Hicks's force which led the Mahdi to put forth his

6 From *Pall Mall Gazette* extra, "Too Late," No. 14.

agents in all parts of the Soudan, and thus to convert a trumpery local rising into a wide-spreading rebellion. So much for our responsibility from a moral point of view. Our political responsibitity began with the order to abandon the Soudan (which was unnecessary interference on our part, inasmuch as the Soudan was practically lost), and was followed up by our objection to the despatch of Egyptian or Turkish troops, our sending Gordon, and our operations for the relief of Tokar and Sinkat. Right through we forced the hand of the Khedive. Why did we not go one step further and force him to cancel the Firman by which he appointed Gordon Governor-General of the Soudan? Had we done this, Gordon would have reverted to his original position as reporter to Her Majesty's Government, or he could have endeavoured to leave Kartoum at once, as his responsibilities towards the people of the Soudan would have ceased. Until we did this we were as responsible to him, morally and politically, as we were to the Egyptian Government. A little decision here might have spared to us Gordon, Colonel Stewart, and Mr. Power; might have prevented the loss of thousands of other lives; might have saved us millions of money.

***

I am only endeavouring to place Gordon's situation and action in a fair light, and I cannot do this without pointing out how greatly England has been to blame in not accepting a responsibility for which she made herself liable. This brings me directly to the second question, which deals with the reason why Gordon, with the promised support of Egypt and England, failed not only to restore order to the Soudan, but even to extricate the beleaguered garrisons. Volumes have been already written on this subject, and there are probably volumes yet to come, particularly those representing that Journal by Colonel Stewart, which was captured by a treacherous enemy, and is now in the hands of Mahomet Achmet, the Mahdi.[7] I will content myself then with an endeavour to supply what I feel is the substance of the answer to be found

[7] See Appendix, p. 360.

in this missing Journal, to the question I have raised. *Gordon was constantly thwarted and never supported* is the summary of a whole, which I will give in detail as briefly as I can.

(1) Gordon wished to visit the Mahdi if he thought fit, but Sir E. Baring gave him a positive order from Her Majesty's Government that he was on no account to do so. Of course, as I have already shown, Gordon, in his position as Governor-General, need not have accepted this as an order, but he was, as he always has been, most anxious to conform to the wishes or desires expressed by Her Majesty's Government, when those wishes affected only a point of judgment, and not a point of duty or a point of honour.

(2) Gordon proposed to go direct from Kartoum to the Bahr Gazelle and Equatorial Provinces, but Her Majesty's Government refused to sanction his proceeding beyond Kartoum.

(3) Gordon desired 3000 Turkish troops, in British pay, to be sent to Suakin, but Her Majesty's Government, advised by Sir E. Baring, who disapproved of the measure, declined to send these troops.

(4) Gordon, being convinced that some government was essential for the safety of the Soudan, suggested the appointment of Zubair as his successor, and gave the most cogent reasons why it was absolutely necessary for the accomplishment of his mission that the appointment should be made. He reiterated his request over and over again from February to December. Her Majesty's Government would not permit the Khedive to make this appointment.

(5) Gordon requested that in the interests of England, Egypt, and the Soudan, he should be provided with a Firman which recognised a moral control and suzerainty over the Soudan. This was peremptorily refused.

(6) Gordon asked for Indian Moslem troops to be sent to Wady Halfa. They were refused him.

(7) In March Gordon desired 100 British troops to be sent to Assouan or to Wady Halfa. In making known this desire to Her Majesty's Government, Sir E. Baring said he would not risk sending so small a body, and the principal medical officer

said the climate would exercise an injurious effect on the troops. These troops were not sent.

(8) Gordon, for the sake of everything and everybody concerned, showed that the Mahdi's power must be smashed. Her Majesty's Government declined to assist in, or even to countenance, the process.

(9) Gordon, in a series of eleven telegrams, explained his difficulties, and said that if Her Majesty's Government would not send British troops to Wady Halfa, an adjutant to inspect Dongola, and then open up the Berber-Suakin route by Indian Moslem troops, they would probably have to decide between Zubair or the Mahdi, and he concluded these telegrams by saying he would do his best to carry out his instructions, *but felt convinced he would be caught in Kartoum.* Sir Evelyn Baring, in his reply to these telegrams, recommended Gordon *to reconsider the whole question carefully, and then to state in one telegram what he recommended!*

(10) Gordon telegraphed: "*The combination of Zubair and myself is an absolute necessity for success. To do any good we must be together, and that without delay;*" and he supplemented this by another telegram, saying: "*Believe me, I am right; and do not delay.*" The combination was not permitted.

(11) Sir Evelyn Baring telegraphed to Lord Granville that General Gordon *had on several occasions* pressed for 200 British troops to be sent to Wady Halfa, but that he (Baring) did not think it desirable to comply with the request.

(12) Gordon desired a British diversion at Berber, but Sir Evelyn Baring replied that there was no intention to send an English force to Berber.

(13) Gordon, foiled on every point, telegraphed a graceful adieu to Her Majesty's Government. Then came the fall of Berber, upon which Sir Evelyn Baring at once telegraphed to Lord Granville that it *had now become of the utmost importance not only to open the road between Suakin and Berber,* "*but to come to terms with the tribes between Berber and Kartoum*"; and Lord Granville telegraphed to Sir E. Baring that "*General Gordon had several times suggested a movement on*

Wady Halfa, which might support him by threatening an advance on Dongola, and, under the present circumstances at Berber this might be found advantageous." ! !

After this, may we not well echo Gordon's sentiments, "What a farce if it did not deal with men's lives"? If Gordon, instead of being *thwarted*, had only been *not supported*, how different might have been the result of his mission to the Soudan! Indeed, one may say how different *would* have been the result! for Gordon has practically said this, and he was a competent and a reliable judge. If England and Egypt had only said, "We will give you no help at all; do what you can with the material you have about you, and do not refer to us until you have succeeded, or until you have failed," I confidently believe Gordon would have at least relieved the beleaguered garrisons of the Soudan, and would have sent down all who wished to leave the country. His weakness was that of trustfulness—the besetting weakness of an honourable man: it had stood him in good stead through his campaigns in China, and through his previous operations in the Soudan; through terrible sufferings, which had often made him wish for death. Then he trusted enemies, and they always enabled him to save life. Now he trusted friends, and they only enabled him to die.

* * *

> "The evil that men do lives after them,
> The good is oft interred with their bones."

Gordon tells us plainly in his Journals how great is the evil done by the policy of Her Majesty's Government, and for how long that evil will live when the Government is dead. Is it not possible to avert something of what is about to happen? Her Majesty's Government are, I believe, beginning to realise how thoroughly correct Gordon was in his views, and how mistaken they were in not following his advice at the time he gave it. At all events after he was dead they expressed their intention of doing much he recommended while he lived. They have been always very late: too late to save Gordon's life, and too late to save the lives of many thousands. May they not be yet in time to prevent some of the evil that must live after them? I think Gordon tells them in his Journals they may, and I think he also tells them how. It is impossible to read carefully what he says without feeling that he did not expect to live long, and that he had a distinct presentiment he would die at Kartoum. At all events there is a strong undercurrent of this presentiment all through, and it even rises to the surface every now and then when he appears to be taking a hopeful and almost a cheerful view of the situation. At times it carries all before it, as for example when he emphasises the possibility of the fall of Kartoum under the nose of the expedition, and again in the words with which he concludes his sixth and last volume; but then, on the other hand, it is often quite out of sight, especially at such times as he is discussing his position as Governor-General, and turning over in his mind the expediency of appointing Lord Wolseley or Sir Evelyn Baring as his successor. But, whether on the surface or deep down, I think it is always there, and I feel sure that some of his numerous efforts at a solution of the Soudan problem were intended as final instructions for Her Majesty's Government, to be read after his death or after the fall of Kartoum. The days of prophecy are gone, and I do not at all wish to place Gordon in the light of the ancient orthodox and professional seer, but in considering his career one cannot avoid being struck by the remarkable way in which the lost gift of prophecy has been replaced by the power of combining knowledge with judgment. It would be well if Her Majesty's Government would bear this in mind, and lay down a distinct line of policy and action with regard to the Soudan, which should be based upon what Gordon recommends. The recall of the troups from the Soudan may have been necessary to meet the exigencies of the moment, or it may not; but it is a pity it did not precede Lord Wolseley's letter to Cassim el Mousse Pasha:—

We mean to destroy the power of Mohammed Achmet at Kartoum, no matter how long it may take us to do so; you know Gordon Pasha's countrymen *are not likely to turn back from any enterprise they have begun until it has been fully accomplished.* When that happy event takes place I hope to be able to establish you amongst your own people, and that you and all others will realise that the *English nation does not forget those who serve it faithfully.*[8]

***

General Gordon's Journals are sufficiently characteristic to enable those who read them with care to know their author perfectly. The first volume is alone a very complete introduction, in which each succeeding page brings you to a closer intimacy. If a friendship is not established before reaching the sixth, then all that is noble and chivalrous in man can have no charm. Examples of his rare genius, his nobility, his honesty and his marvellous energy are to be found throughout, but, in pointing out a few characteristics, I will confine myself to the first volume, as I propose to refer chiefly to special points of military and political interest in the others.

In this first volume then we have an interesting instance of Gordon's nobility, when he declines to have anything to do with certain doubtful proposals made by the apostate Europeans in the Mahdi's camp, for he declares "treachery never succeeds; and it is better to fail with clean hands than to be mixed up with dubious acts and dubious men. Maybe it is better to fall with honour than to gain the victory with dishonour, and in this view the Ulema is agreed, for it will have nought to do with the proposals of treachery."

The generosity of his feeling towards the enemy is shown when he says: "I do not call our enemy rebels, for it is a vexed question whether we are not rebels, seeing I hold the Firman restoring the Soudan to its chiefs." His consideration is apparent in his regret at not being more considerate; and his tolerance in the desire to spare even the lives of traitors.

His views on hypocrisy are humorously expressed when he is speaking of the Mahdi's trick of bringing tears to his eyes by the use of pepper under his finger-nails, and, as tears are considered a proof of sincerity, he recommends the recipe to Cabinet Ministers who wish to justify some job.

His severity is evident in his remarks on diplomatists, whom he considers most unsatisfactory men to have anything to do

8 *Egypt*, No. 9, Encl. 3, 43.

with in their official capacity; and his irritability peeps out when he says: "Egerton must have considered I was a complete idiot to have needed permission to contract with tribes to escort down the refugees. I hope he will get promoted, and will not be blamed for overstraining his instructions."

His religious earnestness is everywhere apparent, and he delights in endeavours to interpret Scriptural passages, especially such as are more or less paradoxical.

As an example of his humility I select the passage where he says: "If we will be with our Master we must be like Him, who from His birth to His death may be said to have been utterly miserable as far as things in this world are concerned. Yet I kick at the least obstacle to my will." His desire to help every one is to be seen on almost every page, and his forethought, energy and judgment are also everywhere. His notions of chivalry do not permit him to countenance the distribution of honours to men who only do what he considers to be their duty, and he does not approve of the Victoria Cross being given in cases of *noblesse oblige.*

His determination often prompts him to speak very plainly: "If you remove me from being Governor-General, then all responsibility is off me; but if you keep me as Governor-General then I will, *at the cost of my commission* in Her Majesty's service, see all refugees out of this country." His satire is generally severe, but there is nearly always a cheerful or a good-natured ring in it. The following is a fair example:—

I am sure I should like that fellow Egerton; there is a big-hearted jocularity about his communications, and I should think the cares of life sat easily on him. He wishes to know exactly, "day, hour, and minute," that I expect to be in difficulties as to provisions and ammunition.

Now I really think if Egerton was to turn over the "archives" (a delicious word) of his office, he would see we had been in difficulties for provisions for some months. It is as a man on the bank, having seen his friend in river already bobbed down two or three times, hails, "I say, old fellow, let us know when we are to throw you the life-buoy; I know you have bobbed down two or three times, but it is a pity to throw you the life-buoy until you really are *in extremis*, and I want to know *exactly*, for I am a man brought up in a school of exactitude, though I did *forget* (?) to date my June telegram about *that Bedouin escort contract.*"

He is a strict disciplinarian, and never hesitates to rebuke laxness in others. "If Abdel Kader is at Kassala,"[9] he says, "what on earth are our people about not to tell me! for of course I could help him. We seem to have lost our heads in the Intelligence Department, though it costs enough money."

His bluntness and honesty are often combined with subtle humour, and an excellent notion of all three may be gathered from the last words in this volume of the Journals :—

As for "*evacuation*," it is one thing; as for "*ratting out*," it is another. I am quite of advice as to No. 1 (as we have not the decision to keep the country), but I will be no party to No. 2 (this "rat" business), 1st, because it is *dishonourable;* 2nd, because it is not *possible* (which will have more weight); therefore, if it is going to be No. 2, *the troops had better not come beyond Berber till the question of what will be done is settled.*

* * *

The interest of the second volume is great from a military point of view, but its value is somewhat lessened by the fact that Gordon's instructions and suggestions were based on the assumption that the relieving force would reach him some two months earlier than it did. During those two months the conditions around Kartoum materially changed, and with these altering conditions Gordon had to reconsider many of the manœuvres he at first suggested. The political interest chiefly consists in the strong recommendation that the country should be given to the Turks, or that Zubair should be established as Governor-General at Kartoum, and that the Equator should be given to himself. "I will (D.V.) keep it," he says, "from Zubair;" that is to say, he will guard the country against all slave-hunters. In this volume Gordon declines the imputation that the Expeditionary Force has come for him, and shows how, to save our national honour, it has come to extricate the garrisons of the Soudan. Of the troubles these garrisons were causing him we get a fair notion, but his complaints seem to be only a safety-valve for his humour. He knows the men about him are treacherous and liars, but he almost seeks excuse for them when he says: "Man is essentially a treacherous animal; and although the Psalmist said in *his haste*, 'all

[9] General Gordon had been incorrectly informed by his spies about Abdel Kader, who had not left Cairo.

men are liars,' I think he might have said the same at his leisure." This volume concludes with a new effort to solve the Soudan problem by suggesting the Khedive should replace him at once by appointing Abdel Kader Governor-General.

***

This solution is fully discussed in the opening of Vol. III. It is not one in which Gordon will participate, but it may prevent his being antagonistic to the relieving force. Unless he is deposed nothing will induce him to leave the Soudan until he can extricate the garrisons. In removing him from the Governor-Generalship and in replacing him by Abdel Kader, the Government would be utilising a man whom they could mould to their own shape. Of course this solution was, as Gordon says, in some degree "a trap," but it recommended itself as the only way out of the difficulty, if the Government decided to abandon the garrisons.

The only creditable solution, Gordon still affirms, is to be found in handing the country over to the Turks with a subsidy or a sum down; and he supplements his argument by a programme showing how by this action Her Majesty's troops could leave the Soudan with honour before January 1885. "I think this would read well in history," he says. "Her Majesty's Government, having accepted duties in Egypt, and consequently in the Soudan, sent up a force to restore tranquillity, which having been done, Her Majesty's Government handed over the government of the Soudan to the Sultan." The necessity for this solution is the result, in Gordon's opinion, of the indecisions of Her Majesty's Government, and he enumerates with great care the causes which have hampered his action and thus required the despatch of a relieving force. This volume is perhaps more cheerful in its tone than any of the others. The presentiment that the expedition will be too late to prevent disaster is rarely evident, and the advance of the Mahdi promises to decide, at all events, the fate of those who are shut up in Kartoum. "A month will see him defeated or victorious, as God may will it," and with this philosophical consolation Gordon ceases to discuss the future of the Soudan, and begins an interesting detailed account of the offensive and defensive manœuvres which are taking place in and around Kartoum.

*
* *

In the fourth volume—the shortest of all—Gordon continues his narrative of events, and shows how numerous and how wearisome are the internal troubles with which he has to contend at Kartoum. Treachery is silently at work, while indolence, selfishness, and dishonesty make those who are not treacherous almost useless. He is the referee of every petty dispute, as much as he is chief justice, administrator, and commander-in-chief. The people demand his decision on every point, political or personal, and wish to leave it to him to do or not to do, irrespective of his knowing anything of the merits of the case they bring before him. His counsellors say: "Do what you think right, you will do better than we;" and his reflection is, "I, poor devil, do not know where to turn." Then in sorrow he exclaims, "Oh, our Government, our Government! What has it not to answer for? Not to *me*, but to these poor people. I declare if I thought the town wished the Mahdi I would give it up: so much do I respect free will." It is doubtless these internal troubles which lead him to say: "It is of course on the cards that Kartoum is taken under the nose of the Expeditionary Force, which will be just *too late*."

*
* *

In Vol. V., which begins on the first day of the Arab New Year, the arrival of the Mahdi at Omdurman is reported. The treachery referred to in the previous volume had led General Gordon to make numerous arrests—a necessity he deplored; but these arrests in all probability saved the fall of Kartoum on October 21st, for the Mahdi had evidently speculated on either a rising in the town on that day, or on the gates being opened to him by some of those who were then imprisoned. On this day Gordon also received the news of the treaty concluded between King John of Abyssinia and Admiral Sir William Hewitt, and his anger at the injustice of such a treaty is as apparent as is the bitterness of his satire: throughout the whole volume, indeed, he cannot get away from this subject, and, though the frequent effort to dismiss it in disgust from his mind is evident, he continually reverts to it. He considers it discreditable, and does not hesitate to say so. Moreover, he contends that by the Treaty of Paris, and also by that of Berlin, the integrity of the Ottoman Dominion is guaranteed by the Powers, and that it is therefore a farce to say Egypt ceded Kassala.

His views on the whole policy of Her Majesty's Government are summed up in an imaginary scene in the House of Lords. "The noble Marquis asked what the policy of Her Majesty's Government was? It was as if he asked the policy of a log floating down stream—*it was going to sea*, as any one with an ounce of brains could see. Well, that was the policy of it, only it was a decided policy, and a straightforward one to drift along and take advantage of every circumstance. His lordship deprecated the frequent questioning on subjects which his lordship had said he knew nothing about, and, further, did not care to know anything about."

Fielding, had he been alive, would have envied Gordon the completeness of this humorous satire. The results of the policy, as far as it has gone, he shows to have been the loss of some 80,000 lives and the effectual restoration of the slave-trade and of slave-hunting: "a miserable end to diplomacy when it would have been so easy in 1880 to have settled the Soudan with decency and quiet, giving up Kordofan, Darfur, the Bahr Gazelle, and the Equator."

* * *

In the latter part of Vol. V., but especially in the early part of Vol. VI., Gordon fully realises the *Abbas* catastrophe. He knows Stewart and Power are dead. There is no expression of personal regret, though he is "sorry for their friends." He loved them both, and he pays the highest tribute he can to their merits; but he is sure that in their present they are happier than in their past. Moreover, he had done his best, for every precaution human foresight could conceive he had taken; having done this, the rest was in the hands of God, and the disaster was "ordained." But these views do not prevent him from courting all inquiry; and he even holds a court-martial on himself. His verdict is, that if the *Abbas* was attacked and overpowered, *he is to blame;* but that if she was captured by treachery, or if she struck a rock, *he is not to blame.* In the one case he should have foreseen the chance, and prevented her going; in the others he could foresee nothing. It was out of his power to avert treachery; and the *Abbas* drew under two feet of water, and was accompanied by two sailing boats.

He explains with care and clearness why Stewart and Power left him; they went of their free will, not by his order; for he would not "put them in any danger in which he was not himself." If they went they did him a service, for they could telegraph his views; if they stayed, they could not help him. They could go in honour, for they had promised the people nothing; he could not go in honour, for he had promised them himself. If Gordon were alive, and thought any one could misinterpret what he says, and thus cast a slur on the memory of either Stewart or Power, he would be greatly pained. His love and admiration for them both was evident; and he knew that, had it been their duty to remain, they would have stayed to die with him at Kartoum. "If Zubair had been sent in February, when I asked for him, we would not have lost Berber, and would never have wanted an expedition;" and, if Berber had not fallen, Stewart and Power would have been alive. Zubair had been his almost first request, and he never ceases to regret that one who had devoted his life to the Soudan should not have been allowed to comprehend its requirements better than those who sat in Downing Street.

Within a week of beginning this volume of his Journal, Gordon expected the town of Kartoum to fall; the recovery of an enormous quantity of stolen biscuit enabled him to hold his own for more than another month. During this time a notion of his troubles may be gathered from what he says up to December 14th; his real suffering must for ever remain unknown. That it depended upon the suffering of others we may feel assured; he never knew what it was to feel for himself. He felt for his country; he felt for all he tried to help, and if he was among such as were killed first, his dying thought would have been, "What is to be the future of all I leave behind?"

*
* *

In his Journals—his last words—those familiar with his character and life will see Charles Gordon true to himself to the very end. They will see in him the same ardent passion for justice and for truth; the same scorn for wrong-doing and deceit; the same gentle pity for the sufferings of all, and the same mercy and forgiveness for his foes: and with all this is combined the perfection of humility, and the sense of imperfection. There is no impatience, save with those who wronged his honour and the poor people for whom he died; there is no unrest, for he neared that "life of action" for which he had long yearned; there is no sorrow, no dark doubt, for Charles Gordon was with his God.

A. EGMONT HAKE.

GENERAL GORDON'S POSITION AT KARTOUM.

Only a very few words on my part are necessary in laying these Journals before the public.

On New Year's Day, 1884, General Gordon arrived at Brussels from the Holy Land, and at once commenced his arrangements with His Majesty the King of the Belgians to proceed to the Congo.

After visiting England once or twice, he left this country for Belgium and the Congo on the morning of the 16th January.

On the 17th January he was recalled by telegram. He reached London on the morning of the 18th, and was on his road to Kartoum upon that evening.

At this time he felt quite confident of success, his instructions being that, by restoring the ancient families, whose territories had been seized by the Egyptian authorities, to their former power, he would be able to extricate the Egyptian garrisons and civil *employés* with their families, and remove them to Lower Egypt without difficulty.

During the voyage, however, from Brindisi to Port Said he prepared a Report or Memorandum, dated 22nd January, in which, reviewing these instructions, he drew attention to some of the difficulties and complications which were likely to arise in carrying out the policy of Her Majesty's Government, and asked for their support and consideration in case of his being unable to fulfil their expectations with exactness; and Colonel Stewart, in his separate observations of the same date, pointed out that, in view of eventualities for which it would be impossible to provide, the wisest course was "to rely on the discretion of General Gordon and his knowledge of the country."

General Gordon, it will be seen, accepted—and disclaimed the right to express any opinion of his own upon it—the policy of leaving the Soudan. It appeared to him then that to reconquer that country and restore it to the Egyptian Government without securities for a just and honest administration would be iniquitous; that, on the other hand, to secure that object would involve an expenditure of time and money which could not be afforded, and consequently he then came to the conclusion that the Soudan might properly be restored to independence, and left to itself.

It will be seen, however, that he did not, after his return to the Soudan, remain long of that opinion. His heart warmed at once to the people whom he had faithfully governed, and whose affections he found, or at all events believed, were constant to him.

It is necessary here to explain that General Gordon had not intended to go to Cairo, but to proceed *viâ* Suakin and Berber. On the invitation, however, of Sir Evelyn Baring, he went to Cairo and accepted at the hands of the Khedive a Firman appointing him Governor-General of the Soudan, without which he could have exercised no control over the Egyptian authorities employed in that province.

It was no part of General Gordon's character to form a definite opinion from imperfectly known facts, and to adhere obstinately to that opinion, notwithstanding the evidence of altered circumstances and new elements.

We need not therefore be surprised to find that, on arrival at Abu Hamed, on the 8th February, finding the state of the country to be less disorganised than he had supposed, and adverting to the confusion which must ensue if all traces of the Khedive's Government were suddenly effaced, he made the suggestion that a sort of suzerainty should be kept up, and that the chief officers of the Soudan should continue to be appointed by the Khedive, a complete and abrupt separation being thus postponed, although the control to be retained would be more nominal than real.

This feeling in General Gordon's mind grew rapidly stronger as time went on. When he reached Berber he saw still more clearly the position he was in, and became impressed with the impossibility of carrying out his mission with credit, unless he was able to secure to the provinces of the Soudan some sort of government in the place of the one it was intended to withdraw.

Accordingly, upon the day of his arrival at Kartoum (the 18th February), General Gordon, after pointing out to the Government the difficulties that surrounded him, inasmuch as the garrisons and *employés* were to be removed, when all form of government would disappear, urged in the strongest terms he could employ that power should be placed in the hands of a single man, and that the man to be chosen should be Zubair Pasha.

Now it may be remarked that although Zubair was one of the most noted slave-hunters that had ever existed, yet his ability and influence could not be surpassed, while even the Khedive could not lay claim to any such proud descent—Zubair being a direct descendant of the Abbassides.

This recommendation was rejected by the Government although renewed over and over again in a most persistent manner by General Gordon, backed up by Sir Evelyn Baring, who, on the 9th March, says : " I believe that Zubair Pasha may be made a bulwark against the approach of the Mahdi. Of course there is a certain risk that he will constitute a danger to Egypt, but this risk is, I think, a small one; and it is in any case preferable to incur it rather than to face the certain disadvantages of withdrawing without making any provision for the future government of the country, which would thus be sure to fall under the power of the Mahdi."

I must admit that, up to the end of July, I was of opinion that if Zubair had been sent up General Gordon's life would have been in danger. On the other hand, I am aware that a Cabinet Minister of high position was, from the first, in favour of sending Zubair up, and so indeed was Lord Wolseley.

At the beginning of August, General Gordon, having again begged that Zubair might be sent to Kartoum, I used my endeavours to secure the attainment of that object, but without success. It was now apparent that General Gordon could not in honour leave until some form of future government had been determined upon.

Zubair's appointment having been disallowed, the only alternative seemed to be the Turks, and the suggestion was made that they should occupy the Soudan. Anything, in fact, to secure the country against anarchy and its reversion to barbarism.

It must be borne in mind General Gordon did not ask that an expedition should be sent; on the contrary, he deprecated sending any, unless for the purpose of saving the garrisons and of establishing some form of government.

The proposed movement of two squadrons of cavalry from Suakin to Berber is outside the question. It was to save Berber they were applied for, not for the relief of Kartoum. General Gordon's message was, "Send troops (200) to Berber, or you will lose it!" It is fair to Sir Evelyn Baring, to add that on the 24th March he said, "Under present circumstances I think an effort should be made to help General Gordon from Suakin, if it is at all a possible operation."

If General Gordon had known how much in unison Sir Evelyn Baring's advice had been with his own, and what support he had received at Sir Evelyn's hands, he would have been eager, had his life been spared, to acknowledge that co-operation.

Before concluding, I must say a few words with respect to the severe comments which occur in places throughout the Diaries, upon the meagre information he received from the Intelligence Department,[1] in connection with which the names of Major Chermside and Major Kitchener are mentioned. Now, with regard to the former of these officers, he was at Suakin, and therefore does not come into the question. With respect, however, to Major Kitchener, I am persuaded that he did all in his power to get messengers into Kartoum, in the same way as General Gordon fancied he got them out; and yet how few succeeded in reaching their destination. In the same way too as General Gordon fancied his messengers had reached, so did Mr. Egerton fancy his had been successful, for at the end of July he hinted that General Gordon could have

[1] This department must not be confounded with the one associated with the Quartermaster-General at the War Office.

sent messengers out, in the same way as others had got in, and yet at that date only one had done so. It is due to Major Kitchener to say that from the time he went to Dongola he certainly kept us acquainted with the position of affairs at Kartoum in a manner most reliable, and deserving of much credit.

With these prefatory remarks I leave my brother's Journals to speak for themselves. He shows, to my mind, with the utmost clearness the position in which he was placed, and reiterates over and over again that nothing will induce him to leave Kartoum until he has secured the safety of all those who have stood by him. He says, "I will end these egotistical remarks by saying that no persuasion will induce me to change my views; and that, as to force, it is out of the question, for I have the people with me, at any rate, of the towns which hold out; therefore, if Her Majesty's forces are not prepared to relieve the whole of the garrisons, the General should consider whether it is worth coming up. In his place, if not so prepared, I would not do so. I do not dictate; but I say, what every gentleman in Her Majesty's army would agree to, that it would be mean to leave men, who (though they may not come up to our ideas as heroes) have stuck to me, though a Christian dog in their eyes, through great difficulties, and thus force them to surrender to those who have not conquered them, and to do that at the bidding of a foreign Power to save one's own skin. Why, the black sluts would stone me if they thought I meditated such action."

Up to the 14th December General Gordon could have got away at any time, had he been so inclined; in fact, he says, "As for myself, I could make good my retreat at any moment I wished." After that date we know nothing. No doubt Omdurman fell at once, and in all probability the Island of Tuti followed soon after. General Gordon must then have seen that no relief could reach him, provisions were rapidly running out, treachery, as he well knew, was at work, and the end came.

He writes to his sister on the 14th December: "God rules all; and as God will rule to His glory and our welfare, His will be done. I am quite happy, thank God, and, like Lawrence, have tried to do my duty."

In conclusion, I will add in General Gordon's own words, "It is, of course, on the cards that Kartoum is taken under the nose of the Expeditionary Force, which will be just too late. The Expeditionary Force will perhaps think it necessary to retake it; but that will be no use, and will cause loss of life uselessly on both sides. It had far better quietly return with its tail between its legs; for, once Kartoum is taken, the sun will have set and the people will not care much for the satellites. If Kartoum falls, then go quietly back to Cairo, for you will only lose men and spend money uselessly in carrying on the campaign."

H. W. GORDON.

THE MISSION OF COLONEL SIR CHARLES WILSON,

R.E., K.C.M.G.

Very severe criticisms have been made upon the manner in which Sir Charles Wilson carried out the duties that had been entrusted to him, with regard to communicating to General Gordon at Kartoum.

The charges made against him may be with advantage restricted to two :—

First—The delay in not proceeding to Kartoum at the latest on the morning of the 22nd ; and

Second—In not having pushed on to Kartoum itself in order to ascertain General Gordon's fate beyond a doubt.

Sir Charles Wilson left England in order to assume the position of Head of the Intelligence Department, and also with the tacit understanding that he was to be specially employed in order to open direct communication with General Gordon.

Having this special object in view, Sir Charles Wilson accompanied Sir Herbert Stewart's force towards the Nile, and, when that gallant and highly-distinguished officer was wounded on the 19th January, he found himself in command.

Now this force, which did not equal a British battalion upon its war strength, was hampered with a number of wounded officers and men, some of whom were with it, while others—the bulk—were in a zereba constructed at some distance in its rear.

Sir Charles Wilson, however, advanced to the Nile, where he bivouacked for the night ; and on the morning of the 20th he returned to the zereba, and brought back with him to Gubat the wounded who had been left behind.

Early in the morning of the 21st, General Gordon's steamers appeared, and landed their soldiers, who took part in the operations of that day.

Reports now reached Sir Charles Wilson that, exclusive of the Arabs in Metemma, large numbers were advancing from the North and from the South. It therefore became imperatively necessary for him to secure the safety of those who were under his orders before he could proceed upon his mission.

Accordingly, on the morning of the 22nd, he made a reconnaissance towards the North, and, finding no enemy, he turned his attention to the South.

The whole of the 23rd was occupied in making arrangements for the proper protection of his force, and he could not have left before the morning of the 24th.

It may here be observed, in confirmation of the report of the Arabs advancing from the south, that Sir Charles Wilson, on his road to Kartoum, saw a body of men at a place on the left bank of the Nile, about twelve miles south of Gubat.

It is really beyond the question to consider what General Gordon's position at this time was at Kartoum. When General Gordon sent down his last journal, on the 14th December, he stated he could not hold out for more than ten days, and he was in daily expectation that the Fort at Omdurman would fall; while even then, with that Fort in his possession, he considered it would be very hazardous for any steamer to attempt to come up to Kartoum. On the 28th November he says: "I hope the officer in command will clear Halfeyeh before he pushes on to this, for he may get a shell from the works at Omdurman (not the Fort) into one of his steamers. I do not like to risk sending the *Bordeen* steamer down to give the warning. If the steamers do come up, and have not the sense to stop at Halfeyeh I shall endeavour to warn them. The danger is at the Ras or nose, on the junction of the Blue and White Niles. The proper thing to do would be to clear Halfeyeh camp of the Arabs before coming on here. You could then communicate with Kartoum by land, and avoid running the gauntlet of Arab guns in penny steam-boats."

Now if General Gordon so expressed himself on the 28th November, two months before Sir Charles Wilson got to Kartoum, and when the fort at Omdurman and the island of Tuti were both in the General's hands, what must have been the state of affairs when both those positions had fallen and were in the possession of the Arabs?

Returning to Sir Charles Wilson's progress with his detachment of only twenty men, when he got to the point of danger, as pointed out by General Gordon, he found himself under a cross fire of artillery and musketry from all points of the compass, including Kartoum itself. Under such circumstances he had no alternative but to retire, since, had he continued his journey, he could never have secured his retreat.

Consequently I cannot but express my feeling that on neither head of charge does any blame attach to Sir Charles Wilson.

H. W. GORDON.

DESCRIPTION OF THE JOURNAL.

[Lieut.-Colonel Stewart kept a complete journal of events that occurred at Kartoum from the 1st March to the 9th September, upon the night of which day he left.]

General Gordon, who had assisted in great measure in the preparation of this Journal, describes it as a perfect gem.

It was in duplicate, and was captured when Colonel Stewart was murdered; and, according to Slatin Bey's account (who at the time was with the Mahdi), is now in his (the Mahdi's) possession.

General Gordon's Diaries are in six parts.

The First is from the 10th of September to the 23rd of September, and contains 78 pages.

The Second is from the 23rd of September to the 30th of September, and contains 41 pages.

The Third is from the 1st to the 12th of October, and contains 85 pages.

The Fourth is from the 12th to the 20th of October, and contains 32 pages.

The Fifth is from the 20th of October to the 5th of November, and contains 93 pages.

The Sixth is from the 5th of November to the 14th of December, and contains 104 pages.

The First, Second, Third, and Fourth Diaries are addressed to Lieut.-Colonel Stewart, C.M.G., or the Chief of the Staff. The Fifth is addressed to the Chief of the Staff of the Expeditionary Force for the relief of the garrison, and the Sixth is addressed in the same way.

The First and Second Diaries were sent on the 30th of September by steamer for Berber *viâ* Shendy.

The Third was sent by the steamer *Towfikia* on the 12th of October to Metemma.

The 4th was sent to Shendy in a steamer on the 21st of October.

The Fifth left in the steamer *Bordeen* on the 5th of November for Metemma;

And the Sixth also left in the steamer *Bordeen* on the 15th of December.

Each Diary has the same remarks—sometimes repeated three times, on the outside of the Journal, to the effect that "it should be pruned down prior to publication."

The Journals or Diaries were handed over to Sir Charles Wilson on the 22nd of January, at Metemma, by the officer commanding General Gordon's steamers.

The Journals were, in my opinion, properly considered by the Government as official documents (see letter accompanying the last Journal), and were handed over to me with the remark that, "So far as Her Majesty's Government had a desire in the matter, it was for the publication of the whole Diary; but they did not wish to interfere with my discretion."

The note at the end of the first Journal evidently implies that when the Government have done with the Journals, then Miss Gordon is to have them.

The publication being, therefore, in my hands, I have arranged with Messrs. Kegan Paul, Trench & Co. for their issue in a very nearly entire state, only some six or seven pages being omitted, which contain, in my opinion, no matter of public interest; while, with regard to names, those who are well acquainted with the affairs of Egypt can fill up the blanks without difficulty.

It is to be hoped that strenuous endeavours may be made in order to obtain Colonel Stewart's Journal, together with those of General Gordon from the 15th of December to the day upon which Kartoum fell, as well as that of the Doctor promised to the *Times*.

The Cairo telegrams alluded to in the Diaries have not been handed over to me.

H. W. GORDON.

POSITION OF THE STEAMERS,

DECEMBER 14, 1884.

Abbas . . .	Lost, with Col. Stewart.
Bordeen . . .	Metemma, took down Journal VI.
Chabeen . . .	In dock, Kartoum.
Fascher . . .	Captured at Berber by Arabs.
Husseinyeh . .	Sunk off Omdurman.
Ismailia . . .	At Kartoum.
Mahomet Ali . .	Captured up Blue Nile by Arabs.
Mansowrah . .	Metemma or Shendy.
Monsuhania . .	Captured at Berber by Arabs.
Saphia . . .	Metemma or Shendy.
Talataween[1] . .	Ditto ditto.
Towfikia . . .	Ditto ditto.
Zubair . . .	Kartoum.

Resumé—

Lost	6	
At Kartoum	3	—1 in dock.
At Metemma waiting for Lord Wolseley	4	
	13	

[1] Sunk by a cannon-shot off Shendy.

BOOK I.

On outside wrapper (a glass-cloth):

No secrets as far as I am concerned.

C. G. GORDON.

LT.-COLONEL STEWART, C.M.G.

or

Chief of the Staff, LORD WOLSELEY, G.C.B.

Soudan Expeditionary Force.

JOURNAL OF EVENTS—KARTOUM, VOL. I.

From 10th Sept. to 23rd Sept., 1884.

On Cover at back:

GENERAL GORDON'S JOURNAL

From the 10th to 23rd September, 1884.

N.B.—This Journal will want *pruning out* if thought necessary to publish.

C. G. GORDON.

10/9/84.

Edwd Weller. lith.

London; Kegan Paul, Trench & Co.

JOURNAL.

Vide note as to pruning down on outside.—C. G. G.

September 10.—Colonel Stewart, MM. Power and Herbin, left during the night for Dongola, *viâ* Berber.

Spy came in from South Front, and one from Halfeyeh reports Arabs will not attack, but will continue the blockade.

Sent off two sets of telegrams by a spy, who will go to Shendy.

Yesterday, when the messenger went out to deliver my answer to the Arabs, in response to Mahdi's letter, though he had a white flag, they fired on him, and tried to capture him. They use the white flag, and find it respected by us, and that we let their men go back. They chain any men we send to them.

It is wonderful how the people of the town, who have every possible facility to leave the city, cling to it, and how, indeed, there are hundreds who flock in, though it is an open secret we have neither money nor food.[1] Somehow this makes me feel confident in the future, for it is seldom that an impulse such as this acts on each member of a disintegrated mass without there being some reason for it, which those who act

[1] The military, civilians, Ulema, inhabitants and settlers in Kartoum telegraphed on August 19th to the Khedive as follows: "Weakened and reduced to extremities, God in His mercy sent Gordon Pasha to us in the midst of our calamities of the siege, and we should all have perished of hunger and been destroyed. But we, sustained by his intelligence and great military skill, have been preserved in Kartoum until now."—*Egypt, No.* 35, *p.* 112.—Ed.

have no idea of, but which is a sort of instinct. Truly I do not think one could inflict a greater punishment on an inhabitant of Kartoum than to force him to go to the Arabs.

Halfeyeh reports that Faki Mustapha, who was in command of the Arabs on the west or left bank of the White Nile, wishes to join the Government. He is informed we are glad of it, but wish him to remain quiet, and to take no active part till he sees how the scales of the balance go; if we rise, then he can act, if we fall he is not to compromise himself; but what we ask him is to send up our spies, which he can do without risk.[2] The same advice was given to the people of Shendy, who wished to issue out and attack Berber.

The runaways of Tuti[3] wish to come back, which is allowed.

The "matches" used for the mines are all finished, and we are obliged to go back to powder hose, and unite the mines in families of ten.

Rows on rows of wire entanglement are being placed around the Lines. General Gordon's horse was captured by the Arabs in the defeat of El foun; the other staff horse got a cut on the head, but is now all right.

The Mahdi is still at Rahad.[4] The answer to his letter (*vide* Colonel Stewart's journal) was sent open, so that the Arab leaders could read its contents.

With respect to letters written to the Mahdi and to the Arab chiefs, commenting on the apostacy of Europeans, they may, and are, no doubt, hard, but it is not a small thing for a European, for fear of death, to deny our faith; it was not so in old times, and it should not be regarded as if it was taking off one coat, and putting on another. If the

[2] In this passage we have an example of the old and perfect fairness with which General Gordon dealt with others. Before allowing Mustapha Faki, the neutral, to join his ranks and aid him against the Mahdi, he must first himself be satisfied that such a step would not endanger Faki Mustapha's life. Success or failure was still doubtful. This, of course, he could not tell Mustapha, but would it be right and just to use him while such a doubt existed? Gordon was of opinion that it would not, and thus he bade Mustapha wait events, and do for him that only which involved no risks.—ED.

[3] Tuti is an island at the junction of the White and Blue Niles.—ED.

[4] Near El Obeyed and about 200 miles from Kartoum.—ED.

Christian faith is a myth, then let men throw it off, but it is mean and dishonourable to do so merely to save one's life if one believes it is the true faith. What can be more strong than these words, "He who denies Me on earth I will deny in heaven." The old martyrs regarded men as their enemies who tried to prevent them avowing their faith. In the time of Queens Mary and Elizabeth, what men we had, and then it was for less than here, for it was mainly the question of the Mass, while here it is the question of the denial of our Lord and of His passion. It is perhaps as well to omit this, if this journal is published, for no man has a right to judge another. Politically and morally, however, it is better for us not to have anything to do with the apostate Europeans in the Arab camp. Treachery never succeeds, and, however matters may end, it is better to fall with clean hands than to be mixed up with dubious acts and dubious men. Maybe it is better for us to fall with honour, than to gain the victory with dishonour, and in this view the Ulema of the town are agreed; they will have nought to do with the proposals of treachery.

No doubt the letters to the Arabs will make the Arab chiefs work on the Europeans with them, to take an active part against us, by saying to those Europeans, "You are cast out;" but the Arabs will never trust them really, so they can do little against us.

We had a regular gaol delivery to-day, letting out some fifty, and are sending to the Arabs about nine prisoners whom it is not advisable to keep in the town. A donkey quietly grazing near the North Fort, exploded one of the mines there (an iron alembic which belonged to the time of Mahomet Ali, and had been used for the reduction of gold; it held some 10 lbs. of powder); the donkey, angry and surprised, walked off unhurt! These alembics are of this shape, braced by iron straps together. It is extraordinary that after a good deal of rain, and three months' exposure, the domestic matchbox should have retained its vitality.

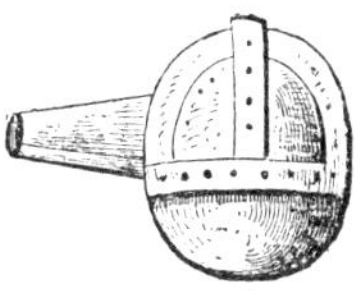

The school here is most interesting, as the scholars get a certain ration. It is always full, viz., two hundred. Each boy has a wooden board, on which his lesson is written, and on visiting it the object of each boy is to be called out to read his lesson, which they do with a swaying motion of body, and in a sing-song way, like the Jews do at the wailing place at Jerusalem and in their synagogues, from which we may infer this was the ancient way of worship, for the lessons are always from the Koran. Little black doves with no pretension to any nose, and not more than two feet high, push forward to say the first ten letters of the alphabet, which is all they know.

We have completed the census (*vide* Colonel Stewart's journal),[5] and have 34,000 people in the town.

September 11.—Stewart's steamers, which had been delayed at Halfeyeh[6] owing to some machinery accident, left last night for Berber.[7] Spy reports that one of captured steamers at Berber is disabled by the Arabs.

When Cuzzi[8] came to the Lines yesterday, the officer Hassan Bey made him walk over on his knees in order to pass into Lines, pointing out to him that the Lines were thickly spread with fearful mines. Cuzzi asked what one would do when the Nile fell, and was told that these new mines would be put down as the river fell. Hassan Bey put Cuzzi into a hut, and questioned him as to the whereabouts of the Mahdi. He said first he was at Duem,[9] and when pressed he agreed the Mahdi was in Kordofan, and had not moved. He said the Mahdi had not more than two regiments; that he had lost heavily in fighting the mountain tribes of Nuba, and had not much ammunition left; that Waled a Goun had some 200

[5] *Vide* Sir Henry Gordon's Prefatory Note.—ED.

[6] A small town eight miles north of Kartoum.—ED.

[7] Berber is about 200 miles from Kartoum.—ED.

[8] English Consular Agent at Berber. According to M. Herbin's telegram from Kartoum received by M. Barère on 22nd September, 1884, Cuzzi had gone to Kordofan, but whether free or as a prisoner was not stated.—*Egypt*, *No.* 35 (1884), No. 142.—ED.

[9] Duem is a town on the White Nile about 100 miles from Kartoum.—ED.

regulars with him, 10 mountain guns, and 2 Krupps, but only 5 boxes of mountain gun ammunition, and 3 boxes of Krupp, and 5 boxes of Remington. (The Arabs captured at our defeat at El foun 75,000 rounds, so that will help them.) Waled a Goun wanted to go to Giraffe, where Abou Gugliz was defeated, but Abou Gugliz said it would never do. Cuzzi looked pretty miserable. Outside the Lines were three Arabs and Zarada (a Greek); they waited for Cuzzi. Soon after Cuzzi had left for the Arab camp, two dervishes came in with the Mahdi's letter (*vide* Colonel Stewart's journal), and a dervish dress from the Mahdi to me. They were given the letters I had received for Slatin for Cairo, and my answer to the Arabs; also the horse head-stall which Abou Gugliz had lost, at which they were amused, and went off to the Arab camp. I sent out my letter in answer to the Mahdi (*vide* Colonel Stewart's journal) with a slave, upon whom they fired. *Talataween* and *Bordeen* left for Sennaar this morning to bring down dhoora.[10] Letter written to the Sheikh el Obeyed[11] proposing "we should mutually remain quiet, &c., &c., with relation to one another, as we are rendering the country a desert."

Jer. xvii. 5. "Cursed (*thus saith the Lord*) is the man that trusteth in man, and maketh flesh his arm, and whose heart departeth from the Lord;" therefore *cursed is he of the Lord*, who hopes by any arrangement of forces, or by exterior help, to be relieved from the position we are in. Jer. xvii. 7. "Blessed (thus saith the Lord) is he that trusteth in the Lord, and whose hope the Lord is," therefore blessed is he "of the Lord" who makes all his arrangements of forces, without any reliance on such arrangements, or on any exterior help, but trusts in the Lord.[12] How impossible for man alone

[10] A description of millet.—ED.

[11] The Sheikh el Obeyed declared for the Mahdi in March 1884.

[12] At first sight there might seem something of a contradiction in these sentiments, but, when weighed, they will be found consistent and sound. They convey an idea which was constantly at work in General Gordon's mind, and this to the effect that man should make every effort towards the attainment of perfection, and then, and not till then, leave the issue to God; that he should, in fact, draw on all earthly resources—as the instrument of God—and that, these exhausted, he should then look to Heaven for aid not to be drawn from earth.—ED.

to accept these views, for with what heart can he make his arrangements if he does not trust in their success! Curious verses, Ezekiel xxix. 10–14,[13] as to Egypt being waste for forty years from the Tower of Syene (Assouan) to frontier of Ethiopia; it is certainly the Soudan which is meant, and it is in a fair way of being a desert.

A Dervish came in with a letter from Abdel Kader, the Sheikh on the White Nile, which, with answer, is annexed;[14] he also brought a letter from the messengers who brought in the Mahdi's letter on 9th September (*vide* Col. Stewart's journal). They said they had not received my answer, which it will be remembered was sent out by a slave, whom they fired upon. This man also brought in a letter from a Greek, Calamatino, who begs to come in and tell me important news for all Europe. His letter and my answer are annexed.[15]

It will be noticed that Cuzzi adds "he is going to Berber to-day," so he may meet with Stewart. They might have gone down together had they mutually known of one another's departure.

A soldier captured at Obeyed came in, and reports that his comrades would come in *en masse* if we would let them come at night. Abou Gugliz denies that the head-stall I sent to him is his.

I put down our defeat at the Dem or head-quarters of Sheikh el Obeyed to two things—1. A lot of Kartoum pedlars went out to loot, and they broke the square. 2. Mahomet Ali

[13] "Behold, therefore I am against thee, and against thy rivers, and I will make the land of Egypt utterly waste and desolate, from the tower of Syene even unto the border of Ethiopia.

"No foot of man shall pass through it, nor foot of beast shall pass through it, neither shall it be inhabited forty years.

"And I will make the land of Egypt desolate in the midst of the countries that are desolate, and her cities among the cities that are laid waste shall be desolate forty years; and I will scatter the Egyptians among the nations, and will disperse them through the countries.

"Yet thus saith the Lord God; at the end of forty years will I gather the Egyptians from the people whither they were scattered:

"And I will bring again the captivity of Egypt, and will cause them to return into the land of Pathros, into the land of their habitation; and they shall be there a base kingdom."—ED.

[14] Appendix A and A 1.

[15] Appendix B.

Pasha captured a lad twelve or fourteen years of age, and the little chap spoke out boldly, and said he believed Mahomet Achmet was the Mahdi, and that we were dogs. He was shot! Before I heard of our defeat I heard of this, and I thought "THAT will not pass unavenged." There was an old belief among old Christians that every event which happens on earth is caused by some action being taken in heaven; the action in heaven being the cause of the event on earth, *vide* Revelations, when at the opening of seals the trumpet sounds, etc., etc., all events exercised in heaven are followed by events on earth. This being the case, how futile are our efforts to turn things out of their course. Vials are poured out on earth whence events happen. To me, it seems little what those events may be, but that the great object of our lives is how we bear those events in our individuality. If we trust in the flesh, thus saith the Lord, we are cursed; if we trust in Him we are blessed. I cannot think that there are any promises for answers to prayer made for temporal things; the promises are to hear prayer, and to give strength to bear with quiet what may be the Will of God. A vial is poured on earth; events happen; one is furious with the British Government for these events; but if we were logical, we should be furious with the pourer out of the vial, and that we shrink from being, for He is the Almighty who pours out the vial.

This afternoon another mine blew up at Tuti; the victim was another donkey, who, however, did not get off so well as his colleague of the North Fort, for he lost his hind quarters, and was killed.—R.I.P.

We cannot help thinking something has happened in Europe of a startling nature, and which is known to the Arabs in an indistinct way, for they evidently look on the game as theirs, and that without fighting, of which they show no sign. Abou Gugliz (in remonstrating with Waled a Goun, who wished to descend a river) told him "that his forts were better than any at Cairo, but that the soldiers came over them, like afreets;"[16] so says the Dervish who came in to-day.

[16] "Go, and with ghouls and afrits rave."—*The Giaour.*

We decided to-night to send out a letter to Arabs, saying that though we will not admit any European into the place we will permit an interview, with any European they may wish to send to a flag placed in front of Lines, with the Greek Consul and Greek Doctor.

September 12.—It is most dispiriting to be in the position I am, if it was not good for me, when I think that, *when I left*, I could say, "no man could lift his hand or foot in the land of the Soudan" [17] without me (Gen. xli. 44) [18] and now we cannot calculate on our existence over twenty-four hours. The people are all against us, and what a power they have; they need not fight, but have merely to refuse to sell us their grain. The stomach governs the world, and it was the stomach (a despised organ) which caused our misery from the beginning. It is wonderful that the ventral tube of man governs the world, in small and great things.

One of Seyd Mahomet Osman's family, come in from Shendy, reports Osman Digna, as writing to Berber, reporting the arrival of the English at Suakin, their purchase of camels, and advance. The Arab chief of Berber assembled his subordinates and told them this, also of the advance of the troops from Debbeh commanded by English (Wood's force) and recommended them to collect their men. The two captured steamers at Berber are on opposite sides of river.

Sent out letter to the Arabs to-day, saying I would let the Greek Consul come out and meet the Greek who had written to me; the Arabs, this time, did not fire on the flag of truce.

Church parade of Arabs on south front, but very far off.

The man from Shendy reports that all the right bank of the Nile is quiet. We have sent out an escort to try and capture Cuzzi, who is on his way to Berber.

It certainly is a curious exemplification of how very lightly religions sit on men, and to note the fearful apostacy of both

[17] These words may be taken literally. Such was Gordon's power and influence in 1879, when he resigned the Governor-Generalship of the Soudan.—Ed.

[18] "And Pharaoh said unto Joseph, I am Pharaoh, and without thee shall no man lift up his hand or foot in all the land of Egypt."—Ed.

Mussulmans and Christians, when their lives or property are menaced. There is scarcely one great family of the Soudan, families who can trace their pedigree for five hundred years, who have not accepted Mahomet Achmet as Mahdi, to save their property, though they laugh at the idea afterwards. I am using this argument with them, in saying, "You ask me to become a Mussulman to save my life, and you yourself acknowledge Mahomet Achmet as the Mahdi, to save your lives; why, if we go on this principle, we will be adopting every religion whose adherents threaten our existence, for you know and own, when you are safe, that Mahomet Achmet is *not* the Mahdi."[19]

One of our captured soldiers from Obeyed came in from Waled a Goun, and four others with a woman came in from Faki Mustapha (two of the last were men slaves of the unfortunate Hassan Pasha Ibrahim, who was executed); they report food scarce in the Arab camp, and that many are striving to run away, owing to the way they are bullied.

Ulema are writing letters to Arab chiefs, protesting against their acts, as being contrary to Muslim religion.

The Greeks and other prisoners in Obeyed, &c., complain bitterly of their privations and ill-treatment by the Arabs, in the letters they sent in here to other Greeks.

I was awakened this morning by a woman crying out "My son has been murdered, and I demand justice." Her little *only* boy had, it appears, been in one of the Arab water-wheels, which are moved by oxen, and a man had pushed him off; his skull was partially fractured, but he had been in hospital for some days, and we hoped for his recovery, when inflammation set in, and he died. He was a nice little bright-eyed, chocolate-coloured child of eight years old—the mother is a widow. One is drawn towards the children of this country, both browns and blacks—the former are of a perfect bronze colour.

[19] "Everything one does is known, and the only regret of the people is that I am a Christian. Yet they would be the first to despise me if I recanted and became a Mussulman."—*Extract from General Gordon's Letter, dated Kassala, December 7th,* 1877.—Hill, p. 300.

The browns and blacks bear their wounds without a murmur; the poor fellaheen soldiers yell upon the slightest touch to their wounds.

One of the Arab chiefs came to the Shoboloha defile, and tried to raise the people to occupy the passage; the people refused, and the Arab chief went off.

There is a negro soldier in hospital with a cut on the nose from a sword; the cut has entered the nostrils, giving him four openings instead of two—it is on the bridge of the nose (if a negro nose can be said to have a bridge), and the man's cheeks are untouched.

One man received a wound in the chest; he lived eleven

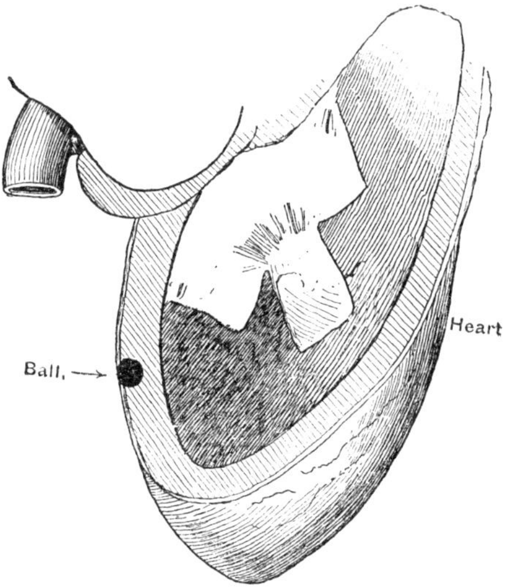

days, and died. The doctor found a bullet lodged in the centre of his heart, in wall of ventricle. The doctor has this heart in spirits. It was a ball weighing the same as our Martini-Henri bullet.

The negro soldiers are wonderfully clean, while the fellaheen and Turkish lot are just the reverse; the former have the gloss of a well-cleaned and polished boot, such as the little London shoeblack loves to turn out for a penny.

A Greek came in from the Arabs to-night; I sent the Greek Consul to see him on the Lines, where he will stop for the night.

I saw the Ulema [20] to-day, and lamented to them the degeneracy of the *Faith*, when Christians become Mussulmans to save their lives, and Mussulmans become the followers of the False Prophet, to save their property. They are going to preach against this, but I fear much that when it is a question between Allah and their goats, &c., they will be inclined to look after their goats, as a rule. I am afraid we are much the same, and would prefer 50,000 men at our backs, than any Scripture promises; it is only when we are pushed into a corner, and cannot get the 50,000 men, that we turn to the promises—at least, that is so to a great extent with me. There is no doubt that success makes men hard on their fellows, while misfortune makes them soft. (One has only to study the demeanour of a Cabinet Minister, or a Colonel while in office, or out of office, to be convinced of this truth.)

I do not believe that fanaticism exists as it used to do in the world, judging from what I have seen, in this so-called fanatic land. It is far more a question of property, and is more like communism under the flag of religion, which seems to excite and to give colour to acts which men would otherwise condemn.[21]

I am sure it is unknown to the generality of our missionaries in Muslim countries, that in the Koran no imputation of sin is made on our Lord, neither is it hinted that

[20] "I have upset so many vested interests, that the only people I can count on are the Ulema, to whom I gave back all their ancient privileges, which had been taken away from them by Ismail Pasha Yacoub."—*Extract from General Gordon's letter dated Kartoum, May 4th*, 1877.—ED.

[21] "If fighting occurs, it is the Soudanese conservative of their property fighting the Soudanese communists, who desire to rob them."—*Extract from General Gordon's Memorandum received by Sir E. Baring, February* 4th, 1884.—*Egypt, No.* 12.—ED.

He had need of pardon, and, further, no Muslim can deny that the Father of our Lord was God (*vide* Chapter III. of Koran, "the Family of Imuran"), and that He was incarnated by a miracle. Our bishops content themselves with its being a false religion, but it is a false religion professed by millions on millions of our fellow creatures. The Muslims do not say Mahomet was without sin, the Koran often acknowledges that he erred, but no Muslim will say "*Jesus sinned*." As far as self-sacrifice of the body, they are far above Roman Catholics, and consequently above Protestants. It is positive trouble when one calls one's servant to be continually told he is at his prayers, and one cannot think that this is an excuse, for it can be no pleasure to be in a constrained position for a considerable time, unless one had some faith in those prayers. The God of the Muslims is *our* God. And they do not believe that Mahomet exercises any mediatorial office for them. They believe they will stand and fall by their own deeds: in fact they are as much under the law as the Jews.

During our blockade, we have often discussed the question of being frightened, which, in the world's view, a man should never be. For my part I am always frightened, and very much so. I fear the future of all engagements.[22] It is not the fear of death, that is past, thank God; but I fear defeat, and its consequences. I do not believe a bit in the calm, unmoved man. I think it is only that he does not show it outwardly. Thence I conclude no commander of forces ought to live closely in relation with his subordinates, who watch him like lynxes, for there is no contagion equal to that of fear. I have been rendered furious, when, from anxiety, I could not

[22] "We have, thank God, passed our dangers. Whether they were imaginary or not I do not know, but we were threatened by an attack from thousands of determined blacks, who knew I was here. Now very few Englishmen know what it is to be with troops they have not a bit of confidence in. I prayed heartily for an issue, but it gave me a pain in the heart like that I had when surrounded at Masindi. I do not fear death, but I fear, from want of faith, the results of my death—for the whole country would have risen."—*Extract from General Gordon's letter dated Toashia, July 11th*, 1877.—ED.

eat, I would find those at the same table were in like manner affected.

The Greek Consul came back from seeing the Greek, who brought a letter[23] from Waled a Goun, asking me to surrender. I answered as per margin,[24] saying I did not see it. The Greek's object was to get us to surrender. He says: Lupton,[25] of Bahr Gazelle, has come down to Shaka, with his men to surrender, and that Emin Bey of the Equator is said to be also captured. The Greek says, "Cuzzi left yesterday for Berber. Slatin Bey[26] was in Kordofan. The Mahdi was on his way here." According to the Greek Consul, this man came in to get money for the Greek prisoners, and for little else. I have left the Greek Consul to do what he likes with regard to this.

There was an earthquake, lasting some seconds, at 9 P.M. to-night; like the other ones, it was from south to north.

When one thinks of the enormous loss of life which has taken place in the Soudan since 1880, and the general upset of all government, one cannot help feeling vicious against Sir Auckland Colvin, Sir Edward Malet, and Sir Charles Dilke, for it is on account of those three men, whose advice was taken by Her Majesty's Government, that all these sorrows are due. They went in for the bondholders, and treated as chimerical any who thought differently from them . . . . by letting Sir Auckland Colvin and Sir Edward Malet stay in Egypt when he went there, got let into their ways. Time has shown the result of their policy, and we shall hear of them no more. In a minor degree the *Times* correspondent at Cairo and Alexandria is a sinner, for he backed them. We are an honest nation, but our diplomatists are conies, and not *officially* honest.

September 13.—Sent out notifications to all the authorities in Egypt and the Soudan to search Cuzzi closely, for I think

[23] Appendix C. [24] Appendix C 1.

[25] Lupton Bey was Governor of the Bahr el Gazelle.—ED.

[26] According to a telegram from M. Herbin to M. Barrère, Slatin Bey, formerly Governor of Darfour, had by this time joined the Mahdi, and by him had been placed in command of the Kordofan cavalry, which force was supposed to represent the most formidable contingent of the Mahdi's army.—ED.

he is an emissary of the Mahdi; this can be done under pretence of customs. I am inclined to think that Cuzzi betrayed Berber to the Arabs, for how else can the different treatment he received from the Mahdi from all other Europeans be accounted for?

Five of our soldiers captured at Obeyed came in to-day; they report the Arabs not strong, and not meditating immediate action (they brought their arms with them); they say the Arabs knew of our expedition to Berber.

The Ulema sent a letter[27] to the Mahdi to-day; these letters are interesting, for they show the views of these people.

The steamers are reported to have passed the Shoboloha defile safely; they ought to be at Berber to-day.

Note that I do not call our enemy rebels, but Arabs, for it is a vexed question whether we are not rebels, seeing I hold the Firman restoring Soudan to its chiefs.

The Greek who came in yesterday told the Greek doctor here that the superior of the mission at Obeyed *alone* has kept his faith; his name is "Luigi Bonomi;" the other priests and nuns all have become Muslims (so he says); the nuns have nominally married Greeks to save themselves from outrage. He says Cuzzi received two horses, a wife, a slave, and $60[28] from the Mahdi, with whom he was on the closest terms of intimacy. He says, Slatin had 4000 ardebs[29] of dhoora and 1500 cows, and plenty of ammunition when he surrendered; he has been given eight horses by the Mahdi (all this information must be taken with reserve). The Greeks here made up £38 for their compatriots in captivity, and the Austrian Consul sent $100 to the mission at Obeyed.[30] I gave the Greek $5, which I expect was wasted, and I doubt if the

[27] Appendix D.

[28] Dollars.

[29] An ardeb is equal to five bushels.

[30] The Names of Mission at Obeyed.

Prêtres à Kordofan.

1. Don Luigi Bonomi, *Superior.*
2. Don Guiseppe Ohrwalder.
3. Don Paulo Nusignoli.
4. Fra Isodoro Locatelli.
5. Fra Guiseppe Regusto.

Sœurs.

1. Teresa Grigolini, *Superioress.*
2. Fortunata Corce.
3. Catarina Chincherini.
4. Cometta Çorsi.
5. Elizabetta Venturini.
6. Maria Caprini.

Greek will not keep all the money he has received. I grudge the $20 I gave Cuzzi, for I expect he is a vile traitor. I expect he gave the Mahdi all the ciphers; fortunately he had not the Foreign Office cipher, which Stewart has carried off. Had I known this information about Cuzzi I ought to have decapitated him, but it is as well I left him to his fate.

If what the Greek says is true about the apostacy of all but Don Luigi, what a spectacle! for certainly these people came to this country with more faith than those that stay at home; they could not expect any comforts in it, but much self-denial. Some of those nuns had as much as £1000 a year, which they left to come here. Of course the Greek's statement is open to much doubt.

Slatin's name is Abdel Kadi; Cuzzi's name is Mahomet Yusuf. Mahdi proposes I should put myself, on my surrender (?) under Abou Gugliz, who is a *notorious breaker* of the Dervish rules. I forgot in my letter to remark on this. It appears each of these men have a spiritual adviser with them, who acts as a spy as well.

Two more of the Obeyed soldiers escaped this afternoon; they say the Arabs meditate putting a gun on the Blue Nile above Bourré, and another in front of south front of Lines, with the idea of bombarding the town.

Psammitichus[31] besieged Azotus or Ashdod for twenty-nine years (according to Herodotus). What a life for the people of Azotus! One is tired enough of this, and we have only had six months of it. Azotus or Ashdod is a miserable little village between Jafa (which, by the way, is called after *Japhet*, the son of Noah) and Gaza.

The black soldiers who come in are generally old acquaintances of mine, *i.e.* they know me, while their black pug faces are all alike to me. I like the Chinese best, then the pug-faced blacks, then the chocolate Soudan people. I do not like the tallow-faced fellaheen, though I feel sorry for them.

Ezekiel xxix. and xxx. are interesting, for they show Egypt to be doomed to be the basest of kingdoms, the slave of

[31] King of Egypt.—ED.

kingdoms, never possessing a ruler of its own race (Mahomet Ali was a Sandjak[32] of Salonica, and an alien to this land). The judgments on this land are on account of its cruelties in respect to the slave trade. Berber (which Colonel Stewart ought to pass to-night) is 200 miles from Merowé, where the cataracts cease, thence there is open water to Dongola, 150 miles distant from Merowé; he ought there to find the telegraph open, and so on the 20th of September he ought to be in communication with Cairo and Europe.

One thing puzzles me is, if it was really determined to abandon the Soudan to its fate, why the people of Dongola and of Senheit were not withdrawn, when the determination was taken; there could be no possible object for keeping the peoples in those places. I think if, instead of "Minor Tactics" or books on art of war, we were to make our young officers study "Plutarch's Lives," it would be better; there we see men (unsupported by any true belief, pure pagans), making *as matter of course*, their lives a sacrifice, but in our days it is the highest merit not to run away. I speak for myself when I say I have been in dire anxiety, not for my own skin, but because I hate to be beaten, and I hate to see my schemes fail; but that I have had to undergo a tithe of what any nurse has to undergo, who is attached to a querulous invalid, is absurd, and not to be weighed together. When I emerge all are complimentary; when the invalid dies the question is, what should be given to the nurse for her services. We profess to be followers of our Lord, who, from His birth, when He was hunted, till His death, may be said to have had no sympathy or kindness shown Him, yet we (and I say myself especially) cry out if we are placed in any position of suffering, whereas it is our *métier*, if we are Christians, to undergo such suffering. I have led the officers and officials the lives of dogs while I have been up here; it is spurs in their flanks every day; nothing can obliterate this ill-treatment from my memory. I may say that I have not given them a moment's peace; they are conies, but I ought to have been more considerate. It is quite painful

32 The commander of several companies.—Ed.

to see men tremble so when they come and see me, that they cannot hold the match to their cigarette. Yet I have cut off no heads; I only killed two Pashas, and I declare, had it not been for outside influences, those two Pashas would have been alive now; they were judicially murdered.[33] Happy, as far as we can see, are those men who swing in small arcs; unhappy are those who, seeking the field of adventure, swing from the extremes of evil and good. The neutral tint is the best for wear.

What a contradiction is life! I hate Her Majesty's Government for their leaving the Soudan after having caused all its troubles; yet I believe our Lord rules heaven and earth, so I ought to hate Him, which I (sincerely) do not.

I hear Hansall, the Austrian Consul, is disposed to go with *his seven female attendants* to the Arabs. I hope he will do so.

Heaps of cattle come in every day, but very little grain. Seyd Mahomet Osman has sent word to his people to go to Kartoum for refuge; this is pleasant for us! but it shows his confidence in our future, and it is a great honour to me, who (thank God) am given faith to outspeak "I am a Christian,"

[33] "Surviving Soudanese declared that the two Pashas in command charged back into their own square; the soldiers, recognising them, opened their ranks to let them through; and into the gap thus made the rebel cavalry followed. The treachery, doubtless pre-arranged, was complete in its success, but retribution was close at hand. When the battle was over these two traitors, Said and Hassan, came into Gordon's tent, and the General offered them drink. They refused; Gordon's secretary, divining the reason, drank first, and the Pashas, who had suspected poison, followed suit. During the remainder of that day they lay hidden in their homes, for the soldiers were crying aloud for vengeance, and would have murdered them at once had they appeared in the streets. The next day they were tried by court-martial, and found guilty of communication with the enemy and of having treacherously murdered their own men. In the house of Hassan a great store of rifles and ammunition was discovered; and it was proved that both he and his colleague had stolen the two months' pay given to the troops on account of six months' arrears. They had also taken into the field with them seventy rounds of cannon ammunition, instead of eight, the usual number, so that the rebels' guns might be well supplied for future attacks on Kartoum. The trial was long and patient, but the verdict was apparent from the beginning. Hassan and Said were found guilty, and on the same evening, amid expressions of universal delight, they were shot by the men they had betrayed."—*The Story of Chinese Gordon, pp.* 92-3, v. ii.—ED.

to have obtained such confidence from a man, who would, in the times of my glory, scarcely look at me.

One of his (Seyd Mahomet Osman's) men going down to Shendy (where his sister, a very plucky woman, lives) was taking down a pair of slippers for her, and he brought them here; I wrote my name on the inside of each, and told him to tell the "Sitt," or lady, when she put them on, she put her claw on my head; the man came back the other day, and said the "Sitt" was delighted with the idea.

What a row the Pope will make about the nuns marrying the Greeks! It is the union of the Greek and Latin churches.

September 14.—Yesterday evening the Arabs fired four cannon shots towards Lines on south front, but they did not reach the fortifications.

Halfeyeh[34] reports the assembly of the Arabs, with a view to attacking that place. A party has gone out to see what truth there is in this report.

Four other men came in from the Arabs to-day; they had little to say, beyond that the Arabs meant to maintain a blockade, and not to attack directly.

The Arabs killed four soldiers who tried to escape, but those who came in say this will not stop their coming.

A man I sent out to Waled Mocashee, who fought with Waled a Goun (*vide* Stewart's journal), was caught with my letters by Arabs, and was on the eve of being hung, when my letter arrived, in which I remonstrated with the Arabs for ill-treating my messengers, on which they pardoned him, and let him go. This man says the Greek, who came into the Lines yesterday, was sent off to Kordofan on his return to the Arab camp. The Arabs would have been quite justified in executing the man above alluded to, for he was a genuine spy; my remonstrance to them was with respect to their treatment of *direct* messengers I sent to them; there is considerable doubt that even Waled Mocashee ever did fight with Waled a Goun.

In my letter to Sheikh Abdel Kader, I proposed to him to

[34] *i.e.* Natives from Halfeyeh report.—Ed.

come in and see me; the Arab chiefs asked him to go, but he would not; it is well known we have refused to give in.

If it is possible to get rid of the bitter feelings existing between the two great sections of the Soudan people,[35] it will go a great way to pacify the country; by degrees this may be done.

Meat has fallen from 10*s.* per lb. to 2*s.* per lb.

The steamer *Towfikia*, which went up the Blue Nile to Giraffe, fell on the Arabs, and drove them off from collecting grass and wood (one is thankful for small mercies in these times).

The word "Islam" means the resigning or devoting oneself entirely to God and His service, *i.e.* self-sacrifice: consequently a true Christian is of the Islam religion, as far as the name goes (this is Sale's translation of the word Islam).

It is curious how quick the people forget their disasters and losses; it is only ten days ago that we lost in killed nearly one thousand men, yet no one speaks of it now; it takes about four or six days to obliterate the bitterness of a disaster.

The old bugbear of the defection of the Shaggyeh has sprung up again. Saleh Pasha, who is a prisoner with the Mahdi, has written to his brother to say he and the Mahdi are coming, and that he is not to join me. These sort of things, which are taken up as gospel truth by those around me, are one of the most disagreeable parts of my position; those who will one day declare that the Shaggyeh are faithful, will two days after urge one to take the sharpest measures of repression against them, which is, to my mind, just the way to push them into rebellion, if they had any tendency that way (I mean by rebellion, joining the Arabs).

Saleh Pasha's brother came in to-day to see me; he has heard that his brother is with the Mahdi at Schatt, a place inland from Duem, on White Nile. He seems to think this is authentic; if so, we shall have the Mahdi here ere long; he has been there nine days.

The news of the near approach of the Mahdi has not

[35] Those for, and those against the Mahdi.—ED.

troubled me, for if he fails he is lost, and there will be no necessity for an expedition to Kordofan; if he succeeds, he may, by his presence, prevent any massacre. I have always felt we were doomed to come face to face ere the matter was ended.

I toss up in my mind, whether, if the place is taken, to blow up the palace and all in it, or else to be taken, and, with God's help, to maintain the faith, and if necessary to suffer for it (which is most probable). The blowing up of the palace is the simplest, while the other means long and weary suffering and humiliation of all sorts. I think I shall elect for the last, not from fear of death, but because the former has more or less the taint of suicide, as it can do no good to any one, and is, in a way, taking things out of God's hand.

Schatt is twenty miles inland from Duem, which is one hundred miles from here, on left bank of White Nile.

The Greek who came in told the Greek Consul that the Mahdi puts pepper under his nails, and when he receives visitors then he touches his eyes and weeps copiously; that he eats a few grains of dhoora openly, but in the interior of the house he has fine feeding and drinks alcoholic drinks.

The Greek says the Mahdi has lots of letters from Cairo,[36] Stamboul, and India; that his constant conversation is Kartoum, and his chance of its capture.

After this pepper business! I think I shall drop any more trouble in writing him letters, trying to convince or persuade him to reasonable measures.

The Greek told the Greek Consul that the Mahdi was perplexed to know what on earth I was doing up here, as I had no part or lot in the Soudan. I expect this question is more perplexing for others than the Mahdi (myself included). I must confess that the pepper business has sickened me; I had hitherto hoped I had to do with a regular fanatic, who believed in his mission, but when one comes to pepper in

[36] "I strongly suspect that he (the Mahdi) is a mere puppet put forward by Elyas, Zubair's father-in-law, and the largest slave-owner in Obeyed, and that he has assumed a religious title to give colour to the defence of the popular rights."—*General Gordon's view as expressed to the Editor of "Pall Mall Gazette" on Jan.* 8, 1884.—ED.

the finger nails, it is rather humiliating to have to succumb to him, and somehow I have the belief that I shall not have to do so. One cannot help being amused at this pepper business. Those who come in, for pardon, come in on their knees, with a halter round their neck. The Mahdi rises, having scratched his eyes and obtained a copious flow of tears, and takes off the halter! As the production of tears is generally considered the proof of sincerity, I would recommend the Mahdi's recipe to Cabinet Ministers, justifying some job. The nails (so say the Greeks) must be long! to contain the pepper.

September 15.—Another escaped soldier came in this morning; reports that they are waiting orders of the Mahdi, and do not mean to attack the Lines. Charity thinketh no evil. She was not in the Soudan, for I declare, what with the tricks of the officials here, Charity would have had a bad time of it.

They say the Mahdi, when he goes out and sees a woman carrying a jar of water, rushes at her and begs to be allowed to carry the water. He rushes up to the Sitt[37] even as I do, only I have not tried the water-carrying.

It appears that the pepper business is of old date in the Soudan, and not invented by the Mahdi.

The strength of Eastern potentates is the seclusion they live in; they are sacred. Once they are known, they are done for, and perhaps the Mahdi coming here will do for him. As long as he could put the misdeeds of his subordinates on them, he was all right, but when the people see that he does nothing to rectify wrongs, his prestige ought to go.

This afternoon one of Seyd Mahomet Osman's family came up from Shendy; he reports the Stewart expedition having passed Shendy,[38] that they captured a large boat with grain and twenty-four slaves, which was collecting taxes for the Arabs. He reports as true the arrival of troops at Dongola; that the Mudir of Dongola has quieted his province; that the Arab chief Mahomet el Khair, of Berber, on hearing troops had come to Dongola, sent round to collect the Arabs, pro-

[37] A woman.—ED.
[38] Shendy is ninety-five miles from Kartoum.—ED.

mising them $20 a month, half responded to the call, and came to Berber and asked for their pay. Mahomet el Khair sent them to a house where he said the money was (the Government money, the celebrated £60,000 which was given to me at Cairo!) When they entered the house, no money was found, and Mahomet el Khair explained it by saying the devil had caused it to enter the earth! He then *pretended* that the Mahdi had sent for him, and bolted. He seems to have seen he could not hold out. If he goes to the Mahdi, and does not account in some better way for the disappearance of the money, I fear it will go hard with him, for the Mahdi, although he allows certain freedom in miraculous events, is likely to be chary in allowing such events among his followers, especially when they affect his pocket.

Another captured soldier escaped and came in. He says the Arabs begin to notice these diminutions of their men, and to be very strict. Nearly all the soldiers knew me personally in Darfour.

As for the £60,000 which has been lost and stolen by Soudan Arabs, it is only a tithe of what has been stolen from the Soudan by the Egyptian Pashas, that effete race, so I do not regret it.

We hope to finish another of those small steamers in twenty days, like the *Abbas* (which went down to Dongola with Stewart), and in another forty days to complete another one, this will complete the four steamers bought by Colonel Prout[39] in 1878; one of them, the *Mahomet Ali*, is in the hands of the Arabs, having been surrendered by Saleh Bey.

I should not be surprised if Berber surrendered to Stewart's expedition. It was a miserable defence it made, and the people were never very much inclined for the Mahdi. I cannot help thinking Cuzzi was at the bottom of its surrender.

The *Towfikia* steamer went up above Giraffe to-day, fired on some Arabs and captured a cow. Four of the captured soldiers of Obeyed escaped here; they had little to say, beyond

[39] Colonel Prout was appointed by General Gordon to the command of the Equatorial Provinces at the date of the latter's resignation in the autumn of 1876.—ED.

that they had been very miserable, and that the Arabs hoped we would surrender.

I sincerely hope that Berber will surrender to Stewart's party; it would be a great feather in his cap.

The majority of the soldiers who come in bring their rifles.

Haunting the palace are a lot of splendid hawks. I often wonder whether they are destined to pick my eyes, for I fear I was not the best of sons.[40]

"Enough for the day is the evil thereof," but I cannot help feeling appalled at what is to happen; even if we do manage to extricate Kartoum from its troubles, we will have to quiet down all the countries around Sennaar and Kassala, and to withdraw from the Bahr Gazelle, and Equator (for I do not believe the Greek's story about those lands being evacuated). Then comes the question of whether the prisoners in Kordofan are to be left to their fate. If Her Majesty's Government has entered the field this is impossible, and if Her Majesty's Government prevent Egypt extricating them, then it is virtually Her Majesty's Government who leaves them to their fate. Besides this, there is the terrible outlay of money (which has to be met) for current expenses. Also who is to govern the country. All idea of evacuation *en masse* must be given up, it is totally impossible, and the only solution is to let the Turks come in, or else to leave me here, the very thought of which makes me shudder, or to send up Zubair Pasha;[41] in both cases a subsidy of £100,000 is needed per annum.

September 16.—The man left in charge of the Roman Catholic Mission's garden is furious with the Austrian Consul for taking those $100 he sent to the captives at Obeyed. He says that had he known they had become Muslim he would have sent them poison. The $100 came from the sale of produce of the garden. Whether his anger is owing to his bigotry, or to the having to give up the $100, is a question.

40 "The eye that mocketh at his father and despiseth to obey his mother, the ravens of the valley shall pick it out, and the young eagles shall eat it."—Prov. xxx. 17.—ED.

41 Zubair is the correct spelling. It must not be forgotten that Zubair is of very high family, being a direct descendant of the "Abbassides."—ED.

He says he cannot leave, for he is in charge of the Bishop's robes. I expect he holds on to the garden, whose dates alone sold for over $1600.

A woman escaped from the Arabs this morning.

The notes to Sale's Koran, chapter xix., entitled "Mary," are very interesting, as containing the Muslim view of our Lord's conception. The sixteenth chapter of Koran, entitled "the Bee," is considered to allow Muslims to apostatise, if forced by violence to do so (*vide* Sale's notes with regard to Moseilama), though it is more meritorious not to do so. So the Muslim here are well off in this respect, *vis-à-vis*, the Mahdi.

Faki Mustapha, who commanded on the left bank of the White Nile, and who retired into the interior, was expected to come over to us. He however has written a letter[42] in abusive terms to Cassim el Mousse, in which he maintains that Mahomet Achmet is the Mahdi. Another soldier came in with two rifles. *Towfikia* went up the Blue Nile, and took on board two runaway slaves. Another man came in with a letter from a man who is a prisoner with the Arabs, which letter says positively that 22,000 troops are at Dongola, and that the Mudir of Dongola is at Merowé, and is pushing on his men.

The soldier who brought in *two* rifles accounts for it by saying he started with his companion to come; that his companion got frightened and dreaded to delay, so they sat down and his companion went to sleep; so my friend thought it was time to be off, and that it was as well to take his comrade's rifle with him!!

September 17.—I have the strongest suspicion that these tales of troops at Dongola and Merowé are all gas-works, and that if you wanted to find Her Majesty's forces you would have to go to Shepheard's Hotel at Cairo.[43]

The reports of the advance which we get from Seyd Osman are never supported by any written evidence from Dongola,

[42] Appendix E.

[43] Lord Wolseley and staff left Cairo for Wady Halfa ten days after Gordon wrote those words.—Ed.

and I expect they are invented. Whether the resurrection of Stewart, Power, and Herbin will have any effect remains to be seen, but, ill-natured or not, it is my firm impression that Her Majesty's Government will be most disagreeably surprised by their emerging.

If Stewart gets down, he ought to be in communication with Europe on the 22nd of September, and Power's telegrams ought to be in *Times* 23rd September. It makes me laugh to think of the flutter in the dovecot which will follow. "*That beastly Soudan again!*" (Africa has indeed been a "beast" to our country, as one of Dickens's characters called it.)

Egerton's telegram,[44] carefully written in cipher (and equally carefully without date, but which we ascribe to June), respecting the contracts to be entered into with the Bedouin tribes to escort us down ("and be sure to look after *yourself*"*!*) might have been as well written in Arabic, it would have produced hilarity with the Mahdi. Two escaped soldiers came in with little news, they came with their arms.

A man came in from visiting the Sheikh el Obeyed. He says that the Arabs lost very few in their attack on Mahomet

[44] Lord Granville on May 17, 1884, instructed Mr. Egerton to communicate the following message from Her Majesty's Government to General Gordon :—

"Having regard to the time which has elapsed, Her Majesty's Government desire to add to their communication of the 23rd April as follows :—As the original plan for the evacuation of the Soudan has been dropped, and as aggressive operations cannot be undertaken with the countenance of Her Majesty's Government, General Gordon is enjoined to consider and either to report upon, or, if feasible, to adopt, at the first proper moment, measures for his own removal and for that of the Egyptians at Kartoum who have suffered for him or who have served him faithfully, including their wives and children, by whatever route he may consider best, having especial regard to his own safety and that of the other British subjects.

"With regard to the Egyptians above referred to, General Gordon is authorised to make free use of money rewards or promises at his discretion. For example, he is at liberty to assign to Egyptian soldiers at Kartoum sums for themselves and for persons brought with them per head, contingent on their safe arrival at Korosko, or whatever point he may consider a place of safety ; or he may employ and pay the tribes in the neighbourhood to escort them. Her Majesty's Government presume that the Soudanese at Kartoum are not in danger. In the event of General Gordon having dispatched any persons or agents to other points, he is authorised to spend any money required for the purpose of recalling them or securing their safety."—*Egypt*, 22, 1884, *No.* 22.—Ed.

Ali Pasha; that they will wait till the river falls ere they try and close in on Kartoum.

The righteous indignation, expressed on the publication of that slave circular, which did nothing more than say "that the treaty of 1877 (declaring that the slaves would not be *allowed to be sold after* 1887) would not be put in force," is rather amusing to think over (a *pact with the devil*, as, I dare say, some called it), when one thinks that the probability is the whole country will be a nest of slave hunters and banditti.

They say the Mahdi means to take up his quarters on the left bank of the Nile, so as to have his retreat clear to Kordofan in case of accidents.

The *Towfikia* steamer went up the Blue Nile, and found the Arabs near Giraffe, with three guns, which fired five or six rounds at the steamer, but did no harm.

The pomp of Egerton's telegram, informing me "that Her Majesty's Government would (really!) pay on delivery so much a head for all refugees *delivered* on Egyptian frontier, and would (*positively*, it is incredible!) *reward* tribes with whom I might contract, to escort them down."

It was too generous for one to believe! Egerton's chivalrous nature must have got the better of his diplomatic training when he wrote it! The clerks in my divan, to whom I disclosed it, are full of exclamations of wonder at this generosity! Egerton must consider that I was a complete idiot to have needed such a permission. I hope he will get promoted, and will not be blamed for his overstraining his instructions!

Another soldier escaped with his wife; he says: The Arabs brought three guns down to cover their foraging party, and have taken them back, which is a relief to me.

I own to a great fear that Stewart's journal will not be published *in extenso*, but will be doctored; if so, it is a great pity, for there are lots of nice things in it. For really it is my journal as much as Stewart's, though he wrote it.

When the escaped soldiers come in, they pay me a visit, and are given a dollar, made to look at their black pug faces in the mirrors, which are in the palace, and asked their opinion of the reflections. Some stare with wide open eyes, for *they have never seen themselves before.* They generally approve of the reflections, especially the black sluts, who think themselves "Venuses," and shove their hands into their mouths, which is a general sign among blacks of great modesty, like the casting down of the eyes with us.

Faki Mustapha's letter[45] caused great commotion among the Ulema, for he says, "He will destroy the Korans, and shut the mosques, and listen only to the Mahdi."

There is a tone in Egerton's telegram[46] which grates on me; it is, *to me*, as if he said, "You have got into a mess, and although you do not deserve it, I am willing to stretch a point in your favour, and authorize you," &c. And in the previous part (the author unknown) of the telegram, it is as if I was enjoying this wretched fighting up here. I declare it is Egerton and Co. who made the mess, and would like to hang its fabrication and solution on me, not that I mind the burthen, if they did not send such telegrams (the Co. are Malet and Colvin).[47]

I must say I do not love Diplomatists as a rule (and I can fancy the turning up of noses at my venturing to express an opinion of them), I mean in their official attire, for, personally, the few I know are most agreeable (and I specially except Alston, the chief clerk, and Weller, the hall porter, who has, of late years, become quite amiable); but taking them on their rostrums, with their satellites, from their chiefs down to the smaller fry, no one can imagine a more unsatisfactory lot of men to have anything to do with. I have seen . . ., . . ., . . ., . . ., at different times, and when one left their august presences, one marvelled at the policy of Great Britain being in such hands. Lord Hammond was a Tartar, and one knew he was to be respected.

One would not so much mind if they did not inoculate with their virus those who get employed by them, but I have found Stokes of the Suez Canal, Wilson of Anatolia, and many others (I may say Stewart), all impregnated with their ideas

[45] Appendix E.
[46] *i.e.* The telegram given on page 27.—ED.
[47] See *ante*, note on page 27.—ED.

of sun worship and expediency. I own to having read with pleasure the "Queen's Messenger" till Lord Carrington stopped its publication, and Marvin's work on Public Offices.

A man has come in who says Stewart and his steamers have captured a large convoy of two hundred camel-loads of stuff belonging to the Arabs. They had passed Shendy, and had not been fired upon.

The Mahdi will be furious.

I do not think the resources of this place are known. We can turn out 50,000 rounds of Remington ammunition a week, there are some 10,000 rounds of mountain-gun ammunition in store, and if the Mahdi takes Kartoum (which will entail the fall of every town in Soudan) it will need a large force to stay his propaganda. According to the Greek he meditates an invasion of Egypt and Palestine, where they are all ready to rise.[48] All the steamers on the Nile, even below Assouan, are but crockery, if struck by a mountain-gun shell; consequently, if the people rose at Esneh they could, by the Mahdi sending down two guns, stop the river. The further the Mahdi is off from the people who rise, the stronger he is; here we are near him, and hear all about his festivities and pepper business; at Esneh this would be lost in the mists of distance, still more so at Cairo and in Palestine. What have we done in Lower Egypt to make them like us? Not a single thing. We have foisted Europeans on them to the extent of £450,000

[48] "The danger to be feared is not that the Mahdi will march northward through Wady Halfa; on the contrary, it is very improbable that he will ever go so far north. The danger is altogether of a different nature. It arises from the influence which the spectacle of a conquering Mahommedan Power, established close to your frontiers, will exercise upon the population which you govern. In all the cities in Egypt it will be felt that what the Mahdi has done they may do; and, as he has driven out the intruder and the infidel, they may do the same. Nor is it only England that has to face this danger. The success of the Mahdi has already excited dangerous fermentation in Arabia and Syria. Placards have been posted in Damascus calling upon the population to rise and drive out the Turks. If the whole of the Eastern Soudan is surrendered to the Mahdi, the Arab tribes on both sides the Red Sea will take fire. In self-defence the Turks are bound to do something to cope with so formidable a danger, for it is quite possible that if nothing is done the whole of the Eastern Question may be reopened by the triumph of the Mahdi."—*General Gordon's views, as expressed to the Editor of the "Pall Mall Gazette."*—Ed.

a year; we have not reduced taxes, only improved the way of extorting those taxes. The Mahdi says, "I will take one-tenth of your produce, and I will rid you of the 'dogs'"—a most captivating programme! If well led, and once he takes Kartoum, the combined forces of France and England will not be able to subdue him, unless they go at his nest. From a *professional military point of view*, and *speaking materially*, I wish I was the Mahdi, and I would laugh at all Europe. Query (believing all the above as I do)—would I be justified in coming to terms with Mahdi, on the understanding that he should let down all refugees (on the Egerton contract arrangement), while I should give over to him, unhurt, all warlike material in Kartoum?

Certainly, according to the letter, I would be justified in so doing; and *then* what! of what I feel sure will happen, *i.e.*, a rising in Egypt occurs, what will my nation say? (for Egerton will disappear by some appointment in Chili) they will say it is my fault; but (*D.V.*) they shall not say so, for I will not give up the place except with my life. It cannot be too strongly impressed on the public that it is not the Mahdi's forces which are to be feared, but the rising of the populations by his emissaries. I do not believe he had four thousand men when he defeated Hicks. We have to think what would a garrison of ten thousand men do in Cairo if the population rose.

Had Zubair Pasha been sent up when I asked for him, Berber would in all probability never have fallen, and one might have made a Soudan Government in opposition to the Mahdi. We choose to refuse his coming up because of his antecedents *in re* slave trade; granted that we had reason, yet as we take no precautions as to the future of these lands with respect to the slave trade, the above opposition seems absurd. I will not send up A. because he will do this, but I will leave the country to B., who will do exactly the same.

September 18.—Men came to Halfeyeh from Shendy, and report in further detail, the attack on the market of Metemma,[49]

[49] A town nearly opposite to Shendy, on the left bank of the Nile.—Ed.

and capture of a lot of things. They report also the arrival of troops at Dongola, and their advance towards Berber (saying that a reconnaissance was just pushed out to ascertain if Kartoum had fallen or not). Three escaped soldiers came in from Arabs; they report that a lot of troops are at Fashoda.[50] I suppose those from Equator or Bahr Gazelle; it appears they have been at Fashoda some little time, and have lots of cows, &c. They did not like to come on, for they did not know if Kartoum existed.

10 A.M.—A fight is going on between the *Towfikia* steamer and five hundred of our men and the Arabs, near Giraffe. The Arabs are retiring towards the White Nile. I sent out the men to get wood, &c. The Arabs did ditto, thence the collision.

The three men who came in to-day, say the Arabs, seeing the numbers who desert them, take the rifles from the men at night, and give them out by day.

These men say the Mahdi knows of the advance of the troops on Berber, and is in a way about it.

Yesterday, previous to hearing the news of to-day, I had arranged for the departure of the Greek Consul and subjects to the Equator, and then their retreat, *viâ* Zanzibar, but it will now be held in abeyance, till we see the corroboration or not, of this advance of troops to Berber.

The following meditations as to the future, may save a good deal of talking: therefore I write them. Supposing it to be true, an expeditionary force comes to Berber, composed of partly British troops. What will result? The Mahdi's people will retire still further into the interior, and some of his people will come in. The chief of the expeditionary force will say, "Now the road from Kartoum to Berber is open, retire the garrison." He may say, "I will give you three months to do it in." Well, we send up steamers to the Equator and Bahr Gazelle, and the garrison of Kartoum marches on Sennaar and we get down the refugees, and garrisons from those places. Of course the moment it is known we are going to evacuate, we

[50] An old hot-bed of slavery on the White Nile.—Ed.

drive all neutrals, and even friendlies of the country into the arms of the Mahdi, for they will calculate "We are going to be left, and consequently we must, for our own interests, do something for the Mahdi, in order to hedge our position." This means that arrayed against our evacuation will be the mass of those living in our midst, and who are now with us. This is disagreeable, but one cannot help seeing that it is quite impossible to keep British troops after January. Therefore I maintain we must instal Zubair with a subsidy or give over country to the Sultan with a subsidy. There is no option. If it is determined to do neither, but to evacuate purely and simply, then when the Sennaar garrison is brought down, give me the steamers, and the black troops, who are willing to go, and let me take them up to Equator, while the expeditionary force goes down to Berber. I must say I think this will be a mistake, to leave the prisoners in Obeyed, and to let the Mahdi gain Kartoum.

As for Kassala, it must be relieved, by a separate expedition from Massowah and Senheit. Supposing the evacuation, and non-establishment of a regular government (under Zubair or the Turks) is determined upon, the Mahdi would, on taking Kartoum, think twice of moving on Egypt, if I was on his rear at Equator, with all the steamers.

No one can feel more strongly than I do, that January must see any British troops, who may come up on their way down to Egypt, *coûte que coûte.* This must be so, therefore I keep on, about giving the country to Sultan, or installing Zubair, with subsidies.

In the serail, we have a Turkey cock and five Turkey hens. They were all very tame, but having put the Turkey cock's head under his wing, and swung him into sleep, on one occasion, he is now shy to come near me; however, if one goes to his wives and scratches them he is furious, and comes up with his neck of all colours, but keeps out of range. I am sorry to say that one of his wives, having sat with patience for three weeks on eggs, and brought forth two chicks, *he killed them;* such is the accusation lodged against him by the cook. I think a Turkey cock, with every feather on end, and all the colours of the rainbow on his neck, is the picture of physical strength; his eye is an eye of fire, and there is no doubt of his being angry when he sees his wives touched. I am one of those who believe in the fore and future existence of what we call animals. We have the history of man, shaped in the image and likeness of God. He had breathed into him the breath of God, and became alive, while the waters and earth were told to bring forth animals *that had life already* (Gen. i. 20). "That hath life." Take Psalm viii. "What is man, Thou hast put *all things* under his feet." What a fall there is in the next verse, "*All sheep and oxen,*" and turn to Hebrews ii. 8, where the same Psalm is quoted, and where *all* things are subject to Him. All principalities, powers, and every existence are under Him. Why did the Psalmist go out of his way to quote "sheep and oxen," unless they were (so to say) the incarnation of those powers and principalities? Man, however much he has fallen, has the grand pre-eminence over all creatures, *he was shaped* (the word is the same as is used for a potter making a clay vessel) *in God's image and likeness*, and it is only God who could have so shaped him, as it is only God who knew His own likeness. Also when our Lord took our form (which he still keeps) as man, in Him dwelt the fulness of the Godhead, so that there is no doubt (as he differed only from us in being sinless) that man is capable of containing the fulness of the Godhead. Our belief is that *as man* our Lord governs heaven and earth, not a sparrow falling without His permission; this being so, the *capacity* of man must be such as to allow of his being so endowed as to rule all events in heaven and earth, for it is distinctly said our Lord was incarnated in a similar body to ours, except without sin. Our Lord, who is now man for ever and ever, is not likely to have taken a form which contained any hindrance to His fulness of His Godhead, therefore the form He took must be perfect, and as our difference between Him and us is our sin (which He has taken away), we, in our turn, must be capable of realising His fulness of Godhead, and my belief is that our future happiness is in being finite intelligences. We will keep on to all eternity, grasping the infinite knowledge of God which we are so formed as to be able to do, but which will last for ever inasmuch as He is infinite. When one gets on these subjects, and has to come down to this dreadful Soudan question, it is depressing; so also is the thought that misery here is our lot, for if we will be with our Master, we must be like Him, who from His birth to His death may be said to have been utterly miserable, as far as things in this world are concerned: yet I kick at the least obstacle to my will.

I certainly will, with all my heart and soul, do my best if any of Her Majesty's forces come up here or to Berber, to send them down before January, and will willingly take all the onus of having done so. Truly the people are not worth any *great* sacrifice, and we are only bound to them because of our dubious conduct in Egypt, to which bond there is a limit, which I fix in January. As for the Kordofan Europeans, with one exception, they have denied their Lord, and they deserve their fate in some measure.

September 19.—The ex-Khedive always said that the great difficulty of governing the Soudan, was the want of means of easy access, so he went into a great scheme of railways; he always said that the Government was bad because of the immunity which Governors enjoyed, owing to his being unable to control them. The Soudan, if once proper communication was established, would not be difficult to govern. The only mode of improving the access to the Soudan, seeing the impoverished state of Egyptian finances, and the mode to do so, without an outlay of more than £10,000, is by the Nile.

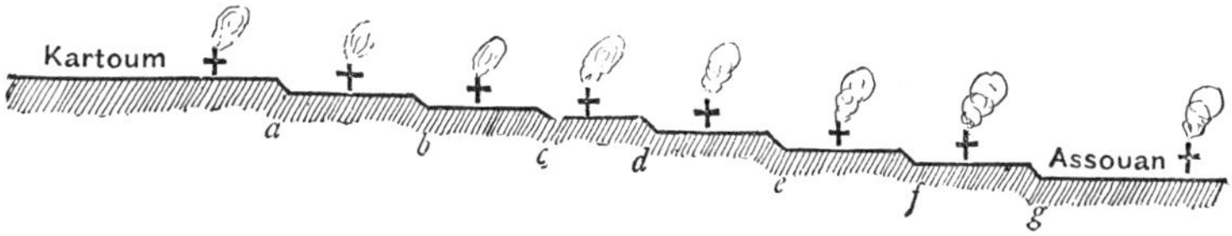

Take this section to be the bed of Nile from Kartoum to Assouan, *a b c d e f g* the cataracts; place steamers on the open spaces between cataracts, build small forts at cataracts, and a sure and certain road is open for ever.

The same crews would do for these steamers, for a weekly service would suffice. Camels should be placed at the cataracts for the transhipment of goods from steamer to steamer.

After the first outlay, which certainly would not be more than £10,000, for we have the steamers (I think £5000 would be enough), the thing would pay itself. Of course, it would be better to make loop tramways worked by animals, than to keep camels at the cataracts. I worked at this idea quietly for the time[51] I was in the Soudan before. Colonel Mason went down and examined the cataracts between Hannek

[51] "Ismail, the ex-Khedive, fully considered that, to maintain his hold of the Soudan, he must improve his communications with it and Egypt proper. Unfortunately, in his wish to bring the Soudan trade down the Nile through Egypt proper, he was led to abandon its natural outlet by the route from Berber to Suakin, across the 280-mile desert, and determined to make a railway through the desert along the Nile past the Cataracts from Wady Halfa to Hannek, a distance of 180 miles. Contracts were made, and some £450,000 were spent on the line; but financial difficulties arose, and in 1877 it came to a standstill some fifty or sixty kilometres south of Wady Halfa. It was evident that on this grand scale the continuation of the line could not be hoped for, so I studied the question. There was the line made from Wady Halfa for say fifty miles; and therefore 130 miles remained to be got over before this barrier of desert was passed. By the researches of Colonel Mason and Mr. Gooding, and also by my own personal examination, the river for this 130 miles was shown to be not continuously encumbered by rocks. There were, as it were, long strips of open water between the ridges of rocks,—one of these strips was forty miles in length. Now steamers built in England had in full flood been hauled up every one of these ridges, and had thus been brought to Kartoum and had plied to Gondokoro. My idea was to bring up small steamers during high Nile, place them on all the open strips of water of any reasonable extent; and thus work them from ridge to ridge in these open spaces. I proposed further to have only one crew, and to ship them from steamer to steamer so as to save expense. At those places where the ridge was of any great length, I proposed to use tramways to get over the space between the debarking landing-place of one open water-way to the embarking wharf of the other open water-way. Thus, by using the water-way where open, and tramways where the river was encumbered, I should get over these 130 miles. I calculated that the cost of all this work, steamers, and tramways, &c., would be £70,000, while the railway, if carried, would have cost over a million and a half. However, the revolts, troubles of different kinds, and other things, prevented this being carried out, and the controllers would not take it up; so, after an expense of nearly half-a-million, the railway exists with its end *en l'air*, with its valuable stores perishing, while Egypt proper has no more hold over the Soudan than was had by Ancient Egypt."—*See* "*Colonel Gordon in Central Africa*," *p.* 315.—Ed.

and Wady Halfa, and he found one space of open water forty miles in length. The Wady Halfa railway might be produced some nine kilometres, and brought down to river bank. The mass of the misfortunes of the Soudan arose from this idea of utilising the Nile not having been carried out, but one had to work at it quietly, for Cairo was bent on the Wady Halfa railway over which such sums had been spent. I even took one steamer up from Wady Halfa to Dongola (*i.e.* Mr. Baird, C.E., did so), to begin the chain of steamers.

No church parade to speak of; Arabs are now visible only on the south front, four or five miles distant. Arabs did not bring their gun down to the Blue Nile to-day, and no escaped prisoners came in. To-day is the Muslim Sabbath, and there is no office work. (Not that there is much on other days; however, one never sees any one from morning till night).

This has given me time to think over the outburst of indignation *in re* the slave circular. We did not see the papers, so can only guess what they said, but expect that this diabolical fact caused upraised hands in horror, "Was the world coming to an end?" What complete rubbish! Was it not announced openly that the Soudan was going to be abandoned, and consequently that the Soudanese were to be allowed to follow their own devices (which are decidedly slave-huntingly inclined)? What possible influence could my saying that that feeble Treaty of 1877 was not going to be enforced, have on people who were going to be abandoned? The sole and only object of my mission was to get out the garrisons and refugees without loss of life. And in saying what I did I merely told the people a platitude.

Baring deigned to say he would support me! Of course, that was an enormous assistance, to have his approbation. I expect that my asking for Zubair to come up was the last drop in the cup, and henceforth I was a complete pariah, yet, in reality, if the Soudan was to be abandoned, what difference could it possibly make whether Zubair or the Mahdi carried on slave-hunting, for, according to all accounts, the Mahdi is most active in this direction (so says the Greek). We had decided to abandon the Soudan, and to leave it to its own devices; the only obstacle to this were those *horrid* garrisons; once we could get them out, then chaos might reign, for all we cared. The Arabs, foolishly, would not let us return, consequently the present position. Zubair's coming up, when I asked for him, would have, I think, saved Berber, and greatly facilitated the getting down of *those* garrisons, which we only care for, because it is a *palpable* dishonour to abandon them, "they ought to have surrendered at once, troublesome people that they are, giving so much bother!"

Stewart will bear witness that my whole efforts have been, and will be, directed to carry out my instructions, viz., the withdrawal of the garrisons and refugees, and had it not been for the defeat of Mahomet Ali Pasha, I should have got out at least two-thirds of those at Kartoum and Sennaar. I was engaged in a certain work, *i.e.*, to take down the garrisons, &c. It suited me altogether to accept this work (when once it was decided on to abandon the Soudan), which, to my idea, is preferable to letting it be under those wretched effete Egyptian Pashas. Her Majesty's Government agreed to send me. It was a mutual affair, they owe me positively nothing, and I owe them nothing. A Member of Parliament, in one of our last received papers, asked "whether officers were not supposed to go where they were ordered?" I quite agree with his view, but it cannot be said I was ordered to go. The subject was too complex for any order. It was "Will you go and try?" and my answer was, "Only too delighted." As for all that may be said of our holding out, &c., &c., it is all twaddle, for we had no option; as for all that may be said as to why I did not escape with Stewart, it is simply because the people would not have been such fools as to have let me go, so there is an end of those great-coats of self-sacrifice, &c. Place before men the chance of success by holding out, and the certainty of death, or miserable captivity, if they give in, there is not much credit in holding out. I must add *in re* "the people not letting me go," that even if they had been willing for me to go, I would not have gone and left them in their misery. I think I say truly, I have never asked for a British expedition. I asked for two hundred men to be sent to Berber at a time when, Graham having beaten Osman Digna, one might have supposed there was no risk for those two hundred men, and I asked for Zubair.[52]

Baring offended Cuzzi, who revenged himself by betraying Berber. Baring *openly* announced "that no troops would come up to Berber," which was a gratuitous act on his part. We may be sure Cuzzi (who loves Baring) did not fail to tell this to the Mahdi, yet Baring pitched into me for indiscretion in asking *openly* for Zubair,[53] which I did on *purpose*, in order to save Her Majesty's Government the odium of such a step! As for Zubair's refusing to come up (as Cuzzi says he did), I put it down to some palace intrigue, and consider (if it is true) he was forced into saying so. If any Expedition comes up, I am grateful *officially* for the people's sake, but I consider that it is a *right* they possess, for, had not Egypt been interfered with, somewhat more than seven persons would have come up here, as reinforcements, between 21st November, 1883, when Hicks' defeat was known, and 19th September, 1884. *I* am grateful *personally*, because, as surely as the chief of that expedition comes up, I will put on him the burthen of the Government (doing what I can to help him). I am unable to forget the sufferings of these peoples, owing to our want of decision *in re* Zubair, and no soft words will obliterate those sufferings from my memory. It is not over praiseworthy if one holds out, when, if you do *not*, your throat is cut.

I am deeply grateful to those who have prayed for us.

Any expeditionary force that may come up comes up for the honour of England, and England will be grateful, and I can hang the yoke of Government on some one else, for the solution of the problem.

Any one reading the telegram [54] 5th May, Suakin, 29th April,

[52] "On the 18th Feb., the day General Gordon arrived at Kartoum, he recommended in the strongest manner that Zubair should be sent up, and gave his reasons in detail."—*Egypt, No.* 12, 1884; *Enclosure in No.* 114.

"On March 9, Sir Evelyn Baring recommended that Zubair should go up, such a recommendation being in harmony with the policy of evacuation."—*Egypt, No.* 12, 1884, *in* 115 *and* 222.—ED.

[53] This cannot be traced.—ED.

[54] Egypt, 1884, Nos. 201–56. See also Egypt, 1884, Nos. 35–166.—ED.

Massowah, and *without* date, Egerton saying, "Her Majesty's Government does not entertain your proposal to supply Turkish or other troops in order to undertake military operations in Soudan, and consequently if you stay at Kartoum you should state your reasons," might imagine one was luxuriating up here, whereas, I am sure, no one wishes more to be out of it than myself; the "*reasons*" are those horridly plucky Arabs.

I own to having been very insubordinate to Her Majesty's Government and its officials, but it is my nature, and I cannot help it. I fear I have not even tried to play battledore and shuttlecock with them. I know if *I* was chief I would never employ *myself*, for I am incorrigible. To men like Dilke, who weigh every word, I must be *perfect poison.* I wonder what the telegrams about Soudan have cost Her Majesty's Government? It has been truly a horrid question. There is the Town El Obeyed and the Sheikh El Obeyed; there is the Helouan of Cairo and the Helouan of Kartoum. Sanderson must have a hard time of it. "The *city* moves about!" "Why, if Helouan is attacked, Cairo must be in danger! Send for Wolseley! Kartoum forces defeated by Sheikh el Obeyed! Why, the town must have moved! Is not El Obeyed the place Hicks went to take? Most extraordinary! Send for Wolseley!"

"Eureka, I have found it out; there is a *man* called *El Obeyed* and a *town* called *El Obeyed.* When a movement occurs, it is the *man*, not the *town*, which has moved!" After *this* I shall hesitate to ask for any appointment from Foreign Office, and I shall get no more crisp bank-notes, as I used to do from old Cunnynghame in 1858–59 (when Alston was a boy, so to say), in those dingy rooms in Downing Street, now pulled down. One can fancy them saying "That brute of a Mahdi!" "That horrid resurrection of Stewart, Power, and Herbin at Dongola!" It will destroy all the *well earned repose* of Her Majesty's Government. As Sir Wilfrid Lawson (he is an *irregular*) said, "One day you will groan when you hear of Tel el Kebir." I think of *all* the pusillanimous *businesses* which happened in 1882 the flight of the Europeans from Alexandria before these wretched fellaheen troops, was the worst. Why, had they barricaded their streets, they would have held Alexandria against 50,000 of these poor things (like Abbot did his hotel and the Egyptian bank their offices). A more contemptible soldier than the Egyptian never existed. Here we never count on them; they are held in supreme contempt, poor creatures. *They* never go out to fight; it would be perfectly iniquitous to make them. We tried it once, and they refused point blank to leave the steamers. We are keeping them in cotton wool to send down to Baring (if he has weathered the storm?).

"Blessed is the man who does not sit in the seat of the *scornful*" (Ps. i. 1). I own it is not right to scoff at one's superiors, but I do not do it in malice, and I hope those who are remarked upon will not be offended. Life is a very leaden business, and if any one can lighten it, so much the better. Because I criticise Baring, Egerton, and the Foreign Office, it is not that I think I am their superior, but because I would like them to see how others, outside themselves, view things. Because I may differ with them it is no reason why they may not be right, and acting uprightly, and I may be utterly wrong. I am sure the "Siren" Malet is conscientiously sure all he did in Egypt was right; if visited in Brussels one will see, at a glance, he is plainly content.

One of the most amusing things which struck me in Palestine, exemplifying how little worth the world's praise is, was an article in the *Times* describing the making of a D.C.L. at Oxford. Sir Charles Wilson received this honour. The *Times* in remarking on the affair, mixed Wilson, R.E., up with Rivers Wilson of National Debt Office, and spoke of his "financial capacities" in Egypt. Of course Wilson, R.E., could not help thinking he had been robbing Wilson of National Debt Office of his renown, while Rivers Wilson felt hurt at being robbed of it. Two people were accordingly put out; while the innocent writer in the *Times*, when penning his article, was thinking how he could meet his rent (this is pure supposition). We may be quite certain that Jones cares more for where he is going to dine or what he has got for dinner than he does for what Smith has done, so we need not fret ourselves for what the world says. The article in the *Times* was a Mordecai to Wilson, R.E., and quite destroyed the pleasure of receiving the D.C.L.; yet the writer in the *Times* did all he could to exalt Wilson, R.E. I think the Press is first-rate, to ventilate articles; but when "we" come out, and praise or blame, I do not care a bit for "we"; for I have seen the "We's," and found them much as myself. I would never muzzle the press or its correspondents; they are most useful, and one cannot be too grateful to them (I own this more than any one), but I certainly think, that their province does not extend to praising or blaming a man, for by praising, or blaming, an assumption is made of superiority, for the *greater* only can do that, to the *inferior;* and no newspaper can arrogate that its correspondent is superior to the General (though I declare I think, sometimes, it may be the case).

Take for instance our defeat here, on the 16th March, which is put down to the treachery of the Pashas. Ten thousand articles in the *Times* will not make me think that their execution was not a judicial murder, yet probably the *Times* may say, I was justified: it alters not the affair with me, it is simply my intelligence against that of their correspondent; if the *Times* saw this in print, it would say, "Why, then, did you act as you did?" to which I fear I have no answer.

September 20.—Six escaped soldiers came in this morning with their arms; they say that the others meditate a general rush for the Lines to escape, that the Arabs are quite astonished at our being so quiet, and believe a mine is being driven under them. The men who came to-day said the Mahdi is still at Rahad! *not* at Schatt. One of these men was a perfect peacock with the patches on his dervish dress. Yesterday evening, while a gale was blowing, Waled a Goun took out the Krupp, meaning to bombard us, but he then took it back on Abou Gugliz' remonstrances, who said that we had stayed quiet for months, that he had made splendid fortresses, and that on one day we had burst on him, and broken him up.

A curious letter [55] was found written, just before Hicks'

[55] Appendix F.

forces perished, by a high officer; it is in the terms, "Stranger, go tell the Lacedemonians we lie here, in obedience to their laws."

I have in a previous page abused the Egyptian soldier, but it is not just, for what possible interest can they take in warlike operations in the Soudan? The English beat them in Egypt, and then sent them up here to be massacred in detail. One may say the massacred ten thousand of Hicks' army, at any rate, showed they could die, if they could not fight.

When we got hemmed in, a lot of slaves belonging to masters in Kartoum got cut off. They have been coming in in driblets ever since, and we made the men soldiers, and the women were freed; this of course bore hard on their masters, who thus lost their slaves, so I have determined to compensate these masters, at rate of £7 per man, £5 per woman, being an inferior article. Certainly I would make "Plutarch's Lives" a handbook for our young officers; it is worth any numbers of "Arts of War" or "Minor Tactics."

Some accounts in the *Gazette*, describing reasons for giving the Victoria Cross, are really astounding, such as a man who, with another, was sent out on a reconnaissance, this other was wounded, and his companion waited for him, and took him on his horse, saving his life! What would we have said, had he left his companion? Lots of these cases pass by unheeded, which, if read by "Plutarch's Lives," would be simply a man's duty. A soldier is bound entirely to his work as a soldier, be can never do more than his duty, and his *métier* is the Field; therefore he deserves nothing, for he is already paid for that *métier*, and not for garrison or home life. The original idea of the Victoria Cross was to give the subaltern officers, non-commissioned officers, and men a decoration, which would take the place of the Bath, to ranks below that of Major, which by the statutes of the Bath could not be done; then came the mistake to give the Victoria Cross for deeds of *éclat*, and so now it is. I like that old Iron Duke with his fearful temper: he told a friend of my father, who was bewailing his long and meritorious service, "That he ought to be —— glad the country had kept him so long." I wish Wolseley would take up this line, and get some quixotic chivalry into us: that it is possible I feel sure, for we are the same men as before. In three campaigns, out of four of late years, no officer or soldier has gone through such privations or dangers, as are gone through by our naval officers and sailors in gunboats, in various parts of the world, yet these latter would be scoffed at if they pleaded these privations, in order to get reward. A man defends a post, if he loses it is throat is cut; why give him a Victoria Cross? and if given, why not give it to all who were with him? they equally with him defended their throats. The men I should like to see cross-questioned on the country they are in are our Generals, whose whole time is taken up in their offices with courts-martial, &c., &c., an occasional day being devoted to moving men about in formations, which are never put into execution in the Field? The *métier* of a General is the Field, not the office; it is as if all their time is to be taken up with the horse in the stable, not in the country, whereas the latter is the most important. I should like to see Wolseley trot out the generals over their districts; ask them the routes, their proposed distribution of men in case of attack, and water-supply to Forts. I do not think it is generally known that if a gunboat cut the sea-wall near Cooling on Thames, the Cliffe and Shornemead Forts are cut off from main land, and that the Thames would come up to high lands, and be ten miles wide. There is one man only that I know who has the gift of questioning, because he knows every part of the coast, Sir W. Jervois; and if Wolseley has not the time, he would do schoolmaster. Of course, this is all fearful treason and presumption.

Spy in Halfeyeh states Stewart's steamers have recaptured the two steamers I had lost at Berber, and had no fighting to speak of; that the English troops are advancing on Ambukol,[56] half way between Debbeh and Merowé, and had defeated the Arabs.

[56] About 180 miles from Kartoum.—ED.

A young black soldier has just escaped from the Arabs; he was pursued by three horsemen and some footmen, and he kept blazing away at them till he got into the Lines. He says he killed two of his pursuers.

I wrote a letter [57] to Abdel Kader, the old sheikh on South Front, and sent him a packet of soap with the letter, as he had lamented to one of our men, who had escaped, that he had none. I daresay he will think the packet is a mine!

I have ordered the sale of five hundred ardebs of Government dhoora: no one family to purchase more than two ardebs.

The capture of the steamers at Berber cuts off the Arabs of Berber from those on other side.

With the young soldier who escaped were three others, but their hearts failed them, and they were recaptured. I fear they will suffer, but no physical suffering will change the heart, hence I do not believe in purgatory.

The *Towfikia* steamer went up to Giraffe, and as the Arabs had a sort of sneaking affection for the place, we put down twenty self-exploding mines, to deter them from going there. The worst of it is, our domestic matches have run out, and we cannot make any substitute, so we have to fall back on the powder-hose, connecting groups of ten. I think good wire entanglements, with mines, will defend any place, if one has anything like moderate troops behind the parapet. Wire entanglement ought to be twenty yards in depth, mixed with it the earth-mines. No field artillery will neutralize their effects, and only a continuous bombardment of days would destroy them.

A man has come in from Shendy, who corroborates the advance of the Expeditionary Force and the defeat of the Arabs. Another came in, who says the *Abbas* passed down safely, and that the steamers *Mansowrah* and *Saphia* are on their return, but says nothing of capture of the two steamers at Berber.

Another escaped soldier came in.

The Arabs took the man with the flag of truce (I sent out

[57] Appendix G.

with letter to Abdel Kader, the old sheikh) into their Lines; he took a *letter* from the Ulema to the Mahdi.

Tolerably good information says that the Mahdi has written to the tribes about here, telling them to submit to our authority, and to fight no more, to pay taxes, &c.; that if he is the Mahdi, then Turks and all men will eventually acknowledge him, without any more fighting, &c. We have this from two separate sources. I think he feels that to fail here would lead to his fall, and so he will come to terms in order to keep Kordofan, as I originally proposed to him.

Faki Mustapha (the man who commanded Arabs on left bank) has sent in to say he never wrote the impertinent letter E,[58] to which his seal was not.

The doctor took a stone as big as a swan's-egg from a man to-day.

There is nothing like a civil war to show what skunks men are. One of my greatest worries are the Shaggyeh, who are continually feathering towards me, or towards the Mahdi. I expect both sides despise them equally. According to history, the same thing went on during the reign of James II. When William of Orange landed, Queen Anne's husband the Prince of Denmark did not show well in the affair, and I expect that the Empress Eugenie could say a good deal for "Rats," during her time. I must say I cordially hate them, and if I had my way, I would smite the Shaggyeh, but policy says "give them rope." I have told them distinctly, that I know it is self-interest alone which rules them, which however is a platitude, for it governs most of us.

September 21.—Six more escaped soldiers came in with their rifles to-day. They say the Arabs are furious at losing their Peacock dervish (who was one of their officers) yesterday, and also at the constant desertions, and have written to the Mahdi to ask whether they are to kill these blacks or not. The Mahdi hired one thousand camels at $3 a head, to bring dhoora to the Arab camp, but the people who engaged to do

[58] Appendix E.

this, bolted with the money and the camels into the interior. The Mahdi is at Schatt.[59]

Messengers have arrived at Omdurman, saying that mixed force of British and Indian troops at Debbeh, on the Nile, north of Dongola, and that they had defeated a party of dervishes.

The Greek, who came in a few days ago from the Arabs, said the Mahdi had given Cuzzi an ointment to rub on his body, which would keep him in odour of sanctity!

Halfeyeh reports a foraging party of Arabs between Halfeyeh and Shoboloha.[60]

The three messengers fron Dongola came in with two cipher telegrams from Egerton of same import, not legible, for want of cipher which Stewart carried off. Some photograph letters which I could only partially make out, and notes from Floyer,[61] and Kitchener,[62] saying forces were coming up. Letter from

[59] Between forty and fifty miles west of Duem.—ED.

[60] A pass about midway between Shendy and Halfeyeh.—ED.

[61] "*London*, 12*th*.—Debates on Egypt, House of Commons, subject Egypt. Gladstone declined communicate Northbrook's instructions. Declared Anglo-French accord dead letter.

"13*th*.—Financiers—German, Austrian, Russian—attack England's attitude. Conference considered must lead coalition against England. Fitzmaurice stated British Government not prepared change advice given Egypt withdraw from Kartoum.

"13*th*.—Parliament closed till 15th September. Message hopes mission Northbrook suggest useful counsels. England will continue to fulfil public duties imposed upon her by events in Egypt.

"17*th August*.—The 88th, 46th, and 56th regiments, with expedition of 19th Hussars and corps of Mounted Infantry, go to Halfa.

"*London*, 19*th*.—General Earle commands expedition Halfa. Buller chief of staff."

"DEAR GENERAL GORDON,

"I send you the above as the last public news we have heard. I have been appointed Inspector-General of the Soudan Telegraph, but at present I can't get beyond Debba to inspect them, as Mr. Hudai has captured the Merowi telegraph office, and the Sirdar will not let us advance. I am ordered back to Halfa, and am leaving by boat this morning. With kind regards to Colonel Stewart, "Yours sincerely,

"E. A. FLOYER.

"Debba, 22nd August, 1884."

[62] "DEAR STEWART,

"Can I do anything for you or General Gordon? I should be awfully glad if you will let me know. The relief expedition is evidently

Mudir Dongola saying he had beaten the Arabs four times before the British advance! I have made him Pasha, and asked for the Order of St. Michael and St. George for him from the Khedive. I have ordered *three* guns to be fired from all the guns at 4 P.M. as a salute, and to warn the Arabs something is up. I shall send down spies to-morrow. I gave the *three* £50, and gave them each £10, with promise they will be paid £10 more when they get to Dongola. They say they had nothing given them on starting! which is curious if true.

Three more escaped soldiers came in this afternoon. They say the Arabs have disarmed all the black troops, and have told them to go where they liked, so I expect we will have a lot in to-morrow.

We fired a salute of three rounds from each gun on Lines, to let the Arabs know of the advance expeditionary force. The men who came in say the Arabs were fully expecting an attack, and were in a great way.

I send down to-morrow a telegram to Cairo, which will settle the business as far as I am concerned. It is thus couched: "If you remove me from being Governor-General then all responsibility is off me; but if you keep me as Governor-General then I will, *at the cost of my commission* in Her Majesty's Service, see all refugees out of this country.

The Arabs in reply to this salute of three guns fired nine shots against the Lines to-night, two of which passed over our Lines—a sort of revenge for our salute.

The man who went up with the letter came back with two letters [63] and the soap, *which was refused.*

Our salute, which was replied to by the Arabs by shotted guns, made us fire shotted guns in reply; and the "man who came in with the soap" says our guns killed twenty men,

---

coming up this way, but whether they will go by Berber or attempt the direct road from here I do not know. The Mahdi is in a bad way; he has abandoned Parfur, and has no reinforcements to send to Kartoum and Sennaar, which are asked for. "Yours always,

"H. H. Kitchener."

[63] Appendices K and L.

which I fear is an exaggeration. This man says the Arabs are in a bad state, with little food. They threatened to kill him. I sent out letter [64] in answer.

September 22.—One escaped slave came in to-day. The Berber steamers are said to be coming up river. Sent out two hundred men from Halfeyeh to drive off foraging parties of Arabs investing roads from that place to Shoboloha.

The *Saphia* and *Mansowrah* have returned from Berber. *They passed the Abbas*, that is about all, and I am grateful for that. They carried out my orders. Colonel Stewart's letter [65] reports in detail. The steamers lost three killed, and had four wounded. They saw the two captured steamers under the bank.

N.B.—When self-acting mines are placed, it is as well to connect them with twine to facilitate taking them up.

September 23.—The men who went out to drive back the marauders between Halfeyeh and Shoboloha have come back. They drove back the Arabs and captured a lot of things.

During the blockade here, viz., from say March 12th till to-day, September 22nd, we have expended—

3,240,770	Remington . . .	cartridges.
1,570	Krupp gun . . .	
9,442	Mountain gun . .	

Of the Remington cartridges perhaps 240,000 may have been captured by enemy, so that we fired 3,000,000 away; and I expect the Arabs lost perhaps 1000 in all. Each Arab killed needed 3,000 cartridges. We have left here—

2,242,000	Remington . . .	cartridges.
660	Krupp gun . . .	
8,490	Mountain gun . .	

and we turn out 50,000 Remington cartridges a week.

Fifty Arab horsemen came down on our foraging party who were outside Bourré, but the steamer drove them back.

No escaped soldiers came in to-day. I expect they are all close prisoners.

[64] Appendix M. [65] Appendix N.

There are fifty nuggars at Berber with the Arabs.

I am sure I should like that fellow Egerton. There is a light-hearted jocularity about his communications, and I should think the cares of life sat easily on him. Notice the slip in margin. He wishes to know *exactly* "day, hour, and minute" that he (Gordon) expects to be in "difficulties as to provisions and ammunition."[66]

Now I really think if Egerton was to turn over the "archives" (a delicious word) of his office, he would see we had been in difficulties for provisions for some months. It is as if a man on the bank, having seen his friend in river already bobbed down two or three times, hails, "I say, old fellow, let us know when we are to throw you the life buoy, I know you have bobbed down two or three times, but it is a pity to throw you the life buoy until you really are *in extremis*, and I want to know *exactly*, for I am a man brought up in a school of exactitude, though I did *forget* (?) to date my June telegram about *that Bedouin escort contract*."

Turn to page 40, "Send for Wolseley," &c. I see that they did send for him just a month before; "nasty moving cities, and *very* nasty Soudan."

Egerton's cipher telegram,[67] which I cannot decipher through

[66] "Dear General Gordon,

"Mr. Egerton has asked me to send you the following:—'August 30th. Tell Gordon steamers are being passed over second cataracts, and that we wish to be informed through Dongola exactly when he expects to be in difficulties as to provisions and ammunition.' Message ends, 'Lord Wolseley is coming out to command. The 35th Regiment is now being sent from Halfa to Dongola. Sir E. Wood is at Halfa. General Earle, Dormer, Buller, and Fremantle are coming up Nile with troops. I think an expedition will be sent across from here to Kartoum, while another goes with steamer to Berber. A few words about what you wish done would be very acceptable.' "Yours,

"H. H. Kitchener, R.E.

"Debbeh, August 31st."

[67] "Cairo, August 20th, 10.30 P.M.

"To General Gordon,

"445737—905309—185115—417291—552676—792996—271381—511906—689363—945242—226739—648255—102037—626054—535222—672318—277535—134971—467430—203151—804960—483289—681510."

The following was written on the back of this cipher telegram:—

"Your letters of 13/7/84 and 20/7/84 have been received, and their contents telegraphed on. The last news here is the 35th Regiment has

Stewart having taken the book, is short, but I feel sure is weighty, and I regret deeply I cannot get at its contents, which I think would afford matter for amusing comment.

The Mudir of Dongola sent me a telegram which is on other side.[68] He tells me of the extreme anxietude which pervaded Cairo (when they heard Berber had fallen, and it was rumoured Kartoum had ditto), for the retirement of the Dongola people. "Throw things into the river," &c., "but come away," "we are very fond of you," "useless to stay," &c., &c. The Mudir laughs over it, I think, and saw the kind instruction, "raise barrier on barrier between Kartoum and its sister beleaguered cities and Cairo; let us hear the last of these moving cities and Helouans." What awful disgust at this resurrection! I made the Mudir a Pasha; he was an old officer of mine. When I came up I ordered him down, as my orders were to *organise country with Soudanese employés*, not that he was bad. Cairo (how they must wring their hands over it now) remonstrated and asked me to leave him, which I did, and he saved Dongola, and indirectly Kartoum, for had I put a native in he would have gone over to the Mahdi, like Hussein Pasha Khalifa did, and then I really think that the tomb would have been securely sealed, and R.I.P. to all of us. When one thinks that *Cairo saved us* by interfering with my removal of this man, it must add bitterness to the cup they have to drink! The telegrams about this man's reinstatement, and my answer, are in Stewart's journal about the month of March.

I am arranging attack on Berber with four steamers and Krupps, as soon as steamers come from Sennaar.

Spies with letters started for Dongola yesterday.

I hope Stewart will get hold of all copies of telegrams sent

been ordered to advance from Halfa to Dongola at once. General Earle commands expedition, Buller C. of S., Dormer and Fremantle brigades. All coming up. Lord Wolseley leaves London directly to take over supreme command. All well here. Mudir working well. No danger. Sir E. Wood is at Halfa sending on troops. "H. H. KITCHENER.

"Debbeh, 29th August, 1884."

[68] Telegram Mudir of Dongola, saying Cairo Government had shown pressing benevolence for him to evacuate and thus *rivet* the "*tombstone*" over Kartoum.—ED.

to us from Cairo for his journal, and which the Arabs captured (lovely reading!), also that he will find out result of Hewitt's Mission to King John, and of Baring's negotiations for opening of "the road from Suakin and Berber," he spoke about on the 29th of March! which caused hilarity up here, and which led to his angering Cuzzi, who, idiot-like, questioned the sagacity and success of the step, and, getting turned out, paid us both (in all probability) by betraying Berber to the Arabs.

Egerton is a statistician, he evidently is collecting material for some great work. What earthly use is it to us for Egerton "to know exactly our want of provisions," when he is 1500 miles away! I am vexed at not getting at the pith of his cipher telegram, all I can see is that 7775 (Zubair's name) is *not* in it.

I am preparing to clear out of the palace, *in toto*, leaving the telegraph only, and go into the Mudiriat, so there will be plenty of room for the staff, if they come up, which is even now a question to me.

From Lord Northbrook coming out, I infer that Baring has returned to Cairo, and that my friend Egerton has gone back to the Acropolis. I hope he will say a good word to the King of Hellenes in favour of Leonidas, the Greek Consul here, who has behaved worthy of his ancestor of Thermopylæ, on a small scale.

I have a firm conviction we will not do anything in Egypt that will succeed, unless we fall into accord with France, which would not be difficult to do.

Arabi Pasha's private secretary, who even Stewart with all his Job-like patience had to give up as a bad job, came today to say "he was starving," so I have given him £10 a month again. How he ever got on with Arabi is a wonder; he and Stewart used to spend hours, hob and nob, translating Arabic letters, and then Stewart found out that the man had just exercised his own imaginations and taken not the least pains to give the sense of these letters' contents.

The Shaggyeh are breaking my heart with their family quarrels. I shall go to Halfeyeh (*D. V.*) to-morrow to see after them.

They captured five men who had been pardoned, and had gone back to the Arabs, and want me to kill them, which I refuse to do, for who are the rebels? we or the Arabs. I am responsible for the judicial murder of the two Pashas; beyond this I have put no man to death.

I think Colonel Stewart is hard on our men as to their cowardice; they are not heroes, I grant, but they are not, to my mind, entire cowards; "they do not see it," that is all; but if they are put in a position where there is a chance, a *fair* chance of success, they will take advantage of it and be plucky. The Chinese are of the same temperament. "No two piecey man can stay one place, supposing you come, I must go." This is an acknowledged maxim in the East.

A spy came in, and says that Sheikh el Obeyed has news in his camp *that Abdel Kader Pasha* (what a bother for Sanderson all these Abdel Kaders who he may mix up with the one of Algiers) *is with troops at Kassala.*

Two more mines exploded at Omdurman when they were being taken up to renew the fuses, but did no harm.

I saw the Shaggyeh chief Abdul Hamed to-day. He says that Said and Ibrahim Hassan Pashas [69] were *not guilty*, and that the Arabs looted their houses when they heard they had been killed by me, which they would not have done had they been really in communication with them. I shall send for their families and give them each £1000, which is all I can do.

The *Towfikia* went up and had her usual fight with the Arabs.

Report is that a soldier has taken the breech pieces of the two Krupp guns with the Arabs, and has run away, rendering them useless.

If Abdel Kader is at Kassala what on earth are our people about not to tell me? for of course I could help him. We seem to have lost our heads in the Intelligence Department, though it costs enough money.

As for "*evacuation*," it is one thing; as for "*ratting out*,"

[69] The two black Pashas condemned to death by court-martial for treachery on March 20th.—ED.

it is another. I am quite of advice as to No. 1 (as we have not the decision to keep the country), but I will be no party to No. 2 (this "rat" business), 1st, because it is *dishonourable;* 2nd, because it is not *possible* (*which will have more weight*); therefore, if it is going to be No. 2, *the troops had better not come beyond Berber till the question of what will be done is settled.* So I will end this book.

C. G. GORDON.

23 *Sept.*, 1884.

N.B.—To be copied and read by Colonel Stewart, if he likes, and extracts given Mr. Power (as by promise). Afterwards to be given to Miss Gordon, Southampton, if not wanted by that Foreign Office.

BOOK II.

Upon outside wrapper:

COLONEL STEWART, C.M.G.,

OR

CHIEF OF THE STAFF, SOUDAN EXPEDITIONARY FORCE.

JOURNAL EVENTS, KARTOUM, 23 TO 30 SEPT., 1884.

Contains no secrets as far as I am concerned. Official parts those not scratched through. Contains map of Berber; large scale.

CHIEF OF THE STAFF, SOUDAN EXPEDITIONARY FORCE.

For LT.-COL. STEWART, C.M.G. If not with the army, for GENERAL LORD WOLSELEY, G.C.B.

On Book itself:

II.

GENERAL GORDON'S JOURNAL.

FROM 23 SEPTEMBER TILL 30 SEPTEMBER.

C. G. GORDON.

N.B.—Will require pruning down if published.

C. G. GORDON.

23/9/84.

Upon inside:

II.

GENERAL GORDON'S JOURNAL.

FROM 23 SEPTEMBER TILL , 1884.

N.B.—It will require to be pruned out, if published.

C. G. GORDON.

23/9/84.

JOURNAL.

September 24.—My view is this, as to the operations of British forces. I will put three steamers, each with two guns on them, and an armed force of infantry at disposal of any British authority, will send these steamers to either Metemma, opposite Shendy, or to the cataract below Berber, to there meet any British Force which may come across country to the Nile. These steamers, with this force coming across country, will (*D. V.*) capture Berber and then communicate with Kartoum. The steamers will have a month's provisions. I would not attempt to pass the *bulk* of British Force across country, only the fighting column, to co-operate with the three steamers. No artillery is wanted with either force; it is not needed in any way in this country. When Berber is taken I should keep the bulk of the forces there, and send up the fighting column to Kartoum, after having arranged for its provisions, for I cannot feed them; then, in combination with us, clear out rebels from A to B,—an affair of a week; then decide on your future policy. It is absolutely necessary to understand that we cannot hurry over this affair.[1] If we do we will incur disaster. I have spoken of the division of British forces into two lots, one a small fighting column co-operating across country with the steamers, which will meet them, where you like, on the left bank of the White Nile; the other, composed of bulk, *without artillery*, coming up right bank of

[1] *I.e.*, the future of the Soudan.—ED.

the Nile. Now if I were doing this, I should, by the *Abbas* steamer, work up by Merowé,[2] Abou Hamed, to Berber, by a *series of small stations* with small garrisons. I should at once get on each step of the Nile ladder steam launches from Cairo, &c., and put them in the open strips as previously explained in page 49 of my journal, Vol. No. 1.[3] I then have my route open to Dongola where the bulk of the forces remain.

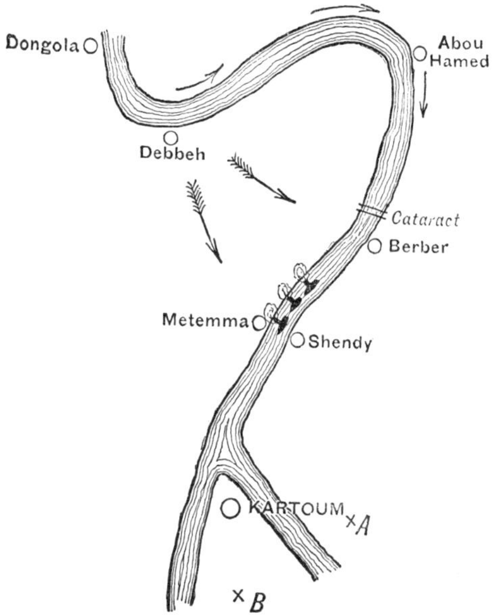

Saying the chain of posts is established, that, in the interim, the Arab forces at A and B are dispersed, then you say *evacuate.* Well, without moving the bulk, and, with the aid of the fighting column, you can get down the Sennaar lot, while steamers can bring down the Equator and Bahr Gazelle garrisons. Now this will take at least six months from the *present date* (for you will *not* come for *a month*). You then begin your downward march, and are harassed all

[2] *I.e.*, Fourth Cataract.—Ed. [3] *I.e.*, p. 35.—Ed.

the way,[4] and the Mahdi will say he kicked you out. You see you are in for six months, and if you evacuate all your prestige vanishes. It is therefore, I say, either, when once you have got up to Kartoum, give the country to the Turks, or else establish Zubair, and (instead of expending time in going up to Sennaar and the Equator) combinating with us,

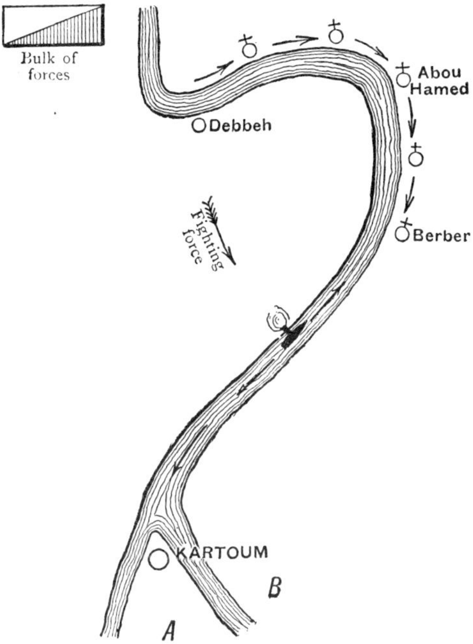

commence an attack upon Kordofan. You must be here six months. How will you spend the time? Will you at the end

[4] "In Colonel Coetlogon's opinion the rebels will retire south on the approach of the British, and await events. General Gordon would certainly refuse to go unless the population and garrison were guaranteed safe departure. The population and garrisons of Kartoum and Sennaar amount to about 40,000 to 50,000 souls, and it would take two years to remove them. As the places become evacuated the rebels would enter and become hostile in front and in the rear."—*Times*, 13 *Sept.*, 1884.—ED.

of six months allow it to be said you are kicked out, or will you not establish some government and retire with dignity. The *cost* is the same in both cases in money; but in honour one costs a great deal more. If Zubair falls, after some time, what is it to you? You did your best and save your honour, and you save a mint of difficulties and troubles, which these expeditions to Sennaar and Equator involve. You will not be obliged to go fifty miles beyond Kartoum.[5] As for the Equator, give it to me, and I will (*D. V.*) keep it from Zubair. It is a thousand pities to give up Kartoum to the Mahdi when there is a chance of keeping it under Zubair.

The fighting force can take the guns of the steamers, if they need artillery; they are very good guns and have field carriages with limbers. I shall not send down the castellated barges or the Krupp guns. Should you cross the desert *en masse*, the way to guard your communications is to occupy, with a company, all the wells in a good large radius, for the Arabs cannot come down on your line of communication, not being able to get water. This is the only way to deal with the Bedouins, or slave hunters.

The elephants came up by the wells of Gabra,[6] direct from Debbeh to Kartoum. Care should be taken on approaching Omdurman, for there are rather a timid lot there (fellaheen).

You must consider whether you will not send down those dreadful Bashi Bazouks, the scum of Alexandria, and the fellaheen soldiers, on arrival, for they are of little use, and eat us up.

For my part, I should not hesitate to ride down with three hundred men (having taken precaution to have made arrangements with the Kababish tribe) from Kartoum to Debbeh.

There is no difficulty in making flying bridges across the Nile with the country boats, however wide, using telegraph wire twisted in six or eight strands.

[5] General Gordon proposed to the Government to give to the King of the Belgians the Bahr Gazelle and Equatorial provinces, and from the first time he suggested the appointment of Zubair, he had determined to defend those provinces from all slave raids.—Ed.

[6] The Gabra wells are about thirty miles to the north-west of Kartoum.—Ed.

Seyd Mahomet Osman's little boy, aged nine years, was caught by Arabs, and behaved like a hero: "He was not going to be a Dervish. He was as much the Mahdi as Mahomet Achmet; and they might kill him if they liked, &c. He was going to stay with the Government and Gordon Pasha." They left him alone.

The Sandjak described the scene as splendid: the little fellow with flaming eyes, gesticulating and stamping with fury.

"U. S. C.,[7] 6.30 P.M.—Did you ever hear of such a thing ——[8] is appointed —— to ——. A more barefaced job never *was* perpetrated. Why, the man has done nothing, *absolutely* nothing. Atrocious! But *what* can you expect? The whole lot of them are off again, a regular autumn flight! What! eh! *you will see them all at Christmas*" (waxing more wrath). "I declare I have half a mind to go to the Mahdi," &c. Page interrupts: "Lady —— is waiting in the brougham." Collapse and exit.

I cannot too much impress on you that this expedition will not encounter any enemy worth the name in an European sense of the word; the struggle is with the climate and destitution of the country. It is one of time and patience, and of small parties of determined men, backed by native allies, which are got by policy and money. A heavy lumbering column, however strong, is nowhere in this land. Parties of forty or sixty men, swiftly moving about, will do more than any column. If you lose two or three, what of it—it is the chance of war. Native allies above all things, at whatever cost. It is the country of the irregular, not of the regular. If you move in mass you will find no end of difficulties; whereas, if you let detached parties dash out here and there, you will spread dismay in the Arab ranks. The time to attack is the dawn, or rather before it (this is stale news), but sixty men would put these Arabs to flight just before dawn, which one thousand would not accomplish in daylight. This was always Zubair's tactics. The reason is that the strength of the Arabs is their horsemen, who do not dare to act in the dark. I do hope

[7] United Service Club.—ED.
[8] The blanks are General Gordon's.—ED.

you will not drag on that artillery: it can only produce delay and do little good. I can say I owe the defeats in this country to having artillery with me, which delayed me much, and it was the artillery with Hicks which, in my opinion, did for him.[9]

Ten thousand times better for us to perish than for you to run the risk; and besides that, I have a confident belief we will not (*D. V.*) perish. The usual hammer and tongs fusillade will go on, but they will not attack the place, and we will not go out against them; while you will creep on quietly and safely, and send out your feelers, making raids upon these Arabs. I would let Buller have full swing for all these little biting expeditions. I believe he is well off (and I think not married, which is an enormous advantage); and he and his subordinates will learn scouting, &c., in a good school. It is this very same warfare we will have to exercise if ever we would oppose Russia in her advance on Afghanistan—*i.e.*, of going up and landing in the Persian Gulf, and cutting in on their flank. So it will be a good school for him and his.

The wretched peasant, with that filthy cloth, which you see, is a determined warrior, who can undergo thirst and privation, who no more cares for pain or death than if he were of stone. The young fellows even have a game by which they test who will bear the lash of the hippopotamus' whip best. They are in their own land; the pains of war are their ordinary life; and

[9] The following extract from Herodotus is pasted on the opposite side of page in the original journal: "The spies having seen everything returned home; and when they reported all they had passed, Cambyses marched against the Ethiopians without making any provision for the subsistence of his army, or once considering that he was going to carry his arms to the remotest parts of the world; but as a madman and not in possession of his senses, as soon as he heard the reports of the Icthyophagi he set out on his march . . . but before the army had passed over a fifth part of the way all the provisions were exhausted, and after the provisions the beasts of burden were eaten. Now if Cambyses had then led back his army he would have proved himself a wise man. He, however, went on; but afterwards none, except the Ammonians, and those who have heard their reports, are able to give account of them; for they neither reached the Ammonians or returned back, but the report was that heaps of sand covered them over and they disappeared." General Gordon has written against this extract: "Hicks' army disappeared. This expedition was made into these lands."—ED.

they are supported by religion of a fanatical kind, influenced by the memory of years of suffering at the hands of an effete set of Bashi Bazouks. No; if our Kentish or Yorkshire boys are to come up to help me, it is not with my wish, unless with the greatest precaution. Thank God we have few Europeans here, and those I can (*D. V.*) care for, and you need not fear for our retreat; and if we die, why, when we entered the army we sold our lives at so much a day. I verily believe no merchant would give me £200, which, to me, is the current value of *the man* in this world.

It is the most extraordinary thing, quite incomprehensible, that with only one exception, that of Zubair's man who came from Cairo (with Egerton's famous despatch about contracts), not one single messenger has entered this place on the proper initiative of outsiders. It has been invariably *my* messengers, who were sent out by me, from Kartoum, who did bring me any news. It would seem as if those outside seemed to think it was my duty to send out and bring in news for myself, and that they had nothing to do with it. Either these officers outside do not care to spend a sou in spies to give me information, or else they think it is a matter of supreme indifference, whether I know what is going on or not; and I must say when my messengers do come back, they bring me scarcely any information of import. There is a lot of "I hope you are well," &c.; men like Kitchener and Chermside might be expected to have more brains than that.[10] If I had not exerted myself in the spy business, we never would have had a word, I verily believe. I never saw such a poor lot as these outsiders. Even if they had had to pay £20 out of their own pockets, one might have expected them to do it, considering the circumstances. They might have been paid back. But neither Her Majesty's Ministers in Cairo, nor these men have seemed to care a jot to inform us. Silly foolish questions are all we ever have got from them, and it is not to be wondered at, that I am indignant with such unpatriotic conduct, and not inclined to be over civil beyond my duty.

[10] General Gordon was under the impression that Colonel Chermside was at Debbeh, whereas he was, in fact, at Suakin.—ED.

I never saw such a feeble lot in my life! One has only to compare the telegrams, &c., we sent down, with the *rubbish* sent in by *our own messengers I* paid for.

Two children and three escaped soldiers came in to-day from the Arabs, but had no news.

Read "Floyer's" telegram, with Kitchener's note to Stewart on same paper—it perfectly exasperates one. Kitchener asks Stewart "what he can do for him"—nothing of what has gone on with respect to the Soudan since Graham's expedition. Of course men are not *obliged* to write at all.

I altogether *decline* the imputation that the projected expedition has come to *relieve me.* It has *come to SAVE OUR NATIONAL HONOUR in extricating the garrisons, &c., from a position our action in Egypt has placed these garrisons. I was relief expedition No.* 1. They are *relief expedition No.* 2. As for myself I could make good my retreat at any moment if I wished. Now realise what would happen if this *first relief expedition* was to bolt and the steamers fell into the hands of the Mahdi: *this second relief expedition* (for the honour of England engaged in extricating garrisons) would be somewhat hampered. We the *first* and *second* expeditions are equally engaged for the honour of England. This is fair logic. *I came up to extricate the garrisons and failed. Earle comes up to extricate garrisons and* (*I hope*) *succeeds. Earle does not come to extricate me.*[11] The extrication of the garrisons was supposed to affect our "national honour." If Earle succeeds the "national honour" thanks him and I hope rewards him, but it is altogether independent of me, who for failing incurs its blame. I am not the *rescued lamb*, and I will not be.

Had Gessi dared to have communicated with me like these men have, he would have heard of it; but he never did.

The *Towfikia* steamer went up and saw no Arabs at Giraffe to-day.

Look at this: I send down a spy, A. Kitchener and Co.

[11] The primary object of the expedition up the Valley of the Nile is to bring away General Gordon and Colonel Stewart from Kartoum. When that object has been secured no further offensive operations of any kind are to be undertaken.—*Egypt, No.* 35, 1884; *No.* 157.—ED.

send him back with answer. If Kitchener and Co. thought, they would know that A., being seen passing to and fro, must incur suspicion; however, A. happily gets through *with risk* (not having, by the way, had one penny from K. and Co.); then all communication stops till I send down B. What is K. doing at Debbeh? that he could not write a better letter than to tell me the names of the generals and regiments—a matter of the most supreme indifference to Kartoum.

September 25.—Arabs came down to the Blue Nile in some force, but the *Mansowrah* going up, and our men pushing along the bank, they all fled. I am going to Halfeyeh to see the Shaggyeh, who are the worry of my heart. Having gone down, I found a very fair market, and the Shaggyehs less irritating than I expected to find them.

Question. What was the policy of her Majesty's Government in sending up General Gordon?

Answer. To endeavour to retire the garrisons *by quiet means.*

Question. What is the object of General Earle's expedition?

Answer. The same. General Gordon having failed.

Question. If General Earle's expedition is for the retreat of General Gordon and ends there, what is the result?

Answer. Her Majesty's Government agree *that they abandon the garrisons.*

There is no possible escape from the situation.

According to accounts from Bourré, the Arabs had come down in some force at night, and had hid in villages near Bourré, meaning to fall upon our foraging parties; they did not bargain for the *Mansowrah* coming up with her two guns, and so caught a Tartar when they emerged to attack our men, and went off in great confusion and some loss.

An escaped soldier came in from the Arabs—no news. He was so dreadfully itchy, I could not keep my patience, or keep him in my room. He saw himself in the mirror, and asked who it was; said he did not know! and really he did not seem to know. It stands to reason that in countries where there are no mirrors, every one must be a complete stranger to himself, and would need an introduction.

I wrote to Waled a Goun, Arab commander-in-chief, as follows:—"I went to Halfeyeh to see Shaggyeh, found five men there; they wanted me to kill them, for being of your family, who had gone back to you after pretending to join me. I questioned these five men; they said they could not bear the smell of you, and that the Shaggyehs had wanted their things, and so had invented the accusation. I have no scales to weigh the truth—perhaps Mahomet Achmet Mahdi has—so, as you have sent me many soldiers of late, I send you these men. I have taken the body of your Peacock" (alluding to the man who came in with the wonderful Dervish dress), "but I send you the plumage of your bird on another body." I have put the dress on one of the men I sent out.

"Why did you run away so swiftly to-day? was Abou Gugliz there? It could not be you, for you said so much about your desire to die at the fortifications."

"As for knowing the truth in the Soudan it is impossible, for the devils of lying and robbery are riding all over the country."

I gave them a dollar each; they leave to-morrow. I have also given them a captured Arab flag and a captured Dervish cap each, so they will go out a grand procession, and as it is their Sunday (Friday), they will arrive at church parade.

Thousands of cranes, with their curious cry, are passing over every day ("The cranes of Ibycus." Few ever read Schiller's poems. I only know Bulwer's translation, but they have grand things in them. "The Veiled Image of Truth at Sais," "The Ring of Polycrates," for who can bear *plain truth?* Who can bear *success?*)

The notables were in a regular state about my going to Halfeyeh to-day. A deputation came to prevent it, but it was of no use. The Mudir threw himself down and embraced my feet, begging me not to go; but, as I thought his solicitude was actuated more by the wish to prevent me going to where he has, I expect, been robbing right and left, than my security, I did not attend much to him. I should break the hearts of our F.O., for I say openly, "As your Government is bad, and will give you nothing when you are decrepit, rob away gaily, but with wisdom, and do not let me hear of it."

The Arabs will be in an awful rage to-morrow with the procession of the five Dervishes with captured flags, &c. You can scarcely imagine the state (well known to Stewart, Power, and Herbin) one gets in, when one is constantly hearing explosions; what with the guns, mines, and musketry, one's nerves get strained, and nothing can drop without one thinking it is an explosion. What the Russians underwent at Sevastopol must have been terrible. As Hansall, the Austrian Consul, says, it is *abrutissant*. It has slackened off now, but still any loud noise, in this clear air, makes me jump (*i.e.*, be, for a moment, afraid) like any man who rides knows, when his horse, at it were, sinks completely beneath him, on a sudden start.

I look forward to the advent of some of the Royal Navy more than anything. There are such a lot of splendid cutting outs and surprises to be made by the steamers, and the steamers are first-rate in every respect. Each steamer is worth two thousand men, if well handled, and they have all on board grub and ammunition, and want no commissariat officers.

If I were Earle, I would leave all the principal medical officers at Dongola, and only take on the lowest ranks of the Army Medical Department.

The Principal Medical Officers are bores and croakers, and want all sorts of attention. A man is a fool or a physician at forty years of age. All in this country you want is to *keep the communication open*, and Cockle will do that. As for wounds, there will be none, *for Arabs give no quarter;* neither will we, I expect, if we go over one hundred miles of desert.

At Halfeyeh to-day, going round the Fort, a tallow-faced Egyptian dashed out with the most fearful whine. I tried to calm him, no good, so Cassim el Mousse, the Shaggyeh Meleh, interfered; no use! the man (?) threw himself on the ground, and deluged himself and me with dust, so Cassim gave him a wipe over the head with his Hippo whip, and I ordered him to be taken out of the ranks and brought to Kartoum; *en route* my cavasses came and remonstrated, saying he ought to be secured, for he was the most notorious thief of Alexandria; so, justly or not, I have put him in prison.

F 2

It would be a great mistake to think the troops are down in the mouth. We have certainly lost a lot; but the men are as determined as ever, and only think it their due if they are aided. Stewart talks of their cowardice, but it is a cowardice of calculation, and it would be a great mistake if the expeditionary force *for the extrication of the garrisons* comes up here, and thinks the men are going to say they are *in extremis*. (I leave out Cairo troops and the Bashi Bazouks.) The black soldiers do not think they have been beaten. There are not many armies which would bear with the equanimity these troops do, the loss of say one-fifth of their numbers *killed*, which was the case in one defeat (only twenty days ago) of Mahomet Ali Pasha.

The steamers from Sennaar will I think be in to-morrow.

The question to-day at Halfeyeh was this. Certain heads of families had gone over to the Arabs with Saleh Pasha (we put a sponge over that affair), and their adherents, being in Kartoum, had not gone over (not their fault); those who had gone over with Saleh Pasha, afterwards came over to me, and asked for their adherents to be given back to them. To this the chiefs of families, who had been in Kartoum and who had kept these adherents under them, objected, so it became a question what to do. I decided to ask each man his desire. "Will you go with A. or B.?" The men came in at the door, and after having elected, they went out of the window, for there were not two doors; they elected as they wished, and went out of the window. Some came in and thought that all that was required of them was to come in at the door, and go out of the window as quickly as possible without answering! I do love to study mankind; he is far better than any landscape. These fellows knew well enough I was going to put their decision on them and tried to avoid giving any, as to with whom they would go. It was somewhat of a gymnastic process for them to go out of the window, and they made a good mess of it; but if I had let them go out of the door by which they had entered, inextricable confusion would have occurred. As it was, we had resurrections at the door of those who had departed by the window, which caused some bother. The two rival chiefs were present, and one's object was to prevent the elector looking at either while he elected; sometimes it was necessary to secure that the pug-face was fairly on the clerk, the electing officer, who asked the question A. or B. I will back the eye for knowledge more than any other organ. A man who does not look you in the face in answering is ninety-nine times in a hundred a liar.

September 26.—There is one great question, and if you know a person, say K., is faithless and is seeking his own, ought one to be down on him? We have an example in our Lord. He knew Judas was going to betray Him, yet He did not denounce him; from which I infer, if we know even that K. is going to rat, or be faithless, unless he, K., gives positive proof of such intention, we ought to treat K. as J., of whom we have no suspicion of treachery. I am inclined (satanically I own) to distrust every one, *i.e.*, I trust every one. I believe that circumstances may arise when self-interest will almost compel your nearest relative to betray you to some extent. Man is an essentially treacherous animal; and although the psalmist said *in his haste* "all men are liars," I think he might have said the same *at his leisure.*

"You may depend upon it, I will do my best for you" —to chief clerk W.O. "Why, if you give it to *him* we must give it to more than forty. It is out of the question." What is the result? Why the *him* will go to his club and say, "Why I was promised it and did not get it." Whereas if he had weighed the words, he would have seen he was promised only "the best he could do." This is a breach of confidence, but it is an example. A man long ago dead —— was asked by a lady to recommend her son for an appointment —— (who was most honest), wrote saying so-and-so wants such and such a thing, but that he did not think the young man for whom the appointment was solicited was worth much. —— wrote to the lady to say he had done his best. Unfortunately he placed the letters into wrong envelopes. The lady never looked on —— again. Well, I suppose —— was treacherous to the lady. He might have refused to write, but he did more—he did the young man *harm* by saying *he was not worth much.*

I like to take things in a light-hearted way. I like the tacit contract, "that if you are useful to me I will use you"; and "*that*" (with full belief) "if I cease to be useful to you you will leave me." I try and act, "do to others as they wish you to do to you." I would never put a man in any position I would not put myself.

Although man is the essence of treachery, I believe every man *wishes to be honest; his interests prevent him.*

The five men went out to Arab Lines with their Arab flags, on which a church parade, which was going on, dispersed.

It is a curious fact that any effort to relieve the garrisons made from the outside is contemporaneous with the *expiration* of the period stated in March of the time they could hold out, viz., six months. There are some ugly suspicious circumstances all the way through! The consequence will be a far greater expense. Had efforts been made quietly between March and August to span with proper transport between Wady Halfa and Hannek,[12] much of the present difficulties to an advance would have been got over, and security would have been felt everywhere that efforts were really being made. There is a humility in Baring's telegram asking my advice as to routes for access to Kartoum. "Sir E. Baring having gone to London, I am charged by Her Majesty's Government to tell you to keep them informed not only as to immediate but as to any prospective danger at Kartoum, that you should advise them in order to be prepared for any such danger as to force necessary to secure your retreat, its amount, character, route for access to Kartoum, and time for its departure. Her Majesty's Government does not entertain your proposal to supply you with Turkish or other forces for the purpose of undertaking military expeditions, such being beyond scope of your commission, and at variance with the policy which was the purport of your mission to the Soudan. If with this knowledge you continue at Kartoum, you should state cause and inten-

[12] Upper part of Nubian Desert.—Ed.

tion with which you so continue."[13] If the telegrams I sent down in March to Baring are referred to, it will be seen I had already[14] informed him of all he could possibly want to know, and I specially said that the expedition by the route of Wady Halfa would be (as it was at that epoch) a mere picnic party.

Man proposes—God disposes. Any one who two-and-a-half years ago had said that the Gladstone ministry would not only go to Egypt, and, not content with one expedition to the Soudan (Graham's), would go in for *two expeditions*, would have been scouted as a madman; and it certainly is curious that Mr. Gladstone, in "—— *Review*"[15] of 1878, combating Mr. Dicey's ideas for the annexation of Egypt, should have stated that this *annexation was impossible on account of the Soudan!*

There is one thing, which, in the opinion of the world, would expunge all disagreeables from the whole question, *i.e.*, if the abolition of slavery were proclaimed. It would be a difficult job, but would be possible if we took our time, and at Lord Mayor's dinners, &c., it would be a platform no one could come up to.

4 P.M. Steamers from Sennaar in sight. Now we shall be all together again, thank God!

The Arabs off the south front are all agog at sight of the steamers coming down. Those on the Blue Nile are firing

[13] From British agent and Nubar Pasha to General Gordon, sent 5th May from Suakin; reached 29th of July.—ED.

[14] Telegram from General Gordon to Sir E. Baring dated Feb. 27, 1884, says: "You have to say whether the partial evacuation of the Soudan fulfils your objects,—if it does not, then you must act by Indian Moslem troops from Wady Halfa; and do so at once by sending detachments of troops to Wady Halfa."—*Egypt, No.* 12 (1884), *Enclosure* 1, in *No.* 229. And again, on Feb. 29: "Should you wish to intervene, send 200 British troops to Wady Halfa and adjutants to inspect Dongola, and then open up Suakin-Berber road by Indian Moslem troops. This will cause an immediate collapse of the revolt. Whether you think it worth while to do this or not you are, of course, the best judge. I can only tell you the *modus operandi* of an expeditious intervention. If you decide against this you may probably have to decide between Zubair and the Mahdi. Zubair with £100,000."—*Egypt, No.* 12 (1884), *Enclosure* 5, *No.* 229.—ED.

[15] 'Nineteenth Century,' August, 1877.—ED.

on the steamers. I sent up *Mansowrah* to help them. The Arabs are in the houses. Expenditure of ammunition is enormous, I should think. The three steamers have passed the place where the Arabs are. They came down one by one, which was not wise.

From the top of the Serail one commands view all round for miles.

It will be a satisfaction to Her Majesty's Navy to know that it is our navy which has, humanly speaking, saved us. It really is a splendid fleet and naval arsenal. The steamers have come in; the Arabs were numerous and had five guns; seven of their shells struck the steamers (Arabs had also two rocket tubes). The steamers brought down 2000 ardebs, and report Sennaar well off, and no Arabs in arms in all their district. Seyd Osman Mahomet is said to have occupied Katarif with his men. A sheikh has promised to capture the steamer *Mahomet Ali*, which is up the River Dinder, and to hand her over to the Sennaar Governor. Wad Medinet did not fire on the steamers, but brandished spears, &c.; our loss in passing the gauntlet was three killed and eight wounded.

The Arabs have no conscience; they make my captured soldiers serve the guns, and otherwise act against us under pain of death!

I declare my people do, in a feeble way, what is wanted, and do not deserve the character of cowards; they bear defeat far better than other peoples, and they are good-tempered over it. *We* English are the cream, all acknowledge that, but we will not exist on two dates a day, as these men do, without a murmur.

The steamer *Bordeen* was struck by two shots, one near water-line. The *Ismailia* steamer received three, the *Talatawee* steamer received two shots. Happily all got down safe. The Arabs fired from guns and rifles with fury—we could see that from the roof. All the steamers have got small-pox from bullet-marks! Our chief of the arsenal, Hussein Bey, had been sharp enough to have bits of old tents ready to stop shot-holes. Had we not had these we might have lost the *Bordeen* steamer.

The Arabs had three forts (breastworks) along the river-bank, rather above Giraffe. I mentioned that we lost three killed and eight wounded; *now mark this*, on their way down the steamers met three escaped soldiers from the Arabs; they took them on board, and, odd to say, of those killed and wounded, were these three men, two having been killed, and the other badly wounded! This is remarkable. If we could believe it, *we are as safe in the fiercest battle as in a drawing-room in London.*

September 27.—I have arranged to send down three steamers to Shendy to co-operate with Dongola forces, and to raise the Shaggyeh tribes. I have sent out a man to warn Dongola of this fact. He carries no letters, only a small slip, stating he is a "true man."

It is of no use sending up to Sennaar again for dhoora, for we have no money to pay for it, and it is a risk with these Arab guns. Steamer *Ismailia* received three shells; steamer *Bordeen* two; steamer *Talataween* two. Some made tremendous holes, and one in *Bordeen* was close to water-line; it is wonderful how they escaped. The poor escaped soldiers were asleep in the hold, when a shell entered and burst; two were killed, one was seriously wounded.

Two men came in from the Arabs. One said he was the Mahdi, the other said a courier had come to the Arabs, saying the English were at Berber; they knew nothing of yesterday's fight.

Our steamers are of about the same consistency as the Thames steamboats, so you may imagine the risk there is of putting them under artillery fire.

Towfikia steamer went up the White Nile exchanging musketry fire with the Arabs.

My beautiful steamers, which used to be comparatively sweet, now stink like badgers. As for the swell *Ismailia* she is a cess-pit.

Several other shots struck the upper works of the steamers; evidently they were under a nasty fire, and as for bullet marks they are spotted all over. Among the three killed (two of them escaped soldiers) one was a little boy.

Another slave came in at Omdurman, but had no news.

Great female sqawking under the window of the Serail, approaching to yells. On examination I find the noise comes from a black female fighting the cavass. On enquiry I find my lady had gone down to buy dhoora with two dollars in her hand, and had been pushed by some ungallant fellow, and the dollars fell into the river. Though I do not see that the responsibility was upon me, I gave her the two dollars, and comforted her black soul. It would be a comfort if all the troubles of life were got rid of so cheaply.

Having undergone considerable anxiety owing to the Shaggyeh tribe in our Lines during the blockade, we got rid of them to Halfeyeh as soon as we could.[16] But when they got to Halfeyeh, and met their brethren who had been with the Arabs, and who had come over to us, the former were seized with distrust of the latter, and so we are obliged to bring these latter into Kartoum. I do not think it any risk, for the Shaggyeh have lied so very much to the Arabs that nothing would ever make peace between them, so I do not feel any discomfort about them.

It is not comfortable to see your steamers with a hole in them through which you could push your head and shoulders and that not a foot above the water-line. The *Bordeen* had that, the shell came in on one side and burst on penetrating the other plate of the other side.

To my mind, these Egyptian mountain guns are far preferable to those steel guns of ours, with their wretched small calibre, and I would prefer a smooth bore howitzer to an Armstrong for these wars.

I made Nutzer Bey a Pasha for his Sennaar trip, and send him down with Cassim el Mousse to Metemma to await ad-

[16] A telegram from Mudir of Dongola says that "on the 24th July, the Emir Abou Kanga and his army, who had come from Kordofan, were slaughtered, and that before the messenger quitted Kartoum another fight occurred, in which the son of Sheikh Sid and his followers were killed on the 30th August, and the siege raised. This is confirmed by a letter sent to me by Cassim el Mousse Bey, stating that he and his soldiers were at Halfeyeh, and that the Shaggyeh tribe and people had come in and tendered their submission.—*Egypt, No.* 35, 1884, *No.* 133.—ED.

vance of Her Majesty's forces. Ibraham Tongi and Mousse Beys refused, or rather declined to go unless also made Pashas, which I did not see, so these worthies stay here.

Chermside to Kitchener.—"Well you know I had to send on the telegram, and I added I hoped Stewart was well. That fellow Gordon takes exception to this, and says *va sans dire*, that I could not have wished that Stewart was ill. Most unjust. Had I added anything to this telegram, I might have got into a row, which would never do, but what was the use of pampering to inordinate curiosity?"

Kitchener to Chermside.—"Well he pitched into me for asking Stewart to tell me if I could do anything for him (the communications being so easy), and for telling *him* the names of the Generals (to my mind a most important matter, for it would strike terror among the Arabs), *he* says *he* does not care who the Generals are (which is sheer heresy and perfectly sickening). I shall write nothing more to *him* except the purest official documents. It is very clear his liver is out of order, to go and attack officers of his own corps like that. It is atrocious!"

September 28.—Two women and a man came in to-day; they say the Mahdi is not at Schatt, but at Rahad. Hussan Effendi and another directed the guns against the steamers. The women say the Arabs had three guns, not five. The Arabs did not lose many from their people's accounts. Among the three guns there was a Krupp, they say.

Say for a moment that the object of Her Majesty's Government is simply to enable me to retreat, and is irrespective of the retreat of the garrisons—then all the loss of life in this neighbourhood on both sides was thrown away, inasmuch as if I had not come there would have been a speedier collapse, without the loss of life (at least such is probable). The Government may say that they had reasonable hopes that I would succeed; I will neither say I gave them such assurance or that I did not give it. I think I was neutral in giving or in not giving such assurance.

When the steamers get to Shendy, they will be only 150

miles from Ambukol, which is a little higher up the Nile than Debbeh (35 miles). Three more slaves came in from the north; they had run away from their master, and will enter the army. I expect we shall have lots of this sort of thing.

Arabs show no disposition to close our road to Shendy as yet, and I believe the country up to that place is with *Kartoum* (I cannot say *the Government*, for I do not know what the Government is).

One of the greatest sinners in the way of getting Egypt into financial difficulties (whence all this trouble) is . . . who in the Crimea used to sell cheeses and other things at exorbitant prices.

Sir Samuel Baker will be disgusted to know that the crack vessel he got from Samuda, the *Ismailia*, the biggest of his lot, is the worst of the larger *fighting* steamers. She is a good yacht, but nothing more. All these steamers we owe to Sir Samuel Baker.

A Frenchman, Monsieur de Bizemont, brought up the steamers from Cairo, through all the cataracts. Monsieur le Blanc was with him. Mr. Higginbotham, C.E., took the steamers in sections across the Korosko desert.

September 29.—To-morrow is Bairam. I have made Ferratch Pasha take over the festivities. The *Talataween*, *Mansowrah*, and *Saphia* (*D. V.*) leave for Shendy to-morrow night with 100 men on board of each. Cassim el Mousse goes with them. I send a slip to Lord Wolseley, to be forwarded with a spy. The two journals of events from 10th to 30th September, and map of Berber, will go with steamers, in hopes of their being able to find a more secure road of sending them to Debbeh or elsewhere.

I found we had 700 bags of Indian rice in store. I have issued it on account of pay to the troops, at two okes[17] per dollar. They will sell it at three okes per dollar. It wipes off my debt to them, and they will gain.

[17] An oke equals 3½ lbs. troy.—ED.

An escaped soldier came in, and says Mahdi has had three messengers from Metemma, saying British troops were coming up in shoals, and so he had a dream, in which he was ordered back to Kordofan.

I hope the officers and men of Her Majesty's forces will be considerate to the Egyptian soldiers and sailors; *they do not understand English*, but as they have done some good service, I hope they will be kindly treated. They are a trying lot, as I well know, but if it were not for them, our soldiers would have to tramp many a weary sandy mile. It is one of my joys that I never have to see Great Britain again. I hope to get out of this affair, and either go to the Congo, *viâ* Equatorial Province, or by Brussels. At any rate I shall never have to undergo the worries I underwent during the week I was in England this year. I say this in order that those who may have to do with me may know how very determined a man's will must be who does not wish (and indeed *will not ever*) go back to England again, and to whom continuance in Her Majesty's Service, except for the honour of it, is a matter of indifference.

I am now going to be egotistic, but it will save a mint of trouble, and I may be pardoned, considering the circumstances. By being so I may save myself what I should much regret, a quarrel.

My idea is to induce Her Majesty's Government to undertake the extrication of all people or garrisons, now hemmed in or captive, and that if this is not their programme, then to resign my commission and do what I can to attain it (the object). As long as a man remains in Her Majesty's Service he is bound to obey the orders of his superiors, but if he resigns he cannot be held as insubordinate if he disobeys. Of course it may turn on the question of whether once having entered the service of Her Majesty's Army, one is free to leave it at one's will. But we officers are not like the private soldiers engaged for a term of years, and perhaps one may risk dismissal if the cause is worthy of it— which, I think, the question of abandoning the garrisons is.

I say this, because I should be sorry for Lord Wolseley

to advance from Dongola without fully knowing my views. If Her Majesty's Government are going to abandon the garrisons, then do not advance. I say nothing of evacuating the country, I merely maintain that if we do so, every one in the Soudan, captive or hemmed in, ought to have the option and power of retreat. Having given them that option and power, I have nothing more to say, and I would not care whether the country is evacuated or not.

It is a miserable country, but it is joined to Egypt, and to my idea it would be difficult to divorce the two.

I will end these egotistical remarks by saying that no persuasion will induce me to change my views; and that as to force, it is out of the question, for I have the people with me—at any rate of the towns which hold out. Therefore, if Her Majesty's forces are not prepared to relieve the whole of the garrisons, the General should consider whether it is worth coming up—in his place, *if not so prepared*,[18] I would not do so. I do not dictate, but I say what every gentleman[19] in Her

[18] The position of the garrisons in Darfour, the Bahr-el-Gazelle and Equatorial provinces renders it impossible that you should take any action which would facilitate their retreat without extending your operations far beyond the sphere which Her Majesty's Government is prepared to sanction.

As regards the Sennaar garrison, Her Majesty's Government is not prepared to sanction the dispatch of an expedition of British troops up the Blue Nile in order to insure its retreat.

From the last telegrams received from General Gordon, there is reason to hope that he has already taken steps to withdraw the Egyptian portion of the Sennaar garrison.

You will use your best endeavours to insure the safe retreat of the Egyptian troops which constitute the Kartoum garrison, and of such of the civil *employés* of Kartoum, together with their families, as may wish to return to Egypt.

As regards the future government o :the Soudan, and especially of Kartoum, Her Majesty's Government would be glad to see a Government at Kartoum which, so far as all matters connected with the internal administration of the country are concerned, would be wholly independent of Egypt.—*Lord Wolseley's Instructions*, *Egypt*, *No.* 35, 1884, *No.* 157.—ED.

[19] "I am strongly against any permanent retention of the Soudan, but I think we ought to leave it with decency, and give the respectable people a man to lead them, around whom they can rally, and we ought to support that man by money and by opening road to Berber. Pray do not consider me in any way to advocate retention of Soudan; I am quite averse to it, but you must see that you could not recall me nor could I possibly obey

Majesty's Army would agree to—that it would be *mean* (*coûte que coûte*) to leave men who (though they may not come up to our ideas as heroes) have stuck to me, though a *Christian dog in their eyes*, through great difficulties, and thus force them to surrender to those who have not conquered them, and to do that at the bidding of a foreign Power, to save one's own skin. Why the black sluts would stone me if they thought I meditated such action. Stewart knows all this and used to groan over perversity.

September 30. The Arabs fired seven shells last night at 9 P.M. which fell inside the Lines, but did no harm. To-day being Bairam, they fired four rounds in their camp—a salute I suppose.

The spy who came in yesterday, says the report is rife that Seyd Mahomet Osman's men have entered Katarif.

The three steamers will leave here to-day for Shendy at 4 P.M.

I shoved off the Bairam reception upon Ferratch Pasha, who held it upon the Lines. I am not up to these affairs, and I think he likes them.

As soon as ever I hear of the arrival of troops at Berber, down will go the Greeks, Bashi Bazouks, and Fellaheen soldiers with a month's provisions. The people of Berber then can send them on, as best they can—they will be off my hands. I have everything ready to send them. We have no telegraph wire left up here to repair the lines, so Floyer had better see to it; all ours has been used in the wire entanglements.

---

until the Cairo *employés* get out from all the places. I have named men to different places, thus involving them with Mahdi; how could I look the world in the face if I abandoned them and fled? As a gentleman, could you advise this course? It may have been a mistake to send me up, but having been done I have no option but to see evacuation through, for even if I was mean enough to escape I have no power to do so. You can easily understand this; would you do so? If you were the people of Kartoum, you would, like they would, make terms with Mahdi by making me backsheesh Mahdi."—*Gen. Gordon to Sir E. Baring, Kartoum, March* 3, 1884; *Egypt, No.* 12, 1884; *No.* 231. This telegram, forwarded by Sir E. Baring to Lord Granville, was received by H. M. Ministers on March 11, 1884. On April 3 Mr. Gladstone stated in the House of Commons that "General Gordon was under no orders and under no restraint to stay at Kartoum."—ED.

The troops on board the steamers are Fellaheen soldiers. If Berber is captured, better take them out and keep them (they are part of their way to their homes), and replace them with such black troops as may be released at Berber; but see after these white soldiers' pay, and rations, and do not neglect them.

We do not want to be told the steamers are dirty, for we know it.

If coming up, see beforehand that Arabs have not a gun or guns at the Shoboloha Pass, and if wood has to be looted, loot those people on the left bank of the Nile, *not* those on the right.

I do not care much to have Wood's men here; there will be sure to be rows between them and our blacks, and they are not favourites in the Soudan. Still less do I want to see Bashi Bazouks, or tribes who have been taken into our pay, for they will rob right and left.

I have prepared the beads, copper rods, uniforms, &c., to send up to the Equator as soon as it is possible. Report says the garrison of the Equator is at Fashoda.

The sister steamer to *Abbas* will be finished in twelve days. We made, or rather Hassan Bey made, a first-rate crank.

Remember, we have very few dollars here, and gold is depreciated in value. We have only £1,000 in the treasury.

It would be as well to tell the Greek creditors, who may be coming up, that there is not the least probability that the Government, whatever it may be, will look at any of their claims until at least a year has expired.

We have painted the steamers up; they are whited sepulchres.

I hope Ibrahim Tongi and Moussa Beys, who will come down with the first lot, who leave this (after the hoped-for capture of Berber), will be sent on to Cairo at once, and not given appointments, on any consideration, at Berber or elsewhere.

I like trying to find solutions for this Soudan problem. This is the last. Let Towfik Pasha send up Abdel Kader Pasha, as Governor-General, to replace me at once. As soon as the Firman comes, I am out of calculation, and Her Majesty's Government can do what they like, for Abdel Kader will follow their dictum. Such an act would not in the least vex me. Lord Wolseley can then do what he thinks fit with respect to the Soudan, the abandonment, and all the etceteras, and I am free of all responsibility to the people and to the troops, or with respect to the money affairs, dhoora, &c., &c. But in this case, it must be borne in mind, I am not the "rescued lamb," simply having been sent up to perform a certain mission, *i.e.*, extrication of garrisons. I failed, and was replaced by Abdel Kader and a British Force. It is for them to explain any change in their programme.

The same remarks, appended to the end of Volume I., are added to this *in re* Mr. Power and Foreign Office, &c.

C. G. GORDON.

30th September, 2 P.M., Kartoum.

I really think that as Her Majesty's Government and I are in such opposite camps (at least I think so)—*in re* the *extrication of the garrisons*—it would save a mint of trouble if Towfik Pasha were to replace me by Abdel Kader Pasha, with whom Her Majesty's Government could do as they liked. At any rate a scandal would be avoided; and I think Abdel Kader would be well received by all. Of course I should have the privilege of laughing in my sleeve if, after all, Her Majesty's Government found they could not get out without the establishment of *Turks* or *Zubair*, or the *retention of the Soudan* under Egypt. I, therefore, as an adieu, recommend this course, for it opens a speedy exit for me without rows, and clears me of all responsibility whatever.

C. G. GORDON.

BOOK III.

On outside wrapper (a handkerchief):

No secrets as far as I am concerned.

C. G. GORDON.

LT.-COLONEL STEWART, C.M.G.,
Chief of the Staff, or LORD WOLSELEY, G.C.B.,
Soudan Expeditionary Force.

JOURNAL OF EVENTS—KARTOUM, VOL. III.

From 1st Oct. to 12th Oct., 1884.

On cover at back:

GENERAL GORDON'S JOURNAL

From 1st Oct. to 12th Oct., 1884.

EVENTS IN KARTOUM.

It will require pruning down if published.

C. G. GORDON.

1/10/84.

On inside sheet:

EVENTS AT KARTOUM.

GENERAL GORDON'S JOURNAL, VOL. III.

From Oct. 1st to 1884.

If published, must be pruned down.

C. G. GORDON.

JOURNAL.

October 1.—Steamers left yesterday at 3 P.M. for (Berber, *D. V., viâ*) Shendy. Yesterday the steamer *Towfikia* attacked the Arabs on the White Nile, and killed a horse and three men. Steamer *Bordeen* drove back the horsemen on the Blue Nile. The Arabs attacked a village lower down the White Nile than Halfeyeh, and were driven back by the villagers with loss: you may believe as much as you like of this, *but our vessels went out*, that is the main thing.

The more I think of appointing Abdel Kader[1] Pasha in my place, the more strongly does the idea recommend itself, for it does away with all difficulties, and leaves Her Majesty's Government perfectly free to abandon or not as it thinks fit. Abdel Kader Pasha would be under no such obligations as I am to the soldiers, &c., of these beleaguered places, and Her Majesty's Government could put it all on him if any-

[1] Abdel Kader was then Minister of War. In March 1882, he was appointed to succeed Raouf Pasha as Governor-General of the Soudan, and on the 11th of May he reached Kartoum and assumed his duties. He carried on an active campaign against the Mahdi until March 26th, 1883, when Al-ed-Din Pasha was publicly proclaimed at Kartoum, Govenor-General of the Soudan, in his place. In January 1884, Abdel Kader was selected by the Egyptian Government as their envoy to Kartoum. He at first accepted the position and then declined it. Upon this the Egyptian Government requested Her Majesty's Government to select a well-qualified British officer to go to Kartoum instead of Abdel Kader. General Gordon was the officer selected. Thus, in suggesting Abdel Kader as his successor, General Gordon was suggesting the very man whom he had succeeded.—ED.

thing was said. To me it has the selfish advantage of being free at once of a very disagreeable and troublesome position, both personally and publicly.

As for feeling at all vexed at this arrangement, viz. my being put out, I should not, for the only thing which actuates me is this: *I think it mean to leave the garrisons;* but if my superiors decide to do so, and will take the responsibility, then what am I? to dispute their decision, the more especially as I cannot do so without funds, which I have not. I do not dispute but that the withdrawal of the garrisons is not a difficult task, but not impossible; and if not impossible, our honour binds us to fulfil it, and to my mind it is shabby not to do it: but Governments do shabby things, *vide* the Boer business, and if they are going to do it here, the way I have pointed out is the best. There is not the least reason for me to participate in its execution, it would not be fair to try and force me, and another thing is that I would *not* be forced. I believe Her Majesty's Government will adopt this idea, and if they do, I see a vista of an escape with honour and without *fracas* (which is very pleasing), from a position which is not likely to be a feather-bed, and which might require me to go on struggling for over a year, not only against the Arabs, but against the antipathies and ill-disguised hostility of Her Majesty's Government, for certainly they would not be over friendly if forced into a line of action their soul abhors.

I think we are bound to extricate the garrisons whatever it costs; *they do not;* there is no reason for any difference of opinion which cannot exist between a Government and an individual, they simply place an individual who thinks with them, and the matter is done, and this individual is Abdel Kader Pasha. I see no reason to try and force me to do what I do not think right, and which I can consequently do only in a half-hearted manner if I even undertook it, *which I will not.*

As for the effect of my replacement by Abdel Kader Pasha: 1st, it would produce no surprise, for it is well known I and Towfik are not at all friends. 2nd, it is also known that Her Majesty's Government wish to be rid of all responsibility of the Soudan, *in re* the garrisons; therefore the removal of me would be merely the carrying out of this policy. 3rd, Abdel Kader Pasha is the best man they have had up here, and so, till the matter was broken to them, he would be well received. It is not vaunting myself when I say that the general opinion here is this, that Her Majesty's Government would never have sent an expedition up here had it not had me and Stewart here, *sent up by them!*[2] I think they fully realise, that as far as the garrisons, &c., &c., were concerned, were it not for us they might perish as quickly as they liked; they also realise that, unless for the action of Her Majesty's Government at Cairo, assistance would have been sent long ago from Cairo, so it must not be expected of the people to be very grateful. They are glad to get out of their mess, but consider they are only extricated under compulsion of circumstances, and not *con amore.*

If time presses, then telegraph Towfik to make the Mudir of Dongola *Governor-General* (it does not signify who is your dummy, only perhaps he may not be so ductile as Abdel Kader) in my place, and your work is easy, such work as it is.

Personally, I can assure you, I shall be only too delighted, for I could be in Brussels in December, and free, honourably, of the whole affair; you could not possibly expect me to stay after being replaced. *Mark my words, if you have made up your mind, this is the best solution* and avoids all scandal.

Abdel Kader will make out that the Mahdi's government is not really so bad: that it is impossible, &c., &c., to be wandering all over Africa, and his paper on the state of affairs will go down splendidly with the public, and there will be honours all round, and mutual congratulations. The British public accepted, without hesitation, the trial of Arabi Pasha, by Ismail Pasha Ayoub, and Raouf Pasha, *as being a just one!* Why, had they tried an angel, and Towfik had wished the angel *guilty—guilty that angel would have been,* even if

[2] The instructions conveyed to Lord Wolseley by Her Majesty's Government were to the effect that the *primary object of the expedition was to bring away General Gordon and Colonel Stewart from Kartoum.* He was moreover enjoined not to advance further southwards than was absolutely necessary in order to attain *the primary object of the expedition.*—ED.

Michael or Gabriel. Now I have told you how to whitewash I will end this tirade. I will only remark that Her Majesty's Government must not say *I was replaced, because I wished to keep the Soudan*, FOR I DO NOT SAY SO, it is an useless country; what I say is, that it is shabby *to abandon the garrisons*, &c., &c.

I own the proposition I make is in some degree a trap, for I feel confident that there will be no end of trouble, even in placing Abdel Kader Pasha in my place and trying to evacuate; but if you accept it you will do so (after this warning) with your eyes open.

Two women slaves came in from the Sheikh el Obeyed; no news, except that the Arabs with this chief, are very badly off for water.

The following is what I would do, if in supreme command, military and political. Divide the forces into three sections; one, A, to stay at Dongola, half force, and look after communications from Wady Halfa to Berber by river, in those *étapes* or stages already alluded to.

Another, B, to occupy Berber, quarter force.

Another, C, to be a fighting force (quarter force) without artillery, for we have guns up here. With C I would come to Kartoum, coax Arabs down to Giraffe, destroy them, then coax Arabs to El foun and destroy them; then push up to

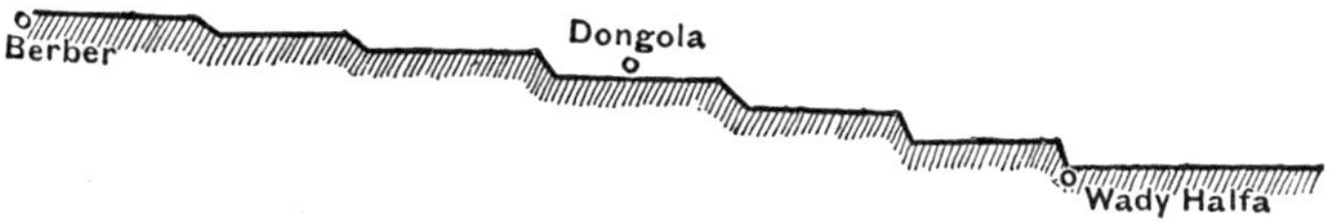

Wad el Medinet and destroy Arabs there, thus opening the road to Sennaar and allowing grain to come down.

By which time you would see your way as to the future. I would restore the telegraph as I went along.

The result of these operations would be the retreat of the Mahdi's Arabs to Kordofan, and the surrender of those in and about Kassala.

Humanly speaking, there will be probably *three* fights, costing each fight, *eight* killed and *fifteen* wounded, as far as experience

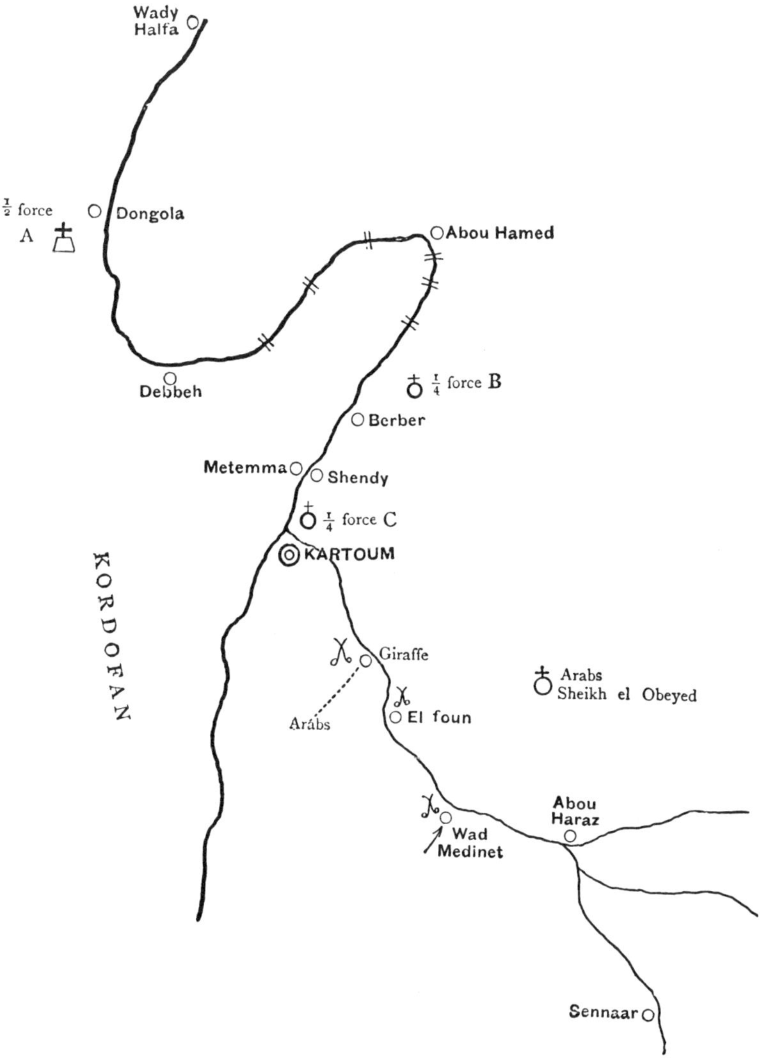
Wady Halfa
½ force
A
Dongola
Abou Hamed
Debbeh
¼ force B
Berber
Metemma
Shendy
¼ force C
KARTOUM
KORDOFAN
Giraffe
Arabs
Sheikh el Obeyed
Arábs
El foun
Abou Haraz
Wad Medinet
Sennaar

goes; not more, and very likely, if the first fight is a good one (and we have a *good* pursuit), there will be no more after it; all the rest will be child's play.[3]

Arabs must have one good defeat, to wipe out Hicks' disasters, and *my defeats.* Berber will be evacuated.

The troops at fight No. 1, *Giraffe*, will go up in the castellated barges (which are real fortresses), and be covered by five steamers, each with two guns, and two barges with a Krupp gun in each (16-pounders), so there would be no risk; none of the Arabs' forts are closed at gorge.

Force need not be more than 1000 strong, *for we could send* 3,000 for the flanks; but, as it would fight on river banks, there would be no fear for flank attack. All could be done in thirty days as far as fighting is concerned. This of course leaves the question of Kordofan unsettled. The Mahdi might come to terms, and abandon his spiritual power, but I doubt it.

The fighting force C probably will be under Buller. *Earle* at *Berber; Dormer* at *Abou Hamed;* and *Fremantle* at *Dongola;* the Sirdar at *Wady Halfa;* Lord Wolseley PARTOUT! Goodenough in command of Royal Artillery; Harrison (in recollection of China) commanding Royal Engineers. I hope Goodenough will not be too proud to use our guns; he will be horrified at the vents, which are from continuous firing [enlarged thus]; we do not rebouch up here, not having bouches.

No one could be astonished at my reluctance to make a bolt of it without the garrisons, for it virtually makes out all our toils, for the last seven months, as utterly useless; we had, to all intents and purposes, better have surrendered months ago. One feels such a mean brute to go egging on men to fight, and then to let it end with a skedaddle.

October 2nd.—A sergeant-major, with a soldier, escaped last night; he reports that the Mahdi came from Obeyed to Schatt, with two ortas of black captured troops, two Krupp guns,

[3] It must be borne in mind that when Gordon wrote this he expected the expedition to reach Kartoum before the middle of November and not towards the end of January. The strength of the rebels had materially increased during December and January.—Ed.

and seven mountain guns; but then the Arab tribes in his rear rose, and that he went back, taking the guns with him, sending one of his Ameers, Abdullah Waled Jubira, to Kalakla with 100 black troops. The sergeant-major reports the Arabs have 140 Krupp shells and 200 boxes of Remington ammunition; that the Arabs did not suffer when they fired on the steamers coming from Sennaar; that, with the Mahdi, are all the Roman Catholic Mission party, *who have not changed their religion:* one nun is exposed to the sun to force her to do so. The man says the other guns are all broken in their carriages, in the Mahdi's fights with the Arabs. The Mahdi takes Slatin and all the Europeans with him when he moves; he reports Waled a Goun has sent the black troops he had with him to the rear, because so many escaped; the Arabs fired a salute of four guns on arrival of the Ameer Abdullah Waled Jubira.

A slave coming in from the left bank reports Faki Mustapha with few troops; says the rumour of the advance Expeditionary Force is rife; says the Arab ferry is at Kalakla; they pass only at night. The sergeant-major says that he is sure the tribes (on the Mahdi's going to Schatt) all rose and pillaged on the road: hence the Mahdi's return towards Obeyed.

The man the doctor operated upon for the large stone is dead.

From what the sergeant-major says, it appears I am not more liked by the Mahdi than I am *elsewhere*—a nuisance! and a bore!

The *Towfikia* steamer went up the *White* Nile, and fired upon the Arabs! The *Bordeen* steamer went up the *Blue* Nile, and fired upon the Arabs! The Halfeyeh people went out and captured a camel! All these things are *hostilities* not countenanced by Her Majesty's Government. This afflicts me, that joker Egerton!

I have sent off another spy to Debbeh, saying that three steamers wait their orders at Metemma, *one hundred and fifty* miles from Debbeh!

The Shaggyeh tribes are giving me bother again with their horrid families down river. They are most exasperating.

A horse escaped from the Arabs, formerly belonging to

Government. It gave *no* information; but from its action, may be supposed *not to believe in the Mahdi.*

Simmons[4] and I agree on one subject—that Egypt is useless to us, unless we have command of the seas; and if we have command of seas, Egypt is ours; therefore it is not worth bothering about. We will never be liked by its peoples; we do not go the right way to be liked. To my mind, if we looked after the Cape and Mauritius, &c., it would be far more beneficial, and less expensive, than wasting our money on Egypt and the Soudan; but because Egypt *used to* be important, we think it is always so. Whereas, the introduction of steam has quite altered its importance, while the creation of other Naval Powers in the Mediterranean renders that sea no longer a question of supremacy of France or England.

I have mentioned reports of troops moving on Kassala, yet not one word is said, either one way or another, by Kitchener. Surely he must know that if this is the case, I ought to be told; or if no movement is being made in that direction, I ought to be informed.

Arabi's clerk, Ahmet-Eff-Awaan[5] (Stewart knows him well)

[4] General Sir Lintorn Simmons, G.C.B.—Ed.

[5] "I have ascertained within the last few weeks that the principal agent in the surrender of the city was not Ferratch Pasha, as originally stated, but a certain civilian exile from Egypt who had acted at one time under Arabi as Secretary of the Ministry of Marine. I know the history of this man well, and can vouch for its accuracy, as I often heard it at Cairo when I was there. Four years or so ago Awaan was an honest and zealous *employé* in the Cadastral Survey under Sir Auckland Colvin—a service which of all others under the Control was the most inefficient, and is now acknowledged to have been so. Awaan, provoked at the waste and mismanagement, one day had the temerity to draw up a memorandum of what he knew and to send it to his chief. The answer was his dismissal. He then appealed to the native press—for there was some liberty in those days—and his grievance made him a hero; and when Arabi came to power he gave him this place as secretary, which he held at Alexandria down to the bombardment. I never heard of his taking any prominent part in the politics of that eventful time, but on Sir Auckland Colvin's landing he was among the first persons arrested. Lord Charles Beresford tried him by one of his courts-martial and found him guilty of exciting to rebellion, or some such charge. He was handed over to the Circassian tender mercies, and, after seventy-four days in irons in the terrible Borgho prison, he was exiled to Kartoum. He was clearly a political prisoner if ever there was one; and when Lord Dufferin promised us the amnesty at the compromise of Arabi's trial, I wrote to him recommending Awaan's case to his special

was, on Stewart's departure, represented to me as in utter misery, so I gave him back £10 a month. *To-night* I heard my friend had been positively preaching for the Mahdi! so I have shut him up. An attempt was made the day before yesterday morning to set fire to one of the houses near the magazine at the Roman Catholic Mission. It was discovered; it was evidently the work of an incendiary. I have ordered all houses to be pulled down in the neighbourhood. This is not comfortable, for it shows we have some evil-disposed people here.[6]

October 3.—Small church parade to-day on South Front. Some twenty-five horsemen came near the Lines, and four shots were fired at them.

An inquiry is going on about the fire near the magazine. Some little suspicion that Awaan is mixed up with it, for his house was near; indeed, it adjoins the place where the fire was. It burned four tents. It will go hard with him if he is found guilty: certainly his preaching in favour of the Mahdi is against him.

I visited the place of the fire, and also Awaan's house. My impression is against Awaan being the culprit; but I have no doubt the Court of Inquiry will find him guilty. Wilfrid

---

attention, and I have his answer, with a memorandum, curiously enough, by the very Sir Charles Wilson who was afterwards to reap such bitter disappointment at his hands. But Lord Dufferin declined to interfere, and Awaan was left at Kartoum to his revenge. On January 26 it was he who, with the English again at his gates, negotiated its surrender to its Arab deliverer."—*Mr. Wilfrid Blunt in a letter to the 'Times' of May* 4, 1885.—ED.

[6] "One of the most painful parts of this business is the constant and continual reports one hears of the intended treachery of this or that influential man. I have, though greatly tried, kept my faith in all men, and have resisted any of those measures which never benefit and which throw widespread alarm throughout the town. Men who belonged to the beleaguered Shaggyeh and who had been shut up with them escaped here without arms, saying that the Shaggyeh had gone over to the enemy, while others would come from them beseeching for aid. I am glad to say that without exception the people of the town and the troops have behaved themselves in a most kind and proper way. This binds me not to leave them until I can do so under Government which would give them some hope of peace."—*General Gordon's telegram to Sir E. Baring, received at Cairo end of March*, 1884. *Egypt, No.* 12, *No.* 287.—ED.

Blunt will be crying out about this ill-used martyr, so will Arabi the blest. I am paying for the houses pulled down. There is no doubt the fire was the work of an incendiary. To-day ends the Bairam.

Stewart will not believe it of Awaan; but it appears that in disputing about the Mahdi, Awaan took off his slipper[7] and struck his opponent—he was so strong in his opinion. A more fawning, wretched fellow one never saw. I should send him to the Mahdi, but that he knows English, and is a born intriguer.

I reason thus respecting the slackness of the Intelligence Department not sending in spies. As noted in the Journal, on an average four or five men come in daily from the Arabs, therefore they do not keep so very strict a look-out; also now there are vast gaps in their Lines around the place, and one may say from here to Shendy is open. It is more difficult to go out than to come in, for in going out one may stumble on some new emplacement of the Arabs, while in coming in a man can ascertain such emplacements beforehand; it is evident also, that as all the information we have had has come from my *return spies*, that no effort has been made by the Intelligence Department. Had that Department initiated any such step in any energy, it is unlikely that all *their* men would have been stopped—my spies get caught, though, *so frequently* passing the Lines of Arabs.

The more one thinks of it, the more impossible does it seem for Her Majesty's Government to get out of this country without extricating the garrisons and establishing some Government at Kartoum; once having, as they have, come up to Dongola, they cannot well go back from Dongola; they must come to Berber, and when once at Berber, as there is the river, they must come up here; once here, they must go to Sennaar or arrange to open this route. It is of all things the most perplexing, and one does not see the end of it, unless we give the country to the Turks. With the best will and with all favourable circumstances, *i.e.*, that it is found

[7] To strike with a slipper during a dispute is with Moslems the greatest insult one man can offer another.—Ed.

possible to abandon, it will take six to eight months, and with a terrible outlay, and one cannot think that even then it is a satisfactory termination if, after extricating the garrisons and contenting ourselves with that, we let the Mahdi come down and boast of driving us out.

If we proclaim the abolition of slave-holding we must proclaim it in Egypt as well, and then the revenue falls. The Turks really seem the only way out of it in a speedy way. It would be cheaper to give them a million pounds than to keep our people up here, and there is no discredit to our arms if we take Berber and open the route to Sennaar, and then leave the country to the Turks, letting them deal with the Mahdi as they like. I think even the gift of two millions to the Turks would be a cheap solution of it, and is also a quick and an honourable one.

As for Her Majesty's Government keeping the Soudan itself, it is out of the question, for you could not get men to serve here except under great salaries and supported with large forces; and as for giving it back to Egypt, in a couple of years we would have another Mahdi; therefore, our choice lies between Zubair and the Turks. Now, the time has gone by when Zubair, almost alone, would suffice; he would now need aid in men, while the Turks would need no aid from us in men. Therefore, give the country to the Turks, when once you have come to Kartoum, with one or two millions sterling (which YOU will spend in three months' occupation up here if you delay), make arrangements at once with the Porte for its Soudan cession, let 6,000 Turks land at Suakin and march up to Berber, thence to Kartoum; you can then retire at once before the hot weather comes on.[8] Let 3,000 Turks land at Massowah and go to Kassala; that saves you that journey. You would be even saved waiting till the troops came from the Equator and Bahr Gazelle.

[8] On Feb. 11th, 1884, General Gordon telegraphed from Berber to Sir Evelyn Baring: "I would not, if I were supreme, try again any Egyptian forces at Suakin, but would engage 3,000 Turkish troops in British pay. That would settle the affair. It would be sufficient for the Padishah's troops to appear to cause a collapse of all fanatical feeling."—ED.

28th October.—Berber occupied.

5th November.—1000 troops at Kartoum. 6,000 Turks land at Suakin and march to Berber. 4,000 Turks land at Massowah and march to Kassala.

8th November.—Defeat of Arabs on South Lines—unless they have bolted.

12th November.—Defeat Arabs near El foun, unless they have submitted.

15th November.—Despatch of force to Sennaar to clear country round Medinet.

1st to *10th December.*—Arrival of Turks at Berber and Kartoum, and at Kassala.

20th December.—Return of Her Majesty's forces to Wady Halfa, leaving 1000 men at Dongola till Turks could come from Berber.

The frontier to be Wady Halfa. All steamers, &c., to be handed over to the Turks. The two millions to be paid in four instalments.

Suakin and Massowah to be free ports under the Turks.

Egypt is responsible for the pensions of those who return to Egypt. Turkey is responsible for the pensions of those who stay in the Soudan. I see nothing to prevent the whole affair being settled by the end of January, and the whole Expeditionary Force from being in Cairo at the end of February.

As for the slave-trade, one cannot help it.[9]

[9] "Several telegrams have been sent from press asking about what I said respecting slaves. The question asked me was this: Did I insist on the liberation of slaves in 1889 as per Treaty 1877? I answered that the Treaty would not be enforced in 1889 by me, which, considering the determination of Her Majesty's Government respecting Soudan, was a self-evident fact. The question is one of slave-holding, not of slave-hunting, and, in my opinion, that Treaty of 1877 will never be carried out in Cairo as to slave-holding."—*General Gordon's telegram to Sir E. Baring, received at Cairo Feb.* 21, 1884, *Egypt* 12, *No.* 132.—ED.

"Let it be known to you all that I have been appointed, in concert

I cannot see why France could object if we let her have some "say" in Egypt. She will thwart all we do there unless we do let her have a "say."[10]

We make up with Turkey by this action, and she would aid us to prevent Egypt being annexed by any other Power.

Remember we have no time to lose—that we must make our choice at once—and that choice must be one of a strong decisive kind, with no shifting hopes of something turning up. Our Expedition is very ticklish, very expensive, and *utterly unremunerative.*

If once our men get sickly up here, and our programme is a skedaddle, the consequences might be most disastrous. The skedaddle programme would cool all the people against us, and strengthen the Mahdi immensely; and then there is no way to avoid the heats, unless by the skedaddle programme; but if you agree with the Turks, you avoid the heats and the skedaddle programme, and have people with you.

I hope I am not going down to History as being the cause of this Expedition, for I decline the imputation. *The Expedition comes up to deliver the garrisons.*[11] I think it would read well in history: "Her Majesty's Government having accepted duties in Egypt, and consequently in the Soudan, sent up a force to restore tranquillity, which, having been done, Her Majesty's Government handed over that government of the Soudan to the Sultan."

Our people may try as they like, they can never govern

---

between the Khedive's Government and the Government of Great Britain, Governor-General of the whole Soudan; and the Soudan has now become an independent State, to govern itself without the intervention of the Egyptian Government in any way whatever."—*General Gordon's Proclamation to All the Notables and Inhabitants in the Soudan, Feb.* 13, 1884.—ED.

[10] General Gordon is here probably quoting the views of Herbin, the French Consul.—ED.

[11] Though, as shown in a previous note, General Gordon was right in assuming no expedition would have been sent had he not been in Kartoum with Stewart, he is also right in saying: "The Expedition comes up to deliver the garrisons," for the avowed policy declared in the instructions of Her Majesty's Government to Lord Wolseley was that steps were to be taken to insure the safe retreat of the Egyptian troops and civil *employés.*—ED.

Egypt and pay the interest; combine with France, and let down the interest to 3 per cent., which we cannot do without France agreeing.

As for any of the men in Cairo now pretending to govern, it is useless; they know nothing of, and have no sympathy with, the country. What can they know of the country, sitting at Cairo? What the people want, is half taxes, and Censors going through provinces remedying evils. Do away with Wood's army, an useless expense. Do away with three-fourths of European *employés*, railway, &c., &c.—cormorants!—ditto, Gendarmerie.

I shall send out three men in different directions to-morrow to Debbeh, with further notifications that three steamers, and each with two field-guns, are at Metemma, Shendy, 150 miles from Ambukol, which is 35 miles higher up river than Debbeh, waiting orders of Expeditionary Force, and saying Cuzzi's baggage is to be searched. I have now done all I can. In ten days' time I shall send a steamer to Metemma with further information. The attempt to fire the magazine has made me vicious with the people. No one in from Arabs to-day. Query, *ominous!*

October 4.—The boiler will be put in the new steamer (sister to *Abbas*) to-day. She will be ready for sea in six days.

Report from Cassim el Mousse late last night. Arabs say Sheikh el Obeyed meditates an attack on Halfeyeh. The trouble these Shaggyeh have given us is beyond description.

Ibrahim Bey Ruckdi, loq. Lutraim: "He called for me at (9 P.M.) 3! in the night; he bullied me to work. Can you imagine such a thing?—it is preposterous. He flew at me like a tiger, because I showed he was unreasonable. It is *Bairam* too: can you imagine such a thing?"

Awaan, Arabi's clerk, has been telling, in the town, that the letters I got saying, "Her Majesty's troops are advancing," were written by him and sent down, and then returned. There is an evident wish to take off his head; but I think he is more fool than knave, and shall try and resist the wish of town.

Saleh Pasha's son telegraphed to me he wanted to come and see me. I answered he might come or *go*, as he liked. He said, what did I mean by "go?" I was much tempted to say, "*Go to your father, who is in chains with Mahdi,*" but resisted temptation, and said, "*Go out of telegraph station.*"

I had to send down ten barges for those creatures at 10 P.M. last night.[12]

No spies in this morning; people will begin to believe Awaan's statement, that he it was who wrote the letters (I pretended to have had) from the English.

A woman just in says there is a report with the Arabs that the English are at Dongola; that a steamer and four nuggars, with English, are at Berber (?) (I expect she has mixed up Stewart's steamer and boats with her story); that the Arab chief of Berber has sent for help, which has not yet been sent him.

One of those large shells was blown up by a boy treading on it; it does not appear to have hurt him; it was in the group of date palms opposite to the Palace.

I confess the shells do not seem so very destructive. Perhaps they are too deeply buried; however, they have frightened people.

A small boy and five men escaped from the Arabs and came in. The Mahdi, with Europeans, is at Schatt; he means to come to Omdurman. They corroborate that some troops went back to Obeyed to put down the rising of tribes.

The boiler has been successfully put in the small steamer.

It is odd how quick the blacks, by instinct, know how to avoid the effects of the shells, by throwing themselves on the ground when they hear the fizz of the quick-match; they all do it, and thus have escaped. Of course it would not do in an assault. The little black chap never ran so fast as he did when he got up after the explosion, never looking behind him. He went to two black sluts, who had been alarmed at the noise, and explained the opening of the ground, &c., with a good deal of gesticulation. They had a sort of Medgliss[13]

[12] See p. 130.

[13] Court of Enquiry.—ED.

on the subject whether it was not time to return home, and pick no more grass, after such dreadful things had happened, and which ended in their doing so, carefully avoiding the scene of the accident.

I expect these improvident people killed over 1000 sheep and goats at their Bairam; the report is that it exceeds that number.

There is no doubt there will be a fearful famine in this country next year, for there are vast districts lying desert which were formerly cultivated.

The party which went to Jaila, the village north of Halfeyeh, which the Arabs had attacked, have come back with the rescued families, and twenty-five cows captured from the so-called rebels. (Query, Who are the rebels, *we or the Arabs?*) (To-day is the 206th day we have been more or less shut up. Delightful life! I wonder what Azotus [Ashdod] felt with its twenty-nine years blockade?)

October 5.—Two men and a boy came in from the Arabs, and report that the Mahdi has made a small advance towards Omdurman. Little else of import. They say Hussein Pasha Khalifa, Saleh Pasha, Slatin, and all the Europeans are with the Mahdi; that Kordofan is in turmoil; that the Arabs say they will wait till they can collect a lot of men, and then will attack the Lines.

If you do not arrange with the Turks you will not get out of the country for a year, and it will cost you twelve millions, and probably then you will have to fall back on the Turks.[14] Whereas if you arrange with the Turks you can get out in January, and it will cost you seven millions, including the two millions you give the Turks. Truly this black sister "Soudan" has avenged her white sister "Egypt."

A scorpion in bath sponge this morning. It stung me upon the finger. I murdered it, and so am quits. I wonder whether any analysis has been made of the scorpion's and the cobra's poison. This is the sixth time I have been stung.

[14] This forecast is in a fair way of being fulfilled.—ED.

A sheikh of the neighbourhood came in, and says a short time ago a Frenchman came up with two Arabs from Dongola to the Mahdi. The Mahdi could not make it out, and asked why he came. The man said he had come up to salute the Mahdi. The Mahdi being suspicious imprisoned him for seven days, and then let him out. He was in a Dervish dress. It is said he spoke to Saleh Pasha and to Slatin in secret, upon which the Mahdi separated these two, and put them in open arrest (is this Rochefort?) My informant says he denied to the Mahdi that the English were in Dongola, but told Slatin and Saleh Pasha that they were there. This man is with the Mahdi now, and is free. It might be Renan,[15] the author of "Life of Jesus," who in his last publication takes leave of the world, and is said to have gone into Africa, not to re-appear again. He was a Roman Catholic priest orginally, is a great Arabic scholar, and evidently a very unhappy and restless man. I met him once in the rooms of the Royal Geographical Society one afternoon, and I remember the Secretary proposing to him to go up to the *top* of that *high house!* to see the observatory. Renan declined. He looked bored and weary in being made a hero of, and when Sir R. Alcock introduced me to him, I suppose he saw my look of commiseration for his trials, and was civil to me. I have often thought we might meet again. What a fearful infliction hero-worship is to its victim. I think it a great impertinence to praise a man to his face. It implies you are his superior, for the greater praises the smaller; and though that may be the case, it is not necessary to announce it to the smaller. Supposing one is wrinkled and grey-haired, it is satire to say you are smooth-skinned, &c., &c., and beautiful, and so it must be with every man who knows himself and who is praised—endurance, self-denial, and twaddle—one would have bolted like a lamplighter if one could, and one could have stood the after criticism.

. . . on going to the trenches before Sevastopol fell out, and said he would not go down. The colonel put him under arrest. He was in a way more plucky to do this than to go

[15] It seems pretty clear that this is Olivier Pain.—Ed.

to the trenches. Self-sacrifice is that of a nurse—ignored (and "paid," of course, what can she want more!). No ones goes into ecstacies over her self-denial.

If it is Renan he will not approve of the pepper system. The man says the Mahdi was perfectly astounded at this Frenchman's appearance, and did nothing but question him. "Why do you come here?" &c., &c. If he comes to the Lines, and it is Renan, I shall go and see him, for, whatever one may think of his unbelief in our Lord, he certainly dared to say what he thought, and he has not changed his creed to save his life.

A black mother and her two sons have come in, and say the Mahdi is at Jura Hadra, twenty-five miles south of Duem. The woman was delighted to see herself in the mirrors, and grinned and smirked at her reflections.

Spies say Nuehr Bey Angara has been sent back by the Mahdi to Obeyed, to put down the rising of the tribes; if he would only *rise* himself, for he is an old friend of mine, the Mahdi would be cut off from Obeyed and be in a bad way.

The steamer *Bordeen* is back from Halfeyeh.

We chose to regard Greece, Spain, Turkey, Mexico, and other lands, as debtors and bankrupts. We did not attempt to saddle the rulers, personally, with the debts of these countries—excepting in the case of Egypt and Ismail Pasha (*i.e.*, we did not turn out the rulers of those states, while we did turn out Ismail), of course it is easy to put it down to his ill-faith. I expect the rulers of those other states were guilty of far worse faith. It is the custom to *say* we acted in the interests of the oppressed fellaheen, but what have the fellaheen gained up to the present time? Where are those millions to come from I have talked of?

Let us consider dispassionately the state of affairs. Does Her Majesty's Government consider they are responsible for the extrication of the Soudan garrisons and Cairo inhabitants? We can only judge that Her Majesty's Government does recognise this responsibility, for otherwise why did they send me up, and why did they relieve Tokar? Once this responsibility is assumed, I see no outlet for it but to relieve the garrisons, *coûte que coûte.* It may be said that the object of the present expedition is for *my* relief *personally*. But how is it possible for me to go away and leave men whom I have egged on to fight for the last six months? How could I leave after encouraging Sennaar to hold out? No one could possibly wish me to do so. No Government could take the responsibility of so ordering me. There is this difficulty: perhaps it would be patriotic to bolt; but *even if* I could get *my mind* to do it, I doubt if it is possible to get *my body* out of this place. Had Baring said in March, "Shift for yourself as best you can," which he could have done, the affair could have been arranged, and we could have bolted to the Equator; but, if you look over my telegrams,[16] you will see I ask him what he will do, and he never answered.[17] The people had not then

[16] Not received from the Government with these Journals.—ED.

[17] "European Consuls came to me to-day with the question whether Kartoum was menaced. I replied that it was not so, directly, but that the road to Berber was threatened. They asked me if I could help them to go to Berber. I replied 'Yes.' There is no doubt that when these Europeans leave, it will be a most significant sign to the people in this town and in the provinces that no assistance is likely to come to Kartoum. Under these circumstances, what do you recommend me to say in order to neutralise the ill-effects of their departure?"—*General Gordon to Sir Evelyn Baring, Kartoum, March* 9, 1884, 11.30 P.M.—*Egypt, No.* 12 (1884), *Inclosure in No.* 242.

"You know exactly the position of the different garrisons so far as I can explain it, and that there is no probability of the people rallying round me, or of paying any attention to my Proclamation.

"If you mean to make the proposed diversion to Berber (of British troops), and to accept my proposal as to Zubair, to instal him in the Soudan and evacuate, then it is worth while to hold on to Kartoum.

"If, on the other hand, you determine on neither of these steps, then I can see no use in holding on to Kartoum, for it is impossible for me to help the other garrisons, and I shall only be sacrificing the whole of the troops and *employés* here.

"In this latter case, your instructions to me had better be that I should evacuate Kartoum, and, with all the *employés* and troops, remove the seat of government to Berber. You would understand that such a step would mean the sacrificing of all outlying places except Berber and Dongola.

"You must give a prompt reply to this, as even the retreat to Berber may not be in my power in a few days; and, even if carried out at once, the retreat will be of extreme difficulty.

"I should have to leave large stores, and nine steamers which cannot go down. Eventually, some question would arise at Berber and Dongola, and I may utterly fail in getting the Cairo *employés* to Berber.

"If I attempt it, I could be responsible only for the attempt to do so.

endured any privation, and I was, as it were, not much engaged to them; but now it is different, especially as we have communicated with Sennaar.

No one can judge the waste of money and expense of life in the present expedition—it is an utter waste of both—but it is simply due to the indecisions of our Government. Had they said from the first, "We do not care—we will do nothing for the garrisons of the Soudan, they may perish; had they not relieved Tokar; had they not telegraphed to me as to the force to relieve me (*vide* telegrams, 5th May, from Suakin; 29th April, from Massowah). Had they telegraphed (when Baring telegraphed to Cuzzi 29th March, which arrived here saying, "No British troops are coming to Berber, negotiations going on about opening road—Graham was about to attack Osman Digna"), "*SHIFT FOR YOURSELF*," why, nothing could have been said; but Her Majesty's Government would not say they were going to abandon the garrisons, and therefore "*shift for yourself.*" It is that which has hampered us so much. On the one hand, if I bolted I deserted them (Her Majesty's Government); on the other hand, by staying I have brought about this Expedition. Baring gave me destinct orders not to go to the Equator without the permission of Her Majesty's Government (*vide* telegrams with Stewart's jour-

---

"Once the Mahdi is in Kartoum, operations against him will be very arduous, and will not serve Sennaar and Kassala."

"*Kartoum, March* 9, 1884, 11.40 P.M.

"If the immediate evacuation of Kartoum is determined upon, irrespective of outlying towns, I would propose to send down all the Cairo *employés* and white troops with Colonel Stewart to Berber, where he would await your orders. I would also ask Her Majesty's Government to accept the resignation of my commission, and I would take all steamers and stores up to the Equatorial and Bahr Gazelle Provinces, and consider those provinces as under the King of the Belgians.

"You would be able to retire all Cairo *employés* and white troops with Stewart from Berber to Dongola, and thence to Wady Halfa.

"If you, therefore, determine on the immediate evacuation of Kartoum, this is my idea. If you object, tell me.

"It is the only solution that I can see if the immediate evacuation of Kartoum, irrespective of the outlying towns, is determined upon."—*Ibid.*—Ed.

nal).[18] I do not question the policy of Her Majesty's Government in not keeping the Soudan. It is a wretched country, and not worth keeping. I do not pretend even to judge the policy of letting the garrisons, &c., &c., perish; but I do say, I think that Her Majesty's Government ought to have taken the bold step of speaking out and saying, "*SHIFT FOR YOURSELF*" *in March*, when I could have done so, and not now, when I am in honour bound to the people after six months' bothering warfare. Not only did Baring not say, "*Shift for yourself*," but he put a veto upon my going to the Equator—*vide* his telegrams in Stewart's Journal. I say this because no one deplores more the waste of money and life in this Expedition, and no one can realise its difficulties better than myself, but, owing to what has past, owing to indecision, we are in for it, and the only thing now to do is to see how to get out of it, with honour and the least expense possible—and I see no other way than by giving the country to the Turks. I am not raising difficulties, or being cantankerous; I wish most sincerely I was out of the place, where from February I have had no peace. The question is how to do so. I may be wrong, but I have a strong suspicion that much rejoicing (*rejoicing* perhaps a *little* for my personal but a good deal for my official safety) would have taken place in official circles had I appeared in the *Abbas* with Stewart; but it was not even physically possible, and I should have been a disgraced man for ever had I been able to do so and had done it. Besides which, we were entirely in doubt as to the intentions of Her Majesty's Government as to letting the garrisons slide or not. I might have been tried for deserting my post, and for letting the steamers and stores fall into the hands of the Mahdi, for that was certain within five days of my quitting the place. What I suspect or

[18] "I have received your telegram of the 9th inst., informing me that you have received a letter from General Gordon from which it appears that that officer contemplates proceeding to Bahr Gazelle and the Equatorial Provinces. I have to state that Her Majesty's Government are of opinion that General Gordon should not at present go beyond Kartoum."—*Earl Granville to Sir E. Baring, Feb. 11th,* 1884. *Egypt, No.* 12, *No.* 4.—ED.

do not suspect, would not justify me in my action, and, as it turns out, my suspicions were wrong, for after Stewart left, I hear a British force is coming up—of course it is a query what is it coming up for? If *for the garrisons*, then I have done what the Government wants, for I have kept the city; if *for me*, then I have done wrong, for I should have come down at all costs; but in one case great inconvenience would have been given; while in the other it is only my life—and if it is *for me* the Expedition comes, it would be better to tell me, "Shift for yourself; we do not mean to extricate the garrisons"—in which case perhaps we may find an issue—at any rate the people will know exactly the state of affairs, and our Government will not be exposed to an unnecessary expense and danger in sending troops up here for *ME*. I should consider Her Majesty's Government were completely exonerated from all responsibility with respect to myself if they sent me that order, "*Shift for yourself;* we *do not mean to extricate the garrisons.*" I should make my arrangements, and (telling the people how I am situated, with no hope of relief for them), should make a bolt to the Equator in six weeks' time. There would be no dishonour in that, for, as I had no relief coming, the only sequel of my staying with them would be to be a prisoner with them, and in fact my presence would only exasperate the Arabs instead of being of any good.

It may be argued, Why not retreat on Berber? I would rather not do that, for I would wish to show in a positive way that I had no part or lot in the abandoning of the garrisons, &c., &c., and, at any rate, I should save the garrisons of the Equator and of the Bahr Gazelle if I succeeded in getting away to them.

October 6.—The steamer *Bordeen* up the *Blue* Nile wasting a lot of ammunition on the Arab foraging parties. No arsenals could stand this drain on their resources. I expect that the *Bordeen* fired fifty rounds to-day.

Three escaped soldiers came in from the Arabs; they say that the Arabs have sent a Krupp and a mountain gun to Giraffe; so that may account for the heavy firing above mentioned. One of the men say the Arabs placed two boats in a position close to the two guns they had brought, in order to entice the steamer to go and take them, thus hoping to sink her. However, I am glad to say the steamer is on her way back. The continual anxiety one is in about these little things is very wearing. One never knows if, through some rash act, I may not lose a steamer, or men may not be cut off. One has no man like Gessi[19] who one can trust for these little expeditions. Steamer *Towfikia* went up the White Nile and fired upon the Arabs. It is just as I thought: the *Bordeen* steamer has come back, having been struck by a shell about a foot above the water-line, close to the cutwater; no one was hurt. All the Arabs are going from the White Nile towards Giraffe. I expect we shall have the old game at Bourré again. In these circumstances you can imagine how very vicious one feels towards Her Majesty's Intelligence Department for not giving us any news. It is not so much for myself as it is for the townspeople.[20]

The steamer reports that the Arabs had five guns. It is evident the Arabs mean to hold the Blue Nile by their force at Giraffe, and I dare not try to dislodge them; they will then communicate with the Sheikh el Obeyed's force, and eventually come down upon Shoboloha or thereabouts; while the Mahdi, coming to Omdurman, will circle us in, a second time.

Owing to a discovered intrigue and the risk of having too much power in the hands of one man, I have sent Ibrahim Ruckdi to Malia as chief clerk, and Gugliz Bey of Malia[21] is made my chief clerk. Nothing like change of air for these fellows.

[19] Romulus Gessi, who was formerly employed as interpreter at the head-quarters of the army before Sebastopol, and who did such excellent work against the slave-hunters in the Soudan as General Gordon's lieutenant in 1878. Gessi was subsequently appointed Governor of the Bahr Gazelle, but was obliged to retire owing to the intrigues of Raouf Pasha. He died at the hospital at Suez in 1881.—Ed.

[20] General Gordon's chief complaint against the Intelligence Department was that they spent no money in bribing natives to try and get messages through to Kartoum; had they done so, many, he held, would have volunteered, and some must have succeeded.—Ed.

[21] The word Malia means Finance Department.—Ed.

As interesting to Stewart, I will mention the intrigue. He knows of the letters which came, accusing Ibrahim Ruckdi of venality. Well, a Medgliss was held, and Mahomet Bey Agad was found guilty of sending the letters. I did not care to push the matter, for, in my belief, Agad was right in his accusation, although he had no right to write anonymously. *Of course* the Medgliss found him guilty, as every Egyptian Medgliss does every one sent before it; so I temporised and hinted to a third person that it would be well if Ibrahim asked pardon of Agad; this hint, being of course a sort of order, he took; but I noticed he was working against Agad; and yesterday he came with a paper against Hassan Agad the Sandjak, putting it forward as Ferratch Pasha's idea to turn Hassan Agad out. I thought over it, and it worried me, the viciousness of the man; but I took no action. However, to-day, as I told him to write another order about the troops saluting me by stopping in the road and saying he was responsible for it, he said, as he turned away, in an impertinent manner, "Am I Commandant of troops?" He was brought back, and, nose to grindstone, was sent to Malia, and Gugliz Bey was brought up to chief clerkship.

I own I am suspicious, *i.e.*, I judge by the eye, by little signs, &c., for I do not know the language; but I cannot help thinking I am more often right than wrong with my suspicions. One comes on a group of clerks, heads all together, in the chief clerk's room; one sees disturbed countenances at once. I cannot help thinking "You are concocting devilry!" and I look out for some "*tricks.*"

Another soldier escaped here from the Arabs, and says the Mahdi is at Jura Hadra, and intends coming to Omdurman. He does not appear to think the Arabs care for the English advance, though they know they are at Dongola, "a far cry," they say, to Kartoum. They consider Hicks's defeat was one over the English troops. One thing is good, viz., that the Arabs came down to Giraffe, for if they stay there, when the British do come they will fall easy victims without any long march inland. It certainly does seem astounding that the Arabs seem so confident when a British force is only 150 miles from them, which is the case, for that distance of 150 miles alone separates the three steamers from Debbeh, which has a waterway to Dongola, and the place the three steamers are at, has a waterway to Kartoum. In reality, with a well-equipped force, Debbeh is not more than eight days from Kartoum at the outside, saying that the 150 miles were made in six and a-half days, which for camels is twenty-five miles a day, very easy marching; while from Metemma to this is 100 miles—a day and a-half for steamers (when I say Debbeh, I mean Ambukol, to which place from Debbeh you have the open river). The appearance of one British soldier or officer here settles the question of relief *vis-à-vis* the towns-people, for then they know that I have not told them lies.

The Arabs fired fourteen rounds at the *Bordeen*. The shell which entered her was a Krupp; the hole is now repaired.

It was an unfortunate remark of Ibrahim Ruckdi, "Am I Commandant of soldiers?" I had dismissed the thought of changing him, having comforted myself that, one way or another, my tenure of office could not be long up here; when he said that, it was like a match in powder; he was brought back, and made then and there to sign his dismissal. I do not think he realised it, even after he had written it. Even to me it was a surprise, for I really had given up all idea of sending him off.

The sister steamer to the *Abbas* will be finished, I hope, in four days. She will be called the *Hussein*, after the head of the dockyard. The other one, also a sister steamer, will be, I hope, finished in six weeks, if we exist that time. Of the two steamers at Berber with Arabs, the *Fascher* and the *Monsuhania*—the latter is reported disabled.

I have ordered *Bordeen* to go on the White Nile on patrol from Kalakli to Shoboloha; the *Ismailia* is at Halfeyeh, *Towfikia* at Omdurman.

The Arabs, who went in numbers to Giraffe to-day, went back to their Dem at sunset.

We have another large steamer, the *Chabeen*, up in our *dry-dock*, which I hope will be soon ready for action.

A man came in from the Arabs; he says Seyd Mahomet

Osman has sent 300 camels to bring his family from Shendy to Kassala (this is a bad sign); he says the English have advanced towards Berber.

October 7.—Ibrahim Ruckdi has fallen from £60 per month to £30. Sixteen soldiers with their arms came in to-day from the Arabs, also one slave; they had not much to say. Arabs had three guns against the steamer yesterday; they kept one gun at Giraffe, where they keep small detachments all night. The Arabs pursued the men escaping, and fired a few rounds, but did no harm; with these men came in four women of theirs, quite a flock.

I really think the Arabs on the south side keep such a way off because they are afraid of the captured soldiers deserting. The sixteen men who came in were splendid fellows, all nearly six feet; they say a body of forty others have made up their minds to come in a mass either to-day or to-morrow.

An Arab of Kartoum came in from Omdurman; says grass huts are being made for the Mahdi's arrival there; man says the Arabs report "English and Turkish troops at Debbeh." *Towfikia* went up the White Nile; saw a few Arabs, who fired on her.

Another soldier has come in—the Arabs will be furious; he says nine others have made up a party to leave the Arab camp. The Arabs spread reports that I kill all who come in; but the whole of the soldiers of the Soudan know me of old, and so the reports are not believed. This soldier was at Berberah when last I saw him. I had moved all the black soldiers from there to Senheit, as the climate did not suit them. It is odd that Berberah, Zeila, and Harrar suits the Egyptian and chocolate faces; not the blacks, who suffer from pulmonary complaints in those parts.

The sputtering of musketry on the Lines this morning quite reminded me of old times. The Arabs fired a good deal at the runaways.

Some of the officers are very anxious to go out against the Arabs, but I do not see it. We are not safe off the river banks, and there is no good risking matters; besides which, we can never, with our force, give them a crushing defeat, which will alone settle the question; and we might, by a small defeat, drive them into the desert, where one could not reach them if other troops come up. We are now thus placed (see

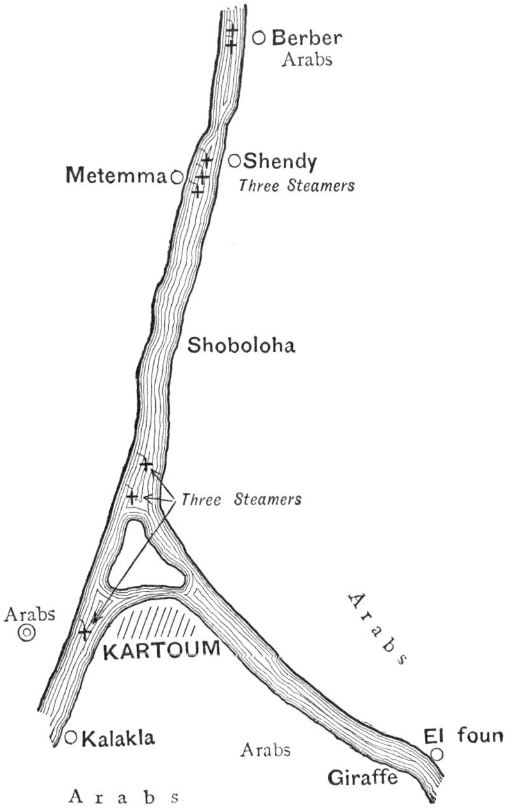

Map), and in four days I shall have four steamers between Shoboloha and Kalakla. In a month I hope two more steamers will be ready: total, *nine*. Arabs have *two* at Berber, *one* at Wad el Medinet; of those at Berber only one is fit for work, the *Fascher*.

I will mention a secret in all Egyptian administrations, *i.e.*,

if you give an order, it is totally inefficient in three days' time if not repeated again and again at intervals; it seems as if its essence evaporated in the heat of these countries. The officers would laugh you to scorn if you said, "Why, I gave a *standing order* respecting this or that." It would be to them perfectly ridiculous and absurd to expect a "standing order" to be obeyed, unless *repeated* at intervals. In most services, standing orders are regarded, but certainly not in Egypt; this is the reason why all those beautiful proclamations and laws issued by the control and their successors, are *dead letters* after ten days; they are constructed for the European Press. What is needed, is continual hammering at seeing your orders obeyed. Saleh Pasha sent a man in with a message to me: "Mahdi is coming with 40,000 men, &c., &c., &c." This is all rubbish. All Kordofan could not produce this number; and if it could, the country could not support them in food for five days.

Fearful row to-night because, after one-and-a-half days' warning, the *Bordeen* was going to start for Halfeyeh, no soldiers were found on board, and this after repeated orders to Ferratch Pasha. Men may say what they like, but one is bound to lose one's temper in such cases. This is the story Saleh Pasha's man tells: "Mahdi with 40,000 men is coming to Omdurman, and will take it; he will then plunge into the river and take Kartoum before the English come." I reply that "the Mahdi is not a fool to think that by plunging into the river he will take Kartoum, neither can he have 40,000 men with him. *Put Saleh Pasha's messenger into chains as a spy of the enemy.*" We have spies direct from the Mahdi's camp, who say "he has not 3,000 with him." This business was going on at the same time as my row with Ferratch Pasha—certainly one is not on a bed of roses in this place.

October 8th.—One soldier who escaped this morning, reports that the Arabs are furious at the desertions of yesterday. Saleh Pasha's messenger (spoken of yesterday), on being put in chains, acknowledges his statement is all fudge about Mahdi's 40,000 men, &c., &c.

A sergeant escaped from the Arabs; he says the Arabs sent up about 200 black soldiers to Mesalamieh to get grain, and they escaped to Sennaar; that Waled a Goun meditates coming over, with two guns, to the old Dem, which was previously occupied by the son of Sheikh el Obeyed, on the north side, near Halfeyeh, which, if he does, will be a great bore for us. The Mahdi is at Jura Hadra; that a man had come from near Berber to say the Expedition was advancing towards that place. One has heard so much of this sort of report that taken with the report of Waled a Goun coming to Halfeyeh, one is inclined to doubt it, for he would not be likely to do that if it was true about the Expedition at Berber.

Sent out spy from Halfeyeh towards Shendy.

Whatever may happen, I hope it will be put to our credit that we gave you the *Abbas* steamer, and placed three steamers at your disposal at Metemma,—when, if we had them we might have cut the route between Jura on left bank of the Nile, and Fakir Ibrahim on the right bank of the Nile,—besides using up 350 soldiers of our meagre garrison in the equipages of those steamers! Truly the indecision of our Government has been, from a military point of view, a very great bore, for we never could act as if independent; there was always the chance of their taking action, which hampered us.

Take the Tokar business: had Baker been supported by, say, 500 men, he would not have been defeated; yet, after he was defeated, you go and send a force to relieve the town. Had Baker been supported by these 500 men, he would, in all probability, have been victorious, and would have pushed on to Berber, and, once there, Berber would not have fallen. What was right to do in *March*, was right to do in *February*. We sent an expedition in March, so we ought to have sent it in February; and then, the worst of it was, that Baker, having been defeated, *when you did send your expedition to Tokar*, Baker's force no longer existed, and his guns resist me at Berber. It is truly deplorable, the waste of men and money, on account of our indecision. Baker's expedition ought never to have been pushed forward, unless by small stages, supported by forts. It had not more than fifteen or twenty miles to go, and that distance ought to be, so to say, sapped.

Take your present Expedition, I do not know (*thanks to that Intelligence Department!*) the details, but it seems to me that till 20th August, or thereabouts, we were supposed to be quietly disposed of, but about that date our resurrection occurred, and then, "Let us have an expedition at once, and send for Wolseley." Had the men at Wady Halfa (Duncan) been told in March (when he came up to Assouan) to make *étapes* up to Dongola, they would have been all ready for the Expedition now. Personally, I do not care, but I think what a perfect mess we would be in, in an European war. I am convinced Wood, the Sirdar, and many others, foresaw what was likely to happen, but they did not consider they were called upon to make a row about it. (Plutarch's Lives are out of print in our generation; we do not like to be what club men call insubordinate, though, of all insubordinates, the club men are the worst.) What is the consequence? Why, an infinite expense and great difficulty. Mark the way the Mahdi treated Cuzzi: is it likely he did it for the love of Cuzzi? was it not because Cuzzi told him of Baring's telegram, "that no troops will be sent to Berber?" Remember, though I put these queries, it is not I who put them: it is *history*. Why did Baker go to Suakin, and Wood, the Sirdar, stay at Cairo? One was chief of gendarmerie; the other was commander-in-chief. It was not a question of police, but of war. If it was right to let Sinkat perish, it was right to let Tokar; if it was right to relieve Tokar, it was right to see after Berber, and thence on to Kartoum, Sennaar, Kassala, Bahr Gazelle, and the Equator. At any rate, *be consistent*. No one can question the right of the Government to decide; but when they decide, let it be a decision. "WE WILL ABANDON ALTOGETHER, *and not care what happens*." That is a decision one can understand, whether one approves or not. We are not the judges; but what we have done is such, that I declare I very much doubt what is really going to be the policy of our Government, even now that the Expedition is at Dongola.

What were my ideas in coming out? They were these: *agreed abandonment of Soudan, but extricate the garrisons*, and these were the instructions of the Government; and I only wish that the public would look over Baring's and my telegrams exchanged from 28th February to 16th March, and see how he answered me:[22] it was as if I was amusing myself up here. And then that light-hearted fellow Egerton adds to it ("that I am in (Capua)"), "What are your intentions in staying at Kartoum?"[23] I should like to see some explanation why no efforts were made for the *relief* of the *garrisons* before August (*not* MY *relief*). Berber was known to have fallen in March; it may be said the season was not good, then why in June does Egerton tell me to make *contracts?* I hope Stewart will *cut out all this biliousness.*

9 P.M. *Telegraph cut with Halfeyeh.* This corroborates rather what this man who came in to-day said, *i.e.* that the Arabs meditate coming again to the Dem, north of this town, which will be a trouble—it will be the beginning of a second blockade, and I hope the *last*, for I declare I do not think I could go through a third *blockade*—siege is too great a word for it.

October 9.—Telegraph repaired with Halfeyeh. The Arabs came down on the Lines with two guns and exchanged some shots with our people. Only waste of ammunition.

One soldier escaped from the Arabs to-day. He came from

[22] General Gordon to Sir E. Baring, March 1st.—"*Re* policy. I maintain firmly policy of eventual evacuation, but I tell you plainly it is impossible to get Cairo *employés* out of Kartoum unless the Government helps in the way I told you." *Inclosure* 1 *in No.* 229, *No.* 12 *in Blue Book No.* 12.

Sir Evelyn Baring replied in a telegram dated March 2nd, 1884:—"I have received your eleven telegrams of the last four days on matters of general policy. I am most anxious to help and support you in every way, but find it very difficult to understand exactly what you want. I think your best plan will be to reconsider the whole question carefully and then state to me in one telegram what it is you recommend, &c."—ED.

[23] Earl Granville to Mr. Egerton, April 23rd, 1884:—"Gordon should be at once informed by several messengers . . . that we do not propose to supply him with Turkish or other force for the purpose of undertaking military expeditions, such being beyond the scope of the commission he holds, and at variance with the pacific policy which was the purpose of his mission to the Soudan; that, if with this knowledge, he continues at Kartoum, he should state to us the cause and intention with which he so continues."—*Egypt, No.* 12 (1884), *No.* 36.—ED.

Sheikh el Obeyed. He says they have got the gun which was captured at Katarif.

The Arabs fired seventeen shells this morning, but did no harm.

Those Shaggyeh! I will back them to try a man's patience more sorely than any other people in the whole world, yea, and in the Universe. It is no use detailing their efforts. I have now sent Moussa Bey down to Halfeyeh. I really believe that they did try the patience of the Arabs, from all I hear; for the Arabs frequently thought of putting them to the sword, and I can quite imagine Arabs having this thought, from the wear and tear they have given me.

Of course the officer on the Lines reports masses of Arabs killed to-day.

Sheikh el Obeyed killed all the prisoners he took (who were inhabitants of Kartoum) in Mahomet Ali's defeat, near El foun. I have ordered the sale of 200 ardebs of grain, no one to buy more than ¼-ardeb.

Stewart will be annoyed at hearing "Ibrahim Ruckdi is *very ill!!!!*" Illness dates from hour of being turned out of head clerk's place; he has not sent for the doctor.

It will be a satisfaction for some to know that, owing to their not sending me any news, I am exposed to hearing all sorts of disquieting rumours from the town, which, though I do not mind them, are not destined to make one's life lighter. The Ulema have been coming here for two days to see me; they have been bothering for more grain, and so I put off seeing them, but I gave them one ardeb a-piece. To-day, however, they pushed an interview, but I still held out, and said they *must* tell my Vakeel what they had to say. After a deal of palaver my Vakeel came in to say, "*that the whole of the town requested I would take back Ibrahim Ruckdi.*" What an idea! I said "The town had better mind their own business, and leave me to mind mine." I think it is lovely! and how Ruckdi must have worked at it during his *severe illness*. Ruckdi had got at my servants. Edrees, the butler, told me, with a look of deepest commiseration, how ill Ruckdi was, on which I laughed. I guessed he was on the sick list, and had asked.

"Yes" (with a deep sigh), "*Ruckdi was very ill.*" "Illness commenced when?" I asked. "Oh, a long time back, but duty and fidelity to *me* had enabled him to crawl through his work," at which I laughed again. Then came the Ulema, with the town petition. I can quite imagine when men have bribed the chief clerk A. to be favourable, that it is a bother to have to go through the same process with chief clerk B. on A.'s being turned out; it upsets all calculations. Ruckdi will return to Cairo with Tongi.

"See-saw,[24] see-saw, why it is enough to kill a fellow. I can't keep my eyes open. I would give a shilling to have an hour's sleep! *Yes*, of course, *you* say it is close at hand, *you black devil!*" "I know your *Kareb* means at least three hours more." "Give you the water-bottle? I can't. I don't dare to touch the rope of this long-necked brute. Hullo: there is some one come a cropper. Rifle 'broken,' of course it is, you cannot fall from a precipice without its being broken." "Hi! stop! Catch hold of the brute; the machufat, as you call it, is slipping round. Can't you stop the brute (noise of a body falling); well there is an end of it. I will walk *now* sooner than embark again on the ship of the desert. Am I hurt? Oh, no, of course not; rather enjoyed sensation. Walks half a mile, boots full of sand, and tries it again."—Scene in Desert: Explorations in Central Africa, by Her Majesty's Army.

The machufats[25] *will* slip forward, and camels *will* object to people riding *on* their long necks; they *will* drop vesuvians on camels, who will not like it; they *will* get galled, and have not glycerine; they will drop their pipes, and not dare to descend for them; they *will* pass baggage-camel with sharp edged boxes which will rasp their legs; as they mount they will go over the other side and swear—oh how they will swear! all their Topies will be crushed—aches and pains in every part of the body (I should be inclined to put them on ambulance saddles, one on each side: awkward if they meet a baggage caravan). "Tired and ill! of course I am tired

[24] Supposed remarks of British soldiers crossing the desert upon camels.—ED.

[25] Saddles.—ED.

and ill after bowing and swaying my body to and fro all night, with my eyes pricking like as from so many needles, from desire to sleep; and you may say what you like, I swear I saw more than one of those skeleton camels get up, and I saw houses as plain as I see you.[26] I was between Scylla and Charybdis. I wanted to sleep, and I was afraid of falling off—shall never forget it."

"Chermside to Kitchener: Any news of *him?*"

"Kitchener to Chermside: Nothing particular; two or three more men down. Steamers at Metemma. Abuse as usual of Intelligence Department. Mahdi doing much better: *he* finds it more difficult to get his letters through, and will have time to get over *his* liver complaint and injustices. Stewart says it was a perfect pandemonium to be boxed up with him when in his tantrums. *I hope you are well. Let me know if I can do anything for you.*"

I think, in the interests of the Telegraph Department, Floyer ought to make officers pay for telegrams like this intercepted one.

A man came in from the Arabs on the South Front. He says the Arabs have imprisoned the regular troops with them; that the regulars want to make a rush for our Lines and to escape to us.

A boy came in four days absent from the Mahdi's camp, which is at a place opposite Gitana. He says the Mahdi is moving along the left bank towards Omdurman, and that he has with him all the Europeans, Elias Pasha, and Slatin; that he will try and take the place before the advance of the English, who are said to be near Berber. Kordofan is quiet. The Mahdi has about three to four thousand with him. The Mahdi says he will cross the river dry-foot—by a miracle.

Sent for the *Ismailia* from Halfeyeh, replacing her by the *Towfikia*. The *Bordeen*, down the river, will go to the same place on her return. Somehow this advance of the Mahdi has raised my spirits; nothing is more dead-like to be shut up as we have been; now, at any rate, a month will see him victorious or defeated, as God may will it. I think he will

[26] Allusion to images produced on the retina by an excited or exhausted brain.—Ed.

try and negotiate, for, of course, Hussein Pasha Khalifa, has told him I had a Firman enabling me to give up the country if I found some one to take it.

"Kitchener to Chermside.—Hurrah! Capital news! The Mahdi has *him* on the hip! he has gone to Omdurman. Bottled *him* up now! We will have no more impertinent remarks about the Intelligence Departments. Dongola illuminated! Regular feast of lanterns! Wish you were here, old fellow; hope you are well! Can I, &c., &c."

I declare Floyer ought to make them pay for these telegrams—intercepted and brought here.

Lord . . . : "Well after a long night comes the dawn, this is somewhat better news. I confess I was never much taken up with Livingstone's explorations, and I never would have believed any one, if he had told me I should be carrying out these explorations with a British army. One must not be ungrateful, but one may be permitted the remark why that Mahdi did not move before he has quite spoilt my holiday; why, dear me, in three months I shall be back in that bear-baiting garden again, being asked questions. What a life! What do you say? I am sacrificing myself for my country. Well, you are right there, I am a martyr, if ever there was one."

The mass of people who have come in from the Arabs, have spread far and wide—what is to be expected from the Mahdi and his Government—so I have no fear for the town, which I suppose has 40,000 inhabitants in it.

The Arabs prevent all coming to me—I prevent none going to them—and I even give them written permissions to go; so I gauge the fidelity of the people.

Small steamer got her steam up to-day, and I hope will be finished in three days, armed and in action.

I feel sure that the Mahdi comes with the idea of negotiating; if so, and one can have reasonable hope of success as to the extrication of the garrisons, I shall negotiate—for up to the present time, my original instructions are not abrogated, and I feel sure Her Majesty's Government will not wish any longer campaign, than is necessary, in these parts, for their honour, but it must be remembered *if*, by negotiating,

I get out the garrisons at the cost of the steamers, &c., &c., I must not be blamed if in the future, by the cession of the steamers and warlike material, Egypt suffers. Her Majesty's Government gave me clear orders, *i.e.*, "get out garrisons and evacuate"—these orders have not been cancelled and are in force. No official notice is given me of an advance of troops or of a change of policy; therefore I am justified in acting on my original instructions. Kitchener's note is not sufficient to justify me in disobeying my regular instructions. Egerton's telegram was not decipherable.

October 10.—The beginning of the year 1302 of the Arabs is on the 21st October. On the 1st, 2nd, and 3rd October were Hicks's defeats. The Mahdi, bringing all the Europeans with him, makes his move look as if he were confident of his success ultimately. All information tends to show that his object is to starve us out. If the man would only drop his prophet's functions, we might come to terms; but he will never do that, I fear. There is one good thing in the Mahdi's coming here—he will be easy of access, if our Government wishes to communicate with him; and also if he is defeated there is an end of him, without going to Kordofan. I suppose our people at Debbeh must be aware of the whereabouts of the Mahdi at any rate.

It is an odd coincidence the advance of the Mahdi and of the Expeditionary Force at the same time, and to the same place (Armageddon).

I have 240 men at Omdurman, and it is pretty strong. It is not likely to be attacked; for if the Mahdi won it, he would not have gained Kartoum, though it would be a trouble, as it would discourage the people.

There is one bother, in any negotiations (which, however, I do not think possible), viz. how far one ought to go *in re* the steamers and warlike store. If I had Zubair here it might be settled, but now the Expedition is at Dongola it is a query what ought to be done.

I have lost seven guns, two on board each steamer, at Metemma, and one on board the *Abbas*.

This morning the Arabs fired six Krupp shells into the Lines, which did not burst.

Not a large church parade either at Kalakla, South Front, or at Faki Mustapha, near Omdurman. Two men came in, one from South Front with rifle, and one from Omdurman; the latter says the Mahdi will come to Omdurman either to-day or to-morrow, and will content himself with the investment of the place. He has with him all the Europeans, nuns and all. The Arabs meditate coming over to the old Dem, near Halfeyeh, but they say it will be the *Arabs of Waled a Goun* who will come, *not* those of the Sheikh el Obeyed; this is odd, and it would seem as if these two parties had fallen out. We know Sheikh el Obeyed did not agree with Abou Gugliz.

People do not appear a bit put out at the approach of the Mahdi; in fact they look on it as a good thing, for they say the affair will be ended here, and there will be no necessity to go to Kordofan.

A very little Arab boy, with large, black, limpid eyes, came in from the Arabs. He had been captured some months ago.

The steamer *Bordeen* is still down the river robbing, I expect, right and left.

A Sandjak of Shaggyeh, who was for months a prisoner with Sheikh Ibrahim (son of Sheikh el Obeyed), told me how this latter used to quarrel with Abou Gugliz, how the latter had taken the gun they had captured from us; and how glad Sheikh Ibrahim was when we beat Abou Gugliz at Giraffe. On one occasion Abou Gugliz put Sheikh Ibrahim in chains.

Four of the Arab Krupp shells fell in the centre of the town—did no harm—(regular bombardment of Paris), moral effect, *nil.*

Little steamer *Husseinyeh* trial trip to-morrow. The Arabs will think one of the large steamers has been brought to bed.

One cannot help being amused at the Mahdi's carrying all the Europeans about with him—nuns, priests, Greeks, Austrian officers—what a medley, a regular Étât major. It will be a great crow for Lord Wolseley if he manages to put an extinguisher on the Mahdi.

Cambyses, son of Cyrus of Isaiah, lost his army B.C. 525, in these deserts, 2409 years ago.

The Mussulman year 1302 begins on the anniversary of Trafalgar. "England *expects*" (does not say even "thank you") "you will do your duty."

Those who were ever quartered at Gibraltar will remember two despatches over the mantelpiece, Collingwood's on Trafalgar; Wellington on Waterloo. What a different tone in them. I cannot help thinking the navy is more chivalrous than the army in all nations; they are more seriously minded, having gone through greater vicissitudes of danger. I noticed flags around Faki Mustapha's tent, and three women came in this evening from Waled a Goun's camp, and reports that the Mahdi came to Omdurman to-day; but a soldier who escaped with his rifle came in afterwards and said the Mahdi had not yet come to Omdurman, but was expected to-morrow.

In five days' time I shall send down the *Towfikia* steamer to Metemma, and order the *Talataween* back. With the *Towfikia* I shall send this Journal up to date. The *Towfikia* will stay at Metemma.

I have placed two of the castled santels at the end of the Lines on the White Nile, the other two are at Bourré. The *Bordeen* steamer is back from Shoboloha; she captured fifteen cows and four slaves. She was fired on from the left bank of the Nile.

Armed the men of the band and made them body guard of Ferratch Pasha.

In future, for the defence of Kartoum, strong forts ought to be built at Shoboloha, on both sides of the defile.

The *Bordeen* telegraphed from Halfeyeh "Important spy captured." I answered, "What did important spy say?" I was answered, "Important spy said that the English had sent out three men to see about roads to Kartoum." This was two and a half hours' work to get this information. It is enough to drive one wild (a very small *mouse* for such a *mountain*). Couriers were sent on horses to and fro for this information. I am going to sit on the captain of the *Bordeen* to-morrow. These people, if they have a grain of information which they (not I) think important, make a perfect Mont Blanc of it, so as to get promotion. What on earth of importance is it to us whether the British general has sent a hundred and fifty spies to look after roads.

The captain of the *Bordeen* gave the names of the spies sent out by the British general obtained from this "important spy," thinking, of course, I should be delighted. These things render one perfectly furious, for, at least, twenty people were kept at work for absolutely nothing; and like a born idiot, there was I, on tiptoe of excitement, waiting information of the "important spy," to end with the news that "three men had been sent out by the British general." Had "this important spy" said the British general had started, it would have been another thing, but that is in the future, and I do not blame the British general for not rushing headlong into these deserts.

October 11.—A sergeant-major came in at Omdurman to-day, he left the Mahdi three days ago. The Mahdi was then one day's march from Omdurman, at the place Stewart met the chiefs when he went up the Nile in March. The Mahdi will be at the camp Faki Mustapha to-night or to-morrow. He has from 2,000 to 3,000 regulars with him, whom he captured here and there. Three Krupp guns and four mountain guns, but has a lot more mountain guns *en route* from Kordofan. With the Mahdi are Hussein Pasha Khalifa, Saleh Pasha, Slatin, and all the Greeks, priests, and nuns, who have become Muslim. A priest and a nun who refused to become Muslim, he left in Obeyed. Nuchranza is with him. He has a mixed multitude with him, who are not over zealous, for he has discontented the people by his exactions. They have plenty of meat, but not much grain. The Frenchman spoken of (and supposed to be Renan by me) has gone away from the Mahdi. Fighting is going on in Kordofan in the Gebel Nubar. Report is rife of the English being at Debbeh. The Mahdi intends bombarding Kartoum from the other side, and trying to demolish the Fort Omdurman. The money captured at Berber has not yet left Berber.

Another soldier came in from Waled a Goun's camp; he says the regulars are all in chains.

The Arabs are making a fort 2,000 yards off the South Front. They fired eight rounds from a Krupp, which entered the town but did no harm.

Four shells entered the town yesterday—one slightly wounded five black sluts, one struck a house belonging to the family of the Mahdi.

Small steamer's trial trip took place to-day—a great success; she snorts terribly.

Two more soldiers came in this morning from the Sheikh el Obeyed. They say he intends coming to the old Dem off the North Fort, where they were before. They say he is not on the best of terms with Waled a Goun. I hope sincerely he will not come opposite to us.

Sent out two men separately to Debbeh, with notification of the arrival of his holiness the Mahdi at Omdurman.

Connected the Fort of Halfeyeh by telegraph to river bank, 1500 yards.

Moussa Bey put in charge of the *Bordeen* and *Ismailia*, and Omdurman and Mogrim.

Ferratch Pasha is made a Ferile (General of Division). I am more generous than Her Majesty's Government (when a colonel, I used to make Generals of Division. The Khedive used to tear his hair over it). It may be that Ferratch Pasha may be sold for $2\frac{1}{4}$$ in a fortnight, if the town is taken, and be carrying water for one of the Mahdi's Ameers. I must say I am against doctors. If a man is suffering intense pain, and is in a more or less desperate condition, I would give as much morphine as would still that pain. It was the custom of the ancients to give to those who were to be crucified a numbing potion, which is that mentioned in Matt. xxvii. 34, Mark xv. 23. Our Lord would not abate, by mortal means, the slightest pang of His passion, and He would not taste it. But in our Lord's case He knew the object of giving Him this potion, whereas a patient need not know it. Our doctors give a composing draught to produce sleep, and I cannot see why they stop at that and do not give a draught to produce insensibility to pain—but I suppose they have rules we know not of. Napoleon at Jaffa asked the principal medical officer a question—whether, with respect to the plague patients (whom he could not take with him in his retreat to Egypt, and they would have had their throats cut had they stayed) it would not be justifiable to give them composing draughts. The principal medical officer answered, "his business was to cure, not to kill." Now Napoleon did not say "do so," but he merely asked the question, inasmuch as it was certain that the throats of those patients would be cut by the Turks if they were left behind. History disputes whether Napoleon did not get another doctor to give the composing draughts, but it is certain that the plague-stricken patients were killed by the Turks (whether under the influence of composing draughts or not it does not much signify). To my mind the principal medical officer was a snob, and took advantage of Napoleon's question to make himself a hero. Napoleon alluded to it afterwards at St. Helena, and I am inclined to believe his version, viz. that he only put the alternative question to the principal medical officer, and did not order the giving of the composing draught. I shall now conclude this Volume III. I have sent 200 men to Omdurman, and am prepared to evacuate Halfeyeh and place its garrison at Goba, if the Sheikh el Obeyed moves to the north of this place.

C. G. Gordon.
12/10/84.

BOOK IV.

On outside wrapper (a handkerchief):

No secrets as far as I am concerned.

C. G. GORDON.

LT.-COLONEL STEWART, C.M.G.,
Chief of the Staff, or LORD WOLSELEY, G.C.B.
Soudan Expeditionary Force.

JOURNAL OF EVENTS—KARTOUM, VOL. IV.
From 12th Oct. to 20th Oct., 1884.

GENERAL GORDON'S JOURNAL.

EVENTS AT KARTOUM.

From 12th Oct. to 20th Oct., 1884.

To be pruned down if published.

C. G. GORDON.

The following note accompanied this Journal, addressed to Lieutenant-Colonel Stewart :—

Kartoum, 20th October, 1884.

MY DEAR STEWART,

Here is the Journal up to date—not much in it. I hear you got down all right. Kind regards to Lord Wolseley. I have given up now all idea of getting information from you all.

Yours sincerely,

C. G. GORDON.

On inside sheet:

GENERAL GORDON'S JOURNAL, VOL. IV.

From 12th Oct. to 20th Oct. 1884.,

EVENTS OF KARTOUM.

Together with a paper, Intelligence Department, on False Prophet.[1]

To be pruned down if published.

C. G. GORDON.

[1] See Appendix, "The Insurrection of the False Prophet."

JOURNAL.

October 12.—Post left for Metemma by *Towfikia* to-day. I am almost decided to evacuate Halfeyeh, and put Shaggyeh, now there, at Goba.[1] I dug up a shell yesterday which was at the foot of a lay figure at north side, and see that the reason of their (the shells) not proving fatal is that they are buried too deep, and their force is expended laterally—a man must be over them to be hurt. Of course this would be remedied in regular warfare. Were I to put them out again, I would lay the shells on the surface of the ground, hiding the fuses or ignitors, and run the risk of their being seen. Men going to assault a place do not pick their steps, as if they were crossing a street. I have ordered the concentration of guns on part of Lines opposite to which Arabs bombard us. I have ordered silence for the two or three first rounds of the Arabs, and then to give them some salvoes.

What with these people's prayers, eating and sleeping, one's patience is indeed tried. I know no people in the world who can take advantage of cover better than them—the cover being "*I am ill;*" that is a settler; for although you know it is the illness of laziness, you can say nothing; if you doubt it, you are universally voted a brute.

When you say to any escaped soldier, "Why do you come here?" he replies, "Why, the Arabs give us nothing. Why,

[1] Goba is on the right bank of the Blue Nile, to the north of Tuti Island, and within two miles of Kartoum.—Ed.

with you I can get this or that." It is merely a question of what they can *get*. The belly governs the whole world.

Have ordered the *Bordeen* steamer to creep up when the moon rises, and attack the Arab ferry at Kalakla.

Went over to Goba, and chose positions for the Shaggyeh tribe. If we evacuate Halfeyeh, we shall have to give up three outer forts, and one central one (Seyd Mahomet Osman's house).

It is quite a danger to pass through the yard of the Palace on account of the turkey-cock (though he has a harem of five); he killed two of his children the other day. I do not know if you have noticed it, but when not angry, or in full dress, the lobes of flesh about their necks are grey; but it does not need half a minute for them to make them of the most brilliant scarlet. I cannot understand how they make part of their heads blue, while the appendages are scarlet. I think the turkey-cock is a bird worth studying; the tuft in front is peculiar to him alone. I know no other bird which has it. I would give him the palm over all birds for pluck.

I have decided to bring those wretched Shaggyeh over to Goba, and have sent boats for them.[2]

I declare solemnly, that if it were not for the honour's sake of our nation, I would let these people slide; they are of the very feeblest nature, and the Arabs are ten times better; but because they are weak, there is so much more the reason to try and help them; for I think it was because we were such worthless creatures, that Our Lord came to deliver us. These Shaggyeh know no shame. It is an unknown quantity with them. What a life one has to live. I wish I commanded the Arabs (speaking professionally). I think it is a great shame not giving me Zubair Pasha, for he would know how to deal with these people. They are the weariness of my life. From February until now they have been one continued worry to me, and I expect they worried the Arabs as much.

I have decided to put the Shaggyeh into the North Fort, and not to occupy Goba. A slave came in from Kerowé; had no

[2] See p. 99.

news. The Arabs did not fire upon the Lines to-day, so concentration of artillery fire on them did not come off. A woman came into the Lines from Waled a Goun with a letter.[3] *Towfikia* was to have left this morning; but late last night, happening to go to the telegraph office, and asking whether she was all ready, the captain replied he had no wood! so there was an end of her start to-day.

I particularly wish to ascertain how many communications were sent me from Cairo or elsewhere in Egypt between the 12th of March, when the telegraph wire was cut, and the present date. I hope Stewart will get this information for me, and not be hoodwinked about it. I should also much like the substance of those communications.

The letter was from Abou Gugliz[4] sending in a woman who had before been a spy. He begs me to become a Mussulman, &c. The woman who brought it, says the Mahdi comes to-night to Omdurman, and that he says, as soon as he comes, *I shall ask to surrender!* The Mahdi says he will write me three letters; he will then wait for five days, and that he will then advance across the river, which will divide for him. Looking at the date which will be arrived at, after these letters are written and the five days' grace have expired, and making allowances for what is meant by the dividing of the waters, it would bring the Mahdi's attack about the 21st October, the New Year's Day of 1302 A.H.

We hear the Arabs are perplexed, because the other day, when they bombarded us, we did not answer. This was my doing to save ammunition. The Arabs asked the regulars with them, "why we did not answer?" and said they were sure the regulars were in communication with us. We are now weighing the pros and cons for not answering the artillery fire of the Arabs, which do us no harm and uses up their ammunition. By not doing so we do not lose the sympathies of the regulars, whereas if we do so we exasperate and render desperate those regulars. We had an instance of that at Bourré, where at first the regulars were well disposed towards us, and came

[3] Appendix P. [4] Appendix P.

over in numbers; whereas after we had killed a lot of them they ceased to come in, and used to fight us with viciousness.

The woman says, beyond the captured regulars, Arabs have no fighting force. These captured regulars are mostly all blacks.

Another *plot!* In town a man was discovered taking out a note couched in mysterious language, from one of the clerks in a Government office. With the note was £34, supposed to be a present to the Mahdi from Sheikh el Islam (the blind man) here. The efforts to square the circle are extraordinary. The people here, I expect, have all hedged. I am going to make a sort of general arrest to-night (similar to that made by Napoleon III. on the night of the 1st December) of all who are supposed to be in communication with the Mahdi. I shall not hurt them, but shall send them out to the Mahdi. (Query, was it on the night of the 1st and 2nd December Napoleon took his foes prisoners, or on the night of the 2nd–3rd December? I think it was the night of the 1st–2nd December, and the so-called massacre happened during the day of the 2nd December. (Vide Kinglake in 'Coup d'état.')

I shall not send out the Sheikh el Islam[5] although he is a disgrace. I asked Mahomet Edrees, my servant, "to become a Christian." He said "he could not." Then I said, "Why ask me to become a Mussulman, when your Sheikh el Islam is prepared to acknowledge Mahomet Achmet as the Mahdi?" 5 P.M.—The arrests are out. Sheikh el Islam, Cadi, and a host of swells are to be kept in their homes—sixteen in all! A good swoop; among them the Mudir Achmet Bey Jelaba. I have made Moussa Bey Mudir. There will be quite a scare about it. I have not sent any away to the Mahdi. The band boys are all armed, and are quite ferocious. It would be a great mistake to come up here and think to find soldiers *in extremis;* they are as cocky as possible. They strut along as if no one was their equal. The blacks are a stubborn race; and if one sticks to them, they will stick to you. *Towfikia* has left for Metemma *at last.*

[5] *I.e.*, the priest.—Ed.

A mouse has taken Stewart's place at table; she (judging from her swelled-out appearance) comes up and eats out of my plate without fear.

The turkey-cock has become so disagreeable that I had to put his head under his wing and sway him to and fro till he slept. The cavasses thought he was dead, but he got up and immediately went at me. The putting the head under the wing acts with all birds, but it is the *cock* alone who gets mesmerised by the chalk lines drawn in front of his beak. How do you account for this?

I believe that a good recruitment of blacks and Chinese would give England all the troops she wants for expeditions, mixed with one-sixth English. As for those wretched Sepoys, they are useless. I would garrison India with Chinese and blacks, with one-sixth English, and no army could stand against us. The Chinese in Shanghai had the greatest contempt for the Bombay Sepoys, and used to knock them about. Beloochees and Sikhs are a different class. I have the greatest contempt for the pure Indian Sepoys. Chinese, or blacks, or Goorkas, or Belochees are far better. The moment he (the pure Sepoy) is off parade, he puts off all uniform that connects him with Her Majesty's Government, and puts on his dish-clout. I hate these snake-like creatures. Any man accustomed to judge by faces sees that they hate us.

I would back the Mussulmans of India against the lot of those snakes. India, to me, is not an advantage; it accustoms our men to a style of life which they cannot keep up in England; it deteriorates our women. If we kept the sea-coast, it is all that we want. It is the centre of all petty intrigue, while if our energy were devoted elsewhere, it would produce ten-fold. India sways all our policy to our detriment. Lord Cardwell replied (when I asked him the question as to the benefit we got from India), "*that we could not get out of it*," and I suppose that is the answer that must be given.

October 13.—Cavalry sortie this morning from Bourré; captured fifteen slaves and killed thirteen men who resisted. This sortie was under Abdoul Hamid, the Sandjak of the Shaggyeh. We lost none.

The Arabs on Omdurman side have spread out their huts in a semicircle (but at a considerable distance) around Omdurman, on the left bank.

Shaggyeh from Halfeyeh will be in the North Fort to-day. The Arabs off South Front, near the White Nile, fired musketry against the Lines, but did no harm.

Last night cavalry Shaggyeh captured three men who were going off to Sheikh el Obeyed from Halfeyeh; they had their arms with them. I have let them go again.

No definite news yet of the arrival of the Mahdi at Omdurman. The Mahdi will be furious with this cavalry sortie; it will be disagreeable news to him on his arrival here.

A man from the Arabs has come in to Omdurman with two letters;[6] it is too late to see them to-night. By telegraph I hear that the man brought two letters for the Commandant at Omdurman from Faki Mustapha, saying the Mahdi was coming the day after to-morrow, and inviting him to submit; so I have told them to send the man off again.

We are a wonderful people; it was never our Government which made us a great nation; our Government has been ever the drag on our wheels. It is, of course, on the cards that Kartoum is taken under the nose of the Expeditionary Force, which will be *just too late.*[7]

The Expeditionary Force will perhaps think it necessary to retake it; but that will be of no use, and will cause loss of life uselessly on both sides. It had far better quietly return, with its tail between its legs; for once Kartoum is taken, it matters little if the Opposition say "You gave up Kartoum," or "You gave up Kartoum, Sennaar," &c., &c., the sun will have set, people will not care much for the satellites. England was made by adventurers, not by its Government, and I believe it

[6] Appendix Q.

[7] Many of General Gordon's "instincts" have been no less remarkable than many of his escapes. In a telegram to Sir Evelyn Baring, dated March 1st, he said, "I will do my best to carry out my instructions, but feel convinced I shall be caught in Kartoum."—ED.

will only hold its place by adventurers. If Kartoum falls, then go quietly back to Cairo, for you will only lose men and spend money uselessly in carrying on the campaign.

October 14th.—I have been obliged to make some more arrests. Report in says many of the people, chiefs, &c., of Shendy come in to the three steamers now at Metemma; also that the steamers have been firing on the Arabs of Metemma; report says that Expedition advance guard is at Abou Hamed, remainder at Merowé; that some English are coming from Kassala with Seyd Mahomet Osman to Gros Ragéb; that the Sakkeyer Arabs meditate a raid on Shoboloha tribes, who are

1 *Daily News.* 2 *Times.* 3 *Standard.* 4 *Pall Mall Gazette.*

favourable to Government. The Arabs fired on the Lines this morning, doing no harm. Made Ferratch Ullah, who used to be at the Palace, a Miralli.[8]

[8] In his 'Wild Tribes of the Soudan,' Mr. F. L. James gives an account of how he and his party were treated by Ala-ed-Deen and the Bey at Senheit. This Bey was no other than Ferratch Pasha, who is said to have opened the gates of Kartoum. "We had engaged camels at Senheit," says Mr. James, "for some weeks' shooting in the vicinity. On our return, a steamer was leaving Massowah for Suez, which we could only catch by taking the same camels on to the coast. Our Shaggyeh drivers objected, saying the road to the sea was out of their country, and their camels were tired—perfectly valid excuses. We offered them half as much again as the proper fare, but they still demurred, fearing that the Governor of Massowah would take their camels, make them carry for the Government, and probably never pay them. On obtaining a letter for the Bey at Senheit (Ferratch), asking (as we fondly imagined) Ala-ed-Deen, who was at that time Governor of Massowah, to let them go free, they

In the two letters,[9] Faki Mustapha says the English are prisoners at Assouan, and that the Arabs had captured *Abbas* with Stewart at Cataract Dar Djumna, below Abou Hamed, *which would be dismal!*

Arabs are keeping a long way off the Lines since the cavalry sortie.

No sign of the arrival of the Mahdi at Omdurman. Very few horsemen to be seen on the South Front. Query, have they gone down towards Berber?

This evening, some twelve of those arrested and allowed to stay in their houses are to be taken to the barracks; I hate those arrests, but one can scarcely doubt so many informants, who declare there was "trahison" meditated, not from any wish to join Mahdi, but for fear I was not strong enough to hold the city, and owing to Awaan's statement, *that he had written the letters* I had received from Debbeh announcing that the Expeditionary Force was coming.

The north side is like a market, with the camels, horses, sheep, goats, donkeys, of the Shaggyehs, who have come up from Halfeyeh, &c.

I confess I am more perplexed about these arrests than I like; is it a good thing? or is it not? If I could be sure that the majority wished to go to the Mahdi, I could make up my mind at once what to do; it would be an immense relief to me; but does the mass wish it? If they do not, I ought to take all precautions against such an event. Then comes the query. Am I not, in these arrests, being made a tool of by the Turkish and Cairo elements? Are they not gratifying spites? Paul said, "*I have learned*" (as in a school) "*in whatsoever state I am to be content.*" I can only say, "*I am learning,*" *but have* "*not learned.*"

No sign this evening in Faki Mustapha's camp of the arrival of the Mahdi.

---

consented to accompany us. On our arrival we presented the letter, which, we found, merely stated that the garrison of Senheit was in want of salt, and that he had better load up the camels with some, and return them to him."—Ed.

[9] Appendix Q.

Heavy thunderstorm and rain this evening, which will be made out by the proselytes of Mahomet Achmet as a proof of his divine pretensions. It is rather bad for our mines.

October 15th.—No spies in—everything quiet. Some begin to doubt if Mahdi is so near.

People say I must have some news of relief, otherwise I would not have made the arrest of Mudir, Cadi and Sheikh el Islam, &c., &c.

I see there was a total eclipse of the moon on 4th October, and there is a partial eclipse of the sun on the 18th-19th October.

I reason thus respecting the arrests: if the people really want to go over to the Mahdi, it will make no difference beyond hastening the event; if they do not want to go to the Mahdi it will make no difference. If there is a minority to go to the Mahdi the arrests have upset their plans, at any rate for a time. To my idea, these people were only *hedging*, in order to be prepared for all contingencies.

Mahomed Pasha Hassan, who is a barometer of fear, approves of the step—so I hear in an indirect way:—*of course* every body approves of it, if *asked* by *me*, for fear of their own arrest.

I had to make three more arrests—when once one begins this detestable practice, one never can stop. As far as I can judge the mass of people approve of the arrests. I am now going on the principle "in for a penny, in for a pound." Wilfrid Blunt will make a nice row about this. It is very odd we have had no one in from the Arabs for two days. Glad to say I found out one arrest not just, and have let the man out.

Jeremiah was arrested over and over again, and let out by King Zedekiah. I wonder how any man can possibly wish to enjoy despotic power: he can never be happy or comfortable if he has any pretensions to a conscience.

2 P.M.—Six flags appeared at Faki Mustapha's camp. Report in town says the Mahdi is at his Isle of Abba, 160 miles up White Nile, attending to the circumcision of his son (poor little fellow). I hope it is true, for it will give us ten days' respite. He may also have another dream there, which

will tell him not to come to Kartoum, or he may persuade his followers to have one to same effect. What a comfort!!!

The Mahdi will make it an excuse that he came for this circumcision from Kordofan to Abba Island (where he received his first revelation that he was the *Mahdi*), if he sees things go against him.[10].

3 P.M.—The six flags at Faki Mustapha's camp have increased to ten (gathering of waters). We have just completed *our* concentration of forces, and the steamers have just come in from their last trip from Halfeyeh. We may now be said to be in fighting trim, close hauled. Small steamer *Husseinyeh* will be completed to-morrow, I hope.

6.30 P.M.—Horsemen riding to and fro in Faki Mustapha's camp. A letter has come in with two men from Slatin. Have received the letter, and send back the men who brought it, at once. "You must remember," says England, "that when you entered my service, I bought you, as far as your body was concerned, giving you at first 5*s.* 3*d.* per diem, when no one else would have given you 1*s.*, giving you also a beautiful plumage and the *entrée partout.* You have advanced now to higher pay, but on *same terms* (your whole life and body). You can never say you have done *more* than your duty. If you do not do it you break your word, and if you do it you merely fulfil your contract, and have no *claim* on me."

The two men who came in with the letter of Slatin were one Arab and one slave. The latter questioned (apart) says that the report is *that the Mahdi will come in two days to Omdurman; that he has not been seen; that the regular soldiers have gone back to Kordofan; and that Faki Mustapha told him* (the slave) *to frighten the Kartoumers.* I am hoping the Mahdi will prove a *bogie!*

Steamers *Bordeen* and *Ismailia* went down below Kerowé to-day, and saw no Arabs on the left bank of the Nile.

The quietude of Sheikh el Obeyed's forces is curious, for

[10] The Mahdi declared that the Archangel Gabriel had twice appeared to him and commanded him to unsheath the sword of faith in order to reform the bad Moslem and to found a Mussulman Empire which would be followed by universal peace.—ED.

they have twice beaten us, *with heavy loss*, though they have been beaten by us, with loss, at other times, but in minor engagements.

I begin to get over my disquietude *in re* the arrests; from what I hear, I think public opinion is not dissatisfied; but really it was a strong measure to arrest Sheikh el Islam, Cadi and Mudir, and sixteen others, and that without turning the two former out of their employ.

A lot of people were pressing for harder measures, but my new chief clerk said "we would wish to leave it to you to do or not to do," which is lively, as I am innocent of what goes on, or who is a traitor, or who is not; if ever there was a happy-go-lucky government, it is this, in Kartoum. I declare that, sometimes, I give a decision, and have no more idea of what the decision is about than a cow; these, however, are exceptional cases. I have had about six bad slips in ten years, not more, and these I have managed to rectify, with loss of prestige. Slatin is *not* with Faki Mustapha, so says the slave. What liars these spies are!

If in two days I find the news correct that the Mahdi is still in Kordofan, I shall let out all the political prisoners (which will shock the townspeople), but will be true joy and delight to me, for it has been a work utterly repugnant to me. I like free will (we left God with *our own free will*, we must return with our *own free will*). I hate a forced subjection, and I feel sure that to let these people out, with free will to go to the Arabs or not, will be good policy. I must say that I feel it a great compliment, when my counsellors say to *me*, "*Do what you think right, irrespective of our advice,*" *when they know I am ignorant of all that goes on, ignorant of the Arabic language, except in my style, ignorant of the Arab customs, &c., &c.* "*You will do better than we do,*" is what they say, and *I, poor Devil, do not know where to turn.* Oh! our Government, our Government! what has it not to answer for? Not to *me*, but to these poor people. I declare if I thought the town wished the Mahdi, I would give it up: so much do I respect free will.[11]

[11] The action of Her Majesty's Government had now raised the question in General Gordon's mind as to whether he was justified in

October 16.—The letters of Slatin have arrived.[12] I have no remarks to make on them, and cannot make out why he wrote them.

Heavy rain last night, I expect there is an end to the vitality of our mines, and we have now no more matches to renew them.

No spies in, no Arabs visible outside their camp: it is pretty certain that the Mahdi has not come to Omdurman.

The Austrian Consul [13] has asked me to let him write to Slatin, and to allow him to give him (Slatin) an interview on the Lines, which I have agreed to and sent out. Slatin's letter to Hansall was quite in a different tone to the one he wrote to me. What astounding lies those spies have told about the Mahdi and his heterogeneous staff being close here.

Noon.—Two spies came in, one from Sheikh el Obeyed, one from Kordofan. The latter says the Mahdi is not coming to Kartoum, but has been recalled to Obeyed on account of the advance of Expeditionary Force; that the Mahdi has withdrawn all the regulars captured here and there from our vicinity to Kordofan; that a lot of the Arabs he forced to come with him have deserted him. That is about all; one feels disinclined to write these histories, which are contradicted a few days afterwards. Certainly the Arabs are very quiet, and one does not see many about. I hope to be able to let out the prisoners on New Year's Day of Arab year 1302, which is on 21st October. I shall make Ferratch Pasha do the honours of the day, I cannot stand these pageants. A woman came in from the Dem on the South Lines; she says a few days ago there was a regular panic caused by report of troops having captured Katarif; half the Arabs went southward. However the report was contradicted and they have come back.

Slatin's letter to Austrian Consul contains the remark "that if he comes over to me I must promise never to surrender the

---

punishing any of the inhabitants of Kartoum who were *hedging* with the Mahdi. He was almost disposed to let them *hedge* if it gave them a better chance of their lives.—ED.

[12] Appendix R.

[13] Hansall.—ED.

city, *as he would then suffer terrible tortures and death.*" He evidently is not a Spartan, he also says "that he changed his religion because he had not had much attention paid to his religious belief when young." If he gets away I shall take him to the Congo with me, he will want some *quarantine;* one feels sorry for him.

Slatin says there is a rumour that a boat of Stewart's expedition, down Nile, was captured by Arabs at the cataract Dar Djumna, below Abou Hamed, but he doubts its truth; this, in his letter to the consul.

The Arabs have not occupied Halfeyeh. The Shaggyeh are pulling down Goba and Hogali, the village opposite the Palace. The village of Omdurman is levelled. The little steamer *Husseinyeh* is finished and armed, and will go up against the Arabs (her virgin trip), on Saturday morning. They have put a little lion as figure-head to it.

Fancy post-office officials (of all people), who have done literally nothing for seven months (not being *able* to do anything), asking for increase of pay!! These people have no conscience. There were very few Arabs to be seen on South Front this day, and few were seen going to Giraffe. At Faki Mustapha there also seems no numbers, in spite of the great array of grass huts erected for the Mahdi. Report in town says that the Arabs in Kordofan say the Mahdi is all fudge, and that they are robbed more now under his name than before, when they were under the Government.

Report says the Mahdi sent Sheikh el Obeyed (the *man* not the *city*) to tell him to come to Obeyed (the *city* not the *man*), and devotes himself to God's service as a dervish. The Sheikh el Obeyed (the *man* not the city)[14] does not see it, for he is very rich (I know it is a horrid nuisance these names, but I did not give them). It would be a charity to execute the *man*, for those who are perplexed, and end the difficulty. We cannot execute the city.

October 17.—Church parade at minimum: that at Faki

[14] These distinctions are in satirical allusion to a mistake made at the Foreign Office.—ED.

Mustapha's Dem some 400: that at South Front not more than a 1000.

Mr. Gladstone has a rival up here in shirt collars: Mohamed Bey Ibrahim appeared to-day with regular wings rather ragged, his collars up to his ears, regular othodox patterns.

I am sending *Bordeen* and *Husseinyeh* up the White Nile to reconnoitre, and the horsemen out towards Giraffe and Halfeyeh.

I shall have nothing to do with Slatin's coming in here to stay, unless he has the Mahdi's positive leave, which he is not likely to get: his doing so would be the breaking of his parole, which should be as sacred when given to the Mahdi as to any other power, and it would jeopardise the safety of all those Europeans, prisoners with Mahdi.

According to all accounts, the cataract at Dar Djumna below Abou Hamed is a very small one, so I am in hopes it is a false rumour that we have lost the boat. A slave came from Faki Mustapha, saying the Mahdi is at Jura Hadra, his people suffering from sickness: many have gone back to Kordofan. All regulars have gone back, they have little grain, and people are discontented. This man brought his rifle in with him; 219 days to-day we have been boxed up; four of the principal men were allowed to be prisoners in their houses, one of these allowed a man to come to him and bribe the sentry with two dollars: this man was whipped off to the prison at once. The Sheikh el Islam let two women come to him, he was only threatened. We caught a man going over to the Arabs to-day, he had under his ordinary costume the Dervish dress. If Zubair was here he would take off heads I feel sure. I content myself with fearful threats, which they know are nothing.

October 18.—The *cavalry* went out towards Giraffe, and captured five *female* slaves! and killed three Arabs, who resisted their being taken. I own I do not feel satisfied with the killing of these men, but I suppose it is *war:* we lost none. The captive ladies had little to say more than the Arabs had two guns at Giraffe.

Bordeen and *Husseinyeh* went up the White Nile, saw no Arabs at first, but coming back Arabs got down two guns and opened fire, they killed one man and wounded another. I had warned these steamers distinctly to keep in the middle of the river, and not to go near the banks. The casualties were from musketry. Arabs fired fifteen rounds (gun), *Husseinyeh* fired ten rounds (gun), *Bordeen* fired ten rounds (gun). I have stopped these steamers going up the White Nile for the future. The officer is entirely responsible for the death of this man, for I had given orders that, *even* if they saw cattle or boats, they were not to be enticed to the banks to get them. I never will believe in ships against land batteries, unless troops are landed, for *unless* a steamer can get close alongside a battery, the battery will hold its own.

October 19.—This morning, in spite of my orders not to leave the Lines, Bourré must needs send out men, and the consequence was that I have a Bimbashi and six men wounded; however I think I have stopped these excursions for the future. The *cavalry* went out from the North Fort to Halfeyeh, and saw no one, and captured a cow!

I hope it will be remembered that with respect to white troops (Fellaheen) on board the now four steamers at Metemma, I make you a handsome present of them (officers and all), and request that if you use the steamers you will disembark those men and take them on your list, for we never wish to see them (and to have to feed them) up here again. *You will be carrying out the evacuation policy!!!* If you do not use the steamers, please send them back *empty of these Fellaheen troops*, but send me *their rifles*. You will soon have a fine contingent? for I have everything ready for a *general discharge of Cairo débris* (Bashi Bazouks, &c., &c.), the moment I hear you are really at Berber; I shall not wait to ask your leave, for I have had enough of the *débris* up here, and you can feed them better than we can; *at any rate, they will be off my hands*, and *on yours*. I hope it will be an understood thing that *every Egyptian soldier* you find *belongs to you*, and that you will not send him back to me. I nobly present you *with them all*, and then, besides that, you have the glory of living representatives of your rescuing expedition. I object and protest against (when once Egyptian soldiers come into your Lines) your returning them to Kartoum. As for their pay, &c., as far as I have been able to order, it ought to be quite clear what is owed them. I have given orders enough about that subject, as Stewart knows. I include *officers* as *well as men*. I want to see them no more. *Pray attend to this request!* [15]

The *Talataween* came in this evening from Shendy; reports Seyd Mahomet Osman has come to Gros Rageb with English troops. English troops are coming from Debbeh by Nile, and have passed Abou Hamed. Arabs captured two boats of Stewart's expedition, by means of the captured steamer *Fascher* above Abou Hamed, which our steamers had seen getting up steam: *vide* my Journal. I had a feeling about this that when the steamers had seen the Arab steamer *Fascher* getting up steam they ought to have stayed and tried to prevent the pursuit. The Arabs have a gun at Shendy, which came from Berber. The English troops are only two days distant from Berber. The steamers had twenty-five wounded, they collected eleven prisoners, and captured four boats. One of our men was killed. The *Towfikia* lost none on going down. I am sending down the *Bordeen* and *Talataween* the day after to-morrow to Shendy, with order to leave one steamer at Shendy, and go on with the other four to Berber, and to remain in its neighbourhood. The *Mansowrah* will stay at Shendy, and the *Talataween*, *Bordeen*, *Saphia*, and *Towfikia* will go towards Berber. I shall keep *Ismailia* and *Husseinyeh* here.

[15] There is a good-natured, and half playful ring about these orders, but the fact must not be overlooked that they are distinct commands. General Gordon, while Governor-General of the Soudan, had the right to issue orders to any one in the Soudan, and no one was more cognizant of this right than he. —Ed.

STATEMENT OF TROOPS, ARMS, AMMUNITION, GRAIN, &c., IN KARTOUM, 19th OCTOBER, 1884.

	No. of Black Troops, Regulars	2316
A	White	1421
B	Cairo Bashi Bazouks	1906
	Shaggyeh	2330
	Townspeople enrolled	692
	Total	8665

A and B will be sent to Berber as soon as it is possible to find Transport, and as soon as you get to Berber.

No. of Guns upon Lines	12
Steamers	11
Rounds Gun Ammunition	21,141
,, Small Arms, Remington	2,165,000
,, Arsenal turns out weekly	40,000

Amount of Grain and Biscuit in Magazine.

Grain	Ardebs	4,018
Biscuit	Okes	349,000
Weekly consumption of Troops	Ardebs	500

No. of Steamers	7
Private Boats	58
Government Boats	53

Money in Specie	£2,900
Paper	£39,195

October 20th.—Here is a summary of reports brought by *Talataween*, which left Shendy four days ago. *Abbas* went down to Hagar Homar with her four boats. She was pursued by *Fascher*, which captured two of her boats, with twelve Greeks. The *Abbas* turned and fired two cannon shots at the *Fascher*, which retired, and the *Abbas* went on her way and was seen no more. She is supposed to have been attacked by Arabs below Abou Hamed and drove off attack, killing seventy-two Arabs, the Greeks captured in the two boats were not hurt by the Arabs. When the *Abbas* got to Debbeh the troops advanced towards Berber. Three distinct parties moving on Berber: *one* through the desert of Korosko (the Arabs have put 1500 men and a gun at Abou Hamed); *one* from Merowé to Berber across the desert (making forts at intervals), and *one* with Seyd Mahomet Osman down the Atbara valley towards El Damer (which place is at the junction of the Atbara with the Nile) assisted by Awad Kerim. The steamers have been bombarding Metemma and Shendy, I expect with no great effect.

To-day came in from Waled a Goun two men and three women. They say the Mahdi is opposite Kalakla, *i.e.* within two miles of Kartoum, few people with him; those who came with him from Kordofan have, in great part, gone back.

In yesterday's skirmish the Arabs lost two men in the steamer fight, the day before they lost more. Waled a Goun has sent his family to Gitana; many are deserting.

An officer and sergeant have escaped and come into Omdurman.

They say that the Arabs of Berber were warned by someone in the town of the descent of the *Abbas*. I have ordered the sale of 200 ardebs of dhoora on the strength of this news. A man, who was at Berber, on board one of the captured steamers says Ferratch Pasha! and other officers have sent news to the Arabs, and that the Arab chief of Berber wrote to Cassim el Mousse, proposing he should kill me, which Cassim el Mousse refused to do. This Mahomet el Khair is a true cur, for I have ever treated him well. I expect if the truth was known very few notables or officials have not been hedging with the Arabs.

The Shaggyeh on the opposite side are yelling, on enquiring find it is for dhoora; they have had their month's rations and the month is not up. I went to the telegraph office and told them that "till the month was up I would give them none, but that the Sheikh el Obeyed had plenty, and that if they liked they could go to him"; no answer was given to this telegram.

The officer and sergeant who came in at Omdurman say the Mahdi with all Europeans, Hassan Khalifa, Saleh Pasha, and *that* Frenchman are opposite Kalakla, and that he means coming to Omdurman, that the Arabs are not in good heart.

The *Saphia* and the *Mansowrah* ought to have laid off Berber, and prevented the exit of the *Fascher* when the *Abbas* went down, but I expect they only cared to come back here. I am much put out at the loss of those two boats. What one has felt so much here is the want of men like Gessi, or Messodaglia, or Slatin; but I have had no one to whom I could entrust expeditions like that. *I do sincerely hope all Egyptians and Turks or Circassian officers and men may be taken out of the steamers and kept by you; it would be too bad to send them back to me.* I do not mean the *captains* or *engineers* of *steamers.* Twenty-two wounded men were brought to the hospital (four were gravely wounded) from Shendy steamer. I wish you to take command of steamers, but do not let any *Khedival authority* do so, *for he will certainly be bribed to let back the Egyptians.* Please acknowledge the receipt of the Journal, of which this is Vol. 4. As far as my experience goes, there are not more contemptible troops, officers, and men than the Egyptians, so beware of them, and, with scarcely an exception, all Turks and Circassians in Egyptian employ are emasculated.

I have prepared to clear out of the Palace, and have five houses ready for occupation. I hope Cuzzi's baggage will be searched, for I feel sure he is a traitor. A slave came in this evening from Waled a Goun with the usual story of the near approach of the Mahdi; that Arabs want food; that regulars mean to desert when they get an opportunity. With the reiterated request that I may not have any *Egyptians, Turks, or Circassians sent back to me,* I end this Journal.

C. G. Gordon.
20/10/84.

The sunset to-night ends the year 1301, and begins 1302.

BOOK V.

On outside wrapper (a handkerchief):

EVENTS AT KARTOUM.

20th Oct. to 5th Nov., 1884.

GENERAL GORDON'S JOURNAL, VOL. V.

The Chief of the Staff of Expeditionary Force for the Relief of the Garrisons.

No secrets as far as I am concerned.

C. G. GORDON.

On cover:

EVENTS AT KARTOUM.

20th Oct. to 5th Nov., 1884.

GENERAL GORDON'S JOURNAL, VOL. V.

To be pruned down if published.

C. G. GORDON.

On inside:

GENERAL GORDON'S JOURNAL.

From 20th October to 5th November, 1884.

EVENTS IN KARTOUM.

The Chief of Staff of Expeditionary Force for Relief of Garrisons.

VOL. V.

To be pruned down if published.

C. G. GORDON.

JOURNAL.

October 21.—Steamers left this morning for Shendy. To-day is New Year's Day of the Arabs, 1302. I think the Mahdi speculated on a rising in the town, but that the arrests[1] have put him out in his calculations.

New Year's gift this morning, in arrival of Mahdi at Omdurman. Not much display. It is reported that he will occupy Kerowé and Halfeyeh at once; so it is as well I got the steamers off before he got his guns down to river bank. They will be safe with you,[2] and very useful.

Two men came in from Saleh Bey of Galabat with the post. They were thirty-two days *en route*. They brought a letter from Mitzakis, the Greek Consul, from *Adowa*, dated 17th August (which told me as much, or more, than Kitchener's letter of 31st August!).[3] Saleh Bey is all right; he has been attacked. Spies say the small steamer *Mahomet Ali*, captured by the Arabs, is now on the Blue Nile, at Abou Haraz. Sennaar is all right.

Mitzakis writes to the Greek Consul here to say that a treaty has been made between Her Majesty's Government and Abyssinia, to give Abyssinia Kassala, Galabat, Katarif, and Bogos! and that the King is preparing an army to go and take possession.[4] What an action. These lands (except

[1] The arrests of the Mudir, Cadi, Sheikh el Islam, &c., who were supposed to be in communication with the Mahdi.—Ed.

[2] *I.e.*, Chief of Expeditionary Force.—Ed.

[3] Appendix Q.

[4] Appendix Q.

Bogos) are entirely Mussulman, having held their own, and are in no way threatened, and WE go and send a wild *so-called* Christian people (who have nothing to do with the quarrel) against these peoples, who have held their own against the Mahdi.

October 22.—I wonder what Saleh Bey of Galabat will say to this cession, after he has been fighting for me. Also what Seyd Mahomet Osman will say after all his trouble.

I can now see why I was kept in the dark.

In one of Saleh Bey's letters he says he sends me a letter from King John. This I have not got; it apparently was not sent.

A man came in with letter from Slatin, in which he says the *Abbas* was captured near Dar Djumna. Stewart killed, with nine men, and all the papers captured.[5]

Three soldiers escaped yesterday from the Arabs. Seven more came in to-day; they had no news. Mahdi and all Europeans are four hours distant. Mahdi has put Saleh Pasha (of Shaggyeh) in chains.

Twenty-six goats came kindly into Lines to-day.

I am very anxious about the *Abbas*; it would be terrible, if it is true, that she is captured.

The cut out pages are, or rather were, a tirade against the cession of Kassala,[6] &c., &c., but as they would be no use now I have cut them out.

I believe Government can, now-a-days, get men to do anything by means of money and honours (*not honour*), and I have a shrewd idea of how this affair will end up here. However, it is not my affair, and I have taken my decision.

Kitchener to Chermside. "He is furious about that admirable treaty of Hewitt's. Fortunate I did not tell him about it. He has the Mahdi alongside now, and can vent his spleen on him. We have got his steamers all but two, and need not care." [7]

[5] Appendix R.

[6] Eight pages of the diary were cut out.—ED.

[7] General Gordon has just stated that a letter received from the Greek Consul, dated 17th of August, contained more news than one he received,

. . . Admirable treaty, let us think—yes, spread of Christianity, regular missionary movement, ancient Christian Church and people. . . . ! get me up a *précis* of this history of Abyssinia, but cut out part of Bruce which speaks of ravages committed by the Abyssinian army on the march. Hewitt, charmed with His Majesty, calls the Queen his mother, &c. Now, if we can *only get* that Mahdi to make a treaty we are safe for six months. Enough for the day is its evil. I declare I am becoming a missionary myself with my quotations and acts.

Graham would be angry if I criticised his despatch, which Slatin sent me. The *Rammer*[8] seems an excellent weapon.

October 22.—It is suspected that the two men who came with letters from Saleh Bey of Galabat are spies of the Mahdi, into whose hands has fallen the letter King John wrote to me; these men came in a very circuitous way from the direction of the Mahdi's camp.

Another soldier and a slave came in from the Arabs just now.

King John and the Mahdi both force men to change their religion; both cut off lips of smokers and noses of *snuffers;* both are fanatics and robbers.[9]

---

dated 31st of August, from an officer in Her Majesty's service. He then goes on to say he sees now (*i.e.*, after reading the Greek Consul's letter) why he was kept in the dark.—ED.

[8] Sir Gerald Graham's despatch.—ED.

[9] "King John issued an edict that if any of his subjects were found smoking they should lose hand and foot. General Gordon in his notes on Abyssinia in 1879, said: 'I write in haste, but I will sum up my impression of Abyssinia. The king is rapidly growing mad. He cuts off the noses of those who take snuff, and the lips of those who smoke. The king is hated more than Theodore was. Cruel to a degree, he does not, however, take life. He cuts off the feet and hands of people who offend him. He puts out their eyes by pouring hot tallow into their ears. No one can travel without the king's order if he is a foreigner. You can buy nothing without his order; no one will shelter you without his order—in fact no more complete despotism could exist.'

* * * * *

"The cruelties the king and his people committed were atrocious. Forty Soudan soldiers were mutilated altogether, and sent to Bogos with the message that, if His Highness the Khedive wanted eunuchs he could have these."—*Hill's 'Colonel Gordon in Central Africa,'* pp. 421–423.—ED.

If the Mahdi has got King John's letter to me, he knows all about the famous, or rather infamous, Hewitt Treaty, which is a trouble. Slatin's letter mentions the "Rapport Militaire"; it seems odd he should have known it was on board, unless the *Abbas* was captured; yet we have two men who declare she passed down. Perhaps the captured Greeks knew of the existence of this famous journal, and told the Arabs of it, or Awaan may have written it; it is odd he (Slatin) says nothing of Power and Herbin.

House of Lords. ... in answer to questions put by the Marquis of ... replied that the noble marquis seemed to take a special delight in asking questions which he knew he (...) could not answer. He could say he had given a deal of time and attention to the affairs of the Soudan, but he frankly acknowledged that the names of places and people were so mixed up, that it was impossible to get a true view of the case (a laugh). The noble marquis asked what the policy of Her Majesty's Government was? It was as if he asked the policy of a log floating down stream; it was going to the sea, as any one who had an ounce of brains could see. Well, that was the policy of it, only it was a decided policy, and a straightforward one to drift along and take advantage of every circumstance. His lordship deprecated the frequent questioning on subjects which, as his lordship had said, he knew nothing about, and further did not care to know anything about.

... to ... Why, I did my best to keep the Hewitt Treaty secret from him. It is no use blaming me. I knew from his telegram he would make a noise about it, and I told Kitchener not to say a word about it. It is that brute Mitzakis who let the cat out of the bag.

A man came in from from the Mahdi's camp, who left this fourteen days ago with my permission to go to the Arabs. He now comes back to see his family in Kartoum. I have told him,—*once out, there is no return!* He is a cool fellow.

The Major wounded at Bourré the other day is dead.

The two men who brought letters from Saleh Bey of Galabat do not like going out on the North Fort side; they want to go out by the West side, *i.e.* where the Mahdi's camp is.

I believe that the Hewitt Treaty will be a complete dead letter, for the Greek Consul says the Admiral gave him (King John) no money, so what was the use of the treaty. I expect King John wrote to me to ask me to give him the taxes of the country ceded, quoting the treaty of Hewitt. As for the King or his men ever leaving their hills, it is out of the question. He might have made a move had he been given £100,000, but no chance of his doing so when he has nothing but this paper treaty. The only place the King could possibly occupy is Senheit, and I doubt his doing that permanently. He will drive out the Roman Catholic Mission at once[10] (part of his missionary movement); the occupation of Senheit just cuts off the safe road from Massowah to Kassala. I declare it is amusing to see what shifts Her Majesty's Government have been put to to get out of their mess.

A slave has come in to Omdurman with another letter from the Arabs. I shall stop this fun for the future.

I feel sure King John gave Admiral Hewitt a spear and shield and the Order of Solomon—vanity of vanities—for the treaty, and I feel also sure we shall see no Abyssinian army in the Soudan. The King will write, or has written, a haughty letter, saying that his mother, the Queen, has given him, &c., &c., and he requests I will send in the taxes *at once*, otherwise he will advance. All T.,[11] and we shall hear no more of His Majesty except groans at my perfidy in not sending the taxes. He is a hopeless sort of man, and never is worth considering.[12] Her Majesty's Government will say: "We made the treaty; it is not our fault His Majesty did not carry it out, on paper; Kassala and all the other places are now under King John, and consequently quite safe." The treaty is worth as much as any treaty made now giving Kordofan to anyone![13]

[10] Mr. F. L. James in his "Wild Tribes of the Soudan," gives an excellent and interesting account of this mission station, p. 210, *seq.*—Ed.

[11] Twaddle.—Ed.

[12] Ismail, the Ex-Khedive, who knew King John well, said to General Gordon, "Never go near him, it is perfectly useless."—Ed.

[13] Of course General Gordon's contention throughout is that giving Kassala, Katarif, Galabat and Bogos, to the King of Abyssinia, is in fact precisely the same thing as abandoning those places.—Ed.

We need now only a treaty with the Mahdi about the garrisons, and then Her Majesty's Government will sleep in peace: *their work is done.* I only say I will have no confidence in any such treaty, and shall take my precautions accordingly.[14]

Letters have come in: one says Lupton Bey has surrendered,[15] and has been appointed Governor of Bahr Gazelle with an adherent of the Mahdi. Another says that he has brought slaves to the Mahdi, and hopes to buy horses with the products of their sale.[16] The Mahdi's letter is to relate how he captured the post, &c., *Abbas*, &c. My answer was, that I did not care who had surrendered and who had been captured. As for these letters, I cannot make head nor tail of them, so I leave them to the Arabic scholars of the Universities.

October 23.—(What a fearful scrawl!) Ten soldiers, with six women came in this morning to Omdurman. I have sifted out the Mahdi's letter[17] respecting the capture of the *Abbas*, and do not believe it; the papers he sent me as being captured in the *Abbas* were never in the *Abbas*, they were taken from a spy I sent out from here, the same man who brought me the news from Dongola of the British advance. He had a bad eye (ophthalmia), and was caught at Metemma and killed, having, when drunk, let out that he had come from me.

The nuns had to walk all the way from Kordofan. The Mahdi has 15,000 head of cattle with him. The Arabs are dying in great numbers from dysentery. The village of Hogali opposite the Palace is levelled. It may not be generally known, but by the Firman which named Towfik, there is an express injunction that no part of the Egyptian territory is to be ceded, except by permission of the Porte. Also by the Treaty of Paris, and also by that of Berlin, the integrity of the Ottoman Dominion is guaranteed by the Powers. What a farce it is to say Egypt ceded Kassala!

[14] Here a page has been cut out by General Gordon himself.—Ed.

[15] Appendix U, *a*, *b*, *d*.

[16] Appendix U, *b*.

[17] Appendix U.

The escaped party, I mentioned as having come in, have arrived at the Palace, nine soldiers, eight women, and two slaves, all old friends, also a *baby!* They say the Mahdi started with 40,000 Arabs and 1,500 regulars from Kordofan, that he has not now more than 5,000 or 6,000 Arabs, and 1,000 soldiers (500 ran away), that they have no dhoora, only 35 boxes (35,000 rds.) Remington cartridges, and 50 shells; they say the other soldiers want to come in, either to-day or to-morrow. The Mahdi says he will go against the English and will not stop at Kartoum. The whole gang were shown themselves in the mirrors. Such a display of ivories was never seen. The baby danced with delight, at seeing itself, *for the first time*, it was like a black slug. The *mother* was, of course, delighted.

The Arab horsemen cut the telegraph which goes out of the Lines at Bourré to the North Fort. I declined to allow its repair since I had lost a major and had six men wounded when last we went out of the Lines, and besides which I had another cable to the north side. No sentries at the North Fort or Bourré, or on the Mudirat; these people are enough to break any one's heart. Fortunately, from the roof of the Palace one watches all these things, and can bully them into obeying orders, but it is (as Hansall says[18]) a *vie abrutissante*, to be always snarling and growling. The *Ismailia* and *Husseinyeh* went down the river, and saw no Arabs on either bank. If these Arabs (one's servants) are not *eating*, they are *saying* their *prayers*; if not *saying their prayers*, they are *sleeping*; if not *sleeping*, they are *sick*. One snatches at them at intervals. Now figure to yourself the position; you cannot do anything with them while in these fortresses *eating*, *saying prayers*, *sleeping*, or *sick*, and they know it. You would be a brute if you did (which I fear I often am). You want to send an immediate order, and there is your servant bobbing up and down, and you cannot disturb him. It is a beautiful country for trying experiments with your patience.

It is very curious, but if I am in a bad temper, which I fear is often the case, my servants will be always at their prayers,

[18] The Austrian Consul.—ED.

and thus religious practices follow the scale of my temper; they are pagans if all goes well.

I must say I hate our diplomatists.

I think with few exceptions they are arrant humbugs, and I expect they know it. I include the Colvin class. The Rothschilds are, I feel assured, giving Her Majesty's Government a lot of bother about the Finance Question. If you had asked . . . at Balaklava the price of a cheese, he would have said £5 5*s.* If you asked him now you would offend him.

October 24.—Arab church parade. Mahomet Achmet and Faki Mustapha, few in number, at Waled a Goun; the Arabs have divided their camp, putting the regulars near the river, in camp apart from theirs, to act as buffers if any attack is made on them.

The Arabs have got a nuggar at Giraffe. A man of Zubair's old force has come in from the Arabs. To-morrow expires the six months for which the notes were issued. We have been boxed up 226 days (seven and a half months); siege of Troy.

The man who came in (Zubair's old soldier) was one of Lupton's men from the Bahr Gazelle; he left five months ago (Bahr Gazelle). He says Lupton is at Shaka, and is Sheikh

Abdullah, so he has changed his religion.[19] I wonder what has become of the garrison of the Equator. Another man has come in.

All that bloodshed in fighting the slave dealers in the Bahr Gazelle has gone, apparently, for nothing![20] There are great doubts if the Mahdi is really near, no one appears to have seen him.

Since the escape of the lot yesterday, the Arabs have taken the rifles of the regulars from them: at the Mahdi's camp, the Arabs have a ferry under our nose, across the White Nile; but I do not like to send up the steamers, for the captains are so heedless.

I calculated that the advance force of troops arrived at Wady Halfa on 22nd September,[21] that they took twenty days from there to Debbeh, so that on 12th October they were at Debbeh (Stewart (*D.V.*) arrived at Debbeh on 28th September), and I calculate they could not be at Metemma—Shendy—before 10th November, which will give them twenty-nine days for 150 miles, thence it is five days here for a steamer, so that 15th November ought to see them or their advance guard.

Extracts from Appendix R.

La Route de Souakim à Berber.

Avant que la bataille de Tamai eut été livrée et gagnée, le Général Herbert Stewart, sinon les généraux Graham et Buller, avaient étudié avec soin la question de savoir si les troupes, ou une partie des troupes, pouvaient marcher jusqu'à Berber *pour aider Gordon à réprimer les partisans du Mahdi dans la région du Nil.* Cette proposition semblait alors si convenable que l'état des troupes les mieux adaptées à une semblable expédition, les dispositions

[19] When a Christian becomes a Mahommedan he has to take a Mahommedan name.—ED.

[20] General Gordon is here evidently thinking of Gessi's glorious campaign against Suleiman.—ED.

[21] The Black Watch started from Cairo for Wady Halfa on September 23rd. The Mounted Infantry reached Deel on September 24th, and 150 men under Daubeny got as far as Tangoor on the 26th. The first steam pinnace arrived at Sarras, which is about twenty miles above the second cataract, on September 26th. Lord Wolseley did not reach Wady Halfa until October 5th.—ED.

pour les approvisionnements, l'équipement, les chevaux disponibles, etc., avaient été l'objet de l'étude journalière des officiers. On se souviendra qu'après Tamai, la cavalerie se transporta aux puits d'Handouk, à huit milles de Souakim. On croyait généralement, alors, que cette marche en avant n'était que la première étape d'un mouvement sur Berber d'une force montée. Pour empêcher toute souffrance provenant d'une disette d'eau, l'effectif ne devait pas être de plus de 500 hommes de cavalerie ; aucune infanterie ne devait faire partie de l'expédition. Il était en outre entendu, qu'en cas de nécessité, un semblable effectif pourrait suivre un jour ou deux après et trouverait également, dans les puits, de l'eau en abondance. Le fait est que les généraux Graham, Buller, Stewart, les colonels Clery, Taylor, et d'autres, semblaient ne pas mettre en doute, si l'ordre en était donné, qu'une succession de détachements, forts chacun de 500 hommes, pourrait être rapidement poussée sur Berber. Le bruit de ce qui se passait parvint rapidement aux oreilles de nos hommes qui étaient à la Zariba d'Handouk, et la plupart des troupiers manifestèrent un désir intense de prendre part à l'expédition. On savait que le Général Stewart avait soumis ses plans pour la marche en avant au Général Graham, et que ce dernier, ainsi que l'Amiral Hewett, les avait recommandés au gouvernement. *Les jours se succédèrent, mais l'ordre du départ n'arrivait pas : quelque empressés de partir que fussent beaucoup d'hommes, si nous avions connu alors la position exacte de Gordon, on eût manifesté beaucoup plus d'anxiété pour l'ordre du départ.* Lorsque cette question était discutée, question qui au moment occupait pleinement nos pensées, entre officiers supérieurs, ils exprimaient l'étonnement que l'ordre fut tant retardé, et que le Gouvernement hésitât davantage. *On n'arrivait qu'à une seule conclusion, c'etait que la position du Général Gordon était telle qu'il n'avait pas besoin d'aide de troupes britanniques venant de Souakim.* Quoi qu'en ait pu penser, après réflexion, le Général Graham, de la possibilité d'envoyer une troupe de cavalerie forte de 500 hommes, en mars dernier, de Souakim à Berber, je suis certain que lui et la plupart des officiers sous ses ordres croyaient alors que c'était une chose sage et guerrière à entreprendre. Nous nous apercevons tous trop tard, que cette simple expédition eût sauvé Berber, Khartoum et Gordon au vrai cœur.

If they do not come before 30th November the game is up, and Rule Britannia. In this calculation I have given every latitude for difficulties of transport, making forts, &c., and on the 15th November I ought to see Her Majesty's uniform. I suppose a part of the force will go to attack Berber on the 10th November (when I calculate they will be at Metemma—Shendy) and that a small party will come on here; so we have now 7 days in October and 15 days in November to wait = 22 days—three weeks to add to the 226 days we have already passed, owing to Baring (who I shall remember) and his peace manœuvres. One of the papers Slatin sent to me, says that Graham was willing to send men to Berber, and could have done it; but Evelyn would not give the order. I asked only for 200 men to be sent there (vide my telegram in Stewart's Journal). I take Slatin's paper out of Appendix R, and put it on the other side.[22] I do not know the date, but I declare that, if my telegrams to Baring are made known, it will be proved Baring knew up to the 12th March the exact position of affairs up here; and therefore, if there was an impression abroad that I did not say, "Send troops (200) to Berber,[23], or you will lose it," he must have suppressed my telegrams.

I dwell on the joy of never seeing Great Britain again, with its horrid, wearisome *dinner* parties and miseries. How we can put up with those things passes my imagination! It is a perfect bondage. At those dinner parties we are all in masks, saying what we do not believe, eating and drinking things we do not want, and then abusing one another. I would sooner live like a Dervish with the Mahdi, than go out to dinner every night in London. I hope, if any English general comes to Kartoum, he will not ask me to dinner. Why men cannot be friends without bringing the wretched stomachs in, is astounding.

October 25.—Three men came in from Waled a Goun; one

[22] The paper referred to is the French extract just given.—ED.

[23] *Sir E. Baring to Earl Granville* (*received March 5th*).

"General Gordon has on several occasions pressed for 200 British troops to be sent to Wady Halfa. I agree with the military authorities in thinking that it would not be desirable to comply with this request."

Sir Evelyn Baring to Earl Granville (*received March 4th*).

"General Gordon and Colonel Stewart strongly urge the desirability, from the point of view of the success of their present mission, of opening up the Berber-Suakin route. . . . I cannot agree with the proposal mentioned in Colonel Stewart's telegram, that a force of British or Indian cavalry should be sent through for Suakin to Berber."—*Egypt, No.* 12 (1884). *No.* 205.—ED.

I sent out again, as I think he is a spy, the other reports that the small-captured steamer *Mahomet Ali* will be down at Giraffe with twelve boat loads of grain, either to-day or to-morrow. I do not even attempt to stop it; for if the Expeditionary Force arrives, we will capture it; I cannot risk steamers against land guns.

Two soldiers came in from the Arabs at Omdurman with their rifles.

A lot of people are moving from the right bank of Nile, towards the Sheikh el Obeyed's (the *man* not the *city*). Are they leaving on account of the advance of the troops? or is it for offensive purposes? or is it a raid which is returning from pillage? We sent up the steamers and stopped the Arab ferry near the Lines. The Arabs are retaliating by putting a gun or two in the old place near the large tree (el Sheddarah). The Arabs fired four shells at the steamers. Soldiers at Omdurman captured two cows, and killed two others. Another slave came in at Omdurman. Yesterday some cows were captured near the South Lines.

What would be the best plan of attacking the Arabs? The object is to give them such a crushing defeat as will put an end to the fighting, and prevent them rallying on Kordofan. The position is thus:—

1. I would attack Waled a Goun at A, and I would cut off his retreat by the sending up steamers to Duem with a small force; the Mahdi's force and Sheikh el Obeyed's force would look on.

2. At the same time I would attack the post at Giraffe. Both operations on the same day with the following troops.

Operations on White Nile.—To proceed up the White Nile by boats, 2000 B. infantry to point X. To proceed along the White Nile, right bank, the cavalry you may have to point X. To occupy with two guns and 1500 men simultaneously the two villages outside the Lines, with the Soudan troops, the troops not to advance, only to threaten, houses loopholed, &c. Three steamers to accompany the force.

Operations on Blue Nile.—To proceed up the Blue Nile or along the bank, 1000 B. infantry, accompanied by steamers and boats, with the Shaggyeh horsemen, some 80, and 1000 men of Soudan troops to Giraffe.

If these operations are successful, then 800 men with four steamers to pursue up the river to Duem.

Expedition towards Sennaar.—The Sheikh el Obeyed will probably surrender at once, then a force of 500 B. I. and 1000

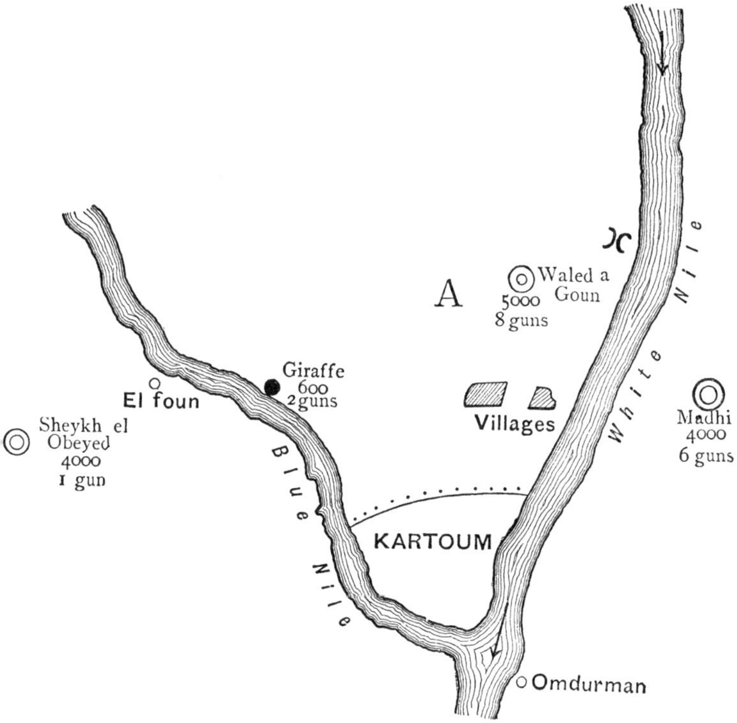

Soudan infantry should go up river to Wad el Medinet, and open the route to Sennaar (while men are sent up to buy corn with them). There appear to be no Arabs in arms between Wad el Medinet and Sennaar, or south of Sennaar. (The Mahdi will at once retreat to Obeyed, *the city.*) This expedition will probably be met at Abou Haraz by the surrender of

Katarif and all that district, and thus the route to Katarif and Kassala will be opened.

These operations will entail the very smallest amount of marching on the troops, and would be completed in three weeks or less.

It must be remembered that in all these engagements in the Soudan no quarter on either side has been given, so it must not be expected that the Soudan troops will give it now if you come; also with respect to the wounded Arabs, if you go and help them, they will (like the Afghans) try and kill your men who make the effort; they are very treacherous, and, worked up by religious frenzy, they think—1. That you only pretend to help them, in order to kill them afterwards; 2. That, being desperate, they think to enter Paradise if they kill an infidel. It seems rather cold-blooded to write this, but it is the character of those whom you are to fight. For my part, I hope they will all run away, for they are only dupes ninety-nine out of every hundred; it is the leaders who are the prime movers. I would give the lives to the leaders if they ask pardon; but I would send them all to Mecca to study Mahdism under the Orthodox. No information as yet as to the meaning of the caravan, &c., which left the Nile to go towards the Sheikh el Obeyed. One of our boats, which was collecting grass down below Halfeyeh, must needs land its crew and try and take some cattle of the caravan. The Arabs turned on them, and killed the Reis. Crew says they killed a lot of Arabs (?). I think these people do really love fighting, if there is the least chance of plunder.

King John (according to the Greek consul) is to be allowed to import arms at Massowah. He will never do it, for he has not money to buy them.

If the Mahdi has got the Bahr Gazelle, and we evacuate the Soudan in his favour, the Anti-Slavery Society may as well close their office as to the suppression of the slave-trade in these parts, especially if we leave him the steamers.[24]

Special Commission, House of Lords. . . . under examina-

[24] Gordon's intention and desire was to have taken the steamers to the Bahr Gazelle, and to have protected that country against the Mahdi.—Ed.

tion, Q. 2389. Did your Lordship know, when in Cairo, that the Fellaheen were being dragged in chains, from their houses, to go and fight the Mahdi, under Hicks, and what steps did you take to prevent it?[25] Did you inform Her Majesty's Government of the facts, and what was their answer?

The Mahdi has moved his ferry higher up river since our steamers went up this morning.

It is a great question of doubt to me, if Public Officials ought so to sink their personality, as to allow themselves to overlook facts, which must strike them, as being not only evil, but also detrimental to our national interests, merely because such facts are likely to be disagreeable to our Government in requiring them to decide on difficult questions. . . . did know of this forced conscription, and so did . . . Did they not see that, to allow such conscripts to go up to the Soudan, was not only cruel, but also politically unwise, for it could not be expected that they would have any heart in the matter? If they had stopped it, Hicks would have never left Kartoum, and his army would not have been annihilated; for it is the defeat of Hicks which gave the Mahdi his great prestige. He had annihilated detachments *before that: after that* he had crushed a huge army. See what it has led to! There are times when men like . . . ought to obey, and there are times when they ought to disobey or else resign. Now, if . . . had only hinted his resignation, the Governments were so placed as to be obliged to listen to him. I have a strong suspicion . . . did know how to act. It was . . . and a wish to be agreeable to Her Majesty's Government which prevented him acting according to his own ideas. Sometimes it is the height of unkindness to be too kind and amiable, and this is one of those cases. History may be misty about it (will not know the thimble the pea is under, for the cards are well shuffled), but there is no doubt that . . . had the destinies of Egypt and of the Soudan in his hands, *far more than Her Majesty's Government*, and he did not succeed. His amiability did for him. It is *not insubordinate* to resign, if you do not agree to a policy,

[25] The fact that the Fellaheen were dragged in chains from their huts, and kept in chains in the streets of Cairo, is well known.—ED.

or feel you cannot carry it out with a whole heart. In military affairs it is different; one is ordered to go here and there, and one obeys (even if one thinks it is unwise, having represented it), but in diplomacy there is no such call, and certainly there was none in the case of . . . who is only an amateur in the Foreign Office Service, an outsider. Had . . . when he came to Egypt cut down the rate of interest by a swoop of his pen to 3½ per cent., who would have said a word; but now it is the difficulty. There would have been a fearful howl from the bondholders, but that would have been all. He dismissed the Control (under the *cover* of Towfik), and could have reduced the interest, and he would have gained the sympathy of all the people. Hicks (who, by the way, never wanted to go to the Soudan) would have held his own at Kartoum, and have worn out the Mahdi, and we would have had none of this late work. I am afraid to say what numbers have been killed through this present policy, certainly some 80,000; and it is not yet over. For my part, I hope they will all run away. We have in a most effectual way restored the slave-trade and slave-hunting, for Her Majesty's Government cannot keep the Soudan, and never will Egypt be able to govern it. The only thing to be done, is to give it to the Sultan. What an end to diplomacy of Her Majesty's Government: and it was so easy when I left in January, 1880, to have settled it quietly, *giving up Kordofan*, *Darfur*, and *Bahr Gazelle*, and *Equator*, with decency and quiet.

I declare I do not see how we will get out of it (the Soudan) even now; allow that you come to Kartoum, that you drive off the Arabs, open the road to Sennaar. What are you going to do? You will say, "Take out those who wish to leave." Well, you begin with Sennaar, and of course will have to fight all the way down. It will take three months. During those three months, how are you to feed Kartoum? for the moment you leave Sennaar you leave your granary. You get to Kartoum, you are face to face with 30,000 people who will not leave, and who are hedging with the Mahdi; and with 3000 Shaggyeh, all armed. You fight your way to Berber; another three months, you have no food at Berber; then it will need another two months to get to Dongola, which (seeing your policy) will be hostile. It is indeed a terrible problem, and I wish I could see my way out of it.

Then you come into the hot months, and low Nile. This time *next year* will not see you out of the Soudan, with decency. Of course you can go back now, but what was the use of coming? *I will not allow that you came for* ME. *You came for the garrisons of the Soudan.* Now, by the Turkish arrangement, if you act promptly, you can get away quietly in January, 1885. It will not cost anything like what it will cost you to keep your troops here for a year, as I fear you must do if you persevere in trying a "*rapid retreat.*"

I can have no object in this advice. I want to get out of the affair, but with decency. I regret the necessity of an expedition, but if once you come to Berber, and communicate with Kartoum, if you stick to the "*rapid retreat,*" you will not be able to accomplish it, and you are in for a year's stay. While, on the other hand, the giving of country to Turks enables you to get away with credit. Let Her Majesty's Government *find excuses* for it, it will not be difficult for *them.* Put yourself in my position if you say "*rapid retreat, and leave Sennaar to its fate.*" I will say "*No, I would sooner die first,*" and will resign my commission, for I could not do it. If you say, "*Then you are no longer* Governor-General," then I am all right, and all the responsibility is on you (for I could not be supposed, if you turn me out of Governor-General, to be obliged to aid such a movement, which I think is disgraceful). You will then be face to face with the people. I do not say but that Abdel Kader might not aid in the "*rapid retreat*" better than I could, even if I agreed to it (of this you can judge for yourself, at any rate I shall be out of it, and of my engagement to the people).

It may be that all this writing is unnecessary, and that you have other views, but it is as well you know my opinions. *I am secure against any loss, by the King of the Belgians, if I leave H.M.S., therefore I am, so to say, free of H.M.S. If you turn me out of Governor-General I am relieved from all responsibility, as to your action in Soudan, towards the people.* I do not think I am insubordinate in this matter, nor unreasonable. I do not say I would not give *all my services in a subordinate position* to aid you, but it would be against my grain and be very distasteful, and must NOT be in POSITION of GOVERNOR-GENERAL, that must be a *sine quâ non*, and it must be known that I disapprove of the "*rapid retreat.*"[26] I would not say this if I was not convinced that the "*rapid retreat*" is an operation of such difficulty as to make every Englishman akin, and bound to aid one another. If I was Lord Wolseley *I would make* Her Majesty's Government send the Turks here.

I do not advocate the keeping of the Soudan by us, it is a useless possession, and we could not govern it, neither can Egypt (after the late events). I am only discussing how *to get out of it* in *honour and in the cheapest way* (we must remember we caused its troubles), and that way is, either by some sort of provisional Government under Zubair, or by giving it to the Turks; it is simply a question of GETTING OUT OF IT with decency. Zubair would square the Shaggyeh and townspeople and arrange with the Mahdi, and you could get away. He might hold his own if you gave the Mahdi a good defeat ere you left; at any rate it is only by Zubair or the Turks you will get out of the Soudan before November 1885 !!!!!

The Turks are the best solution, though most expensive. *They would keep the Soudan:* give them £2,000,000. The next best is Zubair with £500,000, and £100,000 a year for two years; he will keep the Soudan *for a time.* (In both cases slave-trade will flourish), thus you will be quiet in Egypt, and will be able to *retreat to Egypt in January*, 1885. *If you do not do this*, then be prepared for a *deal of worry and danger*, and your campaign will be *entirely unprofitable and devoid of*

[26] General Gordon intends H.M. Government to understand by this statement, that, in the position of a Major-General in H.M. service, he would give all his services to the retreating expedition, were he ordered to do so, though such an order would be most unwelcome; but that he would do nothing of the kind until some one replaced him as Governor-General. He is really applying to himself the remarks he made a few pages back: "In military affairs it is different: one is ordered to go here and there, and one obeys (even if one thinks it unwise, having represented it), but in diplomacy there is no such call."—ED.

prestige,[27] for the day after you leave Kartoum the Mahdi will walk in and say he drove you out, which is not pleasant in India or elsewhere.

In discussing this question I have entirely put my own peculiar views out of the question: to give up countries which are to some degree civilised, which, if properly governed, are quiet and orderly, to the Turks or to Zubair, and to allow of the slave-trade to flourish again in tenfold intensity, is not a very high *rôle*, but *quoi faire?* We have not the men to govern these lands, we cannot afford the money; consequently, I advise what I have said. When I left the Soudan it was quiet and covered its expenses, and there was no bother to have continued to have governed it. Now it is different, and would need an outlay which our Government will not give. (It is because the cloth is short I recommend the shape of coat to be such.)

It would be nobler to keep the Soudan, but it is too much to expect our taxpayers to agree to (and besides which, "Plutarch's Lives" are no longer in vogue, and "*you must pay me well ere I go to the Soudan*" is the idea). The Soudan could (if cut off from excrescences) be made to pay its expenses, but it would need a *dictator*, and I would not take the post if offered to me.

October 26.—Three women came in from Waled a Goun. The idea is gaining ground that the Mahdi is dead, and that his Vakeel is acting his part. The Arabs are thinking of placing a station at Kerowé.

Yesterday week was the anniversary of Hicks's defeat, 1st November, 1883, though I believe it went on for three days, 1st, 2nd, and 3rd November.

The Arabs have brought a gun nearer Bourré to-day, probably emboldened by absence of the steamers. Two lieutenants, one sergeant-major, two sergeants, one soldier, and one

[27] Up to the present we have neither given the Soudan to the Turks nor have we established Zubair as Governor-General, but we have had "*a deal of worry and danger*," and the campaign has been "*entirely unprofitable and devoid of prestige*."—Ed.

slave came into Omdurman from the Arab camp. They say the Mahdi is alive; with him are Saleh Pasha, in chains, Hussein Pasha Khalifa, Elias Pasha, and all the Europeans. They heard a report (now some days old) that the Expeditionary Force was two days distant from Berber. The two lieutenants were with Hicks; they say the army died of thirst, and scarcely fought at all. With the Mahdi are 5,000 men, of which 1000 are black troops, 150 are Egyptian troops. What little weight do engineers place on the existence of populations in fortresses, yet this existence is all-important; more so than the works. Malta and Gibraltar are weak, because of their civil population.

The Arabs have a big tent at Giraffe this evening. The lieutenants who came in say the Mahdi will try and place a station in the place we drove them out of—on the North Fort—in August last, just before our defeat at El foun. Goba, with the exception of Mahomed Seyd Osman's house and the Mosque, is destroyed. Salaam Pasha's is nearly so.

8 P.M.—Two slaves have come into Omdurman. They say "*the regulars* in the camp of Mahomet Achmet, *the Mahdi, went this afternoon* to the Dem, or camp of ***Faki Mustapha***, and looted it, firing on the soldiers of Faki Mustapha, who resisted the plundering." I fear it is all fudge.

October 27.—One sergeant-major and two slaves came into Omdurman this morning. Sent out two spies towards Shendy.

One thing which (although spiteful) would cause me intense pleasure if the "*rapid retreat*" is carried out, is that the English would just walk into those Shaggyeh and Bashi Bazouks, and bundle them all out, and thus pay them out for the worry they have given me, and for their meanness.

If the Turks come here, you would have scarcely anyone to send down, and you would hand over the Shaggyeh and Bashi Bazouks to the Turks, and all the Divans, &c. Nothing then could be better for you than to get the Turks here. You would get off all responsibility of Kassala and Sennaar, and you would let the Turks and the King of Abyssinia settle about the *Hewitt*

Treaty. You would also get off the bother of the Equator and Bahr Gazelle, if it has not fallen.

You would know exactly what sum you had to pay, and save no end of expense and time and vexation with regard to the settlement of claims. Remember that Baring authorised me to draw more than £100,000; indeed, he said, "Such sum as you need." So you are responsible for paper-money issued.

You would make up with the Sultan, and, as for giving up Suakin and Massowah to the Turks it is nothing; for those ports are useless, except as ports of the Soudan, and would be a bother to you to keep, if the Mahdi has the Soudan. You would be always in strict blockade on land side.[28]

The more I think of it the more the Turk solution appears Hobson's choice. I can see no option, unless, ere you arrived at Kartoum, Kartoum fell, and then, even, it would not look well to go back from Berber, while that even would be dangerous to some degree; for the Dongola people would see you meant to evacuate, and would be hostile. You have gone so far and spent so much that I cannot see anything for it but to go on. And the Turks are the only solution which affords the certainty of being able to stop. I get out of all my troubles if the Turks come, for I shunt them on the Turks, and so do you. The idea is that when the English come here the Arabs will bolt.

Stewart's servant, Macktar, must needs go and marry another wife. How they can go on like this, marrying and giving in marriage, when one can never say that to-morrow is our own, is wonderful. Tangi has taken two wives up here!

The Government shall not get out of the desertion of Kassala (if they take cover under the Hewitt Treaty and say, "we arranged with the King of Abyssinia to look after that country"), if they do desert it, for the King will never move, and all who have ever known anything of Abyssinia must know he can never move. There is a report in town that Slatin has been put in chains. I should not be at all surprised.

[28] We are at present not only in strict blockade on the land side of Suakin, but absolutely besieged.—ED.

The sergeant-major, soldiers, and two men, Shaggyeh, who came in to-day, say that Slatin is not a prisoner. The sergeant-major states that one of our soldiers escaped from Omdurman three days ago. On inquiry I find that it is true, and the officer in command never reported it. The sergeant-major says the Arabs meditate an attack on Omdurman, in consequence of what the deserter told them. This is the *fourth* desertion since March that I know of, and it is the *first* desertion among the soldiers (with saving clause) that I know of. Arabs fired on the Santels [30] at the end of the Lines on the White Nile, and struck one. The Arabs fired fourteen times with Krupp guns; they retired when we fired twice on them; they fired from their old battery near the Tree "el Sheddarah." Some time ago I gave Ferratch Pasha £100 a month, and I afterwards made him a Ferile, or General of Division, for political reasons. He had the cheek to ask me to give him £150 a month (the sum I used to give the Seraskier or Commander-in-Chief in the Soudan in old times, but which was £50 beyond regulation). He put in an application a few days ago for the £150, and forage for eight horses! quite ignoring the state of the dhoora exchequer. I said, "Wait." He was foolish enough to renew the application, which I tore up. He may go to the Arabs if he likes. The Arabs appear to be passing the Blue Nile at Giraffe; they may be going to place a post at Halfeyeh, the Sheikh el Obeyed refusing to send his men there; we shall see to-morrow. It is not from any feeling of respect to the people up here that I urge their relief, but it is because they are such a weak selfish lot, and because their qualities do not affect the question of our duties to them. The Redemption would never have taken place if it had depended on our merits.

I must say I rather revel at the thought of the dismay which will attend the reduction of salaries to quarter their present rate, they have been so very selfish about these things. I believe if the Mahdi would only give them half the present rate, they would go to the Mahdi, but the Mahdi's service is

[29] Barges.—ED.

gratuitous, so there is no fear of that. I go out, a black Bashi Bazouk addresses me on the inadequacy of his pay and rations. I whisper to him, " *Go to Sheikh el Obeyed*," he grins and evaporates. I do not care a bit now. We must either be relieved, or fall, before the end of November, or at the end of November. I am meditating the sending down of " *Husseinyeh* " with this post; if the Arabs come to Halfeyeh I then cut off all hopes of our escape, for the *Ismailia* steamer would not be fit to go down to Berber. The financial affairs up here will be a precious job.

It amuses me to find people here holding on to the delusion that the old state of affairs is likely to come back as to the Government, and saying, " You are going to stay with us as Governor-General, and things are to be as of old." I answer, " I would not take you again at any price after your meanness." They say, " Oh, yes, the people are not well behaved, &c., &c., but you will stay *for the glory of God*" (*i.e.* our interests). They are an amusing lot: Allah on lips, self interest at heart, and such self interest, as is *positively naked*, and they even laugh at it.

A soldier and a slave came in to-night to Omdurman. They say the Mahdi is undecided what to do. The regulars with the Mahdi have been robbing the Arabs, so the Mahdi has taken away their arms.

Spy in from Sennaar fifteen days ago with letters,[30] which say Sennaar is all right. This was in answer to a letter I sent to Sennaar saying, " Expedition was on its way to relieve the *garrisons, so Sennaar depends on me to see after it*."

October 28.—The man who came from Sennaar says the Mahdi has ordered all the Arabs to congregate at Kartoum from all parts. Sheikh el Obeyed has made a station close to Giraffe, on right bank of Blue Nile. They have two boats plying across the river, taking corn from Sheikh el Obeyed to Waled a Goun. Arabs had a reconnoitring party in the ruins of Omdurman village this morning.

One lieutenant, one sergeant-major, four soldiers, and one

[30] Appendix T.

boatman came in this morning from the Arabs at Omdurman. Rumour says the steamers have been looting Shendy (I hope that it will be remembered none of the Egyptian soldiers, officers, or Pashas are to come up here again). The boatman left Berber six days ago. He says the Arabs at Berber have sent the captured money, &c., of Berber into the desert; that Seyd Mahomet Osman, with a mixed force, were two days' march from El Damer; that the five steamers have brought Shendy, &c., into subjection; that the road from here to Shendy is free of Arabs, who have gone into the desert; that only in a certain district *near*, but *higher up* than Shoboloha, there are marauding Arabs, but no great number; that the *Abbas* passed down safely; that the two boats which had wood in them alone were captured, being abandoned on being emptied; that at Dar Djumna a sheikh pretended to be friendly, and tried to capture the steamer, which fired on the Arabs, and killed a lot; that three spies from Seyd Mahomet Osman were captured trying to communicate with Dongola, and were executed; that *a man went with a camel from Berber to Dar Djumna, and came back in one day;* that the Expeditionary Force is at Dar Djumna. The officer reports the Mahdi most undecided, one hour disarming the regulars, and at another hour arming them; the Arabs deserting, and others joining the Mahdi day after day.

A mine was exploded by a man on the north side, and I hear he is dangerously wounded, if not dead. On questioning the boatman again he explained the *Dar Djumna* is not the cataract, but is a place (near the cataract, just below Berber) one-and-a-half days from Berber. They, the Expeditionary Force, had eight steamers (one, the old screw boat of Dongola, I had towed up from Wady Halfa in 1878). The man said the *Abbas* went on to Dongola (why was it not sent up with the others?). I have given half month's pay to all ranks below sergeant-major. I only owe them now half month's pay.

If the General of the Expeditionary Force has sent up a force, *by Nile to Berber*, *to take Berber*, and *then* if he marches across with *bulk of force* from Merowé, in my humble opinion he has done the right thing.

If Berber had not been taken it would have been a picnic. Baring!! Baring!![31]

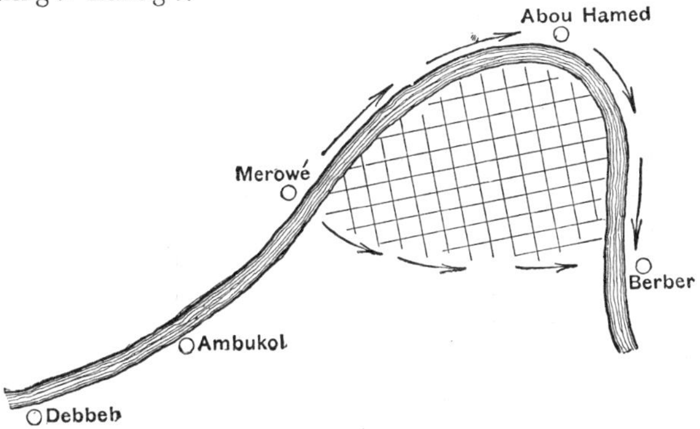

The force going up Nile from Merowé to Berber would have pretty well quieted the banks of the Nile, for the *triangle* contained by *Merowé*, *Abou Hamed*, and *Berber*, so that the bulk of the force, moving from Merowé to the captured Berber, would only be exposed to attacks from the south flank, where there are few people. My experience is that whenever you can possibly do so, never expose yourself to be attacked on all points of the compass; at any rate secure yourself on *one flank*. The force advancing up the Nile were protected on one flank, the Nile; that going across from Merowé to Berber, will be protected on the north flank by the subjugated triangle. Arabs this evening appear not to intend to come to Halfeyeh. They have a station at Giraffe, and another at Kokoo, which is nearly opposite Giraffe, on right bank of Blue Nile. (End of this *blotting paper!*)[32]

Ferratch Pasha tried again in a roundabout way to get the

[31] *Sir Evelyn Baring to Earl Granville.*

Cairo, February 28th, 1884.

"I have the honour to report to your Lordship that, although I did not specially consult General Gordon on the subject of sending British troops to Assouan, he telegraphs to me that if 100 British troops were sent to Assouan or Wady Halfa, they would run no more risk than Nile tourists, and would have the best effect. . . . I certainly would not risk sending so small a body as 100 men."—*Egypt No.* 12, *No.* 170.—ED.

[32] The foregoing portion of the Journal is written on tissue copying-paper.—ED.

£150 a month, forage (*i.e.* dhoora) for four horses, and rations for ten men; he utterly failed, and had to content himself with £100 a month: they are a mean lot. (*Do not let any of those Egyptians* in the steamers *come back here* is my earnest prayer.) (Floyer will be furious at this misuse of telegraph forms.)[33] I am truly delighted that the *Abbas* did not leave the Greeks behind, and only abandoned the boats carrying wood. I hope in fourteen days to have another sister steamer to *Abbas* and *Husseinyeh* completed. I have told them to rivet her only six inches above water line, and to put holdfast rivets for the upper portion which is above water, and which does not require to be watertight.

They say that the *Fascher*[34] steamer had a gun on her; she went aground near Abou Shourim (the Father of the Truth), and got delayed in her pursuit of the *Abbas*. The man wounded by the mine is wounded in the head, chest, and legs; there is not much hope of his recovery.

Awaan (Stewart's friend, the secretary of Arabi) is behaving very badly in prison; he was put in chains by mistake and released, but it has had no effect: he abuses the soldiers. I expect he wrote to the Mahdi and told him of Stewart's departure and of the "Journal." His arrest is said to have been of great effect in the town; he is said to have preached for a long time in favour of the Mahdi.

October 29.—To-day, year 1301 A.H., is said to be about the date of Hicks's disaster; it was on the 1st, 2nd, 3rd November, but with the Arabs it was the 12th, 13th, 14th Moharrem. The news was known in Cairo three weeks after the event occurred; *since that date up to this date* nine people have come up as reinforcements—myself, Stewart, Herbin, Hussein, Tongi, Ruckdi, and three servants, and not one penny of money.[35] Of those who came up, two, Stewart and

[33] This part of the Journal is written on telegraph forms.—ED.
[34] Captured at Berber by the Arabs.—ED.
[35] General Gordon asks in an undated telegram, written after the fall of Berber: "Is it right that I should have been sent to Kartoum with only seven followers, after the destruction of Hicks's army, and no attention paid to me till communications were cut?"—ED.

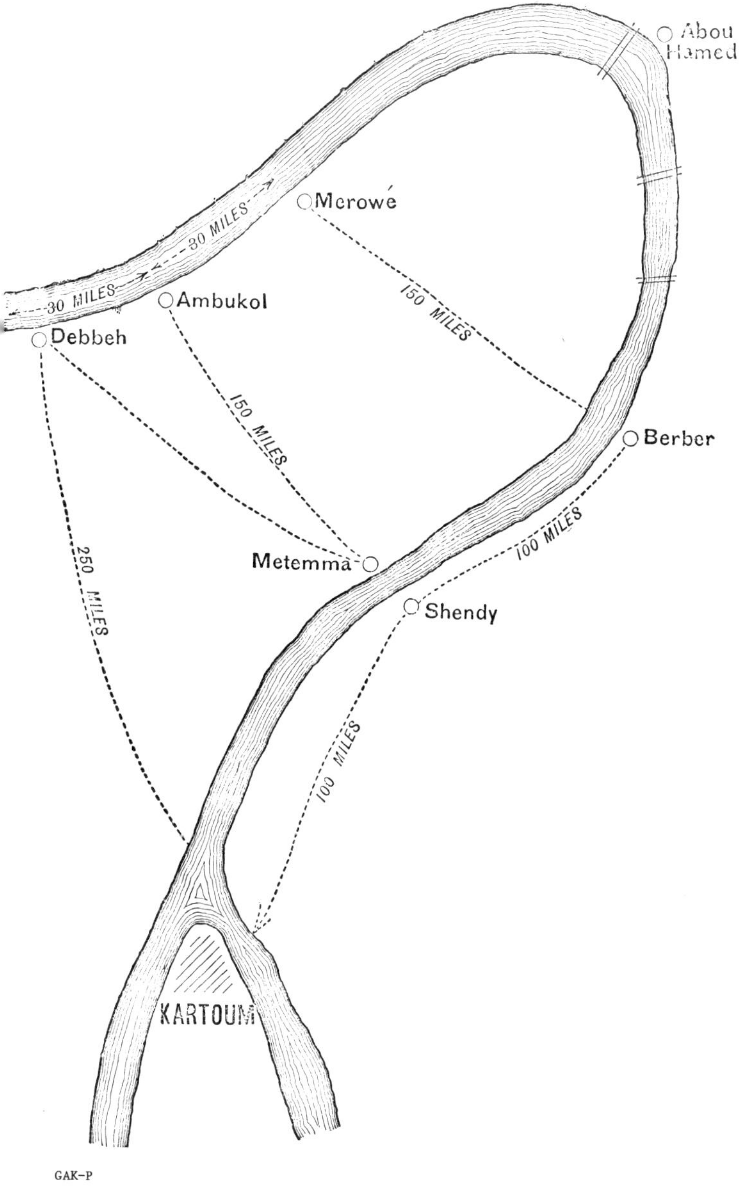
Abou
Hamed
Merowé
30 MILES
30 MILES
150 MILES
Ambukol
Debbeh
150 MILES
Berber
250 MILES
Metemma
100 MILES
Shendy
100 MILES
KARTOUM

GAK-P

Herbin, have gone down: Hussein is dead, so six of the reinforcements alone remain, while we must have sent down over 1500 and 700 soldiers, total 2,200, including the two Pashas, Ibrahim Hardar, and Hussein Cheri, Coetlogon, &c. The regulars, who were in arrears of pay for three months when I came, are now only owed half a month, while the Bashi-Bazouks are owed only a quarter month, and we have some £500 in the treasury. It is quite a miracle. We have lost two battles, suffering severe losses in those actions of men and arms, and may have said to have scrambled through, for I cannot say we can lay claim to any great success during the whole time. Things apparently went against us when we thought we were getting the best of it.

I believe we have more ammunition, Remington (though we have fired three million rounds at the Arabs), and more soldiers now, than when I came up. We have every reason to thank God for his protection. We had many untoward and unexpected misfortunes; the death of Berzati Bey at Gitana; the almost unprofitable first trip of steamers to Sennaar, and their useless delay; our defeat (after El foun victory), by which we lost the active part of our troops, and our fighting Pasha, Mahomet Ali; the surrender of Saleh Pasha and 1500 men, with the capture of the *Mahomet Ali* steamer; the fall of Berber, with two steamers lost. It is really very wonderful that, with such few successes and so many heavy disasters, we should be in the position we are now. Of the reinforcement, Stewart and Tongi got wounded. We have lost three steamers, two at Berber and one at the Blue Nile, and we have built another, the *Husseinyeh*, and hope to have another finished in a fortnight, which makes our loss only one. The defeat near El foun brought about the arrival here of the Mahdi, which might have been very serious, but his arrival has been apparently rendered innocuous. We have £40,000 in Treasury IN PAPER, and £500. When I came up, there was £5,000 in

[36] Formerly General Gordon's under secretary and secretary. He was of old and good family, and greatly respected by General Gordon, who said in 1879: "A few men like Berzati Bey would regenerate Egypt, but they are rare."—Ed.

Treasury. We have £15,000 out in the town in paper money. When I came, we had two Pashas, *Ibrahim Hardar*, *Hussein Cheri;* we have now two, *Ferratch* and *Nutzer Pasha.* Two women, wives of the men who escaped yesterday (with another very small brown baby), came into Omdurman to-day. They say the Arabs are very angry about the desertions; also a boy came in. It would seem, looking over the past months, that, if taken in detail, events have been very much against us; while, if taken generally, we have been most successful. I always had an idea we would not be allowed any success which we could impute to ourselves; that events would be so ruled that we should just *scramble* through and have nothing to boast of. Mahomet Ali Pasha's defeat was owing to his and his men and the people of Kartoum's desire to *loot* Sheikh el Obeyed (the *man*, not the city). It was against my grain, for I wanted to capture Berber, which was the proper military operation to undertake; it was only because they were so anxious, and represented the affair as so easy, that I consented to it. Perhaps, if *we* had taken Berber, Her Majesty's Government would have said that no expedition was necessary for the *relief of the garrisons;* but it would not have been correct to reason thus, for, though Berber might have been taken, we could not have garrisoned it; and it would have been a barren victory, and not have done much towards the solution of the Soudan problem or withdrawal of the garrisons, while it might, on the other hand, have stopped the expedition for *their relief.*

It is the Mahdi's men who have made the station at Kokoo on right bank of the Blue Nile opposite Giraffe, not the men of Waled a Goun; I expect it is to overawe the Sheikh el Obeyed.

The Baggaras on the north side captured this morning three of the Arabs (one is brother of the writer whose things were found on the bank, and whom we supposed to have been murdered); they were stealing three horses belonging to Saleh Pasha. A slave came in from the Arabs at Omdurman; he says the Mahdi says, the Moharrem being a sacred month, he does not mean to fight; he did not act on that view *in re* Hicks; but then Hicks attacked or tried to attack him.

Doubts are thrown on the veracity of that boatman, for he told some few lies about how he went to Berber in a Government boat, which is not true. However, his report cheered us for a time. Some one (Talleyrand?) said, "If a lie got currency for twenty-four hours, it did its work." I am still of opinion, however, if the season was not so far advanced, and the Nile on the fall, that the route by the Nile for a COVERING force was a correct one, but it ought to have been undertaken in July with a rising Nile.

The three men caught to-day say the "*Expeditionary Force is still at Debbeh*," and I expect this is the truth, for the eight steamers coming up the Nile is scarcely possible now, since the Nile is falling. The distance direct from Kartoum to Debbeh is nearly 250 miles, and if the Kababish are friendly, the road is not a bad one; however, I think *Ambukol to Metemma* (could the force know I had the five steamers at Metemma) would be better, for it is only 150 miles, and from Debbeh to Ambukol there is water transport. The road from Ambukol to Metemma does not plunge so deeply into desert; indeed, *Merowé to Berber*, 150 miles, with water transport from Debbeh to Merowé, would be best of all, if the force could cross the Nile at Berber. The only enemy the force will meet with, on any of the three roads, are camel-men and horsemen, till it arrives on the banks of the Nile.

October 30.—This morning the Arabs came to Halfeyeh, capturing some of our heedless people; whether they will stay there or not I do not know—rumour says they are on their way to Shoboloha and Shendy to repel the ravages of steamers.

You have the map made by railway engineers of the route from Ambukol to Metemma, which must have all information, wells, &c., &c. I should put five station forts along the line, and when I made my debouch at Metemma I should split off one detachment to capture Berber, and another towards Kartoum, taking care of any guns in Shoboloha defile (during which passage I should march the men, and not leave them in the steamers or boats). I would make my base at Metemma for all operations in the Soudan connected with the Nile Valley

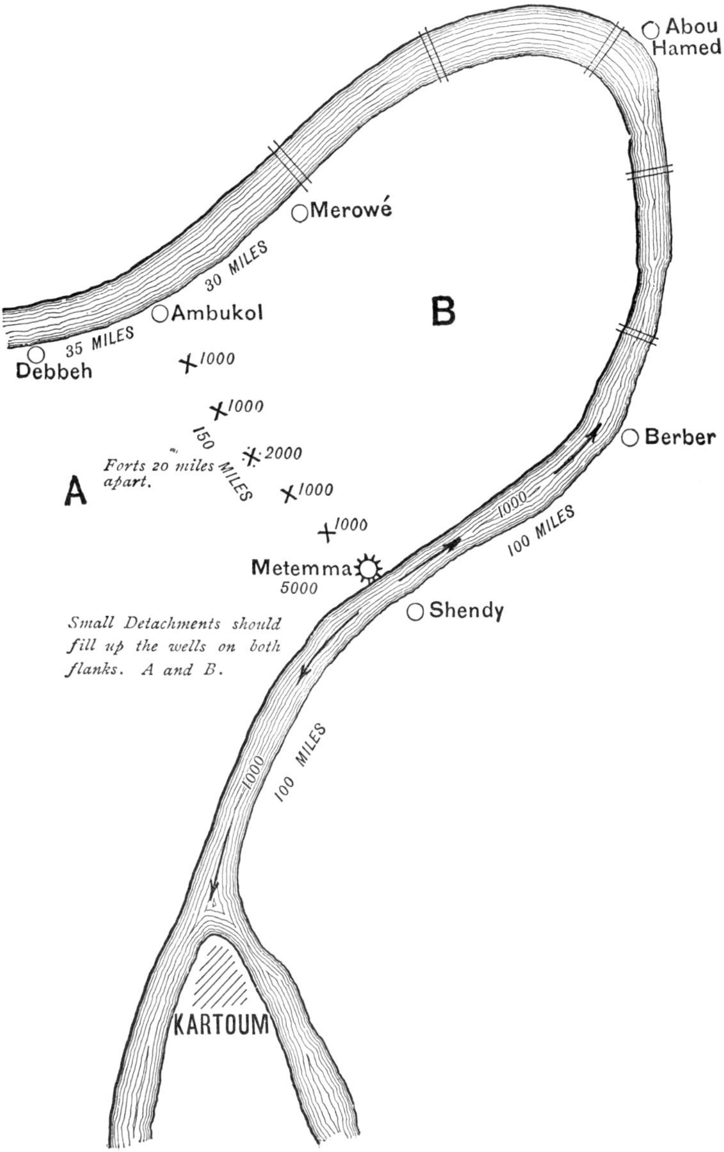
Abou
Hamed
Merowé
30 MILES
Ambukol
B
35 MILES
Debbeh
1000
1000
150 MILES
2000
Forts 20 miles apart.
A
1000
1000
Berber
1000
100 MILES
Metemma
5000
Shendy
Small Detachments should fill up the wells on both flanks. A and B.
1000
100 MILES
KARTOUM

—the numbers I have put for the forts along road are probably in excess of what would be required.

The Arab force which went towards the north (? Shendy) consists of 200 footmen, and 50 horse.

Two men came in from the South Front—they say the Sheikh el Obeyed is with the Mahdi; and Waled a Goun, and Abou Gugliz are at Giraffe. I expect that the Arabs have captured one of our merchant's boats at Halfeyeh.

We have 1300 men in the North Fort, yet 250 Arabs went boldly across our front to Halfeyeh, and we do not dare to show our noses; this speaks for our *morale.*

A slave came in at Omdurman; he says the Mahdi says he will not fight until after Moharrem (to-day is 12th Moharrem).

Arabs fired on the Lines from near the White Nile to-day, but did no harm. Not being able to sleep last night, I was late in getting up, and consequently every one also slept and no proper look-out was kept on the Arabs. I should think I had written about twenty orders about their keeping a look-out, but it is of no use. The Arabs have gone back to Giraffe. I am going to make the officer of North Fort pay compensation for the men wounded, and to the families of those killed, in this raid. The map made by the railway engineers (1874–1875) must have every information as to water supply on Ambukol-Metemma road.

In reality, the relief of the garrisons is only a question of crossing over a *well-surveyed road* of 150 *miles*, at the end of which are found *five steamers* and *nine guns*: of course there is a great deal of trouble in transport arrangements, but no particular danger.

I believe we (*i.e.* those Shaggyeh) lost to-day twenty-three soldiers taken prisoners, one killed, one wounded; seventeen cows, five women, eight slaves, three donkeys, seven horses,[37] twenty-four Remington rifles[38] captured; and this after I had

[37] "Two of these horses returned to-day; as I expect the riders threw themselves off and let their horses loose, and that, too, at a distance so great that the Arabs did not see them!!!"

[38] "I am going to make them pay for twenty-two of the Remingtons, for it appears doubtful if they were captured, inasmuch as to-day they asked me to send the steamer down to look for them. I expect the men simply threw them down and bolted upon the appearance of the Arabs."

repeatedly warned them of an impending attack, and specially warned them last night after the capture of the three spies. They, these Shaggyeh, number 1200; on the other side, with 30 horses, the Arabs were not 200; they made no attempt to defend themselves; dreadful lot, how I look forward to their

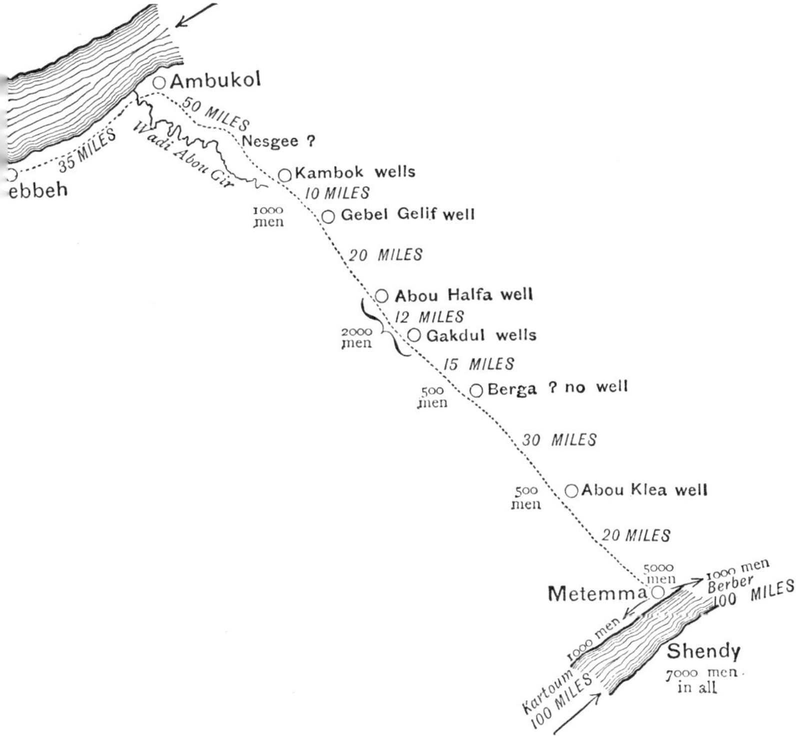

disbandment! Had I left them at Halfeyeh what a time I should have had with them. The Arabs have paid us off with interest for our cavalry raids of a few days ago. If any troops come up, as soon as the environs are clear around Kartoum, I would recommend their immediate disbandment. I cannot see any reason why the "*expedition for the relief of the garrisons*" should not have *captured Berber*, and *arrived at Kartoum on 10th November* (Lord Mayor's Show), which is giving ample time; saying that troops did advance from Cairo on the 15th August, which I guess (from Kitchener's laconic despatch of 31st August) was the case. That strong rumours could not have been known at Debbeh (for at least twenty days) that Kartoum steamers were at Metemma (plundering right and left) is most unlikely, even if my many spies (sent with notes to this effect) did not get through one of their number. These rumours should have pointed out that the Ambukol-Metemma road was THE ROAD to follow [39]—even if not decided on before, which is most probable.

ROUTE AMBUKOL TO METEMMA.—ITINERARY OF ARABS.

Ambukol to Nesgee	24 hours.
Nesgee to Om Halfa	12 ,,
Om Halfa to Gakdul	12 ,,
Gakdul to Abou Klea	18 ,,
Abou Klea to Metemma	12 ,,
Caravan	78 ,,

Wells plentifully supplied.
No wells of import on flanks.

I expect water can be found along Wadi Abou Gir, as water is found at Kambok, which is on a higher level. I shall anticipate no danger for a force of 200 men as far as Gebil Gelif well—that takes 60 miles off this march of 150 and leaves 90 miles.

In the centre you have the wells Abou Halfa and Gakdul, 12 miles apart. This central portion is distant Ambukol 80 miles, Metemma 65 miles. There appear no wells on flanks where Arabs can assemble in any numbers.

October 31.—Three men, soldiers, came in from the Arabs on the White Nile last night. To-day it is $7\frac{23}{30}$ months, or 233 days, since the Arabs appeared in our immediate neighbourhood, since which date we have had no peace.

It will be bitter cold in the desert, and I think, of all the deserts, that of Dongola is the coldest. I do not think I should send Nutzer Pasha and the Egyptians you take out of the steamers down further than Dongola, for the moment, for if you do you will put Dongola on the *qui vive* as to the evacua-

39 See map on previous page.—ED.

tion. Certainly, for those who are for a rapid retreat, having a *tête du pont* (so to say) at Metemma, much facilitates the movement; for the garrisons and the people of Kartoum and Sennaar. Shendy-Metemma is evidently the chief strategical point of the Soudan; for from it you reach Kartoum, Sennaar, and Berber by water, and Kassala by the Atbara valley; but, short of making Fowler's railway to Shendy, I should prefer the making of stations along the Nile, for a peace route and for small forces, as by the Nile you get free of camel transport, which depends on the temper of the Arab tribes; besides, the Nile route is cheaper, and could be put into execution with one high Nile.

The three soldiers who came in last night have one sergeant-major among them. He says Mahmound Khalifa wrote to his father, who is with Mahomet Achmet, in which he says that the English General wants him to get camels in great haste; that he is delaying as much as possible; that the English General wants to go in one body; that he is trying to get him to go in four bodies; *that Mahmound Khalifa* is a traitor, like all his family; and he should catch it, for I expect this information is correct. The sergeant-major says that Mahmound Khalifa is at Dongola or Debbeh. The Mahdi is going into a cave for this month and next; he is now in his cave. All the Europeans are with the Mahdi (not in the cave). Slatin is very good friends with the Mahdi, and *sees him* every day (?). (This is rather against the cave report.)

The mysterious Frenchman is not with the Mahdi, but in Kordofan. The letter which I spoke of as coming from Mahmound Khalifa arrived at the Mahdi's camp fifteen days ago, so left Dongola about twenty-two days ago (9th October). Can it be remembered whether at that time, viz. 9th October, any altercation took place on subject of march?[40] In the

[40] It was at about this date that the recall of Lord Wolseley was generally rumoured at home and abroad. On the 10th of October this rumoured recall was officially contradicted. The *Times*, however, said: "We have every confidence in the veracity and good information of our correspondent, but so incredible did his statement seem at first sight that we have made further inquiries, in order to be quite sure there was no mistake in its transmission."—Ed.

letter is a remark, that the English General said he wished "all to go together, for he would not leave a sick man behind." The man says, Mahmound Khalifa wrote another letter to his father, stating the start from Dongola towards Berber. I can produce the sergeant-major who gave this information.

Church parade much as usual. I expect they exhibited the captives of yesterday. It is extraordinary if we are employing Mahmound Khalifa, when his father, Hussein Pasha Khalifa, is a *so-called* prisoner of the Mahdi. Stewart knows, I think, that the father gave up Berber by more or less treachery.

I hope the Mudir of Dongola will look after this man. The sergeant-major says "that the Mahdi declares" he will execute the Sheikh el Islam (whom I put in prison) for preventing our surrendering, by which bit of news *I read* that an adherent of the Sheikh el Islam got some friends of his to bribe the sergeant-major *to say this* while on his way to the Palace.

Three men more have come in—one sergeant, one corporal, and a slave—from the Arabs at Omdurman. They say many Arabs leave daily for Kordofan; the Mahdi has sent three companies of regulars to bring back deserters; the Mahdi has been taking women from others, which makes the Arabs doubt his holiness; he has only forty rounds for each Krupp gun, of which he has two. The slave was a great fat bull-faced fellow. He was honest, for when I asked him why he came here, he said, "because he got so little to eat with the Arabs." His appearance belied his words. These men said nothing of the cave business. The living skeleton in hospital (Stewart knows him) departed this life yesterday—I will not say, deeply regretted, except by *me in a small way*, for I knew him so long. It turns out that the Shaggyeh chief who commanded in the North Fort slept in town the day before yesterday night, and so was absent at yesterday morning's catastrophe; also the officer Osman Bey, who went down to Berber with steamers to escort the *Abbas* past Berber, and who let the *Fascher* pursue the *Abbas* never reported this man's absence; I have turned them out, and cut them each a month's pay. (No sentry as usual, on North Fort. They are incorrigible. 2 P.M. Though their men have gone to look for missing rifles, I ordered them thirty blows: *i.e.* the sentries.)

Two cows have kindly walked into Omdurman Fort. The Arabs fired a few shots on the Lines near the White Nile, which did not reach them; I expect the Arab chiefs send out the regulars and tell them to fire on the Lines, and the regulars obey orders much as my orders are obeyed here. The North Fort hate my telescope; day and night I work them. It is one of Chevalier's, of Paris, which I picked up here and gave £5 for, it is by far the best glass I ever saw. Commander J. Baker, R.N., has the *best* opera-glasses; he got them from me at Berberah in 1878, in exchange; they belonged to the Egyptian Government. It was the father of Hussein Pasha Khalifa who led the Egyptians into the Soudan in 1823. The

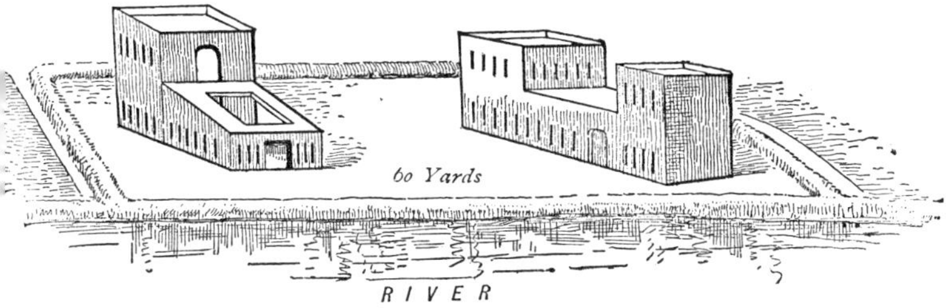

family comes from Assouan, for this, the grant of monopoly of commerce through Korosko desert was given to the family. It was taken away from them in Ismail Pasha Ayoub's time, about 1872, and I restored it to them. I heard the Mahdi gave them this monopoly after the fall of Berber, or rather agreed to their retaining it. I think the only good one of the family was Sheikh Hamid, who died this year. I sent the horsemen of these Shaggyeh out to the scene of yesterday's disaster; they recovered a horse! two donkeys! and three Remingtons! and found the body of one of their slaves. I am going to make them pay for the lost Remingtons, nineteen in number now. I cannot afford to have Remingtons thrown away like that. This recalls to my mind how, when I had 700 men in the North Fort, which consisted of two houses distant sixty yards apart, the great Melon, who was in the house where the telegraph office is, declined to open the door of his house and sent a message to the other house, for fear of the Arabs, who were camped three miles distant. It was like this:

[*See illustration on previous page.*]

I have ever felt the greatest insecurity respecting the Lines, for I believe one hundred determined men would carry them with ease, if they made their attack on the Shaggyeh or Bashi Bazouk part. These creatures used to shut themselves into the houses at about 7 P.M., and never go out till it was broad daylight; they were not eighty yards from the river. The Cairo Turkish Bashi Bazouks, the Shaggyeh, and the Fellaheen soldiers, I will back against any troops in the world for *cowardice!* I expect the reason why the Arabs did not take the three recaptured horses was because they were as frightened nearly as our men (*vide* p. 182); the worst of it is, that it is taken generally as a thing of "*matter of course*" by the Kartoum people, and, one may say, officers; no one is a bit put out or ashamed; it teaches no experience. *Vide* the absence of sentries on the fort to-day, who, I expect, cannot sit down over-comfortably to-night after their thirty blows.

One cannot help feeling amused at these Shaggyeh, for they are the most arrant braggadocios, as are the Cairo Turkish Bashi Bazouks, and when you come up, if you do, you will see how they will exhibit. They have little kettledrums about a span in diameter; whenever I hear them I feel viciously inclined. This dates back many years. The Shaggyeh are very quiet to-day; they are all boxed up in the houses; very few have ventured out more than 2,000 yards. The report is that they are ashamed, which, if words could make them so, they ought to be; but I doubt it. They have not beaten their kettledrums to-night; yes, they have begun to beat them now. On one occasion, when I had two guns in their fort, I had a truly miserable night; for a cow would have taken the fort, though there were 1200 men in it. It was more for the guns than for them that I was anxious. The horse, which was recovered to-day, was saddled and *was* bridled, but, like a wise brute, as he could not eat with the bit in his mouth, he put his foot on the bridle and broke it off. I telegraphed to the rider "that I felt sure he could not look him in the face after leaving him out all night for nothing with the saddle on." [41]

November 1.—The Arabs came up to their old fort in front of Bourré this morning and fired a few shots; they did not stay five minutes there. A Boulak Basha, his son, and two slaves came in to Omdurman and report the Mahdi is in the cave; that Slatin has retained all his property; that the Arabs continue to desert the Mahdi, who sends the regulars after them; that the deserting Arabs fight the soldiers, and have killed many of them; that the Arabs generally doubt the mission of the Mahdi, and wish for the return of the Government. The Mahdi is not going to fight during Moharrem and Saphia months. Two hundred and fifty Arabs deserted yesterday. The Mahdi sent the regulars after them, and four regulars were killed, and the deserters got away. Fifty to one hundred per diem run away. These people are a fine lot. The merchants of the market have been refusing to give more than three and a-half reals for a sovereign, five to six reals being the proper rate; so I captured nine of the chief of them, and have sent them to the Lines with a pretended order to send them out to Waled a Goun, but with orders to keep them on the Lines. I hope this will cure them. I shall let them in again when they sign a paper agreeing to my terms. Of course it is tyranny, but there is no other course to be pursued. The nine culprits, three soldiers with fixed bayonets before, three soldiers with ditto behind, and a mounted cavass on each flank, are wending their way to the Lines through the market. Quite a procession! My servants are my staff. I never hear these sort of things from the officials, who are bribed, I expect, to keep silence.

7 P.M. A small bright fire in direction of and below Hal-

[41] It is interesting to note how often General Gordon breaks away abruptly from a subject which is irritating him, and deals with one which has a touch of humour in it. He never does this when he is discussing or explaining any particular point; it is only when he is thoroughly annoyed with his subject that he suddenly leaves it.—ED.

feyeh, lasting scarcely a minute. I flatter myself I keep a good look out.[42]

Two soldiers came to Omdurman, escaping from the Arabs this evening. Nothing new.

One of the trying things of this existence is the way that one is waylaid as one goes out with petitions for dhoora, and howled at. These are the times when one feels *amiably* disposed towards the gentlemen who have ruled in Cairo for the last seven years.

November 2.—Those men I sent out ostensibly to the Arabs have given in, and I have let them back into town. I hate these coercive measures. But what is to be done? This frightening them is better than putting them in prison, or chaining them. No words are of any avail, or orders. Two dervishes with their weapons presented themselves before Lines this morning, saying they had a letter from the Mahdi for me (at Mesalamieh Gate). I said, "Leave the letter and go back; I will not let you in. It is no use any more writing."

The Arabs fired on the Lines near the White Nile. We answered, and committed some damage, from all appearance; for the whole Dem turned out. I have forbidden all firing on the Arabs, unless they come so near as to injure our people; for I expect this vague firing is only performed by the captured soldiers to conform, in appearance, to the orders of the Arab chiefs.

Letter has come in;[43] it is an address to the whole town; it has no seal, the usual rubbish about the Mahdi being Mahdi, &c. A soldier came in from the Arabs at Omdurman; he says the Mahdi is not in the cave, but in a tent (very stupid man!) Some one has stolen 93,000 okes of biscuit; this robbery took place nearly a year ago, and was only found out two days ago. The people of the town wonder at one's getting no information; the last I had was from Kitchener, dated 31st August and received 17th September, now forty-six days

[42] General Gordon was in the habit of passing a great part of the day and of the night on the roof of his palace.—Ed.

[43] Appendix V.

ago. Had our people sent to Kassala *viâ* Massowah,[44] there is no doubt information could have got through, but it is no use saying any more on the subject. I suppose you acted according to "your conscience, best of your ability, and custom of war in like cases."

3.30 P.M. Sentries off the roof of the North Fort again; sent over to have them flogged!

Rectified list of biscuit is 266,430 okes.

Dhoora is 2110 ardebs in magazine to day—six weeks' consumption!! and then the sponge must be thrown up.

I could write volumes of pent-up wrath on this subject if I did not believe things are ordained and all work for the best. I am not at all inclined to order half rations with a view to any prolongation of our blockade; if I did so, it would probably end in a catastrophe[45] before the time, in which, if full rations are given, we should have exhausted our supplies. I should be an angel (which I am not, needless to say) if I was not rabid with Her Majesty's Government; but I hope I may be quiet on the subject of this Soudan and Cairo business, with its indecision; but to lose all my beautiful black soldiers is enough to make one angry with those who have the direction of our future.

Arabs fired four rounds this evening towards the Lines near White Nile, but did no harm (one shell fell in the town) with their Krupp.

November 3.—Two women and one boy came in to Omdurman from the Arabs; also seven cows walked into the same place. To-day is *our* anniversary of Hicks's defeat. I have let out several of the men whom I had arrested as adherents of the Mahdi; they have had a good warning.

4 P.M. *Bordeen* in sight: I have let out the Sheikh el Islam, Cadi, and the old Mudir. A soldier came from the Arabs to Omdurman; he says Slatin is a prisoner for the last three days.

[44] Massowah is only 466 miles from Kartoum, and less than half that distance from Kassala.—ED.

[45] *I.e.* in mutiny or a stampede to the Mahdi. "The belly governs the whole world."—ED.

With this man came in a spy from the Mahdi, whom I put in prison. The Mahdi has sent regulars to the rear. I shall send down the *Bordeen* the day after to-morrow to Metemma, and shall send the *débris*, Tongi & Co. down with the steamer, and you can send them on to Cairo. I think this is noble on my part, for you get their boats and they use your camels. The post has come in from *Bordeen*. Kitchener's letter, saying "*Abbas* was captured" was a terrible blow (I send back the letters sent to Stewart in envelope).[46]

Kitchener asks who were on board: Stewart, Power, and Herbin, the French Consul, and the Greeks named in the margin on the other side.[47] I cannot understand it, for the general opinion was that the route was quite safe for the *Abbas*, which had a mountain gun and some fifty soldiers in her. I can only put it down to some treachery on the part of the Arabs pretending to be friends.

I cannot decipher Lord Wolseley's telegram,[48] for Stewart took the cipher-books. (Please inform Foreign Office of *this*, for if he [Stewart] is killed, and *Abbas* captured, they, the cipher-books, are in the hands of the Mahdi.) I think cipher-messages are in some countries, like this, a mistake.

The Shendy steamers sent back ten wounded from Shendy, one seriously; and I hear they had five killed. For goodness' sake do not send back any Egyptians, *now* in steamers, to Kartoum; I include Pashas, officers, men, and exclude the sailors, engineers, and captains of steamers.

If *Abbas* is lost, I hope a Court of Inquiry will be held on the departure of Col. Stewart and Messrs. Power and Herbin;

[46] Appendix X.

[47] List of Greeks who were in the steamer *Abbas*, 10 Sept. 1884.

Demitrios Kapnoulas.
George Kepetzakos.
Herial Bolanaki.
Alexandre Genacari.
Nasum Abagui.
Nessim Morinos.
Demitrios Perdicakis.
Michel Nomikos.
Stauros Papadakis.
Jean Prospion.
Demosthen Kapilos.
Demitrios Georgopoulos.
George Kontis.
Xenophon Apostolidis.
George Tantzos.
Jean Stergiou.
Nicolas Kouvaras.
Jean Dermitrzakis.
Michel Chatzi Christodoulou.

[48] Appendix X.

for when they left we had no news of an Expedition of Relief—*vide* my Journal; also it was generally believed that the passage of the *Abbas* down was an absolute certainty without danger. I also add that Stewart, Herbin, and Power left of their own free will, and without any order from me, as the papers captured would show, if ever available. I refused to *order*, but I said, "If you like to go, I will assist you to go. It is at your own risk. The service you will perform is great, and you can do no good here." *I wrote this to Col. Stewart*, in an official letter.

November 4.—I received private letters from Stanley, dated Congo, 5th May, and from Sir S. Baker, 1st June. I like the official note written on the envelope of Sir Samuel Baker's letter to me—"Communications avec la Soudan interrompées." I should think the communications were *interrompées!!!*

The Arabs have one gun at Shendy, and one gun at Metemma; they struck *Mansowrah* four times.

I looked upon the descent of the *Abbas* as a certainty. I looked upon the relief of Kartoum as most uncertain; hence I sent down the cipher-books of the Foreign Office. Perhaps the *Abbas* got wrecked on the cataract. It is very sad. There is a report that the Sheikh el Obeyed is dead; if true, it will simplify that vexed question with Foreign Office of the *man* and the *city*. Arabs fired five shells at the Lines to-day; we answered with two, and they retired. If the capture of steamer is corroborated, tell the French Consul-General that the Mahdi has his cipher, which was with Herbin. *If Abbas was captured by treachery, then I am not to blame; neither am I to blame if she struck a rock*, for she drew under two feet of water; and fifty boats (sailing) used to go down yearly to Cairo, with high Nile; *if they were attacked and overpowered, then I am to blame*, for I ought to have foreseen the chance, and prevented their going. But when they left we knew nothing of the Expedition, and I passed them under escort through Berber, which was the apparent only danger they had to meet. The Mahdi, if it is true that he has captured the

Abbas, found two of his own seals,[49] which we had forged but did not use, also all his letters to me, and the Journal was in most careful detail, hour by hour, so to say. Steamer leaves at daybreak, 5th November, 1884.

C. G. Gordon.

[49] See Mahdi's remarks upon this in Appendix U.

BOOK VI.

EVENTS AT KARTOUM.

FROM 5 NOVEMBER TO 14 DECEMBER, 1884.

GENERAL GORDON'S JOURNAL.

Vol. VI.

To be pruned down if published.

C. G. GORDON.

Copy of letter that accompanied this diary.

KARTOUM, 10 *Nov.*, 1884.

SIR,

Since departure, 10 Sept., of Lt.-Colonel Stewart, C.M.G., I have kept a daily journal of all events at Kartoum, which contains also my *private* opinions upon certain facts, which perhaps it is just as well you should know confidentially. You can of course make extracts of all official matter, and will naturally leave my private opinions out in the case of publication. I have already sent five portions of this journal, and now send the sixth portion.

I have the honour to be,

Sir,

Your most obedient servant,

C. G. GORDON.

The Chief of the Staff,
Soudan Expeditionary Force,

JOURNAL.

EVENTS AT KARTOUM.

November 5.—Steamer *Bordeen* left this evening for Metemma. According to all accounts the presence of the steamers at Shendy and Metemma cause the Arabs great annoyance, for the Arab chief of Berber keeps calling for them to come down and help him; while they say, "If we do, then the steamers will pillage our houses." I cannot get out of my head the *Abbas* catastrophe; that the *Abbas* (with her 970 bullet marks on her, her gun, and her parapets, which were bullet-proof), could be captured by force, seems impossible; that she ran upon a rock seems unlikely, for she had her sides defended by buffers, sunk one foot in water. I also had warned them against ever anchoring by the bank, also to take wood from isolated spots; in fact, as far as human foresight goes, I did all my possible. Why did you let them go? The matter was thus. I determined to send the *Abbas* down with an Arab captain. Herbin asked to be allowed to go. I jumped at his offer. Then Stewart said he would go, if I would exonerate him from deserting me. I said you do not desert me. *I:* I cannot go; but if you go, you do great service. I then wrote him an official; he wanted me to write him an order. I said "No, for though I fear not responsibility, I will not put you in any danger in which I am not myself." I wrote them a letter, couched thus: "*Abbas* is going down; you say you are willing to go in her, if I think you can do so in honour—you can go in honour, for you can do nothing here, and if you go you do me service in telegraphing my views." You will notice the number of Greeks. They were a bodyguard I ordered and paid highly, to prevent any treachery on the part of the crew. Thus the question of treachery was duly weighed by me and guarded against, as far as I could—both on the part of the crew and on the part of the inhabitants—and I told them to anchor mid stream, and not to take wood except in isolated spots.[1]

I escorted them by two steamers past every place where danger could be apprehended, viz., Berber and Shendy. They appear to have been captured in a comparatively thinly populated place, below Abou Hamed. I feel somehow convinced they were captured by treachery—the Arabs pretending to be friendly—and surprising them at night. I will own that, without reason (apparently, for the chorus was, that the *trip was safe*) I have never been comfortable since they left. Stewart was a man who did not chew the cud, he never thought of danger in prospective; he was not a bit suspicious (while I am made up of it). I can see in imagination the whole scene,[2] the sheikh inviting them to land, saying, "Thank

[1] It is impossible to read this without a feeling of admiration for the thorough way in which General Gordon examined into the minutest details of everything himself. Every precaution human foresight could conceive he took to ensure the safety of the *Abbas* and her crew; having done this, her *fate* was in higher hands than his.—Ed.

[2] Compare General Gordon's account with the account given by the Mudir of Dongola:—"A certain Faki Walad Ahmet, who appears trustworthy, has arrived here, stating that he has heard that after General Gordon's return to Kartoum a steamer, with forty men on board, partly Europeans and partly Egyptians, besides five negroes and three servants, arrived at Salamat, where she ran aground, but did not founder. The population, aware of the fate of Berber, and being much alarmed, several persons from the steamer went ashore in order to reassure the natives, declaring that they had not come to make war, but to purchase camels in order to cross the desert to Merawi. The Sheikhs Soliman and Abu Noman, and the uncle of Faki Osman, agreed to see to their conveyance, and provided a guide, who was to conduct the party. Those on board were so pleased with this attention that they presented one of the Sheikhs with a gold sword, the uncle with a silver sword, and the guide with a rich dress, whereupon the Sheikhs requested them to leave the steamer and accept their hospitality until preparations had been completed for crossing the desert. The invitation was accepted, and the party entered a house, where they were all massacred. The Sheikhs afterwards returned

God the Mahdi is a liar"—bringing in wood—men going on shore and dispersed. The *Abbas* with her steam down, then a rush of wild Arabs, and all is over! A spy said something of a chief having pretended to be friendly, and when the *Abbas* was near, rushing on her, but then he said the *Abbas* turned on them, and killed seventy-two or seventy-three (see back page of this Journal).[3] It is very sad, but being ordained, we must not murmur. I look on it as being a Nemesis on the death of the two Pashas.

I do sincerely hope you will have a strict examination into the question of Stewart, Power, and Herbin going down. What makes me think so much of the capture being by treachery is, that the two sailing-boats which went with the *Abbas* have not arrived at Debbeh, for if the *Abbas* struck on a rock, why could not the boats come on? I expect they were all caught at one *coup*. 11 P.M. last night Arabs fired twelve shells into the town from their Krupps on the South Front, they did not frighten us and did no harm. At midnight they fired two or three volleys of musketry with no effect. Four soldiers came in from the Arabs at Omdurman. They state the Mahdi sent a party of Arabs to Sennaar, the garrison sallied out and killed nearly all of them. Also that the Baggara Arabs, under pretence of getting better pasturage for their cattle, asked the Mahdi to let them go from his camp some distance, he agreed, and they have bolted—they are his best horsemen—also that the people no longer regard the Mahdi as before. Hussein Pasha Khalifa is good friends with the Mahdi. The Arabs came near Bourré and fired a few shots, and then went back. I expect that the Arabs sent the regulars out, and go through this as a mere form; one of these men[4] was with Slatin Bey when he surrendered, and says he did so when he had plenty of food and ammunition, and that he (Slatin) is on the best

---

to the steamer and killed most of them on board. Of forty persons only fourteen were spared, and these were taken prisoners." The Sub-Mudir, not knowing if there were any Europeans among the survivors, had sent messengers for further intelligence.—ED.

[3] *I.e.*, details of the fighting strength of the *Abbas*.—ED.

[4] Who came in.—ED.

terms with the Mahdi. We shall not know the truth until the other Europeans get out of the Mahdi's clutches.

Stewart had about £60 in gold with him, and *every paper* connected with our mission. I purposely kept none here, for one did not know what one day would bring forth; when he left on the 10th of September we had lost over 800 men killed, and 978 Remingtons, with a lot of ammunition on 4th of September, only six days before he left. Baker tells me news, he says Clifford Lloyd has left on account of row with Nubar, and that China and France have come to terms.

One shell from the Arabs went over the town and fell in the river.

I have mentioned that Stewart's journal contained all events from March 1st, 1884, to 10th September, and if lost there is only the journal of the Doctor, which begins 7th March, 1884.

I wish the correspondent of the *Times* to know this, and to be told that the Doctor has promised me that the *Times* shall have the first offer of that journal. Stewart was wounded near the Palace, at 6 A.M. on Sunday, 25th May, in the arm (flesh wound). If Sennaar has beaten back the Arabs a second time I cannot see how it is possible to abandon the garrison, and if they are to be relieved, I see at least a delay of four months; all this could be avoided by handing the Soudan over to the Sultan with a subsidy. When Stewart left we were at the lowest ebb, the Arabs from Kordofan had arrived with their guns, and our three steamers were just in from Sennaar, with seven shot holes in them.

Hansall, the Austrian Consul, has a daily journal; Power and Herbin had one also.

I have captured[5] all the European telegrams which we sent and which we received. I shall hand them over to you, as

[5] *I.e.*, collected them from the different offices and officials in Kartoum. They have not been been given over by the Government.—ED.

NOTE.—On the opposite page is an extract from Lord Lytton's speech, cut from one of the papers: "Ask General Gordon, if he ever comes safely home to us, what he and his still unrescued garrison have learned to think of the high sense of national honour, the chivalrous courage, the unflinching good faith of Mr. Gladstone and his Radical Cabinet." (Three cheers were given for Gordon.)—ED.

they are in cipher, and as you may have the F. O. cipher books, you can peruse them. Stewart (as I have said) carried off the cipher books with him; he had two copies of the journal, but I did not like to ask him to leave one here, as I said, "you can send one home, while you keep the copy to refer to."

I send with this the Firman of Towfik and the letters [6] respecting the troops withdrawing, which I received at Cairo on the 23rd January, 1884, and which have not been promulgated.

If Stewart, Power, and Herbin died because they would not change their religion, they are as much martyrs as Peter or Paul.

A black boy of ten years was caught by the Arabs outside of the Lines this morning, collecting grass, and he escaped from them this evening and came back to the town; he is a smart boy.

If the *Abbas* is taken, the Mahdi has the small seal I used in my former time, and he captured at fall of Berber my large seal, so he has both. If it is true, the *Abbas* must have been captured between Abou Hamed and Merowé, on or about the 18th September. Now, on the 18th September the Arabs must have known of Kitchener being at Debbeh, since he wrote to me from that place on 31st August. Probably Stewart was lulled into security in feeling himself so near Merowé, and on account of the news the Sheikh gave him of the advance of the Expedition.

Abou Hamed is one hundred miles from Merowé, which, with the current, the *Abbas* could do in twelve hours, and there is only one small cataract to pass, which is, by all accounts, an easy one. Stewart had a supreme contempt for the Soudanese people, and for their courage, which I do not share. That our men are not heroes I agree, but we had against us the feeling that the Arabs were ten times our numbers, while we had received no reinforcements whatever.[7] If he (Stewart) has fallen, it is because he was carried away by the idea the Arabs would

[6] Appendix Y.

[7] That is to say, the men were depressed by the apparent remoteness of their chance of escape.—Ed

not dare to do anything. Power had the same defect, viz., over-rashness in not considering the material they had to support them. You may be very strong yourself, but your strength is of no avail if you are supported by weaker vessels. The rate of progress of a fleet is decided by the speed of the slowest vessel, so up here one ought to work as if the whole mass was as cowardly as the greatest coward in the force. If the *Abbas* went on a rock she had two boats (which I expressly mentioned to Stewart were to be taken in case of such an accident), and they could have got into them, and, with the current, got down easily. I sent, in 1878, a boat with a large tank, in which were four hippopotami (infants) ; it got down to *Cairo* in fifty days from *here*, and Stewart had the Reis, or pilot of that boat, in the *Abbas*. Humanly speaking, when Stewart left here the condition of Kartoum was desperate ; while, on the other hand, when once the *Abbas* passed Berber, which we escorted her past, the certainty was she would reach Dongola, and even we discussed whether Dongola might not have fallen, and agreed that the *Abbas* even in that case could have got down to Wady Halfa, in which case I told Stewart to go on with her to Cairo. Men may not remember the case of Captain . . . ., who took a middy up against Taepings with him, which middy was killed. Middy's father . . . made a great row about this. Why did . . . take the middy up, &c. I say, in defence of my letting Stewart go, that both he, Power, and Herbin felt our situation here was desperate after the defeat at El foun—that I had, over and over again, said it was impossible for me to go, physically impossible, because even my servants would have betrayed me (even if I had felt inclined to leave), and I would die here (even going so far as to have two mines brought to the Palace with which to blow it up if the place fell). These three men's ideas were that it was shabby to leave me, but when I showed them they could do no possible good by being prisoners, and when I said I shall send the *Abbas* with the Journal, then, first, Herbin, then Stewart, and then Power, said they would go in her. A long conversation took place between me and Stewart, he wishing me to *order*, I declining to do so, on account of eventualities which might arise ; it ended in my writing the letter I alluded to in former pages of the Journal. I avow I was glad they went, 1. because I thought it was quite safe; 2. because I knew if Europe knew of the state of affairs the Government would be shamed into action.

Remember that this was when the last telegram [8] from Egerton was to the effect that "Her Majesty's Government would pay *on delivery* for all who came down, if I contracted with Arabs." Stewart's idea was that every order of Her Majesty's Government, or wish that they expressed, was indisputable. We often discussed the nuisance we must have been to Her Majesty's Government in being sent up here, and I think he was, to some degree, actuated by a desire to aid Her Majesty's Government when he went down, for then it only left one nuisance (myself), and I had so completely exonerated Her Majesty's Government by my letters, and the notes in his Journal, that they might, as far as I was concerned, have let the garrison fall. On my part, I do not think I could have done Her Majesty's Government a better service than to have, at any rate, tried to send Stewart down with Power and Herbin, for certainly it only left a small remnant here of Europeans (*one of whom is mad*), and the French Government could no longer say a word. Next, Stewart knew everything, and could tell Her Majesty's Government the pros and cons, from their point of view, and with feelings akin to theirs, which they would accept from Stewart, and never without suspicion from me (in which they are justified, for I do not look on things from their point of view). I told Stewart also, "I know you will act conscientiously and honourably; but I know your opinions, and, therefore, as you have all my views on the Soudan in your Journal, I beg you will, in answering queries of Her Majesty's Government, make extracts from the Journal, and state 'General G. says this or that,' while you are at full liberty to give your opinion, even if it differs from mine, but let Her Majesty's Government know *when I answer* and *when you answer*." Stewart, the night he left, wrote at my dictation a series of questions, which I answered on half-margin

[8] *Egypt*, 1884, *No.* 22.

of the same paper, and in which I said, "If Her Majesty's Government have not acted up to time when you get down, then it is too late, and it is no use doing anything."

A curious thing has happened; my friend Kitchener sent up the post; he wrapped the letters in some old newspapers (he gave me no news in his letter), the old newspapers were thrown out in the garden: there a clerk who knew some English found them blowing about, and gave them to the apothecary of the hospital, who knows English. The doctor found him reading them, saw date 15*th September*, and secured them for me; they are like gold, as you may imagine, since we have had no news since 24th February, 1884!

These papers gave us far more information than any of your letters. Did K. send them by accident or on purpose? Abyssinian ambassadors in London, Walmer Castle, &c.; my black troops beating back Ras Aloula at Keren, not recognizing the Hewitt Treaty, and killing 194 of the Abyssinians, at Keren, *vide Standard*, 1 and 15 September. Lord Wolseley seen off at Victoria Station, for the *Gordon Relief Expedition!! NO! for the relief of Soudan garrisons.* Khedive expressing delight at seeing Lord N., while during the audience the Khedive displayed great cordiality towards Lord N. Abdel Kader saying you would have four hard fights. I do not believe it.[9]

It appears that these newspapers were chucked out of the Palace; but that a man saw the papers were thrown out, and said to the cavass, "Give me those papers to wrap up tobacco." The cavass gave them, and the doctor's assistant going to the shop saw them, and seeing the date, took them, and then the doctor got them.

I think that the defeat of Ras Aloula, at Keren, if true, is splendid; when the Abyssinian Ambassadors were being enter-

[9] On the page opposite the one which contains this paragraph General Gordon has pasted cuttings from the paper to which he alludes. One of these cuttings says, "An official telegram received here from Wady Halfa states that, owing to the unprecedented lowness of the Nile, no confidence is felt in the practicability of hauling boats over the cataracts till the end of September." General Gordon's comment written against this is: "It was not a low Nile—it was an average Nile, only you were *too late*." —ED.

tained at Walmer Castle. The Hewitt Treaty, instead of aiding us, appears only to have added to our enemies.

It does seem wonderful if Her Majesty's Government have made a treaty with King John to give over Bogos, *i.e.* Keren, *i.e.* Senheit, to him (with other places), that orders were not sent to the fortress to evacuate; but if the papers we secured are true, that Ras Aloula was beaten back, it is evident no such orders were given. What an extraordinary state of affairs! Mitzakis, in his letter to Greek Consul here of date 25th of August, says, *that possession will be taken of Keren* (*i.e.* Senheit, *i.e.* Bogos) *at once*, and then we have the telegram from Massowa that Ras Aloula has *attacked* Keren, and lost heavily (*vide* the *Standard* of 1st September). By these papers, miraculously secured, I see we have made Minister of Interior Abdel Kader Pasha; according to all accounts up here, he is "Abdel Kader and the Forty Thieves *in one*." [10]

November 6.—Three horsemen and four footmen (Arabs) came opposite Bourré to-day on right bank of the Nile, and fired a few shots, and went off on our firing two shots from Krupp. Also, the Arabs came down with their guns to the White Nile end of Lines, and fired on the santals. A soldier of ours came in from Sheikh el Obeyed with his wife and child; he says *Sheikh el Obeyed died* four days ago (to the great relief of Sanderson), now we have only the *city* to deal with. Two more soldiers came in from Arabs at Omdurman. The Arabs fired seven rounds from their guns on the Lines near the White Nile. A post was captured by Sheikh el Obeyed (with European letters, coming from Kassala) just before his death; the porter of these letters was killed.

I expect that the naming of the expedition the Gordon Relief Expedition is because the fiction "*that Her Majesty's Government has no responsibility towards the Soudan and its garrisons*" is going to be held to, and that the object of the expedition *thus named*, will be considered as accomplished, if Kartoum is reached; but in that case, how can the sending up

[10] *See* 'Ismailia,' vol. i., p. 31.—Ed.

Stewart and me be explained? It was certainly because our Government thought they were responsible that we were sent; also if Her Majesty's Government has no responsibility, why did the troops attack Osman Digna, and relieve Tokar?

The Sheikh el Obeyed's death will be a heavy blow to the Arabs, for his following will no longer hold together.

Another soldier, with his wife, has come in at Omdurman.

These men report Sheikh el Obeyed dead, and that he is succeeded by his son Achmet, and that not more than 1000 or 1500 are with him; the Mahdi and the Arabs are against any attack on the Kartoum Lines. A good many Baggara are still with Mahdi, who is daily losing followers.

A soldier was severely wounded this morning at Bourré.

They say Sheikh el Obeyed died of chagrin. He would not go and see the Mahdi, who sent him word to give up all his property.

What a fury King John will be in, if it is true Keren has fired on and killed his men; he will swear it is Towfik's treachery. I wonder who are the Treaty Powers—Towfik and King John, or our Government and King John? Keren is only three days from Massowah, and it is not likely they would invent this telegram. It makes one laugh, to think of this addition to our enemies kindly given us.

The soldier (who came in with his wife and two children) says that Sheikh el Obeyed captured a post with the Arab and European letters; that he sat for some time in a comatose state, and then died; that his people are all dispersing. This is a great comfort, for we will have (D.V.) no fighting there. A soldier and his mother have come in. They say the Mahdi moved his camp to-day four hours further off. This evening the Arabs fired six times, with their guns, on the Lines near the White Nile.

I knew Harrison[11] would come. Extract A[12] on the other

[11] Colonel Harrison, C.B., C.M.G., R.E.—Ed.

[12] At this point General Gordon refers to the newspaper cuttings he has made and pasted in on the opposite page. The first reference is a comment on a telegram in the *Standard*, dated Suakin, August 30th, which runs as follows: "The *Jaffariyeh* overtook *not far* to the *south* of Suakin the three dhows *recently captured* by the rebels. The latter on being overtaken

side shows you, A, if you cannot protect dhows *now*, how will you do so if all the Soudan falls into the hands of the Mahdi? Also extract B, respecting rebellion in Hedjaz, will show all their lands are in a fermenting state, and will be well worked up by the Mahdi if he ever gets to Kartoum. Another man who came in says the Mahdi has drawn closer to Omdurman, and has *not gone further off.* I have an idea the Arabs will make a try to take the place. A soldier was wounded on the Lines near the White Nile this evening; he was fishing, and got hit. It certainly does seem most miraculous that Suakin should be besieged [13] and dhows captured close to it; no lesson has yet been taught these Arabs.

November 7.—We captured two cows to-day at Bourré. Mahdi's camp is now alongside of Faki Mustapha's, which is one hour and a half from the Fort Omdurman.

A large body of Arabs left, with caravan, the Dem of Faki Mustapha, in a north-west direction, towards the Gabra Wells, the Kababish head-quarters. The Dem of the Mahdi is not far from the river, by which I conjecture he has his Krupps in position near there. Church parade going on, average size. I am anxious for the flank of the Lines ending on the White Nile,[14] and have sent up a steamer to stay there. Four soldiers, one slave and two women came from the Arabs to Omdurman.

ran the boats aground, and escaped inland. The crew of the *Jaffariyeh* subsequently burnt the dhows." The italics are General Gordon's. (*b*) refers to a further telegram headed "Rebellion in Arabia," and dated Constantinople, Sunday night: "Fighting still going on in the Hedjaz between the Ottoman troops and the Arab tribes which have revolted against the authority of the Sultan's Government. Matters must be considered somewhat serious by the Porte, for the Government have decided to despatch to the seat of disturbance further reinforcements of Imperial troops to the extent of some two thousand, &c." In an account in a London paper of the departure of Lords Northbrook and Wolseley, General Gordon has marked certain penny-a-line passages, and in all cases where "Gordon Relief Expedition" occurs, he has drawn his pen through this and all expressions indicating that the Expeditionary Force comes to his relief.—ED.

[13] Suakin was at this time besieged on the land side.—ED.

[14] The Lines extended from the Blue to the White Nile, *i.e.* from Bourré to the Mogrim Fort.—ED.

The Mahdi means to attack Omdurman; he has received 120 camels of ammunition; Slatin is in chains. These men say the Mahdi and the Arabs have not the least intention of risking their skins against the fort, but will shove on the Black regulars they have captured. It is like fighting one's own flesh and blood; it is not fair warfare.[15]

If I am inclined to be vicious I have some little excuse, with women yelling for dhoora, under the Palace windows! Church parade to-day, and the approach nearer to us of the Mahdi's camp, and his sending for and getting 120 camel loads of ammunition, does not show he is wanting in confidence, for if he did fear, he would never have sent for 500,000 rounds of ammunition; or if he had sent for it, he would have stopped its coming, had he feared the advance. The fact is that the Tokar affair, with the non-following up of the victory,[16] has given him great confidence, which is strengthened by his Arabs capturing dhows and firing on the Lines of Suakin with impunity. Perhaps the non-firing on Suakin for three days (August 30) means that the Hadendowa Arabs have gone to assist Berber! I wonder whether it has not been observed, that Suakin is perfectly useless if the Soudan is in the hands of the Mahdi. I declare I think he (the Mahdi) has a fair chance of getting to Mecca, if the rebellion in the Hedjaz goes on, and he gets Kartoum.

The Mahdi may, and I daresay has good information from Cairo, as to the intention of the Expedition, or he may reason, "They will relieve Kartoum, leave me alone in my camp, and go back." If the Government instructions are definite, and going to be carried out at any cost, and if they are to the effect that a *Rapid Retreat* is to take place, then nothing more is to be said. All I ask for then, is to be put out of my place here,[17] to go on my way, and be no more employed. That is

[15] General Gordon had great admiration and affection for the Black regulars.—ED.

[16] *Baring to Lord Granville, March 6th,* 1884.

"With reference to General Graham's message communicated to Her Majesty's Secretary of State for War relative to the opening out of the Berber-Suakin route, I wish to say that I do not recommend any English troops being sent to Berber."—*Egypt, No.* 12, 1884, *No.* 214.

[17] *I.e.*, to be removed from my position as Governor-General.—ED.

not an unreasonable demand, for my mission here was a special one, and not obligatory, like a military duty, and in my position of Governor-General I am quite justified in having said and done everything for the people over whom I was placed by Towfik (following the "*fiction*" that he was independent) that I thought would secure them safety. *If it is determined to abandon* Sennaar and Kassala (following the *fiction* that the King of Abyssinia will look after them), also the Equator, *to their fate*, after their gallant defence, there is nothing more to be said, and the sooner this action is performed the better, if it is to be performed at all. To execute the operation, if it is confined to the evacuation of Kartoum, I can be of no possible use, and I do not care to wait and see the Mahdi walk in on your heels into Kartoum, which we have held against him for so many months; neither do I wish to see Her Majesty's forces dogged by these Arabs all the way to Wady Halfa, or to receive the remonstrances of those who have stuck to me. I am sure I have now written so fully on all these subjects that there can be little room for further discussion: you have to make up your mind and act. I have fully expressed my views and desires, and shall *take, or try to take*, very philosophically your decision; though I do most emphatically protest against this abandonment, which will lead to greater disasters, and is unworthy of our country.

The men who came in to-day say the Mahdi will attack Omdurman to-morrow. The following decisions have to be taken if the rapid retreat is carried out:—

1. Are the Government stores to be destroyed?

2. Are you prepared to supply transport for all who wish to go down?

3. Will you disarm the Shaggyeh ere you leave?

4. What will you do with the steamers?

I declare I should tremble to give these orders. As Governor-General *I never would do it.*

5. Will you write to Sennaar and Kassala, and inform them of what you mean to do, and exonerate me?

(A slave came in from the Arabs. He says the Arabs will

not attack the Lines; that the regulars are all over with the Mahdi on the left bank.)

6. Will you negotiate with the Mahdi (no use, I expect) *in re* the deliverance of the prisoners (European) he has with him?

7. Would you object to aiding the black troops to go to Sennaar and to fight out the question, with the view of saving Sennaar and Kassala garrisons?

Two soldiers and one slave came in from Arabs at Omdurman; they say the Mahdi will not attack directly, that Slatin is in chains for writing to Kartoum; also Saleh Pasha. The Arabs fired two rounds from their guns towards the Lines near the White Nile this evening. They fell short.

Supposing Kartoum evacuated, then Sennaar and Kassala fall. The Arabs now fire on the Lines at Suakin, and capture dhows in the Red Sea, and there is a revolt in the Hedjaz. What is to prevent the Mahdi's adherents gaining Mecca, where there are not 2,000 men? Once at Mecca, we may look out for squalls in Turkey, &c.

If decision is taken on the Rapid Retreat proceeding, the consuls should be warned on your arrival.

If the British Government had only given us Zubair Pasha in March, when I asked for him, we would not have lost Berber, and would never have wanted an expedition. We would have beaten the Mahdi without any exterior help; it is sad, when the Mahdi is moribund that we should by evacuation of Kartoum, raise him again. The defect I laboured under has been that I presented no rallying point to the people, not being of their nation or creed.[18]

The Arabs began musketry fire on Bourré at 1 P.M. and before this morning. It was quite like old times, when it used to go on for months. I never got accustomed to it, for I knew what troops we had, and it always murdered sleep.

[18] "In fact, things are not serious, although they may become so if delay occurs in sending Zebehr (Zubair). My weakness is that of being foreign and Christian and peaceful; and it is only by sending Zebehr that prejudice can be removed."—*General Gordon to Sir E. Baring, Kartoum, March 4th,* 1884. *Egypt, No.* 12. *Enclosure* 5, *in No.* 202.—ED.

November 8.—It must be obvious that if Zubair was with you, and installed as Governor-General, with a semi-independent position and a subsidy, in the present decaying position of the Mahdi, and your temporary presence, he would rally around him a huge following, who are now disgusted with the Mahdi and his dervishes, but who will be obliged to hold to him, because you evacuate; even those people with us, we perforce oblige to join the Mahdi. Zubair's installation would save you all the bother of the Sennaar evacuation. You would have only to stay up here a couple of months, and perhaps have to keep a detachment at Berber and Dongola (in order that Zubair might get up more munitions) for a time. You have now boats fitted for the communication by the Nile, *viâ* Abou Hamed, and Zubair could soon put them along the Nile in a chain. As for the slave trade,[19] the Mahdi will be ten times worse than Zubair, and you could make the payment of the subsidy (to Zubair) contingent on his not doing it on any vast scale. The Zubair solution is the sort of half-way house between rapid retreat and continued occupation, either by Turks or yourself.

The Mahdi could never get the people to rise against Zubair; it will be only because they are presented with no rallying point, and perforce they will join him if you leave. They never would have joined the Mahdi if Zubair had come up. It is only because Zubair was not here that Berber fell.

6.30 A.M.—Arabs streaming across from the White Nile to Bourré. Some Arabs on the right bank of the Blue Nile look

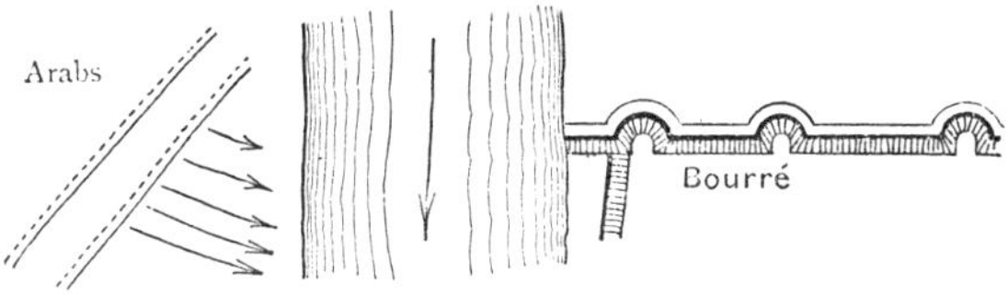

as if they are coming down that bank to the North Fort. I have ordered up the steamers *Ismailia* and *Husseinyeh*. The Arabs have found our weak point, *i.e.* prolongation of our Lines at Bourré, but the steamers will drive them out.

[19] See accounts of slave hunting in the Bahr Gazelle, App. U, *b*.

7.30 A.M.—Fight still going on, steamer coming up the river. 8.30 A.M.—Steamers went up and drove the Arabs off the right bank of the Blue Nile, who were enfilading our Lines. The firing, which has been continuous for four hours, has pretty well ceased. Up to this we have had no killed or wounded, I am glad to say. During the night the Arabs on the left bank of the White Nile (Mahdi's camp) fired three shells against the Lines ending on right bank of the White Nile. A soldier, *fellaheen*, is thought to have deserted to the Arabs last night. 9 A.M.—The Arabs have collected in the vicinity of Omdurman Fort a heap of cows, who seem drawing down towards the fort. I have ordered *Ismailia* to go down. I expect they will drive the cows on to the fort, and try and explode the mines. The Arabs on the White Nile are firing on the Lines with their Krupp. 10 A.M.—Arabs are leaving the vicinity of Bourré, and going back to their Dem near the White Nile. The Arabs near Omdurman village are firing across the river towards Mogrim.

The Austrian Consul when taking his morning ride was surprised at seeing two balls strike the water near, and so he returned. 10.45 A.M.—The *battles* are over, and all is quiet. What a worry all this is! The rockets from Omdurman drove back the advance of the cows; it was an ingenious attempt, if meant.[20]

I expect the Arabs fired away 30,000 rounds to-day. We had *one man killed* in small steamer, and *one wounded*; in the fort we had *two wounded*, and *one man* was wounded by bursting of rocket tube at Omdurman. I hate these rockets with sticks. Hale's are the only decent ones; not that the sticks have anything to do with their bursting. The composition in these climates shrinks away from the case, and the fire flares up the whole of the *exterior* and *interior* of the rocket. I expect we are going to have a series of these festivities, which are so wearisome. In the *Abbas* there was a heap of money orders, &c., connected with the merchants here, so sure did they think she would get down. Six soldiers came in from the

[20] *I.e.* driving the cows down with the view to their exploding the mines.—ED.

Arabs, also four slaves, who report the Arabs are thinking of putting a post at Halfeyeh. (I hope they will not.) The Mahdi has about 8,000 men of sorts with him. Slatin is in chains, also Saleh Pasha. Hussein Pasha Khalifa is great friends with the Mahdi. Omdurman captured sixteen cows when they came near the fort, also one slave. They killed one Arab. The men who came in say the Arabs mean to continue this day's festivities every day. They do not seem to care much about the advance of the expedition, or are uncommonly confident or ignorant. I do not at all enjoy the thought of these *daily festivities*, they are "abrutissant," as the Austrian Consul says.

It is very curious what a very little effect all our immense preparations at Dongola, &c., has had on the course of events; one may say they have not had up to the present the least, while I have weakened myself by sending down my steamers [21] and four hundred men (not, however, of the best quality). I expect we will have the *festivity* to-morrow on the White Nile end of the Lines, which is our weakest part. I must not be blamed at looking forward to a repetition of the past miseries; we truly have had a wearisome time for 241 days! Another soldier has come in; he says the Mahdi thought Kartoum could be bombarded from his new camp, but finds it cannot be done. If Lord Wolseley did say he hoped to relieve Kartoum before "*many months*," he must have a wonderful confidence in our powers of endurance, considering that *when* he is said to have made this utterance, we had been blockaded six-and-a-half months, and are now in our ninth month. I am quite sure of one thing, that the policy followed up till lately (and the policy which may be carried out, of abandoning Sennaar, etc.) is one which will act detrimentally on our army; for what officer, if he was in a fortress, could have any confidence that it might not be thought advisable to abandon him. Her Majesty's Government told me, or rather my friend Baring told me,[22]

[21] The steamers General Gordon sent to Metemma to assist the relieving force.—ED.

[22] *Sir E. Baring to Lord Granville.*

"Cairo, March 13th, 1884.

"I have instructed him (General Gordon) to hold on at Kartoum, until I can communicate further with Her Majesty's Government, and have told

I was not to leave Kartoum for the Equator until I had permission. I have his telegram (so that if it was possible, or if I could do it) if I did leave Kartoum, I should be acting against orders. This Soudan business will cost me £3,000[23] beyond my pay, at least, which I will not ask them or allow them to pay. I shall get it from others, and I shall get another £1000 to buy Stewart's Journal, if he has been killed or captured.

Another soldier is in from the Arabs at Omdurman, which fort has captured four more cows, that is twenty to-day (a cow is worth £20 in town !) £400 ! There is one thing which is quite incomprehensible. If it is right to send up an expedition now, why was it not right to send it up before? It is all very well to say one ought to consider the difficulties of the Government, but it is not easy to get over a feeling, that "a hope existed of no expedition being necessary, owing to our having fallen." As for myself, personally, I feel no particular rancour on the subject, but I own I do not care to show I like men, whoever they may be, who act in such a calculating way, and I do not think one is bound to act the hypocrite's part, and pretend to be friendly towards them. If a boy at Eton or Harrow acted towards his fellow in a similar way, I *think* he would be kicked, and *I am sure* he would deserve it. I know of no sort of parallel to all this in history, except it be David with Uriah the Hittite, and then there was an Eve in the case, who, I am not aware of, exists in this case. Remember, also, that I do not judge the question of abandoning the garrisons or not: what I judge is the indecision of Government. They did not dare say "abandon the garrison," so they prevented me leaving for the Equator, with the determination not to relieve me, and the *hope* (well ! I will not say what their hope was) ("March, April . . . August, why ! he ought to have surrendered; he said, six *months*")—there is my point of com-

him that he should on no account proceed to the Bahr Gazelle and Equatorial Provinces."—*Egypt*, 1884, *Nos.* 12–242.—ED.

[23] The English Government has, in the most liberal manner, stated it will meet any bills that General Gordon may have drawn upon it on his private account, and of which General Gordon has given a list. The Egyptian Government has acted in a similar manner with regard to moneys spent by General Gordon at Kartoum.—ED.

plaint. The second is the FICTION that it is the Egyptian Government which governs Egypt; it is a *silly* story, for every one sees through it. Can one imagine a greater farce than Lord Northbrook asking Towfik for the "assistance of Egyptian Government to carry out this, or that." I expect the two roared with laughter over it (sorry I cannot manage a sketch of the scene). (Baring would *never* laugh, *it is too serious*, like jesting in church.) The third grievance is that Treaty with Abyssinia, under the screen of the "FICTION," (if it is *true* it has been made); *however it is a dead letter*, I am glad to say.

November 9th.—Four soldiers, five slaves, of whom two are women, came in, from the Arabs to-day. Desultory firing *on* and *from* the Arabs at Omdurman, and the White Nile Lines.

Of the men who came in, one is a slave of Slatin Bey. The Mahdi does not mean to fight *direct;* the Khalifas [24] and the Arabs want to fight direct. Omdurman killed some of their men; the Arabs have munitions; Slatin is in chains. These men brought in their rifles. The Arabs lost at Bourré heavily; some bodies came floating down the river to-day. A soldier came in from the Arabs. A few Arabs came and fired on the fort at Omdurman, and wounded a slave in it.

The people up here would reason thus, if I attempted to leave: "You came up here, and had you not come, we should have some of us got away to Cairo, but we trusted in you to extricate us; we suffered and are suffering great privations, in order to hold the town. Had you not come we should have given in at once and obtained pardon; now we can, after our obstinate defence, expect no mercy from the Mahdi, who will avenge on us all the blood which has been spilt around Kartoum. You have taken our money and promised to repay us; all this goes for nought if you quit us; it is your bounden duty to stay by us, and to share our fate; if the British Government deserts us that is no reason for you to do so, after our having stood by you." I declare *positively*, and *once for all*,

[24] *I.e.* the Viziers.—ED.

that I will not leave the Soudan until every one who wants to go down is given the chance to do so, unless a government is established, which relieves me of the charge; therefore if any emissary or letter comes up here ordering me to come down, I WILL NOT OBEY IT, BUT WILL STAY HERE, AND FALL WITH THE TOWN, AND RUN ALL RISKS. These remarks are produced by the extraordinary confidence of the Arabs, combined with the Abyssinian Treaty and other significant remarks in the newspaper Kitchener sent me—Gordon Relief Expedition—who, I expect knows *more* than I do, and that "THAT MORE *is that the Expedition has come up for me personally.*" I hope, if things do come to the worst, and that the Expedition goes back, my steamers (*after abstraction* of the *Fellaheen troops*) will be sent back to this place, with £150,000 which Baring promised me! (or as much as I wanted), and as much provisions as can be possibly spared; also a gun to replace the one lost (or said to be lost) in the *Abbas* trying to *communicate with Europe* and *Cairo.* Unless Zubair is absolutely required at Cairo, I would also like him to come up, or (*to save appearances*) allowed to escape. I hope that Stewart's supposed death, if *by treachery*, will be avenged in a signal way, on the way down.[25]

A boy was captured during the cow business at Omdurman, but he said his father was with the Arabs, so I let him go back.

I have now got all the "telegrams," European, "*sent from*" and "*received in Soudan*" for "1883–84,"—splendid collection, full of interest. What would the *Standard* give for them? However, I think I can afford to be generous, and so I shall send them down with this Vol. VI.[26]

[25] Briefly summarised, what General Gordon says is: "If the Expeditionary Force has come for me alone, I will not return with it: it may go back, while I will remain here as Governor-General, and make the best use I can of the war material which belongs to me while I hold that position. If I am removed from that position by a Firman from the Khedive, I will still remain here, in a private capacity, and devote my life and energy to those people who have devoted their lives to me."—ED.

[26] Not received from the Government.—ED.

The fort at Omdurman captured twenty-one cows this evening; this is splendid—forty-one cows in two days.

The only original document I kept here, and which I was as near as possible giving to Stewart, is the Firman I have already mentioned, which I send with this,[27] proclaiming the abandonment of the Soudan by Towfik.[28] If the Mahdi had got this he would have crowed, though he may know of it, for I showed it, not knowing well its contents, to Hussein Pasha Khalifa (*vide* Stewart's Journal, which went down, and in which I criticise my having done so). I felt inclined to give it to Stewart, who, I felt confident, would get down, because I thought if found with me the Mahdi might say, "Why, you had the order to give up the country from Towfik, and you did not"; but, then, I thought as I shall be killed ere he takes the town it does not make much difference if here or with Stewart, so I kept it. I call attention to the fact that *every document* (except above-mentioned telegrams, of which Stewart had taken copies) went down with him (Stewart), and that will show how sure I felt that he and Power would get down, for otherwise, if I had doubted, I would never have let my original instructions go; now I have not a *single paper*. I cannot quote textually: all went with Stewart; but I have my memory, and I even give you the *Telegrams*. I have not written any despatch concerning Stewart or Power. I dare not, with my views, say their death is an evil;[29] if true, I am sorry for their friends and relations. Stewart was a brave, just, upright gentleman. Can one say more? Power was a chivalrous, brave, honest gentleman. Can one say more? Herbin, I liked very much; he was a most agreeable and gentlemanly Frenchman, and very sharp. The diplomatic

[27] Appendix Y.

[28] The Firman of Towfik respecting the troops withdrawing, which Gordon received 24th January, 1884, and which he did not promulgate.—ED.

[29] It is important there should be no misconstruction placed on these words. Had General Gordon thought their death would benefit the Soudan, he would never have said when he urged their going down, "I you go, you do me a great service, *i.e.* do the Soudan a great service. When he said, "I dare not, with my views, say their death is an evil," he merely meant, "I dare not say that two brave, just, upright men are no happier in the future life than in the present one."—ED.

. . . called him *names* in a telegram; but I found him fairly just,[30] though naturally with a French bias. For my part I cannot see what harm the French can do us if they had a voice in Egypt; and I can see much good arising from it. I declare if they had had a voice in Egypt the present state of affairs would never have existed. If you can find *no chivalry* in your own house, you had better borrow it from your neighbour. We fired yesterday 41,000 rounds of Remington ammunition, and we fired *less* than the Arabs.

November 10.—This morning forty Arabs came down near Omdurman Fort, and fired on it—angry about the capture of cows last evening.

One soldier and one slave came in from the Arabs at Omdurman. Seven Arabs on camels went across from the Blue Nile towards Halfeyeh. I fear a reconnoitring party, previous to their putting a post there. To-day is the day I expected we should have had some one of the Expedition here. Hicks' defeat was known at Cairo on the 21st or 22nd November, since which reinforcements to extent of nine persons reached this place (up to date) from Cairo—" for which the Egyptian Government" (according to the FICTION) " is solely and entirely to blame" !!!!!

The man who was wounded by the mine is dead. If man knew what the future would bring forth he would be pretty miserable. Look at the telegram on other side, written in December 1883.[31] I would not read those telegrams, or Stewart's Journal, for a good deal, when I think how we kept feeding on delusions for so many months. A soldier and slave have come in from the Arabs at Omdurman; five more soldiers and three slaves came in later on in the day; they say Slatin is released from his chains; that there is a rumour of the advance

[30] General Gordon means, in my opinion, "Fairly just in his political views." Herbin was the Editor of the *Bosphore Egyptien.*—Ed.

[31] This refers to a telegram sent by Colonel Coetlogon to Colonel Fraser Floyer, at Wady Halfa, at the above date, which runs: "No fresh news. Anxiously awaiting reinforcements." Underneath this General Gordon has written: "If Coetlogon had only been then informed that there was no intention to send reinforcements (further than nine persons) for (nearly) a year!"—Ed.

of the Expedition direct on Kartoum from Debbeh; that Luigi and Yusef, two priests, are still in Obeyed, having refused to become Muslim; that the Arabs lost heavily at Bourré the day before yesterday. Why Kitchener[32] did not tell me the route the Expedition would take is inexplicable, for it could have done no possible harm, seeing the Mahdi has his spies everywhere, and it was easy to have couched this information in terms I could have understood, and the Mahdi could not have understood. The fellaheen soldier did go to the Mahdi.[33]

November 11.—This morning, 6 A.M., 200 Arabs came to north of Omdurman Fort, and fired vollies towards the village of Tuti and the Fort; the Fort answered, and the footmen of the Arabs retreated; then the Arab horsemen made the footmen go back again, and so on four or five times; at last they retired. We had three soldiers and one woman wounded; only one wound was at all serious. Arabs must have fired five thousand rounds; evidently they do not wish much to fight. Nineteen Arabs came along the right bank of the White Nile from Halfeyeh to Goba, and captured a donkey; this even the Shaggyeh could not stand, and so I suppose one hundred sallied out and some fifteen horsemen; then came a running fight across the plain, but it was evident the horsemen would not head the Arabs; however, from the roof, it was evident four or five Arabs were killed, and the pursuit is still going on. You may imagine the Arabs have a good deal of confidence, for their nineteen men were distant at least ten miles of desert from their camp and were at *a*. They were going along *b b* when they were discovered with the captured donkey. Five at least of these Arabs got away. The Arabs are sure to come down to avenge this. Noon.—Arabs coming down from their camp. *Ismailia* getting steam up. North Fort reports (?) "Captures, 3 Remingtons! 3 spears! 3 swords! and the killing of 20? 5 got away?" The Arabs are halted on the

[32] Major Kitchener did not know it himself.—ED.

[33] A soldier previously mentioned, who was thought to have deserted.—ED.

sand hills. Five soldiers and one woman came in from the Arabs at Omdurman, report, "Arab rocket-tube broken; carriage of gun broken; the Arabs deserting; rumoured advance of the Expedition; quarrels going on; *Slatin in chains.*" The Shaggyeh say they killed twenty Arabs, but they only say they captured nine arms, so eleven must have been unarmed!!!

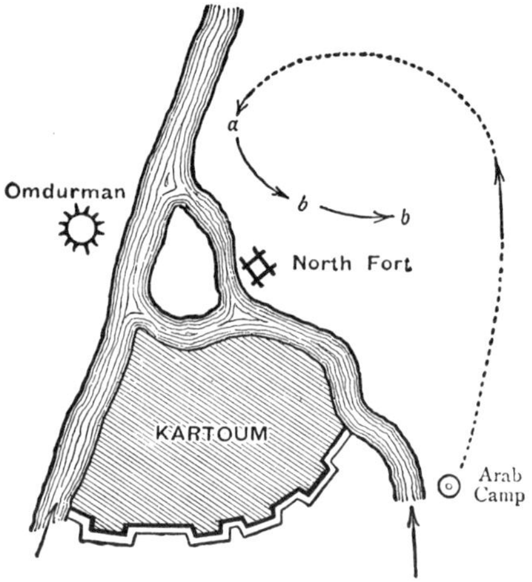

It appears 93,000 okes + 166,000 okes = 259,000 okes of biscuit have been stolen in the last year, only found out now; however, we have now quarter of a million okes, which will see us only for a month or so. It appears that more than thirty of the principal merchants are engaged in the above robbery of biscuit. The process is not finished. One of the greatest problems will be what to do with those Shaggyeh, those Cairo Bashi Bazouks and fellaheen soldiers, whose courage is about equal,—perhaps the palm is due to the Shaggyeh. The twenty cows I mentioned as captured by the men of Omdurman Fort (making up forty-one captured cows, page 217) *were driven in* by five soldiers *escaping from the Arabs* and *were not captured.* They do not stick at a lie (and, in this, resemble some people in high places I know). 259,000 okes of biscuit was a good haul, nearly 2½ million pounds: worth £26,000 now, or £9,000 in ordinary times.[34]

November 12.—Last night three slaves came into Omdurman. At 11 P.M. they reported Arabs meant to attack to-day at dawn. It was reported to me, but the telegraph clerk did not choose to tell me till 7 A.M. to-day. We had been called up at 5.30 A.M. by a violent fusillade at Omdurman. The Arabs came out in considerable force, and, as I had not been warned, the steamers had not steam up. From 5.30 A.M. to 8.30 Arabs came on and went back continually. All the cavalry were out; the expenditure of ammunition was immense. The Arabs had a gun or guns on the bank. Details further on, as the firing is still going on.

10.20 A.M.—For half-an-hour firing lulled, but then recommenced, and is still going on. The *Ismailia* was struck with a shell, but I hear is not seriously damaged. The *Husseinyeh* is aground (I feel much the want of my other steamers at Metemma). 11.15 A.M.—Firing has lulled; it was very heavy for the last three-quarters of an hour from *Ismailia* and Arabs; it is now desultory, and is dying away. *Husseinyeh* is still aground. The *Ismailia* is at anchor. What a six hours of anxiety for me, when I saw the shells strike the water near the steamers from the Arabs; imagine my feelings! We have £831 in specie and £42,800 in paper; and there is £14,600 in *paper* out in the town! I call this state of finance not bad, after more than eight months' blockade. The troops are owed half a month's pay, and even that can be scarcely called owed them, for I have given them stores, and beyond the regulations. Noon.—The firing has ceased, I am glad to say. I have lived *years* in these last *hours!* Had I lost the *Ismailia*, I should have lost the *Husseinyeh* (aground), and then Omdurman, and the North Fort! And then the Town! 1 P.M.—The Arabs are firing on the steamers with their two guns. The *Husseinyeh still aground;* that is the reason of it. Firing, 1.30 P.M., now has ceased. The *Ismailia*, struck by three shells, had one

[34] This recovery of biscuit enabled General Gordon to hold Kartoum until the gates were treacherously opened to the enemy.—ED

man killed, fifteen wounded on board of her; she did really very well. I boxed the telegraph clerk's ears for not giving me the telegram last night (after repeated orders that no consideration was to prevent his coming to me); and then, as my conscience pricked me, I gave him $5. He said he did not mind if I killed him—I was his father (a chocolate-coloured youth of twenty). I know all this is brutal—*abrutissant*, as Hansall calls it—but what is one to do? If you cut their pay, you hurt their families. I am an advocate for summary and quick punishment, which hurts only the defaulter. Had this clerk warned me, of course at daybreak, the steamers would have had their steam up, and been ready. We have a Krupp at Mogrim Fort. Ferratch Pasha reports he has dismounted one of the Arab guns. The Arabs had a show of four hundred horsemen, who kept far off. Telegraph was, and is, interrupted between this and the Omdurman Fort (whether by bullet or otherwise is not known as yet). Considering that the Arab mountain gun can (and has) made holes *two feet square* in the steamer, my anxiety is not to be wondered at. (I feel as if I had walked thirty miles.) We fired eighty-three rounds of Krupp at the Arabs from Mogrim, forty-three rockets. The Arabs fired three hundred and seventy rounds from their guns at the steamers. As for ammunition (Remington), we fired from *our steamers*, forts, &c., fifty thousand rounds; and I certainly think the Arabs fired as much. Omdurman certainly was "OVER-EAGER TO FIRE ON THE ENEMY"[35] in the early dawn, and consequently wasted ammunition. This ends the greatest battle (*as yet*) of our second blockade. Spies (of last night) say it was undertaken against the Mahdi's wish, by his Khalifa or Vizier, who persuaded him to allow it. During all through, the Arabs of the South and East never moved a peg. Like the Chinese, one may calculate, they will never assist one another.

This is our *first* encounter with the Mahdi's personal troops. One tumbles at 3 A.M. into a troubled sleep; a drum beats—tup! tup! tup! It comes into a dream, but after a few moments one becomes more awake, and it is revealed to the

[35] *Vide* General Graham's despatch *in re* Black Watch.—ED.

brain that *one is in Kartoum.* The next query is, where is this tup, tupping going on? A hope arises it will die away. No, it goes on, and increases in intensity. The thought strikes one, "Have they enough ammunition?" (the excuse of bad soldiers). One exerts oneself. At last, it is no use, up one must get, and go on to the roof of the Palace; then telegrams, orders, swearing, and cursing goes on till about 9 A.M. Men may say what they like about glorious war, but to me it is a horrid nuisance (if it is permitted to say anything is a nuisance which comes on us). I saw that poor little beast the *Husseinyeh* (a Thames launch) fall back, stern foremost, under a terrific fire of breechloaders. I saw a shell strike the water at her bows; I saw her stop and puff off steam, and I gave the glass to my boy, *sickened unto death*, and I will say my thoughts turned on . . . more than on anyone, and they are not beneficent towards him. My boy (he is thirty) said, "*Husseinyeh is sick.*" I knew it, but said quietly, "Go down and telegraph to Mogrim,[36] 'Is *Husseinyeh* sick?'" Answer, "No." I asked again; answer, "No." Then telegraph said, "She was aground."

2.45 P.M. The *Ismailia* tried to take *Husseinyeh* off, and got struck twice, in addition to the three times before mentioned, with shells, so she desisted from the attempt. The Arabs are firing on the *Husseinyeh.* I have ordered the Krupp of Mogrim to play on the Arab guns, and shall wait till night to take off the *Husseinyeh.* She is nearer to the *left* bank than to the *right* bank; it is not clear if she is aground or half sunk (equally a trouble). 3.30 P.M. The Arabs are bringing their guns nearer to the aground or half-sunken *Husseinyeh.* The *Ismailia* reports that the two last shells have done her no material damage. 4.30 P.M. The Arabs have now three guns bearing on the *Husseinyeh.* 6 P.M. The firing has ceased. I hope to get the *Husseinyeh* off at night. 7 P.M. The Arabs keep up a dropping fire on the *Husseinyeh,* who, I hear, has two shell holes in her, and has six men, including the captain, wounded. I must say the Arabs to-day showed the greatest of

[36] Fort Mogrim.—ED.

pluck; over and over again they returned to the attack, though overwhelmed with the musketry fire of the castellated *Ismailia.* I think they must have lost heavily, for at times they were in dense groups. I believe that by the *Arabs* we may understand *our own regulars captured in Kordofan and Darfur, &c.* We are going to get the *Husseinyeh* off to-night *if we can.* No Royal Navy vessels would have behaved better than the *Ismailia* to-day; she passed and repassed the Arab guns upwards of twenty times, when any one well-placed shell would have sunk her. Whether the crew knew it or not does not matter. *I did, and felt comfortable accordingly.* The Arab guns were not 1200 yards distant from her, and even less at times. She was struck five times with shell. Remember that the *Ismailia* is only a superior penny boat, and that the Egyptian mountain gun is as superior to our wretched seven-pounders as a three-pounder is to a twelve-pounder Howitzer, both for range and for effect. You want a gun to make a hole, not a gimlet-hole, which these seven pounders do, and what wearisome work to carry them!

All this worry is (humanly speaking) due to that chocolate-coloured clerk of the telegraph not warning me. This evening there was an ominous sign that the Arabs on the Blue Nile knew of our troubles with the *Husseinyeh.* They came up against Bourré, but two gunshots drove them off. At 4 P.M. the Arabs on the right bank of the White Nile fired twelve shells against the Lines, and opened a fire of musketry for a short time, but did no harm. I have given half a month's pay to the *Ismailia* and to the *Husseinyeh* crews, and $2 for the men who have gone to get the latter off; she is *not half sunk*, but *is aground.* There is (8 P.M.) a fire on the left bank of the White Nile, opposite to Halfeyeh. The Arabs got into the ditch of the entrenched camp at Omdurman, which is theirs. We only occupy the Fort, X. Hicks' army were in this entrenched camp. Arabs came to Y.

8.15 P.M. The Arabs have still their guns on the river bank, and are firing at the *Husseinyeh*, whom I am trying, by my men, to get off. Evidently they are not cowed, for generally they take their guns back at night to their camp. Report from *Husseinyeh* steamer:—10.20 P.M., Wounded, 6; killed, 3; efforts as yet are ineffectual as to taking off the steamer *Husseinyeh*.

November 13.—The *Ismailia*, 2 A.M., got struck by *two shells* (?)[37] going to take off the *Husseinyeh*, so we took her gun out, and her crew, and have left her. At 5.30 A.M., the Arabs commenced firing on the Lines at Bourré, and 7 A.M. I see they are coming across to Goba, bringing a gun with them.

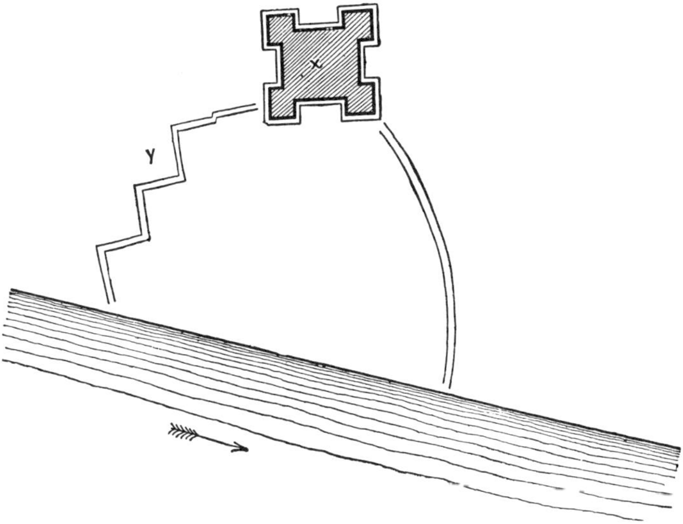

The Arabs at Omdurman are quiet. The Arabs have fired five times with their gun at the Omdurman Fort. The Arabs have got their gun at the village outside Sheikh Ali, near the end of the Lines on the White Nile, and have fired shells at the Lines. Our telegraph was cut yesterday evening with Omdurman Fort, and cannot be repaired (8 A.M.) for the Arabs are shelling that fort. The Arabs, on the North Side, have their gun on the low sandhills some 4,000 yards off, and are shelling us; musketry firing going on at Bourré. The Arabs had their guns last

[37] I expect that this story of *Ismailia* being again struck twice is a fib!

night defending the approach to the *Husseinyeh.* We are repairing the *Ismailia;* the barricade of the steersman of the *Husseinyeh* got struck by a shell. We raised a parapet on the river bank to defend any approach of the Arabs to *Husseinyeh.* Omdurman had yesterday a quarter of a million cartridges—Remington.

Omdurman Fort has one and a half month's supply of food and water; it was a fault to place it so far from the river;[38] yesterday it had not its flag up; to-day it has. The Arabs have sent 250 men to Goba; but the village Hogali, which was the one close to the Palace, having been levelled, they are too far off to do us any harm. There is a report in town the Arabs

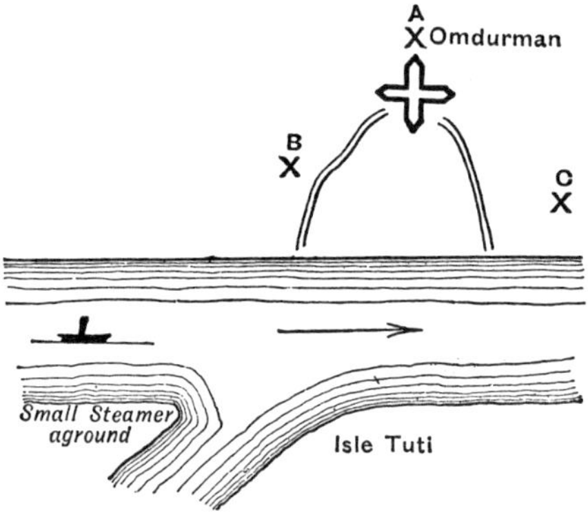

say they will enter it to-morrow, and say their prayers in the mosque on Friday. The Arabs at Goba are wasting a lot of ammunition (Remington), their bullets do not reach us.[39] They will be bothered for water, for we filled up all the wells in Goba. 9.15 A.M. The Arabs have returned from Goba. 10 A.M. They have made a long *detour*,[40] and have gone to the prolongation of our Lines at Bourré, on the right bank of the Blue Nile, where they are firing heavily. I expect we fired 50,000 rounds yesterday, and the Arabs rather more, while to-day the

[38] *i.e.* 1,200 yards.—Ed.
[39] Goba is rather more than a mile from the Palace of Kartoum.—Ed.
[40] *i.e.* to escape the guns of the North Fort.—Ed.

Arabs have fired a great deal. We calculate that with Hicks' army was lost 1,000,000 cartridges, and now it is a year ago, during which time, with the firing there and elsewhere during a year, two-thirds of that million must have been expended, and they have no means to renew the cartridges; they cannot have much more than 300,000 rounds.

The Arabs have now gone from opposite Bourré (11 A.M.), having fired a nice lot of ammunition, and hurt no one in the Fort. Omdurman Fort is still cut off from us; Arabs at A B C. The Arabs certainly got the best of it yesterday, though I expect they paid for it. It appears the *Husseinyeh* got aground through the captain, who was afterwards wounded, not doing what the Reis told him. Fortunately I had foreseen the likelihood of the fort at Omdurman being cut off, and had provisioned it. If the Expedition comes at all, it ought to be here before long. We had fifteen men wounded yesterday, three rather dangerously, and seven were killed. I never feel anxious about any of the fights, except when the steamers are engaged, and then I own I am on tenter-hooks as long as they are out. 1 P.M. The Arabs have got four guns down on the river, and are firing across the river at the Mogrim Fort, which is answering by Krupp and rockets. We are not fortunate with the little steamers I had brought out in sections from England; we have lost, at any rate *temporarily*, one, the *Husseinyeh*; another, the *Abbas*, where is she? And the Arabs have the third, the *Mahomet Ali*, on the Blue Nile. The Arabs fired four guns on the Lines near the White Nile this morning (they fired sixty rounds). Musketry (3 P.M.) going on across river between our men and the Arabs. Certainly we have been left to almost the very last extremity, and I declare I think the year will be complete, from the time Cairo heard of Hicks' defeat, to the time of the Relief Expedition arriving here!!! And I am sure, if an enquiry was made, it would be made out no one was to blame.

The Arabs have eighteen boats plying as ferry from one side of the White Nile to the other. They may try with these boats to get hold of the *Husseinyeh*, or else to board her; there are only some bags of biscuits on board; but as the steamer is blinded, if Arabs once get on board, it would be very difficult to dislodge them, unless we sink the steamer, for they will find the biscuit and so have plenty to eat. Fifteen shells fell into the town this morning, but did no harm.

Nearly all the Arab force which came on the north side to-day were slaves, with them perhaps forty horsemen Arabs. Eventually the Arabs will find out the inconvenience of these Mamelukes.[41] Four bullets came from the Arabs to the Palace to-day—2,800 yards—and came with a good force. A native of Kartoum came and complained he had had nothing to eat for himself and family for four days; they found eight ardebs of dhoora in his house; in another house forty ardebs were found.

November 14.—8 A.M. The Arabs on both sides of the Blue Nile began firing on Bourré at 5.30 A.M., and it is going on now. They kept up for more than quarter of an hour a continuous roll of fire, and have wasted a precious lot of ammunition. They brought down one of their guns and fired a few rounds. Up to this time no one is wounded at Bourré.

Two men crossed from Omdurman, and report Ferratch Ullah as all right, and as having no men wounded in the fort. The Arabs fired their guns on the fort this morning.

An Arab tried to swim off to the *Husseinyeh*, whom (*they say?*) our men shot.

I wonder where King John is, with his 200,000 soldiers?

I argue thus: 1. It would be impossible for the Expeditionary Force, once having come to Dongola, not to move up to Metemma, or to the vicinity of Berber. 2. That once at Metemma, or at Berber, they will find the steamers, and consequently must communicate with Kartoum. 3. Once they communicate with Kartoum they must assume the responsibility of the government of that place (of course, when once that responsibility is assumed, the decision as to what they will do rests with them). 4. It is impossible for them to loiter long on the road between Dongola (or Debbeh) and Metemma.

[41] *i.e.* mounted Arabs.—ED.

5. It will be impossible for them, *owing to the events of the last few days*,[42] to avoid collision with the Arabs around Kartoum. A week ago it might have been possible, but now the Arabs are too close to the town to avoid it. Omdurman Fort being cut off will oblige action being taken to re-open communications. The Arabs *may run away*, but, somehow, since a few days, I doubt it.

A soldier came in from the North Fort from the Arabs this morning.

Another fib—they told me that they had got everything out of the *Husseinyeh* but the biscuit: it appears that the ammunition is still in her.

No church parade on the right bank of Nile (Kalakla), but

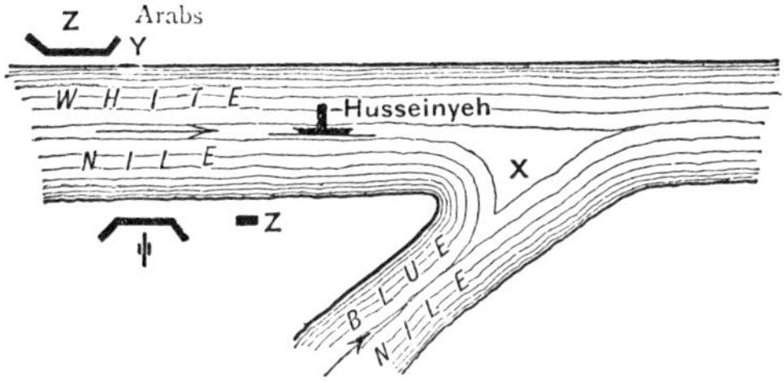

one is going on at Giraffe on the Blue Nile. It appears last night that a boat went off to the *Husseinyeh*, that the men in this boat got frightened at the challenge of our own men and jumped into the water, and left their boat. I went down to Mogrim, and found the *Ismailia* has been struck by seven shells, and is pockmarked with bullets all over. The Arabs (some 400 rifles) line a long trench opposite the *Husseinyeh*: we have erected a parapet on our side opposite her. The Arabs have four guns, from which they kept up a desultory fire, doing no harm. The Arabs' rifle-fire is continuous and futile, ours is less heavy, but I expect equally futile, for the Arabs keep under cover. The Arabs fired regular volleys, upwards of five, while I was there: they appear to delight in the noise. The *Husseinyeh* is about 1,200 yards from the

42 *i.e.* it would have been possible had the force started earlier.—ED.

point X, 800 yards from Y, and 1,000 yards to Z, where my trench is.

Husseinyeh lies just off the end of the entrenchment of Omdurman *entrenched camp.*

She has her stern to the Arabs.

A soldier came in to the North Fort from the Arabs on the

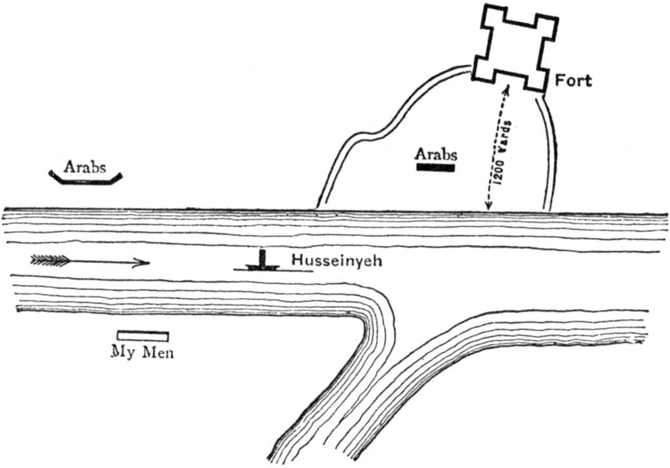

Blue Nile, and reports that a man with letters came the night before last to the fort of Omdurman and called out to the sentries, but before they could let him into the Fort the Arabs captured him and the letters. I hope to be able to-night to communicate by bugle sounds with Omdurman Fort.

Revised list of the robbery; 172,000 okes of biscuit they change every day. We have to-day in the magazine 240,000 okes of biscuit, 1,326 ardebs of dhoora. Have ordered 1,000 okes to be given away, and 4,000 okes to be sold.

The Omdurman Fort is ill placed, as it cannot see the ground down to the river, and is distant 1,200 yards from the river. The Arabs on left bank of the White Nile opposite *Husseinyeh* number 500 (I expect all are my soldiers), and they are so far away from any reserve that it would be easy to crush them before they were aided, *if we dared to try*, which we do not. I was at Mogrim Fort for half an hour, during which time the Arabs fired, as I calculated, fifteen shells and 8,000 rounds, and no one was touched; indeed, where their bullets went I could not see nor hear. No stores could stand that, and up to sundown they were still at it with rifles and guns. Bourré, in spite of all the heavy firing, has no casualties; 80,000 rounds would scarcely cover our *united* expenditure to-day.

Reports from the Arabs at different times said the Mahdi had brought 200 (some say 120) camel loads of ammunition (Remingtons) from Obeyed—say 200, and say that each camel carried 2 boxes, each box 1000, so that he had, before he began, 800,000 rounds; he must have expended in the last week 250,000 to 300,000 rounds, and has left 550,000 rounds or 500,000 rounds. I do not expect he has 200,000 rounds left, which is his weekly expenditure if he goes on at the rate he is going now. We turn out on an average 40,000 rounds a week, and are well ahead of our requirements. Looking at the Arab gunners with my telescope, they never seem to bother themselves about aim, but just to load and fire. It is, of course, different when the steamers are in action. The officer in command of Mogrim Fort was wounded in the arm at sundown. The captain of *Husseinyeh* died to-day. We suppose that on board the *Husseinyeh* are the men I mentioned as having jumped out of the boat last night on the challenge of the sentry, also a soldier of Omdurman who swam off to her with letters from Ferratch Bey, commandant of the fort, so we are sending off a boat to *Husseinyeh* to take them off. A workman in the arsenal was wounded to-day by a ball from Bourré, distant 2,300 yards. The Arab fire on Bourré renders the vicinity of the Palace far more dangerous than Bourré, the balls fall so plentifully around the Mudirat, which is close by, that the Greek consul was obliged to lay to for some time till the firing ceased: it is at least 2,500 to 3,000 yards from the Palace to the place the Arabs fire from.

We have put the gun of the steamer *Ismailia* on the bank of the Nile, to cover the approach to the *Husseinyeh*; the Greek consul says "the balls fall like water" on the road leading to the Palace. I believe a good deal, if you have the ammunition, in the dropping fire of rifles, even at three thousand yards; the balls that fell on the Palace are fairly flattened, showing they have plenty of life to kill. The buglers have communicated with Fort Omdurman, who are all well. 8 P.M. to-morrow, we will have signals with flags. Out of evil comes good—if *Husseinyeh* was not aground, the Arabs, instead of concentrating their force and attention on her, would have devoted it on the fort, which, cut off, would suffer; as it is now, the fort is unmolested. Bullets rained on the hospital yesterday and to-day, but did no harm! I calculate that the *Ismailia* has two thousand bullet marks on her.

November 15.—Last night we sent off a boat to the *Husseinyeh*, and took off the soldier of Ferratch Ullah Bey, who had come from Omdurman, also the ten men who jumped into the water from their boat the night before. Ferratch Ullah writes he is all well; he wants ammunition!!! he had 230,000 rounds three days ago: he says he has now 150,000 rounds, also he has regulars, 470, each 100 rounds, 47,000; he has irregulars, 170, each 200 rounds, 34,000 altogether; in magazine of fort, 150,000 rounds, and with the men 81,000; total ammunition in Fort, 231,000 rounds: yet he calls for ammunition!!! Hicks took 1,000,000. The buglers communicated well with the fort at Omdurman; buglers then spoke the soldiers on Mahdi's side, but they did not answer; we invited them to come over to us.

The five feluccas, which took the men off the *Husseinyeh*, were not seen by the Arabs. I sent an engineer to take off the steam-valves of the *Husseinyeh;* the five feluccas took off, *this time*, everything from *Husseinyeh*, biscuit, ammunition, &c., &c. It appears that the Arabs, who were watching the *Husseinyeh*, had gone off to Kerowé, opposite Halfeyeh; but this is doubtful.

At dawn the Arabs opened a heavy fire with the usual futile efforts on Bourré, also they fired with gun and musketry on Omdurman Fort.

At Omdurman Fort they have had, in the last few days, four killed and sixteen wounded.

A shell from the Arabs struck *Husseinyeh* yesterday, but did no harm, for she is well aground. No wounded at Bourré to-day by the Arab fire.

The Bimbashi, who was wounded in the arm yesterday evening, was lying on his angarep[43] when he was wounded: he thought it a secure place; he died to-day.

The Arabs from Omdurman side of the river have kept up a desultory fire of guns and musketry all day; but at sundown the fire was much heavier, and if the Arabs go on like that for many days, they will be out of ammunition, both gun and rifle.

It has turned out a benefit for us the *Husseinyeh* going aground, for the attention of the Arabs is devoted to her, and they fire scarcely at all on the fort at Omdurman; even if we had her, she could do little good: the other little steamer will be completed in twelve days.

I think I have been rather unjust towards the fellaheen soldier, for though he is not brave enough to take the field, he has done good work on board the steamers, and a good many of their officers and men have been killed and wounded (thanks to the policy that has been followed elsewhere) in a quarrel which does not concern them. These remarks are produced by a visit I made to the hospital to-day, when I saw the mass of the wounded were fellaheen soldiers, whom I put in the steamers, because, when in action, they could not run away, while I kept the blacks for the defence of the Lines. As I was leaving the hospital to-day, a dead man was carried out by four men in chains (convicts) on a stretcher, accompanied by two soldiers with fixed bayonets—to be buried as a dog! This is part of the glory of war! According to the demands for ammunition, we are firing away 40,000 rounds per diem; the officers ask for fresh Remingtons, as by the constant firing those they have are out of order. I feel quite indifferent, for, if not relieved for a month, our food supply fails, and even at the above rate of expenditure of ammunition we have fifty days' cartridges. I like to go down with our colours flying. The Arabs are quite equalling us in expenditure, and they have no

[43] *i.e.* a bedstead.—ED.

reserve of ammunition, or means of repairing their arms. I am going to call the new steamer the *Zubair*, after Zubair Pasha Rahama;[44] the town wanted it called after me, but I said, "I have put most of you in prison and otherwise bullied you, and I have no fear of your forgetting me."

November 16.—The Arabs quiet, little firing at Mogrim; I expect the Mahdi has found out that his men have been making away with his ammunition too fast, even as I have found it out. A small fantasie or church parade is going on near the Mahdi's camp this morning.

The Arabs at the Mahdi's camp have moved the camp further inland; they did this at sundown yesterday. It is on the *tapis* that they may retire altogether; if so it will be glorious. The camp opposite the Lines on South is much diminished, not more than five or six tents. The Arabs there have gone to Giraffe and El foun on the Blue Nile. With the exception of the Arab guns firing on Mogrim, and our guns answering, everything is quiet to-day. In a couple of hours the Arabs fired sixteen shells without the least effect. Their gun ammunition must be nearly expended. A woman was slightly wounded at Bourré this morning. The Arabs work on a regular principle with the captured black troops. They know that they will escape to us if they can, in the first instance, so they keep them on short rations, and promise them full rations if they fight us. They then force them into contact with us for (at first) appearance sake and to get the full rations; when in contact with us we fire on and kill some of them, then their black blood gets up, and they retaliate *en bonne volonté*, and are egged on by the Arabs, who say to them, "Now you have fired on the Government troops you are in for it; the Government will never pardon you," and so thus we get no more deserters. It was the same way at Bourré, before we fired on the Arabs we got plenty of deserters, but when once we gave them a slating no more came in; they are compromised with the

[44] Not because General Gordon held Zubair in esteem, but as a record of how often he had asked for his presence, and of how closely his absence was connected with the welfare of the Soudan.—ED.

Mahdi's cause, and afraid of us if they come in. The Janissaries were the children of Christian parents captured when young, and they fought with vigour against the Christians when they grew up. Scarcely ever is the true Arab in the front, so they say.

We have ninety men in hospital at present, of which fifty-four are wounded. We had one man killed, and one wounded at Mogrim to-day. A woman was wounded in the town yesterday. Report in town says seventy of our captured soldiers have deserted and have entered the fort at Omdurman.

Having been assured by my officers that it was a most terrible risk even to go along the bank near the *Husseinyeh*, even by night, owing to the Arabs' rifle fire, and being extremely sceptical of the past (putting down the information given me as an excuse for doing nothing towards taking off the *Husseinyeh* the first night she got aground; and also as an effort to enhance the danger and daring of those men who did take off the ammunition, &c., the night before last), I went down to-night at 11.30 and found it was all a myth, and that if I wished I could take her off without any risk. However, as she is a target and occupies the attention of the Arabs, who leave the fort at Omdurman alone in consequence of her, I shall leave her as she is. Of course, needless to say, I found all the officers in charge absent; *they had gone home to bed!* However, I am not put out at it. They are, as a rule, the *very feeblest of the conies*, and nothing will change their nature. The *Husseinyeh* lies close to the junction of the White and Blue Niles, and one may say is within our Lines.

I daresay this is a repetition, but if we do get out of this mess it is a miracle, for I do not think a slacker lot of officers ever could be found, but a bad workman always complains of his tools. A good workman turns out good work however rotten his tools may be.

November 17.—It is really amusing to find (when one can scarcely call one's life one's own) one's servant, *already* with one wife (which most men find is enough), coming and asking for leave for three days, in order to take another wife. Yet such was the case, a few days ago, with one of my servants.

The Arabs this morning fired from their guns from Bourré, from the White Nile, and from Omdurman; they are also keeping up a musketry fire. At the Mahdi's camp they had another "church parade" to-day. I suppose they are working up their fanaticism. The Arabs have a Nordenfeldt opposite the little steamer *Husseinyeh.* The town people are pleased at the new steamer being called the *Zubair;* the Anti-Slave Society will be furious.[45] If Zubair had come up, I should have had news long before now.[46] It does seem ridiculous that when our apparent policy is to hand over the Soudan to the Mahdi, who with his people are far more slave hunters than Zubair ever would be, we should not have utilized this man in this expedition. There are about two hundred people on the Isle of Tuti, yet last night an Arab came over, killed a man and carried off three donkeys; they do not deserve the name of men. How Zubair would touch up these fellows; he would go to Tuti and give all the men between eighteen and fifty at least thirty blows of Kourbatch. I am obliged to content myself with lamentations.

("Count the months—March, April, May, June, July, August, September, October, and half November! Why, I declare, it is a breach of contract." [47])

If it be true about the repulse of the Abyssinians at Keren, I expect there were roars of laughter in Downing Street at the greenness of His Majesty the Emperor John (as Mitzakis calls him). It is very odd, but we have had no news of Kassala

[45] "The Committee are unanimous in the feeling that countenance in any shape for such an individual (*i.e.* Zubair) would be a degredation to England and a scandal to Europe."—*Mr. Sturge to Earl Granville, British and Foreign Anti-Slavery Society, March* 10*th*, 1884.—Ed.

[46] *i.e.* Zubair would have been able to obtain it for me.—Ed.

[47] "You will bear in mind the main end to be pursued is the evacuation of the Soudan.

"In undertaking this difficult task which now lies before you, you may feel assured that no effort will be wanting on the part of the Cairo authorities, whether English or Egyptian, to afford you all the co-operation and support in their power."—*Sir E. Baring to Major-General Gordon, Inclosure in Egypt No.* 6.—Ed.

for months, not since September. Baring to Egerton. "You said *it was too dreadful;* what will you say when I tell you he has made sketches of *you* and ME? and how, horrible to relate, put them in his demi-official journal; and we can do *absolutely* nothing, for if he is attacked as being a British officer, he says he made the sketches as Governor-General, and *vice versâ.*"

Independent of my regret for Stewart, the loss of his Journal affects me, for there were lots of things in it of interest. All the Powers (including the Pope, and excluding England and France) were appealed to in a touching memo., to raise an auxiliary force under Baker, &c., &c., and to stop the wave of Dervish fanaticism. I also wrote to the Sultan. I do not know if these appeals ever got through, but Stewart had them all copied in his Journal. Events and my discourses had almost made him latterly as vicious as I am. Baring's ears ought to have burned for the last eight months, he was nicely dissected by us all (Power aiding). If Herbin, the French Consul, had got down Baring would have had a time of it, for Herbin says that Barère, the French minister, went to Baring before Herbin left, and Baring did not tell (Barère) any thing about the evacuation of the Soudan. Of course Baring will shelter himself under the "fiction" that he, as British minister, had nothing to do with it. What a farce, if it did not deal with men's lives.

When one thinks that Baring works harder than a galley slave for such wretched results, one ought to pity him.

I have sent 150 of these superior troops (the Shaggyeh), to the Isle of Tuti, in consequence of the outrage of last night (which I do not believe in, *for that one man came over and killed another man, and carried off three donkeys in a small boat* is absurd). However, the Shaggyeh are safer in the Isle of Tuti than in the North Fort. At 7 P.M. the Arabs came down and fired on Bourré from the left bank of the Blue Nile. The officer (a full colonel of *my* creation), asks me "Is he to fire back?" I said, "Better *not* ask me that question, unless you want to catch it." 7.15 P.M. Omdurman Fort is firing away. I certainly lay claim to having commanded, more often than any other man, cowardly troops, but this experience of 1884 beats all past experiences; the worst of the matter is, that you cannot believe one word the officers say. With respect to the major who was absent from the Fort Mogrim last night, he says he was in the telegraph station, which is a direct falsehood. However, I did nothing to him, more than call him a liar, which he probably considers a compliment. A sort of adjutant-major, whom I had borne with for a long time, told me *two cold lies* in *two days*, so I bundled him out. Can it be wondered at that, after nine months and more of this sort of military worry, and ditto of civil worry, I am heartily sick of the whole affair, and provided *I* am not made a party (and I *will not be*) to a shabby retreat, I should be glad to be out of this place.

The Arabs fired fifteen shells against the Fort of Omdurman; only one seemed to strike the keep; one man was wounded at Mogrim with the splinter of a shell. The Arab gun-carriages must be in bad state of repair, for our carpenters are continually at work making new ones, and the Arabs have no means of so doing. The *Husseinyeh* lies just off the division of the White and the Blue Niles, and not as I showed her position, page 229. All the scratched out portion is abuse of Baring.[48] Some one said, "If you feel angry, then write your angry letter, and then tear it up." It certainly does relieve the mind to write one's bile, and it is good also to scratch it out, for I dare say Baring is doing his duty better than I am; he is certainly more patriotic, if patriotism consists in obedience to the existing Government of one's country.

Doctor reports that the shells and bullets of the Arabs fell all around the hospital this morning, but did no harm, they came from Bourré.

November 18.—Everything quiet all round the place; they fired a few shots with their guns at the Lines near the White Nile.

11.30 A.M. The Arabs on the right bank of the Blue Nile have moved towards the north, and, from the number of porters, I expect they are going to form a camp to the north.

[48] General Gordon has here drawn his pen through some dozen lines of his journal.—ED.

It may be turned as one likes; three prominent undeniable facts exist. Her Majesty's Government refused to help Egypt with respect to the Soudan, refused to let Egypt help herself, and refused to allow any other Power to help her: this cannot be disputed or explained away. Lord Dufferin's despatch was "hands off." [49] The resignation of Cherif was the prohibition of allowing Egypt to help herself. This tardy succour under pressure, and Baring's despatch, establishes the unwillingness to help.

The Arabs have settled down in the old Dem they occupied in March last!! opposite the Palace, and which they evacuated in August; their vicinity will give us more spies, which we have lacked hitherto; this proceeding does not show as if they were much appalled at the advance of the Expeditionary Force. On the 12th March they pitched their tents on the very spot they are pitching them now—251 days ago—during which we have night and day been in hostilities with them, and been obliged to keep on the alert "because of?" "because of?"—"What?" The answer has been worn threadbare.

The Arab guns on Omdurman side firing 1.30 P.M. on Mogrim. They have expended a lot of gun ammunition in last few days. 3.30 P.M. They are still firing; one can distinguish the Nordenfeldt. I remember how, when Hicks left for the Soudan, papers wrote of the great effect that the Nordenfeldts were to have upon Arabs, like the French before the Franco-Prussian war with their mitrailleuses. At 4 P.M. they fired for a quarter of an hour quickly. This was caused by five cows which approached the Fort, the men of which killed three (so to-night they will have meat). The Arabs fired fifteen shells one after the other against the Fort, for the outrage on their property. I shall have to move these superior troops (the Shaggyeh) out of the North Fort, for the approach of the Arabs has filled them with dismay. I have kept moving them from every place the Arabs came near. It is really absurd that one should have to pay and keep such troops. I will say

[49] *i.e.* Her Majesty's Government declined to send troops to the Soudan, yet ordered Egypt to evacuate it, and would not permit Turkish troops to assist her.—ED.

Ferratch Pasha (however irritating he is in some ways) is always the gentleman, which I am sorry to say *I am not*, with the fury I get in on state occasions. A woman came in from the South Front; she says they were all my old soldiers who are fighting on the left bank of the Nile, and that they lost heavily on the day *Husseinyeh* got aground. I am moving *these* Shaggyeh to the Lines; it is no use exposing them to be attacked. The Arabs now on the North Fort opposite the Palace are the men of the Mahdi, not as before, the men of the Sheikh el Obeyed, who do not seem to have entered cordially into the second blockade of Kartoum. We had to-night the Arab forces all around us, and are regularly hemmed in, but the town does not care a bit, and are fighting questions of pay with me, for I am paying in paper the three months' backsheesh I promised them.

The major who was shot when lying on his angarep, and who died of his wound, was 3,000 yards distant from the Arabs. We do not know yet the effect of the rifle in a dropping fire. I offered, in paying the three months' backsheesh to the troops, to give orders for bulk sums £120, £130, but they refused to accept them; they want the *regular paper money*, so I have issued £10,000 more in £50 notes. In this paper money notes *I am personally responsible* for the liquidation, and any one may bring an action against me, *in my individual capacity*, to recover the money, while in the orders it might be a query whether they (the authorities of Cairo) might not decline to pay the orders. Paper money now cannot be bought at a discount. People have tried to buy it up, but they failed.[50] I consider this is very satisfactory for one's credit. Her Majesty's Government, as well as the Soudan people, will not need to name a vessel after me in order to remember me, even if they felt so disposed, which I very much doubt. We shall get lots of spies in now the Arabs have hemmed us in. In these deserts, if you leave a space unguarded you see at once any one moving over it; but if you surround it entirely, there is the usual going to and fro, and thus a spy slips in. I do not think it is realised what

[50] Showing how thoroughly they trusted General Gordon.—ED.

happened in Hicks' defeat a year ago. 10,000 soldiers, including 2,000 cavalry, 4,000 camp-followers, 7,000 camels, perished in two days from thirst;[51] 1,700 rifles, 1,000,000 rounds Remington ammunition, were captured; 7 Krupps, 6 Nordenfeldts, 29 mountain guns, with 500 rounds each, were captured (perhaps 300 men were spared out of the host). Eight Englishmen and 8 Germans were killed, and, according to all accounts, they were so exhausted that they were unable to move. Stewart took great pains to get all the details, and wrote them in his Journal. The Arabs have made a pyramid of the skulls. The major who was wounded at Mogrim was sleeping in the telegraph station in the Fort. He found it hot, and went out and got struck and died. If you went to the Fort at Mogrim you would (on seeing the position whence the Arabs fire) say you were as safe there as in Regent Street. This man was a very timorous man, and had avoided every service of the least danger. It is of no use fighting against your destiny. The doctor described to me to-night the state of the town *a year ago*, when they heard of the defeat of Hicks; and one compares it to our present state, when one may say perfect confidence exists in the town, and every one has gone comfortably to bed—it is a lesson to man to never despair.

November 19.—The Arabs came down, 7 A.M., to Goba, opposite the Palace, and fired, but did no harm; they are pulling down Seyd Mahomet Osman's house, which was spared. Ferratch Ullah did not dare go out for the three cows killed last night. The Arabs had a bugler of ours with them at Goba; he bugled a call "1st Regiment!" and then was apparently stopped, he then bugled "We are strong! We are strong!" I have packed up and addressed to the chief of staff, Soudan Expeditionary Force, "all European telegrams sent *from* and received *in* the Soudan for years 1883–84," and send the box with this portion of the Journal.[52] The Arabs have put a gun in the breastwork on the left bank of the

[51] See Appendix upon the insurrection of the False Prophet.—ED.
[52] These have not been handed over by the Government.—ED.

White Nile below Omdurman Fort, so as to bar the entrance to Kartoum on the north.

We have communicated with Omdurman Fort with flags, it is all right. The Arabs are not firing to-day (since 8.30 A.M.). Twelve days have to elapse ere the month's rations become due; this evening it is reported to me that those utterly useless troops—some fifty Bashi Bazouks—began crying that they had nothing to eat, and even went so far as to throw down their arms; now this is rather too much, considering that they are receiving the full rations of soldiers, and also the pay of men who are supposed to find themselves, so that it is a perfectly gratuitous gift to give them rations at all, or if I do so, I should cut their pay; the best of it is, that I *have given* them full rations for the month, which has twelve days yet to run ere that month is out. I do not know if ever the Expeditionary Force will come here, and I do not know the policy which will be pursued; but there is one thing I think I am justified in demanding, that is the disbandment of these brutes, to whom only yesterday I gave a gratuity of fifty dollars to erect their breastwork—a totally unnecessary proceeding on my part. Of course if I can hand over the government to the Expeditionary Forces' Leader I have nothing to say; he can do as he likes. What irritates me is, that a row like this is aided and abetted by every officer, inasmuch as it is to me the row is brought, they daring not to decide; of course, it must be seen, that situated as we are, if one corps can take rations for a month and eat them in a fortnight, and then get more, it is virtually giving double rations to the troops, for if you gave to one part, all the rest would want it.

November 20.—A caravan of 300 men and twenty camels came up the left bank of the White Nile, from the direction of Metemma. 7 A.M. A soldier who came in from the Arabs, says, "The Mahdi sent 2,000 men down towards Metemma an account of the advance of the Expedition, who are near Berber." Also "reports the advance of King Johannes" (which I doubt). I expect the caravan seen to-day is a caravan with *the money* from Berber. Report in the town says the Arabs have been repulsed three times by the Expeditionary Force. The Arabs are very quiet to-day; their Nordenfeldt kept on grunting at intervals this morning. Four of those precious troops the Shaggyeh (one a Bashi Bazouk), have deserted to the Arabs; it was never reported to me. I have a suspicion that more have gone. We communicated with Omdurman Fort by flag-signals; they are all right. The Arabs fired from their guns on the White Nile, and from the Omdurman side, a few rounds this evening.

It is rather astonishing to find that the row about the rations the night before last, was made by the Cairo Bashi Bazouks, who are completely at one's mercy, for the Arabs would never look at them;[53] they even went so far as to throw down their arms! A volley of lies was told about this affair, trying to prevent me hearing the truth. However, I got at the bottom of it, and have noted my friends. A merchant here had a partner in business, who went to the Arabs eight months ago with £3,000 belonging to this merchant, who coolly asks me to pay the £3,000!!!

November 21.—I do not believe one person has died of hunger during the $8\frac{11}{30}$ months we have been shut up. Ferratch Ullah Bey, in Omdurman, signalled, "Yes, I have 230,000 rounds, but I fire a lot every day." Now this is a corker, for I do not believe he fires ten rounds without my personal knowledge, and I estimate his expenditure of ammunition at under 2,000 rounds per diem. By this I expect he wants me to open the road to him, and ammunition is only an excuse; but I do not care to risk a defeat, or a momentary success, attended with a lot of wounded (we have sixty wounded in hospital now). To-day year came the news to Kartoum of Hicks' defeat. He left this on the 3rd September. The Greek Consul and the Greek doctor describes the arrival of news thus at Kartoum: At night came in the *Bordeen* with Coetlogon from the White Nile. The Greek Consul was in his house. Marquet, the French Consul, came to his house and said,

[53] If they deserted.—Ed.

"Come to my house, by the garden." He went to Marquet's house; he found Hussein Pasha Cheri, Ibrahim Pasha Haidar, Coetlogon, Power, and Hansall. He was told "*Hicks is finished.*" The Consul sent a telegram to Towfik, "Hicks finished." Then Towfik sent a telegram that he would send up reinforcements that night. Towfik had a large party at the Abdeen Palace, and reports were rife that something bad was in the air, but nobody knew anything. *Since that day no aid has come to Soudan.* I hear that the day before yesterday two corporals (one who had come in from the Arabs), five soldiers, and a clerk, all Soudan soldiers, deserted to the Arabs. This was never reported to me. I expect the officers have robbed them.

Ferratch Ullah Bey, of Omdurman, signals he has only 43,000 rounds left. This, out of 230,000 rounds, and I feel sure he tells fibs, and is acting in order to force me to relieve him, which I shall not attempt. He says he has had twenty-five wounded and eleven killed. Church parades all round to-day. The Arabs fired at Bourré and at Tuti this morning.

To-day I discovered a robbery of Ruckdi, my old clerk, about which there could be no doubt whatever, so I have turned him out, and written to cancel his being made a Bey. A woman came in from the Arabs. She says the Expedition left Merowé for Berber, and that Mahomet Achmet will try, on Monday, the 24th November, to take Omdurman Fort. This is disagreeable news! However, I have done what I can, and one can do no more than trust now. What has been the painful position for me is that there is not one person on whom I can rely; also, there is not one person who considers that he ought to do anything except his routine duty. We have now been months blockaded, and things are critical; yet not one of my subordinates, except the chief clerk and his subordinate, appears to day. I had to send for them, and wait till they came, perhaps an hour. "It is Friday, and it is unreasonable to expect us at the office," is what they say. My patience is almost exhausted with this continuous apparently never-ending trial; there is not one department which I have not to superintend as closely as if I was its direct head. The officer who commanded the post from which the men deserted never told me, but says he told Ferratch Pasha. This Ferratch Pasha denies, and so it goes on, tissues of lies, and they no more care about being found out than not. It is indeed hopeless work, and yet, truly, they have been treated most handsomely in every way. Nearly every order, except when it is for their interest, has to be repeated two, and even three, times. I may truly say I am weary of my life; day and night, night and day, it is one continual worry.[54]

Our breastworks at Tuti are bothering the Arabs near Omdurman. A soldier came in from the Arabs; he had nothing to say of importance. We have got a breastwork also towards Goba, on the Isle of Tuti. I have given those improvident troops 15,000 okes of biscuits. I sincerely hope I may never be besieged with such a garrison another time. A slave came in, and reports that "Berber has been taken by the troops from Kassala, and that the Arab Government of Berber arrived at the Mahdi's two days ago (perhaps the caravan we saw yesterday); also that "the four steamers have gone to Berber, *one being disabled, or aground, or sunk!*" If this is the case, it is that brute Nutzer Bey or Pasha who (keeping himself well under cover) has disobeyed my repeated orders as to "not taking the steamers against the guns, but to stay quietly at Shendy and wait for the Expedition." The last order that I sent him was that "I would cancel his appointment as Pasha if he dared to disobey me again." But of what avail is that?

November 22.—Slight firing at Bourré and Goba this morning. A soldier deserted to the Arabs last night, with his rifle.

A soldier and a slave came in from the Arabs. It appears more Shaggyeh deserted to the Arabs than the four I mentioned, but it seems perfectly impossible to find out the truth, or even the number of Shaggyeh there are.

I am terribly anxious for the fort at Omdurman, and am trying to devise some means of occupying the Arabs, and di-

[54] Here succeed some dozen lines through which General Gordon has drawn his pen. Underneath is written "Abuse of Baring & Co."—ED.

verting their attention elsewhere. Omdurman Fort signals they are all right; they had another man wounded. Up to date we have had, passing through the hospital, 242 wounded. We have had some 1800 to 1900 killed (between 17th March and 22nd November).

This is the present state of affairs; the Arab camps are about five miles from the city.

Camp C is on river.

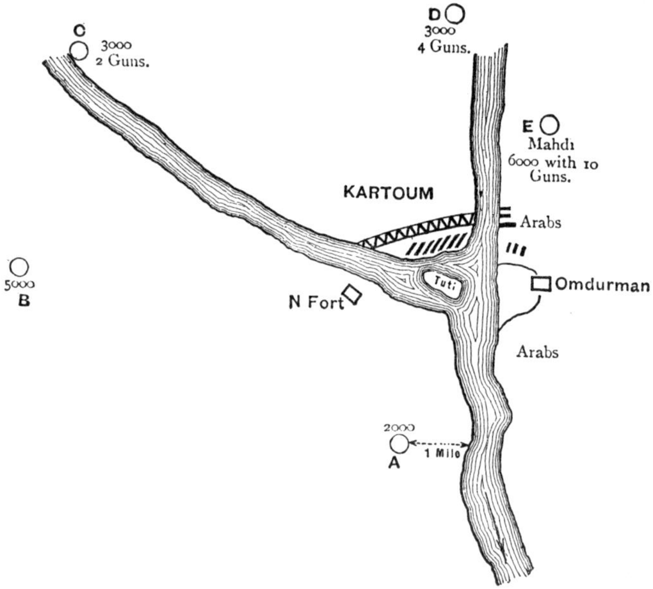

A is one mile from river; camp D and E are three to four miles from the river. Of these numbers perhaps there are 3,000 to 4,000 fighting men, and 600 horsemen to 800 horsemen in the *whole lot.* There is nothing like being precise in these days, and it saves a deal of talking if one knows a man's ideas beforehand. If the Expedition comes here before the place falls (which is doubtful), and *if the instructions are to evacuate the place at once, and leave Kassala and Sennaar, &c., I will resign, and have nothing more to do with the Government of the*

place, or of the Soudan; and this I have a perfect right to do, and no one, not even the Soudan troops or people could say one word. It will depend on circumstances how I shall act *in re* my commission in Her Majesty's service (which I do not hold too fast to, seeing any future employment would not be accepted, even if in the very improbable case of its being offered); but I consider that every officer has a right to resign, and if he resigns he is no longer subject to military orders, and is free to go when and where he likes. It may be argued I was named Governor-General "in order to carry out the evacuation of the Soudan, and that I am bound to carry that out, which is quite correct, but I was named for EVACUATION OF SOUDAN" (against which I have nothing to say), *not to run away from Kartoum and leave the garrisons elsewhere to their fate.*[55] If it is positively determined on *not to look after the garrisons*, and *not* to *establish some sort of provisional Government in the Soudan*, then the course to pursue is *to name a Governor in my place on day of arrival*, and carry out with that Governor that policy which, I have already said, is one of very great danger (putting all the *other* considerations aside). PERSONALLY, looking at the matter from a VERY SELFISH POINT OF VIEW (and seeing I have done my best to prevent this policy being followed, and am impatient to oppose it), I should be much relieved at this *dénouement*, for I should be in Brussels on 20th January.

I have given 6,000 lbs. of biscuit out to the poor (I expect half will be stolen), and I shall sell to-morrow 90,000 lbs. to the townspeople. I am determined if the town does fall, the Mahdi shall find precious little to eat in it. Two soldiers got hold of the head of a shell-rocket fired by Arabs, and, having nothing better to do, they set to work to open it. It burst, and has nearly killed one, and wounded the other—the effects of curiosity!

[55] Sir E. Baring, in writing to General Gordon on the instructions of H. M. Government conveyed to him, says: "You will bear in mind the main end to be pursued is the *evacuation of the Soudan.*"—*Enclosure, in Egypt No.* 6. Sir E. Baring does not say, "the evacuation of Kartoum and the abandonment of all the other garrisons in the Soudan."—ED.

November 23.—A soldier came in at the North Fort from the Arabs; he says the Expedition has captured Berber, and are advancing on this, and the Arabs want to attack Tuti Isle.

The Arabs, this morning, fired from Goba on breastwork of Tuti. The soldier says my noble friend, Nutzer Pasha, kept safely all the steamers at Shendy, and never aided in any way at Berber. The Arabs are (so says this soldier) collecting at Halfeyeh to receive the Expedition, but I do not think it.

Three women came in last night from the Arabs to North Fort; they had been captured during the raid the Arabs made on the Shaggyeh some days ago.

The soldier who came in brought two rifles and two belts of ammunition.

Ferratch Ullah Bey, of Omdurman Fort, reports "he is all right," by signal.

A report has come in that the Expedition had arrived at Metemma, and had encountered the Arabs twice; that a steamer had been sent up to inform me, but the Arab guns had forced her to return; they say that this report has come into the town by men who have friends in the Mahdi's camp, and who had seen some of the Arabs wounded. This news is five days old. Very few Arabs in the camp on the North of the Palace. The Shaggyeh came and asked me to let them go up and pillage the Arab camp as there were so few in it; they knew well that I knew if I did give them leave they would not go, so it was a safe volunteer on their part. A caravan of Arabs came from the North to the Arab camp this morning. The Arabs have only one gun on the Omdurman side now; I expect the rest are taken down against the Expedition. We have only 541 rounds of Krupp ammunition left for our two Krupps. I went to Mogrim, and practised on the Arab house where their gun is, 1600 yards range; we put three shells into it, upon which the Arabs left. I am still apprehensive of an attack on Omdurman Fort, and have the *Ismailia* steamer ready. I have sent down thirty rockets (sky) to Mogrim to be fired off; this will bother the Arabs, who will not know what to make of it, and will think we have got some very important *news*. I know if this happened when *I* was meditating an assault, I should hesitate before I made that assault after the fireworks.

November 24, 6 A.M.—Arabs came down and fired on the Isle of Tuti from Goba. Ferratch Ullah Bey of Omdurman reports all well; another man had been wounded, and one had died. A slave came in from the Arabs on the South Front, who says there is no news of the Expedition in Walad a Goun's camp. 12.15 P.M. The Arabs near Omdurman Fort are retiring from their position near the small steamer, and are burning the straw huts; our men are firing on them, and they do not reply, the *Husseinyeh* steamer has slipped down towards deeper water, of herself. I am sending down the *Ismailia* to reconnoitre. The Arabs have not fired from their gun at Omdurman to-day. It appears the *Husseinyeh* has sunk, so that may be the reason of the Arabs retiring. I expect the Mahdi wanted his troops, who were guarding the steamer *Husseinyeh*, and so he sent off men last night to sink her, and that is the history of the retreat. It is somewhat of a relief to me, for I expect it shows the Arabs will not make an assault on Omdurman Fort. Perhaps our fireworks last night all along the Lines made the Mahdi think I had some great news, which he did not know of; we fired from five places fifteen sky-rockets at one concerted moment. They report from Mogrim that the Arabs retreated *before Husseinyeh* sank, but I expect that is a fib, and that they did not leave till she sank; it is against all reason with a falling river, and, fixed on a level as she was, she sank untouched. The fact is, I expect, that the man put to watch her was asleep, and the Arabs, trying to capture her, drew her into deep water, when the water got into her shot-hole. 1.30 P.M. The *Ismailia* went down to the junction of the Blue and White Niles, and the Arab guns opened on her, so she has come back. I have sent down to make inquiries on the quiet, whether the Arabs returned BEFORE or AFTER the sinking of *Husseinyeh*. The Arabs fired five rounds at the *Ismailia*. The Arabs came back to their breastwork when the *Ismailia* appeared, but on her return they also went back. If *Husseinyeh* had not had a shot-hole in her, the Arabs would have captured her, but, as I had taken her steam-cocks off, they could not use her. We may be able to raise her if she has sunk evenly. The steamer has sunk evenly, for her funnel is above water.

I expect the Arabs put a slave boy to turn the handle of the Nordenfeldt, for it keeps on grunting all day at intervals of half seconds, but does no harm.

November 25.—Arabs came to Goba this morning and fired on the Isle of Tuti for half an hour. It is quite true the *Arabs did work at the Husseinyeh and caused her to sink, and on her sinking they retired;* the sentries in our Lines being all asleep, as I had supposed. Ferratch Ullah Bey, of Omdurman Fort reports all well; he has another death among his wounded. I have promised him three days' pay for every day he and his men are shut up. 1.15 P.M. Steamers in sight; the doctor saw them first. The steamers are firing; only one steamer in sight.

The Arabs had three guns at Halfeyeh against the coming-in steamer. 2.30 P.M. I have sent down the *Ismailia* to cover the incoming steamer. The Arabs are grunting with their Nordenfeldt, and firing from their gun. Mogrim is playing on them with the Krupp, and Tuti with their mountain gun. 2.45 P.M. For the last half-hour the firing on the part of Arabs on the advancing steamer has been most furious with guns and musketry; we replying. I am grateful to say that, after this hot reception, she has got in safe to Mogrim.

If any officer of the Expedition is on board, he will know what it is to be in a penny boat! under cannon fire. The *Bordeen* has come in; she has seven wounded. There are *no Arabs* at Shoboloha, or (consequently) *guns;* the wounded were from two shells fired by the Arabs from Halfeyeh. The Expeditionary Force is at Ambukol (which is LIVELY!);[56] the Arabs had four guns at Halfeyeh; one woman was killed in the *Bordeen:* the letters received by *Bordeen* are of no great

[56] That is to say, the Expeditionary Force was 185 miles further from Kartoum than General Gordon expected it to be.—ED.

import, for they do not tell me the route the Expedition will take, and I have received a later post—that of 14th October.

Two men were wounded at Mogrim to-day. According to the report of the two men who came from Dongola, it is not *certain* that the *Abbas* is captured.

I enclose a telegram,[57] which we cannot decipher. I imagine Colonel Stewart has the key, it being probably Foreign Office cipher.

Towfik, by a telegram, cancels his Firman, which gives up the Soudan,[58] which I have *torn up*, but enclose; (this telegram[59] I received to-day).

A telegram to the Ulema from Towfik says: "*Baring*" *is coming up with Lord Wolseley.*

November 26.—One man came to Goba and fired two shots and retired. The Arabs fired three rounds at Fort Omdurman. The Fort reports all right. Nutzer Pasha reports that the money at Berber has been taken up to the Mahdi. He sends up four wounded. He says the Expedition is advancing in three parties—one to Berber from Ambukol, one from Ambukol to Metemma, and one from Ambukol to Shoboloha. This letter was written six days ago. A caravan came across from the north to the Mahdi's camp to-day. The Arabs at Metemma have crossed to Shendy and gone into the interior. Four fellaheen soldiers deserted from Nutzer Pasha and went to the Arabs—I expect through his ill-treatment of them.

There are three long telegrams in cipher, which I cannot make out, pasted on the other side.[60]

I had a letter saying Government had given Kitchener *carte blanche* to pay the Mahdi up to £20,000 for me; but adds the "writer does not think I would accept such a proposition"; in which he is quite right; neither would the Mahdi.

I like Baker's description of Kitchener.

[57] General Gordon marks on back of this telegram, which is one of three, "Telegraph of which Colonel Stewart has the key." See Appendix X[1].—ED.

[58] Appendix Y.

[59] The one alluded to in former paragraph.—ED.

[60] See above.—ED.

"The man whom I have always placed my hopes upon, Major Kitchener, R.E., who is one of the few *very superior* British officers, with a cool and good head and a hard constitution, combined with untiring energy, has now pushed up to Dongola and has proved that the Mudir is dependable. The latter has given him a letter received from you asking about reinforcements, and stating that you have 8,000 troops at Kartoum, and that Sennaar is still occupied by the Government forces."[61]

There was a slight laugh when Kartoum heard Baring was bumping[62] his way up here, for so we read Towfik's telegram—a regular Nemesis.

I am sure we are deprived of a treat in not being able to decipher the long telegrams on the preceding page. It also is delicious to find not one civil word from any official personage except Kitchener; it relieves me immensely (also I must except Towfik, who in his despatch was civil and polite). Evidently I am in disgrace! How fearful!

According to the man who came yesterday the *Abbas* struck a rock, and the two boats surrendered to the Arabs. I have no doubt but that the Arabs have captured the steamer *Abbas*, for the Arab chief of Berber sent to Cassim el Mousse an impression of the seal I used when I was up here before, and which I sent down by Stewart. Now, it is impossible he could have known this unless he had possession of the seal, for I do not think Stewart knew it. The Arabs at Omdurman have the slave boy grinding away at their Nordenfeldt. I have sent one of our French mitrailleuses down to grind on them. If Baring does bump his way up here as British Commissioner, I shall consider he has expiated his faults and shall forgive him. We seldom realise our position. In ten or twelve years' time Baring, Lord Wolseley, myself, Evelyn Wood, &c., will have no teeth, and will be deaf; some of us will be quite *passe;* no one will come and court us; new Barings, new Lord Wolseleys

[61] This account of Major Kitchener is in a letter from General Baker. General Gordon has cut out the portion of the original letter, and has pasted it in the body of his journal.—ED.

[62] *I.e.* coming up on a camel.—ED.

will have arisen, who will call us "bloaks" and "twaddlers." "Oh! for goodness' sake come away, then! Is that dreadful bore coming? If once he gets alongside you, you are in for half an hour," will be the remark of some young captain of the present time on seeing you enter the Club. This is very humiliating, for we, each one, think we are immortal. That poor old General . . . who for years vegetated at the end of —— street close to Clubs! who ever visited him? Better a ball in the brain than to flicker out unheeded, like he did.

November 26.—The ex-Khedive will chuckle over Baring's ride to the Soudan. I can fancy him twinkling his little eyes over it. He came up in his youth to Dongola with his uncle Ismail Pasha, a slim youth; Halim (the rightful heir to the Khediviat after Ismail) also was here as Governor-General for three weeks, but he bolted back, without leave, from Said Pasha, who was then Viceroy. If Ismail, ex-Khedive, could only get Malet, Vivian, and Colvin to go this ride, I think he would forgive his deposition. I have published the telegram of Towfik to me, and to the Notables (note that in this telegram, Towfik—a year late, it is true—says he is sorry for Hicks's army destruction!), saying he will retain the Soudan. Whoever comes up here had better appoint Major Kitchener Governor-General, for it is certain, after what has passed, *I am impossible.* (What a comfort!)

November 27.—The Arabs fired with artillery and musketry on Bourré for about an hour this morning. They fired three shells, at Omdurman Fort, who signals it is all right.

Two slaves came in to-day; they say the Arabs are wanting in ammunition. I do not wonder at it, at the way they fire away; they say the Mahdi has had a revelation that the Turks will keep the country for eight years, that he is to go back and come again at the end of the eight years.[63] The little

[63] There is some significance in this. The Mahdi in all probability knew General Gordon had recommended Turkish troops being dispatched to the Soudan, and felt he could not hold the country against them, if they came. —ED.

captured steamer *Mahomet Ali* came down near Giraffe last night, and then went back.

If Kitchener would take the place, he would be the best man to put in as Governor-General, but I must confess I think, *with our Government constituted as it is*, that for Her Majesty's Government to take the charge of these countries would be a very serious burden, and that the only solution would be the Sultan taking them over, with a subsidy and the ports of Suakin and Massowah. Judging from Towfik's telegram to me, it would seem that the Hewitt Treaty has fallen through, for he speaks of the retention of Kassala.

Our Government has two courses to pursue, *one* to appoint Kitchener or some other Governor-General, and to be prepared to give him £500,000 a year for two years, for he will never get any taxes worth speaking of; for two years, also, our Government must be prepared to renew the stores, war material, &c., and give 6,000 extra soldiers to the Soudan. Second, to give the country over to the Sultan with two millions and the ports.

To me the last is the best and speediest course to pursue; it rids Her Majesty's Government for ever of any responsibility. If the first course was taken, to my mind, a *sine quá non* for its success would be, *to make up with France in re Egypt.*

There is one other course, an intermediate one, viz., Zubair, with £100,000 a year, and replenished magazines.

About forty females congregated under my window, yelling for food. It delights me to think of the treat Baring will have when he gets here (if ever he does). I do not think there are 500 Arabs in the camp on north side, and no horsemen, though their straw huts extend further than they did in the first blockade. The *Zubair* steamer was launched to-day. With respect to the force of Arabs on north side it may be said, "if so few, why not attack them;" but supposing I was wrong, and they were more than I think, a defeat would cause the fall of the town, therefore I will not risk it.

The Ulema and Notables got a telegram from Towfik excusing himself for his indolence. They came to-day and wished to send an answer, which I agreed to. They did this of their free will, and NOT PROMPTED MUCH BY ME. It will make Towfik hop. Of the Ulema who came, *two* (the Sheikh el Islam and the Cadi) had been imprisoned by me.[64]

November 28.—Fort Omdurman all right. Another of the wounded has died. Two soldiers came in from the Arabs. Small church parades, that on the Blue Nile rather larger than usual. We have to-day in store 174,400 okes of biscuit and 1165 ardebs of dhoora, which is not bad after 261 days' blockade. A slave has come in at the North Fort, and says the Arabs are expecting four steamers to come up. I hope that the officer in command will clear Halfeyeh before he pushes on to this, for he may get a shell from the Arabs at Omdurman into one of his steamers. I do not like to risk the *Bordeen* down by herself to give this warning. If the steamers do come up, and have not the sense to stop at Halfeyeh, I shall endeavour to warn them by a tremendous fire on the Arabs at Omdurman. The danger is at the Ras, or nose (x), on the junction of the rivers. We are protecting the *Bordeen* by casing her steam-chest with wood. The proper thing to do would be to clear the Halfeyeh camp of the Arabs before coming on here. You could then communicate with Kartoum by land, and avoid having to run in penny steamboats the gauntlet of Arab guns.

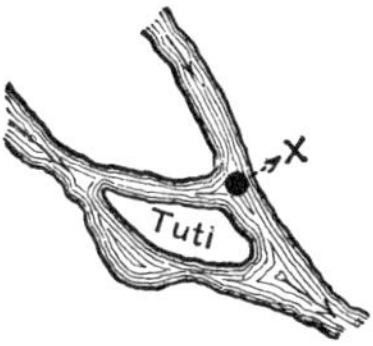

A woman came in from the Arabs. She says yesterday morning a man came to the Arab camp on the north side who said that the Expedition had captured Berber, and that four steamers were on their way here; that the Arabs sent out men to see if this was true, and that it is my own soldiers who are now fighting against us.

If the news that Berber is captured is true, the steamers will be towing up boats (fifty of which are at Berber) and will not be here for some days. 2 P.M. I think the Arabs

[64] They were two of the sixteen General Gordon imprisoned for conspiring with the Mahdi.—ED.

are making an embrasure at Goba, with the view of bombarding the Palace. I can see this with my glass. If they do this, it will not hurt us, and it will take their men and guns from off the river, where their gun-fire is alone dangerous to the steamers. It

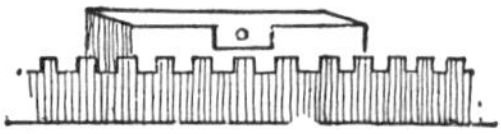

is rather amusing to see the *personality*[65] of this Arab battery. The range is 2,200 yards from here, but as *we* never hit anything we fire at, at that distance, I think I shall be safe in the Palace from the Arab fire. The mountain shell will not penetrate the walls at that distance, as we know from a shell which struck the North Fort some time ago. I expect they will begin to-morrow morning at daybreak. I have fired eight or ten rounds at them; which brought them out to look, but it is quite a chance if the Remington reaches them at that range. There was a time when one would have been anxious for the Palace, but that has gone by. It will not be the first time I have been fired on by my own soldiers, for in China two men of the 31st Regiment were on the breach of Taitsan and one was killed. The other with a shell splinter, was taken prisoner. "Mr. Gordon! Mr. Gordon, you will not let me be killed." "Take him down to the river and shoot him;" and *aside*, "put him in my boat: let the doctor attend him, and send him to Shanghai." He was sent down to Shanghai, and got three or six months' imprisonment by court-martial for deserting, and I daresay he exists at present. His name was Hargreaves. I do not know his regimental number.

Baring to Egerton—"Metemma! at last, after the most fearful sufferings, every bone in my body dislocated with those beastly camels. Found here his Journal, from which it appears that that duffer, the Mahdi, has at last roused himself, but I fear it is too late. As to the tone of the Journal, it is *simply deplorable*, and (do not mention it, please) he has actually made a sketch (brace yourself up to bear it) of our high priest. Excuse more, for what with the bumping of the camel and

[65] *I.e.* the way in which this battery was directed towards that part of the Palace which the Arabs knew General Gordon inhabited.—ED.

the depravity shown by this scoffer, I am more dead than alive." A Bashi Bazouk (no loss), a bugler, and two musicians (of our terrible band) deserted to Arabs yesterday, as Egerton says, it is "incorrigible." This is owing to the robbery of the rations by the officers.

November 29.—Omdurman Fort all right, but three men deserted to the Arabs. Truly this life is almost insupportable: the officers have been robbing the men of their rations, and the storekeeper has been giving them short weight. One feels utterly powerless to contend with these affairs, and unless the Expedition comes soon the place will fall from the venality of these people.[66] They know I cannot possibly find out their misdeeds, and chuckle over it. The Arabs are working away at their battery at Goba.

It is odd that among the despised Egyptian fellaheen soldiers this robbery of rations does not take place. It is only among the officers, &c., of the black troops. 1 P.M. I hear that the soldiers waylay the women, to whom I have given biscuit, and rob them!

I have a strong conviction that neither Baring or Lord W. have taken the precaution of bringing a Firman from Towfik Pasha, giving them a legal status superior to mine in the Soudan. If this conviction is the case (and the fiction of Towfik being supreme ruler is kept up), then it is for me to name the Governor-General, and I feel strongly disposed to print off proclamations to be issued on arrival of Expedition (if ever it does arrive), by which I relinquish the government in favour of the officer commanding the Expedition. Of course, if a Firman is brought, then the situation is different; but *if not brought*, and the *fiction is going to be kept up*, I have a perfect right to vacate the government, and to appoint whomsoever I like, subject to the ultimate approval of Towfik Pasha. It may be that the officer commanding the Expedition may demur to his appointment, but his doing so will not absolve

[66] That is to say, either those who are being robbed and cheated will in their own interest be forced to give up the town to the enemy, or the robbers and cheats will be bought over by the Mahdi.—ED.

him of the responsibility thus officially placed on him if the town falls.

The great question, "Is any officer, civil or military, of the Expedition possessed of a Firman of Towfik?" If not, there is not the least doubt that the *de jure* power is with me to name whom I like (except in the case of a civil or military officer announcing to the people that the British Government has annexed Egypt). There can be no question of military discipline in this, for what has a foreign Power to do with the civil functionaries of Towfik, unless they usurp his (Towfik's) functions?

Two more soldiers deserted to-day. 8 P.M. The Arabs came down to the ruins of village opposite, and fired on the Palace. I sent the buglers up to the roof of the Palace, who by their own accounts killed thousands, and the Arabs retired. I have got so accustomed to the sound of the firing that I can tell when the report of firing is *from Arabs on Tuti or Palace*, or our men *from Tuti* or *North Fort*. Also if it is the Arabs firing on Mogrim or Bourré, or our men firing on them, from these places. According to the directions of the muzzles of the rifles, so are the sounds. I think I would like to be in a real siege, with no civil population or robbers of officers to bully me. To-night a sortie with fifty men would give the Arabs a dose which they would not forget; but it is no use, we are not up to it. The buglers say they killed thirty (! ! !) between them.

November 30.—Fort Omdurman all right. A slave came from the Arabs to it last night. Arabs (10.30 A.M.) have fired two rounds from their ("personality")[67] battery at Goba, but the projectiles did not reach the Palace.

I hear that one of the shells fired by Arabs did reach the town, and fell behind the Palace. They have fired three rounds more, and then the house in which they had their gun fell down. They are now digging away to get out the gun.

[67] "It is rather amusing to see the *personality* of this Arab battery:" p. 256.—ED.

I expect the gun-carriage requires repair, for the house was a good height. 11.15 A.M. Arabs either had another gun besides that in the house which fell down, or that gun was not damaged in the fall of house, for they have just fired another round at the North Fort. Noon. The Arabs fired three more rounds at the North Fort. The shells burst in the air, and the Arabs have now gone to dinner. Another man deserted to the Arabs; he had previously deserted from the Arabs to us. Two of the band reported to have deserted to the Arabs have been found in the town. The Arabs at Goba (whom I do not think number more than 40 ! ! !) fired three more rounds from their gun this evening. I feel strongly disposed to go over *myself* with 100 men (*against* 40 !) and attack them to-morrow. It is simply ridiculous the apathy that is shown. These forty men, which is the outside of their number, are at least four miles from any assistance. The place is so flat and bare that this is a certainty.

December 1.—During the night the Arabs fired on town with their guns. At daybreak they fired from their guns on the Palace and the North Fort, and on Mogrim and Bourré. A caravan of seventeen camels came to the Mahdi from Dongola to-day. The "Nordenfeldt" (Omdurman) has been silent for last three days. Omdurman Fort all right. 10.40 A.M. Arabs just fired one shot, which struck water in front of the Palace; they fired another which burst in the air.

11 A.M. I have sent down the *Bordeen* to entice the Arabs to waste their ammunition, which they are doing.

Towfik's telegram to me, was to-day more fully explained, and I gather that he says Lord Wolseley and Sir E. Baring are coming up, and that they will settle the question of the Soudan. I have replied, that it may be convenient for him (Towfik), but it does not meet the case, unless these two officials have a Firman from him, giving them authority. Now this the two officials will never have, for it virtually would make them *Towfik's subordinates.* It is implied in the telegram, that I am to arrange with these two officials, as to the Soudan. A delightful arrangement for Towfik, but not one so delightful for me; so I have answered him, *it is for him* (Towfik) *to arrange with these two officials, and to send his arrangements in the form of a Firman here.* It is certain that no legal authority exists in the Soudan, expect it is held from Towfik, and unless these two officials have authority from Towfik, they have no authority in the Soudan; now if they hold authority from Towfik, they are under Towfik's orders.

The "fiction" will not hold good in the Soudan. Though I am pretty well dispirited for the last few days, I cannot help laughing at the fearful mess we are in. Towfik is as sharp as his father, and wants to quietly saddle me with the controversy, reserving to himself the right of criticism, but I do not feel inclined to be thus saddled, and I shall perhaps appoint Baring Governor-General, subject to the approval of Towfik, and shall bolt. B. may say he will not take it, but he will have no choice, for, if he does not, he throws away any legal status he possesses. He, on his part, may name some one else, but that will be his look out. My object, of course, is to make tracks, if I can do so (without hurting our country, or being the cause of danger in the smallest degree to our troops), and to leave the onus on Baring and the Ministry. I do not feel so kindly to Towfik as to fight his battles up here, which is what he evidently aims at, neither do I feel inclined to compromise myself by aiding Baring. I have said the only possible solution is the Sultan, let the subsidy be what it may. The fact is, that the Expeditionary Force comes up here as allies of Towfik (unless its Government says it comes up as independent), and as allies of Towfik, it is in all reason subject, as far as civil affairs are concerned, to Towfik; its officers can issue no decrees, except *in his name*, save those which concern military operations. A nice accommodating Governor-General would work this affair, without friction. *I will not*, for I am too deeply involved with the people; but I want (like a rat) to leave the house before it falls, so the best thing is to hint to me, "make Kitchener Governor-General," "*subject to the approval of Towfik!*" Then K. would do all you want, and in a legal way, and you would be happy. Unless you have a superior

Firman to mine, you cannot make K. Governor-General (even if you had ten million troops), unless you declare yourself the rulers of the land, which you will not do, because of the ninety millions sterling of debt on Egypt. 5 P.M. Arabs fired two more shells at the Palace, so I put the three buglers on the roof to practice at them. *They say* they killed fifteen. I would much like to know contents of Lord W.'s telegram to me, also the telegrams in cipher from Nubar and Baring; but I never shall have that pleasure, for I do not expect either this Journal will ever be given back, or if it is, that I shall be lent the cipher books to decipher them. The Arabs fired two rounds at the Palace this evening, one fell in the water in front of the Palace, and one fell in the garden. Two shells fired by the Arabs from Bourré to-day, fell close to the hospital.

To my mind, this is the idea of H.M. Government:—*Expedition comes up to look after British subjects nominally*, but, *in reality, to settle future government of Soudan, under the pretence that Towfik governs.* Towfik telegraphs to me, "that the British officials will settle future status of the Soudan with me *sub rosa*"*!!* now, of course, I may be wrong, but my idea is that the British officials will propose *the keeping of Sennaar, Kartoum, Berber, and Dongola,* the *non-interference with the Mahdi, cession of Kassala to King John, the leaving to their fate the Equator Provinces, &c.* And what the British officials propose Towfik will agree to; but then comes the question, as *I* consider *the proposal is unacceptable* (inasmuch as long as the Mahdi is alongside, no peace is possible), I will not accept it, and will leave A. or B. as my, and Towfik's representative, to carry the proposition out. ("*Après moi, le déluge.*") No one can blame me for this, for I should be a scoundrel if I accepted any proposition which would eventually give trouble to our country.

December 2.—The Arabs fired four shells at the Palace at daybreak with no effect. 9 A.M. They have fired four more; one burst close to my room—a little high. I have put two guns near the Palace to reply to them. Report in town says Waled a Goun's men are passing over from the right bank of the White Nile to the Mahdi's camp on the left bank. Omdurman Fort reports all right. 11 A.M. The Arabs opened fire again on the Palace; we are answering. The Arabs have now two guns firing on us. There is a report that the Arabs of the Mahdi are going north (on the left bank of the White Nile). Noon.—We have silenced our friends opposite, having concentrated a heavy fire on them. I nearly lost my eyes this morning, firing on Arabs, the base of the brass cartridge blew out, and sent the fire into my face; this is a fault of the Remington; the metal case of this cartridge must not be used too often.

Some people ought to have their heads cut off, if there is to be any quiet in the Soudan; I wonder how our Government will be able to allow this to be done under their nose, for however necessary to cut their heads off, looking to future peace of the Soudan, they can scarcely be called rebels, for they may say they were forced into rebellion by the inability of the Government aiding them, and also that they had heard that the Soudan was abandoned. 3 P.M. *Another battle!* with Arabs at Goba, who, however, have no guns—firing terrific. 3.15 P.M. Battle is over, and we have won. Arabs silent. 3.30 P.M. Arabs began it again, by firing their gun. 3.38 P.M. Battle over, an Arab (or most likely one of my men) is standing up, throwing dust in the air (like as Shimei dusting David—"Thou bloody man." 2 Samuel xvi. 8). The Arabs must have used up a lot of ammunition, for they kept up a good fire, though where their bullets went no one could see; the Palace and the North Fort and Muduriat being high, our bullets reach them, but theirs do not appear to reach the river. They have a regular casemate for the two guns, one directed on the Palace and one on the

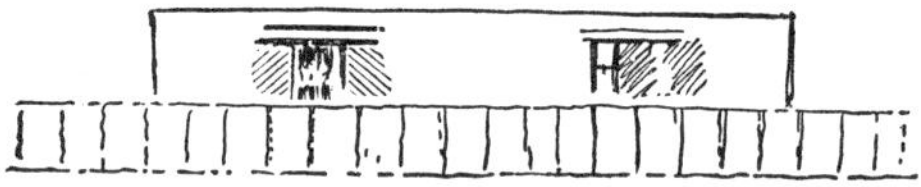

North Fort. They took two days to make it, quite a creditable piece of work, with a screen wall in front. In the Crimea it

was supposed and considered mean to bob, and one used to try and avoid it. . . . used to say, "It is all well enough for you, but I am a family man," and he used to bob at every report. For my part, I think judicious bobbing is not a fault for I remember seeing on two occasions shells like this "●" before my eyes, which certainly, had I not bobbed, would have taken off my head ("*And a good riddance too!*" F. O. would say). I make these remarks with reference to the Arab rifle fire; you can see them with the telescope aim directly at this wing of the Palace and fire, and then one hears a thud in the water; I have got quite accustomed to them now. The mitrailleuse (a Gatling) moved them out of their cover this evening; we have it on the Muduriat. The Palace roof is thus—

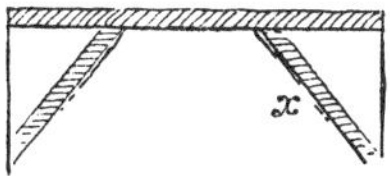

a shell striking x would bring down the roof, so when the Arabs fire, one does not feel comfortable as one hears the shell sighing through the air, till one hears it fall; it is at least 40 feet in height, but with only two storeys. The pasha who built it (Momtoz Pasha) built it without leave from the old Khedive, taking funds which he had no right to; the old Khedive did not see it, and Ismail Pasha Ayoub, who was a prisoner here, split on him; he was tried here, and they say was poisoned, Ismail Ayoub getting his place. Ismail Ayoub was sent up because he did not treat one of the cast-off wives of the old Khedive (whom he was forced to marry) with proper respect; so this wife got up a harem intrigue, and he was exiled.

He (Ismail Ayoub) was a great scamp, whatever was the cause of his exile. He belonged to Kurdistan, and was originally a bugler in Said Pasha's band; and I used to tell him, he was as much a foreigner in this land as I was. He was a good musician, and had learnt French and German. He is now dead. Whilst I was here, I think he was the best administrator the Soudan ever had. He was the Minister of the Interior during Lord Dufferin's time, and wrote the famous despatch about the inutility of using the kourbatch. *He!* who was famous for its use up here, and who, with Cherif and Towfik, roared with laughter over the affair, for Lord Dufferin in the gravest way reported it to Lord Granville, who, I dare say, laughed as heartily over it with Mr. Sanderson. Poor Ismail Ayoub! he was a most agreeable scoundrel; but he came to grief at Cairo in 1883 as Minister of Finance. The bugler "*Almas*" (*i.e.* the *diamond*) telegraphed his *confrères* that he had killed twenty Arabs to-day!!

December 3.—This morning Arabs fired eight rounds at us, and we replied; one of our shells struck their casemate. Numbers of Arabs left Mahdi's camp for the north. Arabs fired nine rounds into the town at night from the South Lines. One shell fell into the garden of the Palace; this from the South Lines. A shell from Arabs at Goba fell in the garden, so it will be seen the attention which is being paid to the Palace.

Twenty shells fell in town yesterday, but none did any harm. I think this is the programme, and though it is of doubtful morality, perhaps it is the shortest route out of a mess. "British Expedition comes up to relieve British subjects in distress, *nothing else;* it finds one of its subjects acting as ruler; it takes him away, and he, on going away, appoints Zubair ruler, subject to approval of Towfik, Zubair having been allowed to come up to Kartoum, as a private individual, to look after his family."

Now who can say anything to the British Government? It has had nothing to do with the appointment of Zubair, or with the Government of Towfik; it came up to relieve its subjects, and "Gordon is entirely responsible for the appointment of Zubair;" "even Towfik is not responsible, for Gordon did it on his own responsibility." This will be a splendid dodge; it first clears Her Majesty's Government of any blame, it puts the blame on me, and in the storm that is caused, I shall have been so effectually blackened that every one will forget the—well! we will not say it in direct words (count the months), we will call the DELAY; in fact, I expect the public will rather blame the Government for having sent any Expedition at all for such a style of British subject; the Government will chuckle over it all, and will preserve the *fiction* that they have nought to do with the Soudan or Egypt.

The Opposition will be perfectly wild at seeing the Ministry get out of the mess, with what one may call really credit, while the Anti-Slavery Society and Europe at large will empty their vials of wrath on me. Towfik and his pashas will wring their hands *openly* over such an act. . . . will get such kudos! For my part I shall get out of any of those wretched honours, for the Ministry will be only too glad to say, "We could not, you know, confer any honours on him after such very disreputable conduct," knowing well enough I would not take them if offered; and as I am not going to England again, and shall not see the papers, I shall not much mind the abuse. I think it is a splendid programme. Zubair must be given either £200,000 or £300,000 a year for two years, replenished magazines, and stores of all sorts, all the Expedition's boats and steamers, &c., &c., and must be aided for two months in small expeditions; besides the £200,000 or £300,000 for two years, he must have down on the nail £150,000 to £200,000.

I must clear, in disgrace, out of the country, to prevent any appearance of any connivance on the part of . . . in this arrangement, which he will or ought officially to deplore. I do not think Zubair will care for the Equator Province; he will agree to give that up; he will agree to uphold the Treaty of 1877 Slave Convention, and laugh as he does so. As for the Bahr Gazelle, I expect the Mahdi has it, and if so, his people will move up there, when Zubair by his politics recaptures Obeyed.

What a fearful row there will be. I know one man who will write: "Better, my dear Gordon, FAR better! to have died, than have so very far departed from the right path; nothing, no, nothing can explain it away. A happy Christmas to you." . . . "This news from the Soudan is very satisfactory; I call it a great triumph, for it not only delivers us out of a dilemma, but it effectually settles our friends, and vitiates anything he[68] may say as to the Delay." Any military operations undertaken after the proclamation of Zubair will be put down "as measures necessary to be undertaken to secure the return, unmolested, of the Expeditionary Force." 5 P.M. Artillery duel going on between our two guns and the Arab gun; our practice is very bad. The shells the Arabs fire from their Krupp gun reach the Palace Garden, but the report of their gun is not to be heard. The Arab shells from Goba fall just about 200 yards short of the Palace: but in its line there is just the second of suspense (after seeing them fire), while one hears the soft sighing of their shells coming nearer and nearer, till they strike. 7 P.M. *Another battle!* (the third to-day). The Arabs came down to the river and fired on the Palace; we could not stand *that*. 7.10 P.M. Battle over; we are as we were, minus some cartridges. 7.20 P.M. Battle begun again, because the buglers played "Salaam Effendina," the Arabs wasting ammunition. 8 P.M. The Arabs are firing from the south at the Krupps on the Palace; they (*i.e.* the Arabs) are at least 4,000 yards distant; one hears the shells burst, but not the report of their gun; they reached the river close to the Palace.

December 4.—Omdurman Fort all right. They had a man wounded yesterday. There was a small battle at Bourré this morning. The Arabs at Goba are quiet after the exertions of yesterday. Firing was heard (on north) towards Shoboloha last night. Report in town says the steamers are near there.

Should the Zubair arrangement be accepted, then comes the question of the military action during two months, at end of which time the Expeditionary Force should be wending its way back. The driving away of the Arabs from the Dem at the north of the Palace will be immediate on the arrival of the troops; the Arabs will then hold on to El foun and to Giraffe. They will vacate the vicinity of Omdurman Fort; 1000 men will deal with El foun and Giraffe, supported by our tag-rag. First Giraffe, then El foun; but at the same time as this takes

[68] *i.e.* General Gordon.—ED.

place, the retreat of Arabs ought to be cut off at Gitana from Kordofan by the steamers and another 1000 men; the Mahdi will return to Schatt, and the town will be free, and all the troops defending the Lines will be available. Then comes the question of going inland and attacking the family of the Sheikh el Obeyed's son, two and a half hours inland, or else going on and attacking Mesalamieh. I think Sheikh el Obeyed's family will give in as soon as the Arabs are driven from El foun (an affair of an hour, *D. V.*). I tried to entice the Arabs at Goba into a fight this evening, but they would not be drawn, and only replied by two shells, which fell in the river. We played on them with the mitrailleuse, and made them move their gun, and then they fired two more shells, one which fell near the Palace in the river. With a good mitrailleuse, and a sharp operator, *with telescope sight*, no gun could be served with impunity at 2,000 yards range, though it could be served *against artillery fire*, for at that range there is plenty of time to dodge under cover after seeing the flash ere the shell arrives. The band, principally of small boys, the men being on the Lines, went on to the roof of the Palace to play (they always come on the eve of their Sabbath, the Friday). The Arabs heard them, and fired a volley at them; they, furious, threw down their instruments, and flew to arms, and a regular fusillade went on for some moments, the other places supporting the fire. The buglers are bugling now "Come to us, come to us," to the Arabs. (The Egyptian Government have the French calls, and can converse by bugle; I do not think we have.) Last night a *renegade* Dervish bugler in the Arab ranks replied, "Come to us, come to us."

December 5.—Small church parades. Three caravans of some size came in from the north to Mahomet Achmet's camp this morning .Two deserters came in from the Arabs. Fort at Omdurman all right. In store 737 ardebs of dhoora, 121,300 okes of biscuit.

We are going to make an attempt to relieve Omdurman Fort (really things are looking very black). The men who came in say the Mahdi is short of ammunition. The Arabs fired three shells at the Palace this afternoon, which fell in the river. A soldier deserted to-day to the Arabs. 5 P.M. The Arabs fired two shells at the Palace, which fell into the water (if *they only* knew! that if they sank the trail they would touch us up! their line is quite correct). 6.30 P.M. Since 3 P.M. we have been firing on them, and they on us, only wasting ammunition, for though our bullets reach them, few of theirs reach us. According to the men who came in from the Arabs, it is the pet detachment of the Mahdi who are opposite the Palace; they do not number more than one hundred, and are principally our Soudan soldiers. I have almost given up all idea of saving the town; it is a last resource, this attempt we make to open the route to the Omdurman Fort.

December 6.—(Certainly every fortified place ought to be provided with a hundred good telescopes.) The steamers went down and fired on the Arabs at Omdurman. We have £150 in cash in the treasury. In the affair to-day we had three killed and thirty-six wounded in the steamers, and Feratch Ullah Bey reports he had five wounded at Omdurman Fort. The Arabs came down in good force, and must have lost.

I have given up all idea of landing at Omdurman; we have not the force to do it. The Arabs fired forty-five rounds from their guns at Mogrim and the steamers. We had two men wounded at Mogrim, and one killed. This is most distressing to have these poor fellows wounded and killed. To-morrow it will be 270 days, 9 months, that we have endured one continuous misery and anxiety. The Greeks who were at Mogrim say at least 300 or 400 Arabs were killed and wounded in to-day's engagement. The *Ismailia* was struck by four, and the *Bordeen* by two shells, but not in vital parts. I visited the steamers, and had weariness of heart at hearing the complaint of the men as to the robbery of their rations by the officers.

December 7.—The 270th day of our imprisonment. The Arabs fired from their guns at Goba 8 shells, one of which fell in the town near Palace, but did no harm. Omdurman reports the fort all right, one more man wounded there. A great force of Arabs strayed down near Omdurman last night, and left at dawn. The cock turkey has killed one of his companions, reason not known. (Supposed to be correspondence with Mahdi, or some harem infidelity.) Report in town that Berber surrendered, "*sans coup férir.*" I hope so. We are going to send the steamers down again to attack the Arabs at Omdurman at noon to-morrow. The Arabs fired nine shells at Bourré, and begun again their practice on the Palace, firing five shells, one of which came close to the roof of Palace.

A soldier escaped from the Arabs and came in; he says the Expeditionary Force has captured Berber. Two soldiers deserted to the Arabs to-day! The Arabs at Goba fired three shells this evening at the Palace; two fell close to it, one fell in the water. One shell from the Arabs at Bourré fell in the hospital. One of the shells of the Arabs this evening struck the building next the Palace, and stuck in the wall, about 9 feet from the ground. A man came in from the Arabs, who says the Expeditionary Force is approaching. I saw a body of horsemen going north to-day, very fast, from El foun. In the *Ismailia* were eighty bullet holes on the water line of her hull; in the *Bordeen* there were seventy-five bullet holes, ditto *in the last engagement!!!* These holes were stopped by screws made for the purpose. As for the bullet marks elsewhere they are not to be counted.

My belief is that the Mahdi business will be the end of slavery in the Soudan. The Arabs have invariably put their slaves in the front and armed them; and the slaves have seen that they were plucky, while their masters shirked: is it likely that those slaves will ever yield obedience to those masters as heretofore?

December 8.—The Arabs this morning fired twelve rounds from guns at Bourré, and five rounds at the North Fort and Palace. Two men came in from the Arabs; they say no Arabs have gone down towards Berber; that the report in the Arab camp was that Berber was captured; this report was four days old. 10 A.M. The steamers are going down to attack. Omdurman Fort reports "*All right.*" 10.30 A.M. The steamers are engaged; the Arabs have two nasty wasp batteries with regular embrasures, quite *à l'Europe.* (Query Slatin Bey's design.) Though we have protected the steam-chests of the steamers, one cannot help being very anxious. The Arabs at Goba are *silent.* Another soldier from the Arabs came in and states report of advance of the Expeditionary Force, who are coming by land. Every time I hear the guns fire I have a twitch of the heart of gnawing anxiety for my penny steamers. 11.30 A.M. The battle is over, and my penny boats are safe, thank God! (not in words only, but from my heart). We had two wounded on board the *Bordeen*, none on board the *Ismailia.* We are meditating an attack with 500 men on the 50 Arabs, who, with their gun, are at Goba. The *Bordeen* was struck by four shells, the *Ismailia* by two shells, one of which destroyed a cabin: they had not much musketry fire, but the Arabs fired a great number of rounds; they had six guns playing on the steamers. At noon Arabs fired five shells at Bourré. In the evening they fired three shells against the Palace from Goba which fell in the town. Had we not cased the steam-chest of the *Ismailia* with wood she would have had her boiler blown up by one of the shells. The Arab rifle force of Goba is completely innocuous; we do not even hear their bullets, yet our bullets reach them, for they cannot stay in the open, and we can see the dust the bullets throw up that we fire. Wadji Barra, an Ameer of the Mahdi, on the north side, sent me a letter[69] asking me to surrender, and saying it is all lies about the Expedition, the Mahdi is evidently (like H.M.G.) offended with my curt answer to his last, and so his holiness will not write direct. Whenever we have what we call a victory we fire some fireworks at the main posts of our Lines, which infuriates the Arabs, and puzzle them as to the reason. They were very angry to-night, and came down in a good number, and fired on the Palace several volleys. I ordered up the three buglers, who put them to flight. The letter Wadji Barra sent me was sent by a woman who came to the North Fort. I telegraphed

[69] In Appendix AB.

the officer "Open the letter and tell me contents." He did so, and I answered, "Send the woman back to the Ameer and tell him to go, &c." I expect this irritated the Ameer, who ordered the advance of his men, and consequent expenditure of his ammunition.

December 9.—A party of sixty men, with ammunition camels, and some horsemen, left the Dem of the Mahdi, and went north this morning. The Arabs on the right bank of the White Nile came over to the left bank of the Blue Nile, and went through some antics, so we suppose something is up. A man was wounded yesterday at Omdurman, which fort reports all right.[70] The Arabs fired yesterday not rifled shell, but round shell, which they must have got at Obeyed, which shows they are out of ammunition of the regulation sort. What called forth the letter from Wadji Barra [71] was a paper I issued [72] to the town, when I received Towfik's telegram saying he would hold the Soudan, and which I gave to a man to send to the Arabs. If Lord Palmerston was alive (or Forster was Premier) he would never leave the Soudan, without proclaiming the emancipation of the slaves. On 18th December, 1862, Lincoln proclaimed abolition of slavery in the United States; this would be a good day to issue such a proclamation in the Soudan. Wadji Barra's letter calls me Pasha of Kartoum, and says I have been deaf to all their entreaties. Stewart left this place *three months ago!* to-day. A man was wounded by the Arab fire at Bourré: they fired twelve rounds from these guns at the Fort. I feel sure that the cause of the Mahdi's coming here is, that he got hold of Herbin's "French Consul's" Journal, written in a hostile critical spirit, and thinking it true, he advanced from Schatt. I expect Hansall, the Austrian Consul, also wrote in the style of Lamentations, for he also sent down a Journal by the *Abbas*. It is remarkable that the very effort which I made to obtain the ear of Europe should have thus recoiled on us. I have for the present abandoned the attack on the Arabs at Goba, as Omdurman is more important,

[70] Letter sent by Wadji Barra in Appendix AB.
[71] Appendix AB. [72] Appendix CD.

and as I expect the Arabs there have taken away their gun; it has not (up to 2 P.M.) fired to-day. I would like to ask the Mahdi—allowing *pro formâ* that he is the Mahdi—what will be his ultimate work? Certainly his present work is not exhilarating, firing on his fellow-creatures night and day. The siege of Sevastopol lasted 326 days. We are at our 271st day. In their case they had always their communication open, and they dealt with an enemy who would recognise the rights of war; whereas we are not so placed. They, the Russians, were united, and had no civil population to deal with; yet I cannot say I think we are over great heroes (the fact is, that, if one analyses human glory, it is composed of nine-tenths twaddle, perhaps ninety-nine hundredths twaddle). We are only short of the duration of siege of Sevastopol 57 days, and we have had *no respite*, like the Russians had, during the winter of 1854–55; and neither Nicholas nor Alexander speculated on (well, we will not say what, but we will put it) "counting the months." Of course it will be looked on as very absurd to compare the two blockades, that of Sevastopol and Kartoum; but if properly weighed, one was just as good as the other. The Russians had money, we had none; they had skilled officers, we had none; they had no civil population, we had forty thousand; they had their route open and had news, we had neither.

December 10.—A slave came in to-day, he had been with Slatin. He says Slatin is still in chains, that there are two insurrections in Kordofan, and rumour is rife that the Expeditionary Force is near. Fort Omdurman is all right. The slave says the Arabs have not much ammunition. The Arabs fired thirty-one rounds at Bourré to-day, and wounded four men (one an officer, a Major Souleiman Effi, fatally). The Arabs have been firing stones to-day. Goba is quiet, they did not fire their gun to-day, or yesterday. I expect it has gone down to the river-bank. The slave who came in says the Mahdi's return to Kordofan is cut off by the insurrection in his rear; so we and he are like two rats in a box. (I wish *he* was *out* of the *box!*) I have ordered the two steamers to stay up at Bourré, towards which place the Arabs seem to be directing an unpleasant degree of attention. (Truly I am worn to a shadow with the food question; it is one continual demand.) Five men deserted to-day. The Arabs shape the stones they fire, like to the shells of their guns; they will soon spoil the rifling of their guns if they continue this.

December 11.—The Arabs fired their gun from Goba three times; one shell fell into the water before the Palace—two passed over it. I put down more mines at Bourré. I have given the whole garrison an extra month's pay in addition to the three months' they had before received—I will not (*D. V.*) hesitate to give them £100,000, if I think it will keep the town.

Three soldiers came in from the Arabs who report advance of the Expedition towards Berber. The Arabs fired fourteen rounds from their guns at Bourré. The officers say that there is a European directing the Arab guns there. (I wonder if it is that Frenchman who came from Dongola, and who, I thought, might have been Renan.) Sennaar is holding out and in great force (so say the three soldiers), so is Kassala. The Dem of the Mahdi is altered in appearance. They say he has sent off the families of his adherents into the interior.

3.30 P.M.—The Arabs fired three shells at the Palace from Goba; two went into the water, one passed over the Palace. This always irritates me, for it is so personal; and from one's own soldiers too! It is not very pleasant also to feel at any moment you may have a shell in your room, for the creatures fire at all hours. The steamers fired on the Arabs at Bourré this morning, and one of the Arab shells struck one steamer, and another struck a santal which we have there to defend the flank; but neither did any harm. Two soldiers deserted to the Arabs to-day—these men are generally those who have before been with the Arabs, and had deserted to us. The Arabs fired another shell at the Palace this evening, which burst in the air.

December 12.—Small church parade. I sincerely hope this will be the last we shall have to witness. We have in hand 1,796,000 rounds Remington ammunition; 540 rounds Krupp;

6000 rounds mountain gun ammunition ; £140 in specie ; £18,000 in paper in treasury ! ! £60,000 in town in paper. 110,000 okes of biscuits ; 700 ardebs of dhoora. This morning I was told a long story of report concerning the Expeditionary Force being at El Damer, near the Atbara river ; of how Berber had surrendered, &c. On tracing it, I found it was a fib put in circulation by one of the chief Ulema, to encourage the people.

3.40 P.M. The Arabs fired two shells at the Palace ; one burst in the air, the other fell in the water in a direct line with the window I was sitting at, distant about a hundred yards.

3.40 P.M. They fired another shell, which fell only fifty yards short of the Palace ; another burst in the air. I have sent the buglers up to stop this target practice. All these shells are in good line for the west wing, in which the Arabs know I stop. They fired seven shells in all in this affair ; though the Arabs have fired over two thousand shells at us, I I do not think we have lost by artillery fire more than three men.

December 13.—The steamers went up and attacked the Arabs at Bourré (certainly this day-after-day delay has a most disheartening effect on every one. To-day is the 276th day of our anxiety). The Arabs appear, by all accounts, to have suffered to-day heavily at Bourré. We had none wounded by the Arabs ; but one man, by the discharge of a bad cartridge, got a cut in neck : this was owing to the same cause as nearly blew out my eyes the other day. We are going to send down the *Bordeen* the day after to-morrow, and with her I shall send this Journal. *If some effort is not made before ten days' time the town will fall.* It is inexplicable, this delay. If the Expeditionary Forces have reached the river and met my steamers, one hundred men are all that we require, just to show themselves.

I send this Journal, for I have little hopes of saving it if the town falls. I put in [73] the sort of arrangement I would make

[73] Appendix EF.

with Zubair Pasha for the future government of the Soudan. Ferratch Pasha is really showing an amount of vigour I did not give him credit for. Even if the town falls under the nose of the Expeditionary Force, it will not, in my opinion, justify the abandonment of Sennaar and Kassala, or of the Equatorial Province, by Her Majesty's Government. All that is absolutely necessary is, for fifty of the Expeditionary Force to get on board a steamer and come up to Halfeyeh, and thus let their presence be felt; this is not asking much, but it must happen *at once;* or it will (as usual) be too late. A soldier deserted to the Arabs to-day from the North Fort. The buglers on the roof, being short of stature, are put on boxes to enable them to fire over the parapet; one with the recoil of rifle was knocked right over, and caused considerable excitement. We thought he was killed, by the noise he made in his fall. The Arabs fire their Krupps continually into town from the South Front, but no one takes any notice of it. The Arabs at Goba only fired one shell at the Palace to-day, which burst in the air.

December 14.—Arabs fired two shells at the Palace this morning; 546 ardebs dhoora! in store; also 83,525 okes of biscuit! 10.30 A.M. The steamers are down at Omdurman, engaging the Arabs, consequently I am on *tenterhooks!* 11.30 A.M. Steamers returned; the *Bordeen* was struck by a shell in her battery; we had only one man wounded. We are going to send down the *Bordeen* to-morrow with this Journal. If I was in command of the two hundred men of the Expeditionary Force, which are all that are necessary for the movement, I should stop just below Halfeyeh, and attack the Arabs at that place before I came on here to Kartoum. I should then communicate with the North Fort, and act according to circumstances. NOW MARK THIS, if the Expeditionary Force, and I ask for no more than two hundred men, does not come in ten days, *the town may fall;* and I have done my best for the honour of our country. Good bye.

C. G. GORDON.

You send me no information, though you have lots of money.

C. G. G.

APPENDICES REFERRED TO IN THE JOURNALS.

APPENDICES TO BOOK I.

APPENDIX A.

Letter to General Gordon from Abd el Kâder Ibrahim.

In the name of God, the Merciful and Compassionate, blessing be on our Lord Mahomed, and peace.

From the servant of his Lord—the Fakeer (humble one) Abd el Kâder Ibrahim, Kâdi (Judge) of Kalâkla, to his Excellency Gordon Pasha, Governor General of the Soudan.

Now this is what we have to state to your Excellency: Your benevolence and compassion towards all are well known, and your special regard towards us is most particularly known to us, and confirmed by deeds since the beginning of your presence in the Soudan both the first and this second time.

That which you have declared in proclamation emanating from you on your arrival in the Soudan this time is known to us both publicly and privately.

But the first conviction in the true mission of this present Imâm, the Mahdi (the expected one, on whom be peace) from the very beginning (first day) of his appearance, forbids us to accept your letters or to reply to you. For we know about him what the Ulema (wise men), who have wandered from the right way, do not know. And as the mission of this Imâm, the Mahdi (the expected one, on whom be peace) is predicted (confirmed) for us and for you in the ancient books, we cannot incline to (receive) your many kindnesses and your regard to us (as shown) by your favours and your bounties, or forsake the command of the glorious and Most High God and of his prophet Mahomed, on whom be peace. We had previously to this frequently communicated with your Highness. And on each occasion we explained sufficiently for him who has a heart (to understand); and in all our communications we made clear unto you the way of peace and salvation. But you have not accepted it; nor have you given your mind to the important object of our call unto you—which is the means of your material and moral salvation from the dangers of this world and the next (and that both) for yourself and for the people of the city—because many of them are our friends and our relations.

But you have rejected what we have demonstrated to you again and again. You have listened to the Ulema whom this world has deceived by its glittering mirage, making them forget both their own souls and the Moslems, for the sake of contemptible riches of this life.

Yet their enmity, and giving of the lie, to the Imâm, the Mahdi (the expected one, on whom be peace), are predicted in the ancient books, and they themselves are aware of this. But if they ignore this let them consider the preface of the book, "Keshef el Ghumma an Jamia el Umma," by Shaàrani.[1]

But you rely upon their sayings and listen to their words, notwithstanding what has been proved and made known to you and to all intelligent people of the calamities and destruction that have befallen the country. This is the very point (acmé) of your error, and of your blindness as to what is right.

But because we have not ceased to compassionate you and the people of the city; and because the supreme Emir Abderrahman el Najoomi, and the Emir Abdallah en Noor and the other emirs with him, have come with a very great host of troops of all the various tribes which have submitted to the Imâm, on whom be peace.

(And because) You are utterly heedless as to (the safety of) yourself and the people of the city, in our exceeding compassion we have written this to you in return for your past regard and favour to us. And we beseech God that it may be accepted (by you).

Besides all this, the noble Imâm himself has arrived at Schatt, and with him innumerable hosts, and he will shortly come with his army to the city.

It is therefore our duty to inform you of this in the hope that you will listen to us, and disregard the words of the seditious; and that you will submit to this Imâm, the Mahdi, because, beyond all doubt he is the Imâm, the Mahdi (the expected one, on whom be peace). And all the Governments (Powers) will be destroyed by his hand; for he is supported and made victorious by the power of God. Be not misled by that which happened in the Desert (Deem) of Jareef and of the East.

For God made the prophet Mahomed victorious, and humiliated all his enemies after his defeat in the raid on Badr and on Ohod, both (which are) well known. And God gave him unbroken victory (success after that) as much as he wished and desired. All (the defeat) which has occurred in the two deserts (deems) before-named is worth nothing (unimportant). It does not equal (counterbalance)

[1] Title of the Book, "The Dissipation of Gloom from all (Mohammedan) Peoples."

a tenth of the tenth of those slaughtered in the day of the battle of Sheikh el Obeyed, as is known to you and the people of the city.

This is our counsel to you, and please God you and the people of the city may accept it.

And know, O Excellency Gordon, that we have communicated with his Highness the Mahdi on your behalf; and his favourable answer has come, (which is) of a nature to please you and give you confidence, provided that you submit and obey.

And this is the communication (of the Mahdi) sent to you by the two Moslem envoys, together with the dervishes, our allies, who now come to you.

(Signed) IBRAHIM ABD EL KÂDER.

Dated 18 Zu'l Kâdi, 1301.
9th Sept., 1884.

Postcript.—We have sent this reply to your Excellency with our allies the dervishes, dispatched from the Lord of all, the Mahdi (the expected one, on whom be peace), and with the two Moslems, Mahomed Yusuf and George Calamatino. And because they were refused at the gates, we now send it back to you with our son Suleiman, specially sent by us, who has a letter from the head-quarters of the Imâm requesting your speedy reply to him.

All the emirs here present have given assurance of safe conduct, in the name of God and of his prophet, to whomsoever you may send for needful negotiations. And if it is agreeable to your Excellency, send for our son and for our friend George Calamatino for complete understanding between us and you, as he is both intelligent and friendly in this matter.

And it appears from your letter that (you consider us) intelligent and understanding; therefore you should have believed our report about this Imâm, that there might be fruit (benefit) derived for all. But we believe that your opinion of us for sense was inconsistent.

Now God is the Director and Guide into truth.

(Signed) IBRAHIM ABD EL KÂDER.

Written the same date.

APPENDIX A[1].

General Gordon's reply to [Ibrahim] Abd el Kâder.

We have received your answer and we have taken note of all you have said.

With regard to the spies of whom you informed us that they were entrusted with delivery of the replies—when (they) these special messengers arrived at the ramparts, we did them no harm.

But when we sent a messenger with our answers you fired with ball upon the slave when he placed the stick upon the ground.

We received the messenger who came to us from you, and he saw that we were well.

It would be better that the messengers whom you send to us should be people of sense, and who know how to behave. As to the Greek whom it is your intention to send to us—the person who has forsaken our religion and adopted another religion—we do not wish to receive him, just as you would not wish to receive a Moslem who had adopted the Christian religion.

A letter has been sent us by this person aforesaid. It shows us that he has important information which concerns the Europeans. But we know that there are many like this fellow, who have information that concerns the son of Najoomi.

But perhaps the information about the Europeans of which he has told us is about the bringing of the European army to fight the son of Weld el Najoomeh after thirty days—for we have now a precious opportunity.

I know that you have been invested with a veil and robes of honour, and you say that Mohammed Achmed is the Mahdi—and I know that there is among you a man of mature age who has spent his life, from his youth up, in Islâm—who would consent to the ruin of the country.

Considering that I cannot bear the sight of that renegade traitor, it is preferable that you should send us a respectable pious man, who may be depended on, to receive 10,000 guineas for the ransom of the Europeans who are to be found there, and we will send them by his hand; and if you say that Mohammed Achmed is the Mahdi, why does he remain in the White (Nile)?—he ought (if he is the Mahdi) to take the whole country.

[The copy above translated is extremely illegible—evidently written in haste—by an unaccustomed scribe; the handwriting is bad and in Turkish style.

We have surmised that General Gordon employed the writer as being trustworthy, for among the inhabitants of Kartoum it must have been possible to find one who could write better.

George Calamatino is evidently the renegade whom the General refuses to admit to his presence.]

APPENDIX B.

Letters from George Calamatino.

Kartoum, 10th September, 1884.

Mr. N. LEONTIDES and B. GEORGOPULO.

Accept our salutes.

I beg (beseech) you on behalf of myself and that of the other fellow-countrymen of mine, of Kordofan and Darfour, to try and induce by any means Mr. Gordon for me to be permitted to see him, as it is of great need and of good to yourselves and of the Government my entering Kartoum; and if Mr. Gordon is not satisfied (with the news I propose to communicate to him), let him imprison me and prevent me going out again. If he permits my entering, do send me a European suit (of clothes), but if he does not, then send out a Greek to meet me; there is no fear whatever his doing so, and he may go back at once. I am waiting for a reply close to the entrenchments.

Your friend,

GEORGE CALAMATINO.

HIS EXCELLENCY GORDON PASHA,

I beg you to give me permission to enter into Kartoum, because I have important matters in regard to all the Europeans who are slaves with the Prophet. If you are not disposed to let me return, I should be disposed and content to remain with your Excellency.

GEORGE CALAMATINO.

Arabic Encampment at Kartoum.
Sept. 10th, 1884.

HIS EXCELLENCY GORDON,

I beg you to accept my most cordial respects. It displeases me that you are irritated; I hope to see you in better moments, and I hope soon for a favourable issue. Health to all and my respects to you.

G. CUZZI.

Answered.

Received your letter, asking to come to Kartoum, to tell me important matters concerning all Europe. I do not want to see you.

10/9/84. C. G. G.

APPENDIX C.

Letter to General Gordon from Abderrahhman en Najoomi and Abdallah en Noor.

In the name of God, the Merciful and Compassionate, blessing be on our Lord Mahomed and peace.

From the slaves of their lord, Abderrahhman en Najoomi and Abdallah en Noor, lieutenants of the Mahdi (the expected one, on whom be peace), to Gordon Pasha. May God direct him to the truth.

What we state to thee is : First, that thou art a stranger in the country and to this government, and thou art intelligent and well informed.

What God wishes to reveal neither men nor demons can keep secret ; and even if they seem to do so God will accomplish His design in spite of the infidels. At thy first arrival at Kartoum the Imâm, &c. (here follow the customary phrases of respect), wrote to thee to surrender to God and his prophet, and informed thee of the truth, in which there is no lie, and assured thee that after that, if thou didst not submit to the command of God and his prophet, the army of God will come to thee and will destroy that in which thou (hast aspired) to share with God thy Creator (in claiming) rule over His (faithful) servants, while the earth belongs to God, and He causes whom He will of His righteous servants to inherit it.

And, nevertheless, thou hast sent to his Highness a reply different from that desired, and the substance of it (is) thy refusal to obey and submit to what he commanded thee to do. Yet in his desire for thy good he waited and delayed a space of time, expecting that thy sense (reason) would return unto thee, and that thou wouldst consider thy ways, nor rely upon this world and its illusions nor on its transitory possessions (wealth).

Time has now been prolonged, and he has become aware of thy firm resolve not to obey and submit. He has now appointed us, the lieutenants above named, and he has supplied us with trusty men from among his companions—men who love death as ye love life, and who count, in fighting you, on the great reward. Death is dearer to them than their wives or the very best of their possessions.

One man of them in battle is better than a thousand of you. He has provided us with weapons of war—in which thou thinkest there is victory—with Krupp cannon, with mountain guns for battle, in which thou shalt taste of evil if thou turn aside from the way of God.

The desire of the Mahdi (&c.) is for thy good. He did not stop at the previous correspondence, but sent you his messengers with his letter, and he especially sent two Europeans to counsel thee and make the truth known to thee; and this out of mercy and compassion to thee and those with thee (to save thee) from destruction in this world and from the evil of torment in the next. Notwithstanding all this thou hast remained stubborn, and hast turned thy back to counsel in thy greed for transitory power, from which thou must soon be removed (by death), either willingly or unwillingly (either peaceable or violent), and thou hast replied to the Lord of all (on whom be peace) refusing to submit, arguing by quotations from the Koran and other prophecies dictated by thy scribes and thy Ulema, and thou reliest on their proofs with which thou art not acquainted. But the fulfilment of those passages is to be found in the Mahdi (on whom be peace) and his honourable companions.

And know, O honourable Pasha, and all erring Ulema who are with thee—for they do know the truth but do not counsel thee (aright), because they love the grandeur and wealth which they have obtained from thee by deceit and sedition.

And listen—if thine understanding be enlightened—to our advice and to what El Jaber our brother, formerly called George Calamatino, will advise thee, so that if thou dost obey and submit to the command of God and His prophet thou shalt save thyself, and obtain the privilege of saving those who are with thee.

Otherwise do not doubt but that thou and those with thee will be destroyed within two days, because the lord of all will, please God, come here, and on his arrival—should he still find thee in rebellion—ye will be destroyed.

Awaiting your decision by bearer.

(Signed.)

Dated 21 Zu'l Kâdi, 1301.
12th Sept., 1884.

Postcript.—We also inform thee, O honourable Pasha, that as for the Ulema who are with thee, and on whose sayings thou dependest, all their children and relations are with the Mahdi, and as soon as distress comes to them they will leave thee alone. Outwardly they are bodily with thee; but inwardly their hearts are with us. The news (information) of the city and of thee is constantly supplied to us by the people of the city. Do not let the Ulema, the merchants and the servants, deceive thee, for when thou shalt fall into the grasp (of the Mahdi) they will not help thee nor protect thee.

Listen to our counsel with an attentive ear.

(Signed) ABDERRAHHMAN EN NAJOOMI.
ABDALLAH EN NOOR.

Same date.

[This letter is more peremptory in tone, and lacks the proper titles of respect given in the former one to General Gordon.]

APPENDIX C[1].

From General Gordon. (Reply to his honour the Sheikh Abderrahhman en Najoomi.)

Your letter sent by Mr. George Calamatino, who is called El Jâber, has reached us. That which you have made known in it is understood. It is true that this is not my country, and I am a stranger in it, but I am deputed as Governor-General here by the two great Governments, and must therefore direct its affairs as becomes my friendship and compassion for the Moslems.

If there be a man who desires to become a dervish we do not hinder him. With regard to the Ulema, you state that they are all liars, and that their words are worthless. But they have said nothing but what they find declared in the books; nay, all the Ulema of Islâm are plain on the subject.

They do not wish to sleep on the (bare) ground, or to be dressed like dervishes, or to change the clothing to which they have been accustomed from the beginning of the Moslem religion.

We have never sent answers to His Honour Mahomed Achmed, or to any others, at dictation of scribe or any of the Ulema, but by help of the Arabic and English lexicon in our possession, dictating them (myself) word by word; and if you do not believe this send us an eminent man, of good sense, to listen to my words, (and hear) whether they are my own or not.

In proof (of what I say) I have received three dervishes from Mahomed Achmed. They had with them the robes (of a dervish), and I spoke to them many words in Arabic, and I refused the garments (of a dervish which had been sent by them). Was that my own doing, or that of any one else?

But as to the cannons and the guns which ye want to fight us with, we have still many like them.

We have seen from the letters we receive that the Mahdi destroys people without cannons and guns, which is true.

As to the words which George, the Greek afore-named, has said, we do not see any advantage in them (of a visit from him).

With regard to the people and the Ulema, of whom you say that outwardly their bodies are with us, but that their hearts are with you, and that in the day of battle they will desert us and flee to you, be it known unto you that we are not keeping them here, nor preventing them from going to you.

Their going, or not going, are both alike (to us). Why do they not go?

(Signed) GORDON PASHA.

Date 23 Zu'l Kâder.
15th Sept., 1884.

APPENDIX D.

Copy of the answer written by the Ulema undersigned, to the Sheikh Abdel Kâder Ibrahim, and to the son of En Najoomi, dated 23rd Zu'l Kadi, 1301.

In the name of God, the Merciful and Compassionate, the Destroyer of him who is obstinate against His religion. Blessing and peace be on our Lord Mahomed and his successors, who have established the foundations and the solid pillars (of the faith).

God has sent down[2] in His glorious book, through which cometh nothing false, neither in its direct teaching nor in what may be deduced therefrom. This has been sent down by the All Wise and All Worthy of Praise (saying), This day I have completed[3] your religion for you, and I have perfected unto you My grace, and have granted unto you Islam as (your) religion; which is the last verse sent down to the Chosen One (Mahomed). After this let no one heed any saying or accept any act which is not dictated in the Book or the Soonna. But if there had been any (fresh) Revelation on which reliance could be placed for superseding any law of the (established) laws of Islam, it would involve accusing the precious Book of lying; for after completion no new thing can be added.

Moreover, it has been unanimously agreed that (anything claiming to be) a revelation of the prophet, on whom be blessing and peace, if its sense differ from the Law, that revelation is not to be acted upon, but must be set aside; and it is one of the absolute conditions of him who contends (for the faith) that he should not violate the unanimous agreement, that he who utters the double confession (of faith in God and the prophet) has (thereby) secured safety for his life and his property, unless by the Law (right) of Islam as is written in the Hadith;[4] and this Law (right) of Islam has been defined in the whole of the true Hadiths (namely) that breach of chastity and murder are contrary to Law (right) and (constitute) apostasy from Islam. And among apostates (is he) who forsakes his religion and causes schism in congregation as is (found) in the Hadiths.

Now this pretender to the office of Mahdi is causing schism in the congregation and has broken the staff (unity) of Islam, and has ruined the abodes of the Moslems, plundered their property, dishonoured their women, and made some tyrannise over others, as is in accordance with their apostasy, because they have made

[2] The Moslems say that the Koran was sent down, every word of it, by the Angel Gabriel to Mahomed.

[3] This verse is considered to be the *completion* of God's final Revelation through Mahomed.

[4] The Hadiths—the authorised traditional sayings of Mahomed and those brought down by Gabriel.

lawful the killing of the faithful, the dishonour of their women, and the plunder of their property, and calling them Kāfirs (infidels) without cause, though these are observing (or defending) the laws of religion, and walking in the firm road (way of truth); moreover, the majority of his followers are sorely troubled by what they have seen of slaughter, infamy, pillage, and taking of captives, nor are they with him body and soul (heartily), the proof of which is that only a few days passed before some of them came to seek assistance from the Government against oppression, famine, and nakedness.

A number of letters have come, some of them from you, in which are a number of erroneous statements, wherein the Sheikh el Akbar says that the Most High God has appointed for the Mahdi a divine host of Ministers (Vizirs), whom God has reserved for him in the depths of His secret councils; He has revealed them declaring and witnessing about the Creation, and that which God has commanded for His servants; also that the Mahdi does nothing except by their counsel; and that they are Persians (foreigners), not one of them is an Arab, yet they speak nothing but Arabic; that they have a chief, Hafiz, who is not of their race, who has never at all rebelled against God; he is the chief of the Vizirs. Their number does not exceed nine, nor is it less than five. To every six there is a Vizir, who has special knowledge and functions. Here ends the quotation.[5]

But where are these foreign Vizirs, and that one among them who professes that he is an Arab? and what about their excess above that number?

And with all this you accuse us Ulema of error from the way of truth, and say that you know what others do not know; whereas, between you and him that has even the very least knowledge, there is a very wide gulf.

And in those letters you address His Excellency the Governor-General (Gordon) as Sáadat,[6] and yet they contain accusations of his being a Kāfir (infidel). Is not this to use terms which contradict each other?

In them you also say that the certain proof as to this being indeed the Mahdi, the Expected One, on whom be peace, was accepted by you at the very beginning of his manifestation, and forbids you to receive letters or to reply to them.

Also in some of your letters you say that you have been among the number of his Vizirs for the last thirty years. How is this after what you wrote lately under your seal to your Sheikh el Obeyed, that whoever believes that this Mahomet Achmet is the Mahdi must needs be a Kāfir (infidel), because there has not come any Hadith, or revelation, or Athar, but shows to all the world the true nature of

[5] In Arabic writing quotation marks are not used, but, at the end of the quotation, they append the words, "End of his words."

[6] Saadat—"Felicity"—is used as a title of honour, and cannot, of course, be properly used for one who is a Kāfir and under Divine wrath.

this man; therefore to believe in him would involve giving the lie to him, on whom be blessing and peace, who is, above all, worthy to be believed?

Here is contradiction! Since your love of the world has actually perverted you even into saying of him, "Peace be on him."[7] ('Alaihy es salaam.)

But the Prince[8] (of the faith), Abd el Ghani, the Nablusi, said in his book, the Hadik en Nadih, the commentary on the Mahomedan religion, No one ought to be distinguished by the salaam (after his name) excepting the prophets, for one cannot say, Ali, on whom be peace (salaam); and this rule applies both to living and dead alike, excepting that a person present may be addressed thereby, for people say, Peace be upon thee. Here ends the quotation.

You have pretended that the coming of the Imam the Mahdi, the Expected One, is proved for us and for you in the ancient books, and that it is impossible for you to incline unto us, and that the hostility of the Ulema against the Imam the Mahdi and their giving the lie to him are both proved and mentioned in the ancient books, and you call the attention of the Ulema to the book *Keshef el Ghummah 'an jamia' el ummah* of Shaàrani. But here, if you meant this for the ignorant who do not know the ancient books or *Keshef el Ghummah*, that might do, for there is not in all the ancient books any reference or allusion which concerns or points to any Mahdi. Nay, it has been denied by the greatest men as being unsupported by any Hadith or testimony, and it originates with the Shiahs, who pretend that our Lord Mohammed, son of the Hanafiyeh, will appear, and also his father 'Ali, in the clouds. But, if we admit the sayings which seem to prove that there will be a Mahdi, where is the Khorassani, brother of him who is appointed Mahdi, who is to prepare the way for him before his appearing? and where is the Safiyān who was to be King before him? and where is the arm which was to appear with the hand pointing (as if to direct)—This is the Mahdi. Follow him? And where is the dwindling of the Euphrates displaying the mountain of gold? Or have you found in him the tokens revealed by the prophet of God, on whom be blessing and peace, that the Mahdi will not disturb any who is sleeping nor will he shed blood. But there are proofs to you and to all that he has shed blood, and has disturbed sleepers to so great an extent that you have made bold to say that he will destroy all governments. Now if what is said about him and what you tell us about him (be true), what would be the fruit of joy and favour to those who submit to him, since the end is destruction?

Now the old books still exist. Produce, therefore, some one who can show us what you have asserted, for we have found no trace of

[7] "Peace be on him" (on whom be peace), the usual formula of salutation to a true believer if alive, and used of prophets when their names are mentioned.

[8] Prince of the Faith—literally, axis or pole.

your assertions as you have set them forth, especially because it is known to everybody who knows this man who pretends to be Mah'di that he has neither tribe nor relations of illustrious origin, and the tribe of which he comes is very small indeed, nor is it (strong enough) to give victory in any matters of religion to him who may come forth from it; and as to his standing alone and separate from any family, which you have put forward as indicating the validity of his claim, that in truth is a notable proof of its worthlessness; for, as the learned Imam Ibn Khaldoon said in his preface, of which we extract a literal copy and send it to you herewith, from which you will learn that he is not justified in his claim, and that the religious mission without (the support of) family will not abide, for every matter of public concern absolutely needs (the support of) family; and a following and mob of ignorant folk cannot be called family; but (the support of) family consists in ancestry and kindred, in whom support is to be found. Let not his pretension deceive you in that he says he is of the house (of the prophet), for this is not known or proved amongst people of position. But, if that were granted, have you seen with him any of the kindred of the prophet who help him to victory? The whole of his arguments in favour of his claim (establish) the contrary, and his proofs and evidences are such as decide against the truth of his claim. And if you had looked with the eye of justice, and followed the right, you would not have believed in this pretension, or have called on people to respond to it, while threatening them with death, pillage and more. But it was your duty to advise[9] the Moslems and not to take up arms against them. Have ye not read, He who kills a believer intentionally merits Jehennam everlastingly, and the wrath of God and His curse are upon him, and great torment is reserved for him? Or (have you read) the Hadith—He who has borne arms against us is not of us? Or the command of the prophet, on whom be blessing and peace (who says), In killing [a Moslem] he has broken the staff (unity) of the Moslems, for their interests are one? And the Hadith—The believer is brother to the believer; he may not oppress him or betray him? And the Hadith—One believer is to another like (the stones of a) building; they support one another? Then he, on whom be blessing and peace (in so saying), clasped his hands (locking the fingers together by way of illustration).

Also the Hadith—He is a believer to whom people have confided their property and their lives, and he has accomplished the Hegira who flees from sin and transgression. The believer is the mirror of the believer, and the believer is brother to the believer who shelters him from harm, and protects him from his pursuers?

Also the Hadith—Whoever casts a look upon his brother believer to terrify him unjustly, God will terrify him in the day of Resurrection?

[9] The argument here rests upon the duty of avoiding force in dealing with brother Moslems, and of using persuasion only.

Also the Hadith—The believers are as one man. If he accuse his head, he accuses the whole body; and if he accuses his eye, he accuses the whole (body)?

Also the Hadith—The (true) Moslem is he from whose hand and tongue Moslems are safe, and the believer is he to whom people have confided their blood (life) and their property?

We have looked at the preface of *Keshef el Ghummah*, and found that the author said in it—The Prophet, on whom be peace, announced to me that this book will remain until the appearance of the Mahdi, on whom be peace, and his followers will profit by it, and by it will be able to dispense with the advice of the Mahdi in most matters of religion, for when he, on whom be peace, is come, he will do away with contradictions and differences of opinion on the earth, so that in his days there will remain none but the pure faith, and the body of the Ulema of his day will be secretly hostile to him.

But there is not found in it that the Ulema err from the way of truth, but (there is found) they are to be excused for their thought when they see him differing in doctrine from the doctrine of their Imams on account of their conviction that there is no authority above the authority of their Imams; yet they would submit to him for fear of his power and through coveting the wealth he possesses, for he and the prophet are brothers, and no one will oppose him but will fail.

Also in the Hadith (it is found) that they (? he) will follow the steps of the prophet, blessing and peace on him; he will be infallible, and he will not decree as to what is lawful or unlawful excepting as he, on whom be blessing and peace, would have decreed if he had been alive. He will not surpass any of their Imams in knowledge and thought in the least. This is what ought to be acted upon, and this as regards him who has attained such a degree of profound knowledge (of religion) that he has arrived at differing (ventures to differ), though the Imams are against him.

But your Imam has not attained this degree of profound knowledge. for he knows nothing of the six sciences on perfection, on which this profound knowledge depends. Besides which, he has forsaken the axioms which are among the essentials of religion.

But the Shaarāni himself, from whose book you quote as guide, has said in his book *El Yawakeet w'el Jowahir* ("Rubies and Jewels") that the Mahdi is to be son of Hassan el Askari, and his birth will be in the night of the middle of Sha'abān, two hundred, fifty and five, and he remaineth until he meets Jesus the Son of Mary. (Shaarāni) said, "Thus was I informed by Sheihk Hassan el Ar'āki when I met with me, and my lord Ali el Khowas confirmed the same." End of the quotation.

Now if his birth was in the year two hundred, fifty and five, and he is to be appointed Mahdi as a youth, as is found in the Hadiths, and (seeing that) from since then that one thousand and forty-six years have passed, while the age of your Imam does not amount to the tenth part of those years, how can you quote the evidence of Sha'arāni on your side and convict us of error by him, while he is quite clear in (saying) that which contradicts this pretension? Whereas if he (the Mahdi) had laid claim to sovereignty, that would have been more agreeable to his (Sha'arāni's) saying:—He has made his claim because the people followed him. For the Governor-General here does not prevent any one from going to him or to any one else, but the roads are open to all who please; notwithstanding which the people do not cease to come in crowds and crowds, desiring the protection of his government; and he protects them, and is beneficent to them, and provides for them; whereas it is just the opposite with those who go to you, even the envoys. And if you doubt this, stop the seizing of booty and the killing of deserters, and pillage after fighting, and see after that who will follow you? For without doubt there are those who do so under compulsion, and are distressed thereat, and wrongly imagine that this is from the Turkish Government. But now we and you are here in the Soudan, and there is not one here of the Turkish Government. If you were to come to Kartoum you would not find a Turk. Why, then, is this war? Is it for the ruin of religion, the slaughter of Moslems, for the overthrow of houses and mosques, for the burning of the books of the religion of Islam and the killing of the Ulema, or to close the way against the pilgrimage of the Hajj (to Mecca)? And this is (your) Mahdi's work!

Now, because it has been declared in the *Sabbeehh* that religion is sincerity to God and His prophet, and His Imāms the Moslems and their people, we have written this unto you, in the hope that you will understand it and will act accordingly before you are hemmed in by the evil of your deeds. And as to this business, since its close and end are close at hand, we remind you thereof, and if that which we have enlarged upon is not sufficient for you, then let your Ulema and your notables come to examine the matter in a place where both parties will feel secure. For there is the Book and the Soonna, and let them bring about union between us, and God will guide whom He will, and cause to err whom He will. But if this does not commend itself to you—although it is enjoined in the saying of the Most High,—if you should differ in anything submit it to God and His prophet, if ye be believers in God and in the last Day;—(then) attend to our proposal and come; let us call our sons and your sons, and our wives and your wives, and ourselves and yourselves, and consult, and lay the curse of God upon the liars.

And be not misled by that which you have mentioned about the slaughter of Moslems in Kordofan and in the engagement with your Sheikh el Abeed, for this is nothing in comparison with what happened to the Moslems in the raid of Tithār and the slaughter of Nebuchadnezzar in the Holy House,[10] and the destruction thereof, and the war of Tamerlane, and others beside, which are written in the books, as will be understood on referring to them; also in the

[10] The argument here is that true believers are sometimes killed, though in the right, as the Israelites were by Nebuchadnezzar.

last war, in which were martyred, by the Beni el Asfar,[11] a number of Moslems past counting. And after the great wars and destruction of countries the Moslems have not seen any result injurious to the faith. Was not the Caaba overthrown by the engines of war? Were not the Imām Hussein and his family slain at Kerbela? Now, if all this proves that he who conquers has right on his side, why, then, did you not follow the conquering government which subjugated the Moslem countries?

Moreover, as to the two engagements you have mentioned, and those who were killed in them, some of them were killed by thirst and some by treachery. And it is well known that war resembles the buckets (on a wheel like see-saw; one up, the other down).

We are ashamed to reply to the foolish comparison you draw about the raid of Badr and that of Ohod, as we are also ashamed to reply to your Imam, who places on a level with the righteous Khalifs those weak (miserables), poor in faith, who are like brute beasts and even more ignorant. Were we to answer that, it would take too long, wherefore we lay hold of the reins of our pen and stop it from running in that Maidān (race-course).

And God will direct in the right way.

Signed and sealed.

Zu'l Kadi 23rd, 1301.
September 14th, 1884.

MOOSA MAHOMED, Mufti of the Mejlis of Kartoum.

SHEIKH EL EMIN MAHOMED, President and Distinguished One (Primus) of the Ulema of the Soudan.

SHÂKIR EFPENDI, Mufti of the Court of Appeal of the Soudan.

SHEIKH HUSSEIN EL MAHDI, Professor of Science at the Mosque.

MAHAMED KHOWAJLI, Supreme Kādi of the Soudan.

APPENDIX E.

Endorsed—

"Letter from Faki Mustapha to Cassim el Moos, Melet of Shaggyehs. No seal to it."

In the name of God the Merciful and Compassionate, the bountifu Ruler.

Blessing upon our Lord Mahomed; and on his successors, and peace.

[11] "Yellow-haired Greeks"—the ancient phrase here applied as "Children of the Yellow (race),' the yellow-haired Russians being meant.

From the servant of his Lord (without Whom he has no strength), the Fakeer of God Ahhmed el Mustafa the humble theologian, faithful to Mohammed, to the beloved and virtuous Cassim el Mousse, the Melek (king) whom may God ever preserve.

After wishing you abundance of peace, I greatly desire (to see) you. May God never separate me from you or deprive me of you. And it is well known to your honour that after seeing you, and (after) your enlisting in our ranks (in faith), besides the previous friendly ties which draw us nearer to each other, that we have been very anxious about you and still think of you night and day; and more especially when you were in Baghshuda, and as was believed, near the Imâm, on whom be peace. Until (we heard that) the Most High God has delivered you in His mercy and goodness; and when you came to this town, inhabited by oppressors. And (when) it was the will of God that thou shouldst enter into this town our anxiety about thee increased on account of what we know of the power of the Mahdi, which no Government can withstand. And when a party of his enemies were destroyed we made inquiries as to those who were slain, being anxious (feeling compassion) for thee.

And we pray to the most High God, publicly and privately, to deliver thee out of it (the city) in safety. And when we heard that you had departed from it to the Halfai, we returned thanks to God for the sake of your children and of our children, (both) for your safety and for your departure from among them. Praises be to God for this. We declare to you, O Beloved! that as to truth (of the mission) of this Mahdi (that) our being in his service is sufficient for you, if you believe in us. Do not pay attention to the Ulema of Kartoum who pretend that Gordon is right whilst he is the most determined of enemies to those who believe in the glorious Koran. But it was predicted, before his appearing, that the Ulema would be hostile to him and that he would kill them. Also that the nobles would be hostile to him and that he would fight them and kill some of them even (if they took sanctuary) under the curtains of the Kaaba (at Mecca).

And this man is that very Mahdi who will perform those deeds. And as soon as we were convinced of the truth of his mission, we arose and submitted unto him. We left off study of the glorious Koran, and the (public) prayers on Fridays, and laid hold of him because he is the unfailing support (= rock, a phrase applied to God). We have not ceased to think of you, and when you were in Kartoum we tried to get the safe conduct, and we obtained it, for yourself and for your property and your children and your wives and all your followers—explicit, sealed and signed, and beyond chance of fraud or pretence. God is my witness in what I say.

I tried to get that good tidings into the town to you, but could not find the way till God heard my prayers and did not disappoint my hopes concerning you, so that your wife and her mother came to the Mahdi, on whom be peace, and I obtained their safe conduct.

I am most deeply anxious about you lest you should be (imprisoned) again with those people, whose ways God hath straitened (who are in difficulties), for the Imâm, the Mahdi himself (on whom be peace), has arrived at Schatt fifteen days ago. And he has honoured us these two days by writing (from him).

If it is in your power to bring away with you all you have of arms and ammunition and ships (steamers), meet us with them—that will obtain for you great honour in the sight of the Imâm, and of his honourable followers; but if not, God will not require of any man more than he is able to do (quotation from the Koran). Then come by yourself, and if you leave behind you any property do not mind it, for you will obtain that at the conquest (of the city) without diminution. Be not troubled as to what has happened between you and the Fakeers in the East. It is a small matter considering the indulgence of the Imâm, on whom be peace. What you did will not be accounted as misdeeds compared with the misdeeds of Salehh Lik when he killed the Yakoobāt, and plundered their property; and the sons of the Mukâtify, and plundered their property, and took their children, although they were noble. In spite of all that, he is nearer than any other man to the Imâm, who has forgiven him, and given him full pardon.

Do not take account of what you have done, but come out to us secretly, if not openly—that we may convince you of the truth (genuineness) of the Mahdi—by whom in His mercy God has strengthened our weakness. But beware of delay, for I fear that after his arrival here you will not find the way (open) to come to us, nor will our entreaties avail.

Do not heed the ignorant talk of the Ulema of Kartoum, or to the pretences (ideas) of people who heed carnal things rather than sacred. Wherefore God has sealed their hearts so that they do not know. They are (foolish) like ostriches, yea they are inferior (to them).

Oh, my beloved, come by yourself—or with those who are with thee if thou canst—but beware!—beware of delay. I warn you earnestly against going back to Kartoum after God has brought you out from thence.

Hasten to us that we may help you before it be too late.

The time of the Turks is over. The rope (line) of their dominion is cut (severed), and what God has cut cannot be mended. Do not hang upon (attach yourself to) that which has been cut, and which is declared by the chosen (people) of God to be indeed cut; as was declared by His prophet, on whom be peace.

Now, according to what we know of your intelligence and knowledge (we say) do not be misled by the changes of this life,—for the days are few. (It is only for a time.) Peace be with you.

(Signed) The Fakeer of God,
AHHMET EL MUSTAFA,
The theologian, the faithful one of Mohammed.
I have no seal.

Dated 19 Zu'l Kâdi, 1301.
September 10, 1884.

Postcript.—I inform you that Gordon and the Ulema of Kartoum have had one of their mails captured in Metemma by a one-eyed man, named Mahomed Ahhmed—(going) to the Governor-General of Egypt (? Cario).

But as to Gordon's letters, he says in them that he and those with him will perish if they are not reinforced within these two months, as they are in want, and have nothing left in their hands but Kartoum only.

The sum of 55,000 guineas at Berber has been taken by the Fakeers, and the letter of the Kartoum people tells him that they have been lost.

From this it is evident to you that there is no help for them. Therefore do not remain with them with your family. The wise man looks after himself.

(Signed) AHHMET EL MUSTAFA.

Same date.

You will receive an answer to his honour Ahhmed Bek Ali Jallâb secretly sent to him, and hand his answer to bearer. Peace (to you).

Same date.

APPENDIX E[1].

A Proclamation from Gordon, addressed to the people of Kartoum, preceded his arrival. He told them that, knowing of the general regret caused by the severe measures of the Government for the suppression of the slave traffic, and the seizure and punishment of all concerned, according to convention and decree, he had resolved that none should interfere with their property, and that henceforth whoever had slaves should enjoy full right to their service, and full control over them. When the terms of this document reached Europe, a storm of indignation was raised against both the law and the giver. Its terms were greeted as an insult to the honour of England, and as a violation of all the traditions of philanthropy. Few paused to consider who was the author of the concession, few to consider what that concession meant; almost all were as ready with their blame as but a short while before they had been prodigal of their praise. The implacable enemy of slavery was now its friend, and in the name of England had declared his change of front. What would the world say to this, and what could England say to the man who, however exceptional his character and career, had thus misrepresented her?

Perhaps this proclamation, in Europe the motive of so much silliness and ill-feeling, did more than anything else towards enabling Gordon to win Kartoum. From the moment it reached the town the attitude of the inhabitants changed; sullen apathy was converted into joyful expectation, and thousands who had been ready to welcome the Mahdi became eager to show homage to Gordon. It was altogether a brilliant diplomatic conception, the work of a man who thoroughly understood the character of the people whom he addressed. It restored to those people rights of which they had been robbed, and which they were now in a position to regain for themselves whenever they would. Yet in the simple gift of what was already theirs lay the opportunity of avoiding much bloodshed and misery—an opportunity which Gordon's insight into national characteristics enabled him to understand, and his rapidity of action enabled him to grasp. By the treaty of 1877, the Soudanese were permitted to hold their slaves until the year 1889; and this treaty was made when Egypt had no notion of relinquishing her possession of the country. Yet it was known to be useless, as its conditions could never have been carried out. The avowed object of Gordon's mission to the Soudan was to remove the Egyptians, and to hand it back to its own children, an operation which in itself involved the permission to hold slaves for ever. Had Gordon said, "I come to concede you the Soudan, which is, when I leave, to be governed as you wish, but after 1889 you must not hold slaves," the Soudanese, and the whole of Europe, would have thought him mad; but as he said, "I come to concede to you the Soudan, which is, when I leave, to be governed as you wish, so that you will have the right to hold slaves as long as you like," it was only the Soudanese who were able to see the sense and value of the concession, and to call its author mad was a privilege reserved for certain European philanthropists.—*The Story of Chinese Gordon*, pp. 70–73. v. ii.

APPENDIX F.

PRIVATE.

From the Mudir of Kartoum to the Governor-General of the Soudan.

This report was made by H.E. Hussein Pasha, Mudir in the neighbourhood of Aloob in Kordofan, and it remained passing from hand to hand among the rebels till we heard of its existence. We demanded it, and received the following copy, which I transmit just as it is.]

On Saturday, 2nd of Moharram, 1301, was accomplished the arrival of the detachment of troops in the vicinity of Aloob, which is near the government seat of Kordofan, by the will of the Creator.

On inspection of them (the troops) it was found that they had suffered from excessive thirst and the not finding sufficient proper drinking water for the detachment, on account of the loss, six days before, of the guide who was appointed to lead the way, and on account of ignorance of the places where drinking water was to be found.

The consequence of which was to throw the square into a state of confusion, to the extent that privates could not recognise their companies nor officers their men. The transport also was scattered —I mean that the animals were scattered singly (without control). It was then that Monsieur Hicks, commander of the detachment, ordered the men and officers to collect in order. But as one of the commanding officers of the detachment disobeyed, he referred the matters to Alî ed Deen Pasha, to see to bringing the detachment into order. But his Excellency answered him that he himself was the commander, and responsible. The consequence of which was to cause universal weakness and paralysis. We met a body of troops and were all surrounded in one place, and on account of what I have said—and for want of water until Sunday, as we did not find enough to last till then—and thus, it was impossible to escape destruction.

But oh, alas for the Government authorities! [12] who are (themselves) secure from danger. But if the will of the Most High God has ordained our death, (so far) delayed, it will be from thirst and not from anything else.

I, the writer of this report, am called Hussein Pasha, Mudir, an officer of the Home Government in the army, a native of Egypt—one of those raised from the ranks; and I adjure you by God, who (may) see what I have written, (if) you are believers in God and His prophet that you will make this known to the Government authorities.

The will of God be done, and there is no escape from the decree of God, Who hears and knows all things. May your life be prolonged.

Written Friday, 19 September, 1884, 8 o'clock 12 minutes.
Marked in the corner 77.

APPENDIX G.

Letter from General Gordon to Ibrahim Abd el-Kader, Kâdi of Kalakla.

This moment we have received a letter from the General of the English troops (stating) that the English troops who arrived in Dongola have killed the Fakih (theologian) El Huda and the

[12] The intention of the writer seems to be to convey reproach of the Government authorities in Cairo, who were responsible for the fate of the army and his own desperate condition. But he seems unwilling to utter a word inconsistent with Moslem resignation or the loyalty of a soldier, though the detachment to which he belonged had been exposed to destruction.

Shareef Mahhmood who was sent from Mohamet Achmet for the blockade of Dongola—and they have (also) killed all the dervishes who were with them; and they are marching straight on Berber; and that the steamers we sent last week have arrived at Berber and found it perfectly desolate and empty. They entered it and seized the two steamers which were lying there. And (the General states) that Mahomet el Khair fled from them, and that before this he had deluded the people and told them to come to him to meet the army ready for Berber; some of them would not go, but some of them went to him, and when they asked him for their expenses he sent them to an empty room to take the cash. When they found no cash there he told them that it was in the possession of a Jin (demon). They were astonished at this. But when they found that the whole thing was deceit from beginning to end they returned to the places whence they came. Now, because you are one of our old friends, and because the brotherhood between us is a fact known to all people, we send you this news which we received seven days ago; and now we have very greatly strengthened the defences of Kartoum and its mines. We are now preparing an earthquake by means of electricity, and I fear for you on its reaching your place; nor do we wish you to be among the others (when it takes effect).

Tell the son of Najoomi and Abu Kerjah to go to Dongola. It is better for them; and later on, when we are arranging matters, we will make them Sultans.

Do not say that Kartoum is starving, or eating dogs and asses. I swear that such provisions are not to be found with you as are to be found in Kartoum—both eatables and drinkables. We do not desire your immediate submission to the Government, lest Mohamet Achmet should suspect you; nor should we wish you to obey Mohamet Achmet, but that you should remain neuter until you see what will happen. As I know that you need soap for washing your faces, I here send you a small box of that wherewith we wash our faces.

Salute the son of Najoomi from me, and tell him (that) to-day there came to us a man from your side, like a peacock, from the quantity of coloured patches ornamenting his mantle, so that the inhabitants were astonished at him.

A letter from the Ulema to Mohamet Achmet is also sent to you. Please forward it to him safely.

30th of Zu'l Kadi.
Sept. 21, 1884.

APPENDIX K.

From Abd el Kâder Ibrahim, Kâdi of Kalakla, to General Gordon.

In the name of God the Merciful and Compassionate.

Praise be to God the bountiful Ruler—with blessing on our Lord Mahomet, and peace.

From the servant of his lord Abd el Kâder Ibrahim—the Kâdi of Kalakla to Gordon Pasha.

Three times have we warned you, sufficiently for people who have sense; and all on account of your friendship for us, of which you spoke in your letter.

This was for your safety and for the safety of the poor and of the Moslems who are with you in the city. But neither our warnings nor our arguments have taken effect upon you.

You write to us every time that you are steadfast in denying (the mission of) this Imâm the Mahdi, on whom be peace.

But nothing has led you to this false conclusion except the enmity between the Moslems and the infidels—and the sayings of the wicked Ulema who are with you at Kartoum as well as the love of supremacy and of this life—and the desire to continue therein. O delusion! delusion! (go to! go to!)

But know that all that thy informants have told thee, and of which thou hast told us, is false; for had there been anything in it we were better informed than (any such things taken place we had better opportunities of knowing it than) thou; because the post and (other) communications pass by night and by day in all parts (of the country) which has submitted to the Mahdi, upon whom be peace. And if such things as you mention were to happen that would not weaken his title to be Mahdi. But the Imâm the Mahdi, upon whom be peace, is victorious; and beyond all doubt he will destroy all rebels and hypocrites, although he were left alone in the world without a man with him, as has been proved by evidence and by eye-witnesses.

Such communications as you send do not please the hearts of the auxiliaries (of the Mahdi)—especially of their Emirs—for by God, they are firmly resolved and determined, and every one of them comes and goes (being) willing to die; and they are not afraid of threats by word or deed. But under all circumstances they trust in God. For this Mahdi is right. English troops or chemicals (electricity) or stores of ammunition will not avail against the Mahdi. What will avail (you) is to return to the truth and cast away what is false; and for all to submit and surrender to this Imâm, upon whom be peace.

There is no deliverance or safety excepting in him; and if you really have friendship for me, as you say, listen to my words and benefit by them, and surrender yourselves with the Moslems,—otherwise the day will soon come when you will learn who has been the greatest liar.

As to the box of soap sent by your messenger, it has reached us, and here we send it back to you rejected; because your sending back the present of the Imâm the Mahdi—upon whom be peace—compels us to return your present. And how could we do otherwise than return it, when you sent back the present of the Vicegerent upon Earth of God, and His prophet, upon whom be blessing and peace? Whereas acceptance of a present promotes goodwill.

In fine, this letter now (last) sent has done nothing but increase the ill-will; for if you and the people of the city had known the facts about the auxiliaries of the Imâm, upon whom be peace, who are now (in arms) against and around the city, you would not have written this, but you would simply have surrendered—if so be that God wills your safety and that of those that are with you.

This is my advice to you. (Surrender.)

God is the guide into all truth, and unto Him all return and submit.

(Signed) ABD EL KÂDER IBRAHIM.

Written last day of Zu'l Kadi, 1301.
Sept. 21, 1884.

APPENDIX L.

From Abderrahhmân en Najoomi and Abdallah en Noor to Gordon Pasha.

In the name of God the merciful and compassionate. Praise be to God the bountiful Ruler, with blessing on our lord Mahomed and his successors, and on whom be peace.

From the servants of their Lord Abderrahhmân en Najoomi and Abdallah en Noor to Gordon Pasha, representative of England and of the Khedive. May God guide him into truth. Amen.

We have to state to you that as to thy presence in the Soudan this last time, and thy first letter to the Imâm the Mahdi, on whom be peace, and as to thine appointment by the Khedive; the Imâm the Mahdi, on whom be peace, has written to thee, and has shown thee the truth in leading thee to God; and also that which concerns thy salvation and that of those with thee, and how thou mayest attain salvation in this world and in the next.

Thou hast replied to his Highness (in a manner) contrary to that (which was) expected (of thee) rejecting the truth, whether for or against thee. After we arrived with our hosts to fight thee and drive thee into submission—willingly or unwillingly—the Imâm, out of compassion for thee and those with thee, a second time exhorted thee to surrender to the command of God and his prophet, and gave thee the covenant (in the name) of God and His promise that if thou didst surrender thou shouldst be (assured of) safety, with thy children, thy property, and all that thou hast, (thus) securing to thee the same (privileges) as to us, and the same (duties) as are required of us.

You have received that letter of his by his messengers the Moslems whom he appointed from thence to advise thee, after our arrival in this (desert) Deem. But neither you nor those with you have accepted the call (wherewith) God and His prophet have called you.

You answered as you did to our lord, and you demanded a thing of Abd el Kâder Ibrahim, when el Jâber the Moslem came (to thee), (who was) one of the messengers sent to thee for negotiation—(but) thou didst send him back. Yet we had sent him to thee in our intention for good and in our goodwill towards thee and towards those with thee. And we wrote to you the advice which reached you. Nevertheless, you did not listen to the truth nor accept it—because the will of God must be accomplished.

We had therefore resolved not to correspond any more with you, nor to communicate with you except by the sword and such like weapons, until we have destroyed your glory and your strength departs (from you) and we pluck you out by the roots when we seize you in our grasp. However, yesterday your messenger arrived with a letter from you to our brother Abd el Kâder Ibrahim, in which you deceitfully counsel him and try to seduce him from his religion, and in which you tell him to desire us and Aboo Kerja to go to the Dâr el Gharb (West) (as being) better for us—because when you are arranging matters you will make us Sultans. But every man of sense knows that all things are in the power of God and not in your hand, nor in that of those who appointed you, nor in that of the English, on whom you depend. And you lie unto the people with you about their arrival (the English) at Dongola, and about their killing Sheikh Ahhmed el Huda and the Shereef Mohammed; and that they were going straight to Berber; and that Mahomed el Khair[13] the Emir of Berber ran away from them, and made fools of the men with him when they asked him for their pay. As to your promise of making us Sultans when you settle the affairs of the country as stated in your letter, and your statement that the steamers sent last week by you had found Berber desolate and deserted, and that the two steamers found there had been captured, we have learned from this letter of yours that the steamers you sent did not seize anything at Berber except only the steamers, and it is known to all the world that the Moslems captured a quantity of Government stores which were in Berber. But you do not mention having seized any of them—only the steamers.

Lying does not become a Pasha such as you.

And we received the day before yesterday a letter from Mahomed el Khair telling us that he was on the shore—both east and west—ready to fight your steamers. And, please God, they (the steamers) with the guns, will not go back to you a second time. But the last will overtake (redeem) the first, and you will not hear of them again. We did not think that with your intelligence and your knowledge that God has strengthened us in His earth, you would have told us lies or tried to frighten and deceive us, and those who

[13] The latest accounts from the Soudan state that Ibn en Najoomi has quarrelled with Mahomed el Khair on account of his peculations.

are with us, by talking of things (already better) known to us, and of which we have constant information, (receiving) news day and night from all parts of the world.

And you seem to have chosen for us, that we should go back to the West (Dâr el Gharb); trying to deceive and mislead us through desire for the life of this world, and (as though) we covet (the dignity) of being Sultans and (to have) dominion. But we call upon thee to come to God and His prophet, and to follow the right faith, and to reject the religion in which thou art, and to adopt the religion of our prophet Mahomed, on whom be blessing and peace; and the fellowship of his Khâlif Mahomed, the Mahdi, on whom be peace. If thou will do this thou shalt have honour in this world and in the next.

Otherwise, if thou dost still look forward to the coming of the English, who, as thou pretendest, have reached Dongola, and are going to Berber, know for certain and be sure—and accept the advice we give thee on the subject—that all the Soudan country, except Kartoum and the towns of Sennaar and Dongola, is all of it in the hands of the Mahdi, and in the possession of his honourable friends. From the extreme border of the Soudan to Suakin, and to Reef, no one shares with them (in the possession thereof).

The Government who sent thee as Governor-General does not possess a single handbreadth of ground.

The English came several times to Suakin. They were killed (fought) by one of the lieutenants there—Oshman ibn Aboo Bekr Digna—who has captured all their armies and the booty thereof.

Therefore, look to thy own safety elsewhere without (relying on) them, and prepare thyself for what may happen to thee before their arrival. For the whole English Government (nation) could not pass by way of Suakin or Dongola. But even if the English were to come God would kill them by the hand of His faithful before they (could) reach you Know that the Imâm the Mahdi, on whom be peace, has sent us for the sole express purpose of fighting thee and as advance-corps to prepare the way of his army and of his Highness.

But whereas thou hast been appointed Governor on behalf of two eminent Governments—and as thou sayest that thou hast come to arrange the affairs of the Soudan—thou wilt not find a better opportunity for carrying out thy intention and desire successfully than (now) in these two days before the arrival of the whole army.

But if thou and those with thee in the town delay—awaiting the English—till after the arrival here of the whole army and the noble presence (of the Mahdi) you will be disappointed in your hope and desire. Therefore it (will be) much better for thee to collect all thy forces and come out to meet us beyond the fortifications, from which we are but an hour distant.

Then thou and thy men may attain your wish, and go back to your fortress, happy in having fought us. But if thou dost delay until the arrival of the whole army and of the noble presence, we are certain that you will not then think of fighting or of hoping to possess (conquer) any more.

It can therefore only be your excessive fear of us which prevents your coming out and fighting us. Soon, please God, thou and those with thee will be in our grasp, and will taste the sore evil (result) of your unwillingness to follow the way of God.

Know oh! Excellency Gordon, that whereas thou hast said in thy letter to Abd el Kâder Ibrahim that thou wast diligently working in preparing an earthquake, and didst fear for him when it should reach him, that thy saying is nonsense, unworthy for an intelligent being to utter.

Has the Earth, indeed, brought out to thee her demons? (for thy service).

Thou hast tried to frighten him by saying that thou wast coming out thyself to fight and kill us, and didst order him to leave us. But this (coming out to fight) would have pleased us better.

The earth is (become) too strait for thee, wide though it be, and thy ways (of escape) are cut off. Look out for thyself (to find) way of escape from the judgments (vengeance) of God and of His prophet. For we have thee by the hair of the head, through the power of God and his will.

As to the answer sent by the Ulema to the Imâm the Mahdi, on whom be peace, we have sent it by a special messenger to be placed in his hands. But do not thou rely on the lies they tell in it, because since the reply which they sent by Jāber the Moslem, in which they denied in the strongest terms (the validity of the claim of) the Mahdi, they sent messengers and letters to the Mahdi, on whom be peace, apologizing for what they wrote to him, and for what they may (in future) write, making oath to him that they are compelled by you to utter these things for fear of their life, and (only do so) pending the arrival of his noble presence, and they pray him not to have any ill-will against them for what they may say.

If thou hast sense, do not regard what they write, but have it sent through you.

And whatever you may find to your interest and for the prolongation of thy dominion, about which thou art deluded, and from which thou shalt soon depart, please God, do it without their advice or counsel, for all they show thee is only deceit, till they (can become) master of their opportunity to join the Imâm the Mahdi, on whom be peace.

As to the favour which God has granted to Sheikh Ahhmed el Huda and Shereef Mahmood and the faithful ones with them to die as martyrs, that is the ultimate object (of desire) for all followers of the Imâm the Mahdi, on whom be peace, and what they have promised him (to do), and what they pray God may honour them (in granting to them).

We pray God to grant us the favour He has accorded to them, and to bestow on us the honours of martyrdom, pleasant in His sight. And we continue in prayer to God to make us among His beloved ones honoured by Him with martyrdom. For He has the power to do this, and to Him it appertains to hear (prayer).

What we have said is enough. God has the guidance in His hand.

(Date and Seals cut off.)

[The length of these letters, and the persuasions used, even the great sheet of paper and the writing of the letters, testify to the great respect in which General Gordon was held.

The subterranean earthquake or mine—to be produced by chemicals or electricity—is mentioned in this letter in reply to the mention made in General Gordon's former letter. These chiefs do not believe he could do such a work except by aid of demons or Jins.

Where, in exhorting General Gordon to surrender, they point out his critical condition, and use the phrase, "*We have thee by the hair of the head*," this is in allusion to the conqueror's hold upon a prostrate foe (by the one lock of hair which Moslems have on their heads), just at the last moment, when the sword is uplifted to slay.]

APPENDIX M.

Letter from General Gordon to the Honourable the Sheikh Abderrahhmân en Najoomi.

Yesterday we wrote to you (as to) the arrival of the English troops in the neighbourhood of Merowé, and to-day also we have received letters from the troops, and herewith we send you a specimen of the correspondence; and although it is very minute we have read it with a magnifying glass. But you must open your eyes well that you may yourselves see its minute letters. English troops have arrived in the neighbourhood of Merowé; ten regiments, infantry, cavalry, and artillery, and the rest are behind them in Dongola and Wady Halfa. (We are informed) that the Mudir of Dongola has killed the Fakir (Theologian), Ahhmed el Huda, and the Shereef Mahmood, who is the uncle of Mahomed Achmed, sent from Kordofan. Every one of their host was destroyed. Other information has reached us by special messenger from Berber, that our steamers have entered and are awaiting the arrival of the army.

Before now we announced in one of our proclamations issued to the inhabitants after our arrival, that we had repeatedly advised the people to give up (their rebellion) but they did not return (to allegiance) and that we should be obliged to bring English troops to this country to chastise the rebellious and bring them to submission. But I suppose you considered these words to be lies until this army arrived near to Berber, (an army) which no strength of theirs could withstand.

A few days ago we sent you notice to go to Kordofan and remain there, and that we would make you one of the Sultans of the West. You had better listen to this advice and go with your men and be happy with them, obeying your Sultan Mahomed Achmed.

Information has reached us that you have made contracts with the Arab sheikhs for bringing provisions upon their camels, (for) about 1000 camels, and (that) the sheikhs received from you a quantity of ready money for buying provisions and ran away from you. All the Soudan soldiers hate you and have come to us ; but if we are bad, as you imagine, these soldiers would not have followed us.

Mahomed Achmed informs us that he ordered Aboo Kerjah to convert us to his faith, but this fellow understands drinking Merissa (*i.e.* date-beer) better than any one else, and we think he may teach us Merissa-drinking.

Please God, the soap we sent yesterday to Sheikh Abd-el-Kader, to wash his face with, may be found like (as good as) the towel which Mahomed Achmed sent to Mr. Costi (Cuzzi) Moosa to wipe his face with.[14]

The guns we fired yesterday were (in rejoicing at) news of the coming army.

Therefore the first and best thing (for you to do) is to consider the news sent you herein enclosed, and arise and go back to your places with whatever you have of guns and such like, as the air is bad here. But Sheikh Ibrahim Abd-el-Kader may remain in his place as his home is in the neighbourhood of Kalakla, and as he is one of our friends and an owner of crops in this district.

But if you do not listen to this advice, one of these days you will arise in the morning and find yourselves in a tremendous earthquake.[15]

As for the cannon you fired at us yesterday, they killed about 20,000 of our soldiers, so that we were altogether tired out with burying the dead, and this is as war should be.

After writing this we received your last letter, and as you do not accept the advice, remain where you are with Sheikh Abd-el-Kader as you now are.

Gordon Pasha in Kartoum.

(Signed) C. G. GORDON.

Date 2nd Zu'l Hejjeh, 1301.
Aug. 24, 1884.

[14] Query—Does this refer to a veil such as dervishes wear, which was sent to a renegade by the Mahdi ?

[15] Reference is here made to the earthquake mentioned in a former letter, as being prepared by Gordon.

(On the back of General Gordon's letter.)

Reply to General Gordon.

In the name of God the Merciful and the Compassionate.

From Abderrahhmân en Najoomi and Abdallah en Noor to Gordon.

Yesterday we sent you an answer to your letter brought to us by your messenger, who is going back, in which we told you to come out of the fortress to meet us in fight before the arrival of the standards (troops) sent to us from the Imâm Mahomed, the Mahdi, on whom be peace, as we are now near to you—within eyesight. And (as) probably you will not have another opportunity after these two days. But you have not done so.

Even to-day we have received your letter and proclamation, both sealed and signed by you, which are not satisfactory answers to our letter. But you put in them nonsense—like unto dreams.

But we are better informed than you; for the hands (power) of the Mahdi, on whom be peace, are over the whole world; and he receives news from all parts thereof.

We are not inside a fortress listening to the sayings of hypocrites, who run away like slaves, and the like—on whose authority you issue lying and deceitful proclamations.

You mention in your answer[16] that you have received a letter from the troops; but on looking at it we find (that it is) a proclamation from you, with your own seal, and not from the army.

How can you say so, and contradict yourself? From this we learn that all your sayings are lies. And after this let there be no more letters or communications between us and you; but (only) war.

The proclamation is enclosed (returned).

(Signed) ABDERRAHHMÂN EN NAJOOMI,
ABDALLAH EN NOOR.

This letter is without any of the usual forms of civility at the top, and is addressed simply "to Gordon," without any title, and on the back of his own letter. It is also written high up, near the top of the sheet, as from a superior to one greatly his inferior.

[16] Evidently a wrong enclosure had been put in by General Gordon.

APPENDIX N.

Letter from Lieut.-Colonel Stewart, C.M.G., to General Gordon.

Island of El Hassa Heya, 4 miles south of Berber,
14th September, 1884.

MY DEAR GENERAL,

You will no doubt be surprised at our not having yet passed Berber, but the fact is, we had several vicissitudes the first couple of days. You know already what happened the first day, how through the ignorance of the captain and the Reis, we ran into the bank and damaged our wheel. The second day the captain ran us on to a mud bank, where we stuck for four hours, and were with difficulty got off by the *Saphia*. This was too much for my patience. I am sorry to say I lost my temper and rather severely handled the individual, turned him out and put the second in command; on the 11th we passed safely through the Shoboloha defile. We saw the broken end of the telegraph cable which is to the south of the defile. Anchored for the night opposite the village of Om Ghirka, and on the right bank, at a small cultivated island inhabited by Shaggyeh, whose chief is Bab Bekr el Mek, a brother of Cassim el Moos. His people received us very well; supplied us with all the wood they could get. The chief came on board, complained greatly of the dervishes, but said, with the exception of the Shaggyehs all the tribes were wholly with the Mahdi. I enclose a letter which he has written you. He begs you will send soldiers, rifles, etc., when he will openly declare himself for the Government. So far as I am able to judge, the Shaggyeh are strong for the Government. At the Shaggyeh villages we passed, the people all showed their joy at our appearance by dancing and shouting. The villages were all along the right bank. The left bank was sullen, if not openly hostile. Bab Bekr reported that a boat full of dervishes had been recently up the river, collecting tithes; the *Fascher* steamer also appears to come up now and then. The Arabs also appear to have received news of our expedition. During that night war drums were being beaten on the left bank. On the 12th we received some shots from the left bank, and about mid-day halted at a Shaggyeh island for an hour or so, where we got some wood. The people were again friendly. Beyond this island we got into the Djaalen country. Passed Metemma, where we saw crowds of people and several flags; were fired on, but distance too great to do any harm. Soon after reached Shendy. Here we were also fired on. The Government house has been loop-holed, and there is a small breast-work wall in front of it. The *Saphia* threw a couple of shells into the town. Saw a man with a letter making signs to us, so stopped a little below the town, but he did not come on. Halted again at an island and looted the village on it; killed a lot of cattle and pulled the houses and Sakkéyés down. We were again fired on from the left bank, and the war drums were beaten all night. On the 13th we found both banks of the river openly hostile. Close to the low hills of Om Ali, on right bank, we saw a gathering of horse and foot; fired at them and knocked over a horseman. Below this point we had to hug the right bank very closely, and some Arabs turned out, ran alongside the steamer, waving swords and lances. We could have knocked them over with the greatest ease, but refrained, as they were so plucky. In the afternoon looted a boat going up with sugar. Halted on right bank about an hour and a half above El Duem. War drums going on all night. On the 14th we spent the day destroying Sakkéyés in a systematic manner, taking them one after another. They gave us a fine supply of wood, without which it would be absurd to go on to Berber. Should think we have destroyed fifteen to twenty Sakkéyés. This evening, when halted, have noticed a number of horse and foot come from the north to the village opposite on right bank. After looking at us for some time they retired, apparently in the direction of Damr. I suppose they came to reconnoitre, and perhaps to attack us while destroying Sakkéyés. To-morrow we shall start before daybreak, and the steamers will escort us to the other side of Berber. I think everything now is in fair working trim, and am sanguine of getting through all right.

At the village of Bab Bekr, an Egyptian soldier came on board who had belonged to the Berber garrison. He had been sold for fourteen dollars to a certain sheikh, who is said to have a lot more of his comrades. I shall send him on as baksheesh to the Khedive. So far as I am able to judge, with the exception of the Shaggyeh, the whole country is with the Arabs; have no certain news about Dongola, beyond that the garrison is strong. Some have told us there is a large Egyptian force there, but others appear to have no knowledge of it. Cannot say much in favour of the men on *Saphia* and *Mansowrah*. They will think of nothing but loot, will not work, and scatter about in the most dangerous way. Omar Bey appears to have little control over them. I must, however, say that both he and the steamer captain have done everything in their power to assist me, and more especially the captain of the *Mansowrah*.

Both Herbin, myself, and Power, wish to be remembered to you. You may depend upon it that I shall do everything in my power to assist you. Thanking you for the very great kindness with which you have overlooked my short-comings, and praying that the blessing of the Almighty may abide with you,

I remain, my dear General,

Yours very truly,

J. D. H. STEWART.

P.S.—How I wish you were with us.

I have advised Omar Bey on account of the very indifferent quality of his troops, who are no better than an armed mob, to be very careful how he lets them land anywhere. He tells me he has now fuel sufficient to remain two days at Berber, and steam again some distance up the river, and that he does not intend to allow them to land. I confess I think he shows his discretion. The incident I mentioned of the Arabs running alongside our steamer, and defying us with sword and lance, impressed me vividly with their daring and recklessness. I am afraid our miserable troops would be scattered as chaff before the wind by them. As far as Shendy you may consider the right bank, if not wholly friendly, is not at any rate openly hostile.

With that exception the whole country so far as I have seen is hostile. The Djaalen have I am afraid gone over heart and soul to the Arabs. All our successes and failures are known everywhere. Mahomet Ali Pasha's defeat is perhaps exaggerated.

I forgot to mention that the country is in fine cultivation, and the people working away at their irrigation as if nothing was the matter. South of Shendy on right bank they did not run away at our approach, and even north of that place some few remained and looked at us unconcernedly. Most however, north of Shendy, ran away, or fired at us.

Letter from Monsieur Herbin, the French Consul, to General Gordon.

15 Septembre, 1884.

MON GÉNÉRAL,

Avant de passer Berber permettez-moi de vous remercier encore mille fois de toutes les bontés que vous avez eues pour moi et de vous affirmer que je n'oublierai jamais le charmant accueil que le Consul de France a trouvé auprès du "Houkumdir," M. Herbin—auprès du Général Gordon.

Malgré les ennuis que vous a causé Mahomet Achmet, je ne regretterai pas, je vous assure, mon voyage à Khartoum, car j'espère que vous me permettrez, plus tard, de vous rappeler que je m'y trouvais en même temps que vous.

Avec les vœux que je fais pour que les événements soient dirigés par Dieu dans un sens qui vous soit favorable, recevez, mon Général, l'assurance de mes sentiments de profond respect et d'absolu dévouement.

HERBIN.

P.S.—Vous me pardonnerez, n'est-ce pas, de vous écrire au crayon.

A Son Excellence,
le Général Gordon,
Khartoum.

APPENDICES TO BOOK IV.

APPENDIX P.

Letter from Abou Gugliz to General Gordon.

In the name of God the Almighty and merciful, and praise be to our Prophet Mahomet and his relations.

From the servant of God Mahomet Osman Abou Gugliz to Gordon Pasha, the beloved by England, and the Khedive, may God beguide him to the true faith. Be it known to you that the bearer, Fatmah, has been seen by the Fakeers, and they thinking she was a spy, they imprisoned her. It is true that she is suspicious, being from the inhabitants of Kartoum. When I saw her I forgave her, and have released her from prison, and left it to her choice whether to remain here or go back to Kartoum—she preferred going back, therefore I send her ; if she is a spy ask her, and she will tell you—if not, treat her as you think right.

23 El Hejah, 1301.
October 13th, 1884.

SEAL.

APPENDIX Q.

From Fakirs El Sayet Eltahen and Hamed Idreer to Commandant Omdurman Fort.

In the name of God, the Merciful and Almighty, praise be to Him and our prophet.

From El Sayet Eltahen and Hamed Idreer to Issat Osman Bey, the Colonel and Commander of Omdurman Station, and to all officers with him, our brethren in God. After many salaams and anxiety to see you, we write as friends and companions of the same religion, and as there has been no animosity or hatred existing between us up to the present day, we inform you that the Government of Egypt is no more under the Turkish Empire, but the English have taken possession of it, and you, being Arabs and Moslems, how would you then remain with the infidels and join Gordon, who has no one except slaves and other very low class of people, and Kartoum being surrounded on all sides with great numbers of troops, notwithstanding the approach of the Descendant of the Prophet, our Iman, and the Iman of all Moslems, Mohamed Achmet, the Mahdi, son of Abdullah, who has come to a very short distance from Omdurman with an unlimited number of troops, how Kartoum can oppose them. When we saw these signs, we have hastened to write to you these lines, and ask you to come with all your belongings and join our Emir, and that you should be admitted into the fellowship and take security. You had better not delay until Wednesday, because the Immaum is expected either to-morrow, Tuesday, or Wednesday. So do not procrastinate one single day. Come before the Immaum comes, and you will be well received and well treated; the same as happened to those who have come before you. You are, no doubt, aware of the mercy of our Emir Ahmad el Mostapha; and the Mahdi has sent orders to the said Emir, and instructed him that all who come out from Kartoum or from the fort should be given security and receive no harm. Therefore, you should send two messengers to meet us, and inform us of your designs; and we hope to be the cause of your safety. Let it be known to you that our Emir is like the ark of Noah—whoever comes to it will be saved, and who refuses will perish in deluge; so do not procrastinate not one day. The Emir was in communication with you at first, to send messengers from your part, in order to come to an understanding; but now there is no time for that. One single day will be enough to cause your perish. On account of friendship we send you this advice; and God is a witness of the truth of our statement. You are strangers in this country, but not strangers to our religion; but Gordon is a stranger to both. Now then, would you leave us and join him? We are told that Gordon Pasha is telling you that the English are coming. What if they come? What can they do to our troops? We are very certain that the English who are at Suakin have all perished by Osman, and those who are at Assouan are besieged there, and have fortified themselves there, and given up the Soudan; so all the projects of that infidel are failing, and also the steamer of Stewart Pasha and the Consul was caught at the cataract, and those who were on board were all killed. We send you also a letter addressed to Ferratch Pasha el Zeeb. Should you think right, send it to him; and, if you fear the result, tear it up and destroy it. Leave the others and come and be saved. We are here near you; come to us secretly, and leave those infidels to their fate. Send Ibrahim your servant, with those you chose to send as messengers, as he is trustworthy, and we can deliver any secret to him. We await your early arrival, so as to go together with Emir Mustapha, on Tuesday the 23rd El Hajah, to the Mahdi. Peace be upon him!

(Signed) HAMED IDREES.
EL SAYET ELTAHER.

From Faki Mustapha to Commandant Omdurman Fort.

In the name of God, &c., &c.

From the servants of God, Ahmed el Mustāpha, the Governor of the Mahdi, on whom be peace, son of El Iffah el-Ameen to Issat Osman Bey Caimmakam of the Omdurman Station, and to all the officers and soldiers, may God direct the right.

Good friends, we have so often called you to God and to His Apostle, and to his Mahdi (Reformer), on whom be peace, in our letters, but you have neither come nor sent us messengers. But inasmuch as the Fakirs performing patrol duty, and the sentinels tell us that you do not fire upon them if they fire at you, and if they pass close by you you do them no harm, hence we hope good of you, and hope of God that you will be directed to the Mahdiship. And now the man of the times has come, the Iman of all Moslems, the successor of God's Apostle our Lord Mahomed the Mahdi [Reformer], son of Abdullah, to a place near to us one day's journey from our camp. Out of solicitude for God's creatures we have taken the trouble to write this to you after having done so already repeatedly; and we have sent you your Brethren, Saddeek, son of Taher, and Hamid el-Shâyib, in order that you should meet them outside beyond the Fakeers, and agree with them on the plan which shall spare your property and children, and write you to us before the arrival of the Mahdi, lest you be lost with those who are lost, which God forbid. You know our solicitude for the people, and that we do not interfere with the property or lives without legal authority. Therefore do not fear us, neither the Imâm, on whom be peace, and who is better than we and better than all God's creatures, excepting God's Prophet. Therefore you shall have security from God, His Prophet, His Reformer [Mahdi], and security from me also, who am God's humble servant. Keep this as a document to witness against us, sealed with my seal, both in this world and the next, that if the least harm befall you, your children, or your property, if you write yourself to me this night, which is the night before Tuesday the 24th el-Hijjah, for fear lest you delay further you will find no other opportunity of reaching us, and will perish. We have already informed you that this Mahdi is the true and expected Reformer who shall possess the eastern parts and the western parts of the earth. Will he therefore be too weak to conquer Kartoum, in which there are only base people and people having no following? And we know perfectly the number; and they are in want of their relief from the North, which has been cut off; and the steamer called *Kartoumiah* has been taken, and the Fakeers have killed those who were in it, and it was sunk over against Gordon like the people of Seba. Do not therefore destroy yourselves with him. Those admonished you out of pity for you that you may be among those who are saved, not among those that perish. If you listen to my words, come out to your Brethren, and afterwards come to us, and we will speak about that which will be for your interest, that is to say, we will agree with you on the delivery of the sentinels by night, so that the morning will find the Fakeers there, and will find you with your property with your Brethren here in the camp, and to-morrow we will meet the Imâm near here, and you will have saved yourselves. But if you reject our words you will rue it, and I have thus admonished you.

(Signed) AHMED MUSTAPHA EL-AMEEN.

October 13, 1884.
23 Hijjah, 1301.

P.S.—Herewith is a letter to Ferratch Pasha el-Zeeb, if you send it by some one who will keep the secret all right. But if any harm come to you therefrom, then let it alone and save yourselves, and if you come to us now, and one piastre of your property be lost, or one drop of your blood, I am responsible, for this is a document against me. Besides, Our Sovereign Lord the Imâm has given security to all who come over to us from the people of Kartoum, and from your fort, and there is no fear.

[L. S.]

APPENDIX R.

Letter from Slatin Bey.

A Son Excellence Gordon Pacha,
Gouverneur Général du Soudan.

EXCELLENCE,

J'ai me permi d'écrire à votre Excellence une lettre en allemande dans laquelle je vous offre mes services. J'ai été obligé d'écrire à votre Excellence en allemande parce que on a brûlé mon Dictionnaire française croyat c'est une livre de prière crétienne. J'espère de trouver l'occasion de m'uni avec votre Excellence et l'acceptation de mes services. J'espère que vous vous portez bien et prie Dieu qui vous donne la siege.

Votre
Dévoué et obéissant serviteur,
SLATIN.

Une de vos Sandechaque, Abdel Habin, a écri une lettre ici demandant le pardon, comme j'entende veulent les Scheigines quitte le Halfai et sê uni avec les partisans du Mahdi pas par l'enémitié contre votre Excellence, non seulement par peure pour leurs femmes et enfants.

J'entends que votre Excellence m'ont écri une lettre, me je ne l'ai pas reçu ; on dit que le Chalifa Abdullah l'a brûlé.

Letter from Slatin Bey.[1]

His Excellency Gordon Pasha, Governor-General of the Soudan:

YOUR EXCELLENCY,

I have learnt through George Calamatino, the bearer of the letter from Mahomet Achmet, that your Excellency, not knowing the true facts of the case, judges my proceedings and capitulation disparagingly. I therefore take the liberty of informing you of the true state of affairs as they are and as they have been, and beg that you may form your opinion of me accordingly.

Since my appointment as Governor of Darfur, I have been engaged in warfare with Sultan Haroun and Dud Benga, and when the revolution, caused by Mahomet Achmet broke out, I was left in Darfur without officers; some of them had been killed, some had been dismissed by the Government, and the few remaining ones were not fit to take a command. At the first outbreak, even of hostilities which were simultaneous with those of Achmet el Arabi in Egypt, I was compelled personally to take a command. After several battles, all more or less unsuccessful, the Arabian officers who bore me a grudge and firmly believed in the victory of Achmet el Arabi over the Europeans, gave out among the soldiers as their opinion, that the cause of my defeat lay in my being a Christian. In order to stifle these injurious opinions, I gave out that I had for some years already practised the Mahomedan religion and now publicly proclaimed my conversion. By this step I had regained the confidence of my soldiers, inspired them with hope, had given them a happy confidence, uprooted malicious intrigues and conducted several successful battles until the annihilation of the army in Kordofan commanded by Hicks.

Whether by my conversion I committed a dishonourable step is a matter of opinion—it was made more easy to me because I had, *perhaps unhappily*, not received a strict religious education at home.

I commanded in Dara against the tribes known to your Excellency as Razagat, H.L., &c., and in spite of great loss of life and want of ammunition, we were full of glad confidence in Hicks' reserves, but after the annihilation of the latter the demoralised troops refused to fight any longer. I had now at my disposal about 700 soldiers, counting sick and wounded, and for each gun ten to twelve dozen cartridges. Officers and men demanded capitulation, and I, standing there alone and a European, was compelled to follow the majority and compelled to capitulate. Does your Excellency believe that to me, as an Austrian officer, the surrender was easy? It was one of the hardest days of my life.

By submission and obedient behaviour I have attained a certain degree of confidence amongst the local magnates, and have thus received permission to write to you, because they are of opinion that by these lines I am requesting your Excellency to surrender.

[1] The following is a translation of the letter alluded to in the preceding.

Should your Excellency not despise my feeble services and small knowledge of tactics, I beg to offer you my help, with no desire for a higher post of honour only from devotion and friendship for your Excellency and the good cause. I am ready with or under you, for either victory or death. My few faithful ones here, my fortune, &c., all—all will I gladly desert to die, if God so please, an honorable death.

Should you accept my services, I beg your Excellency to write me an answer to these lines in French, but in Arabic the following letter :

"Seek to obtain the permission of Seid Mohamed Ebn Seid Abdullah,[1] to come to Omdurman in order to discuss with you the possibility and conditions of surrender."

By showing this letter I hope to obtain permission and opportunity to come to Omdurman and to unite with you. It now remains with your Excellency to accept or refuse my services.

May God give you the victory.

Your Excellency's
Most gratefully devoted,
SLATIN.

Sandjak Saleh Bey, as well as Ata Aga and all other sheikhs here, assure your Excellency of their fidelity and devotion, and regret the miserable circumstances which force them to remain with the supporters of Mohamet Achmet until help arrives in order to preserve their wives and children.

APPENDIX S.

Lettre de Slatin Bey à Mr. Hansall.
(Traduction francaise.)

Le Maigdi vient, mais il n'y a pas beaucoup de monde avec lui, et si les soldats et les habitants de Kartoum sont suffissants et ne partagent pas les avis des rebelles, vous n'avez rien à craindre.

Faites tout ce que vous pouvez, que je remontre personnellement son Excellence Gordon pasha, parce que je puis lui donner des nouvelles plus sincères et plus exacts que ses spiones.

Avisez S. E. que, s'il accepte mes services à Kartoum, je puis la annoncer toujours tout ce qu'il arriverai chez les rebelles.

Mais je désire lui parler d'avance de vive voix.

Faites mes compliments à tous les Européens et à tous les indigènes.

Si les hommes de Kartoum sont bien énergique et bien forts, ils

[1] Slatin's new name.

doivent être bien sûrs qu'ils gagnent tout ce qu'ils veulent. Plût à Dieu que je vous revoir à Omdourman ou à Kartoum. Je désire beaucoup que S. Excellence me donne la promesse, qu'il ne rendra pas jamais le Kartoum aux rebelles, parce que en ce cas je soupirai beaucoup des Arabes, qui vont me tyranniser et me tuer après.

Aussi vos soldats et les habitants de Kartoum doivent prendre patience et attendre un et demi deux mois jusqu'ils arrivent les secours.

Il y a ici le nouvelle, que le petit bateau que vous avez envoyé à Dongola est pris des rebelles à Wady Gama, mais ce nouvelle n'est pas bien sûr, parce que quelques autres disent le contraire.

THE INSURRECTION OF THE FALSE PROPHET, 1881–83, TO THE DEFEAT OF HICKS'S ARMY.[1]

FOR many years the creed of Mahomed has been making immense strides in Central Africa, where it seems to have a peculiar fascination for the native races. The number of converts has been estimated at from eight to twelve millions, and the idea of the regeneration of Islam by force of arms has gained a strong hold among them. On the appearance of the False Prophet in the summer of 1881, thousands flocked to his standard.

The person in question is a Sheikh named Mahomed Achmet, the son of a carpenter, and a native of Dongola. He was born about the year 1848, and educated in a village near Kartoum, where he studied religion. In 1870 he became a Sheikh, and after a short stay at Kaka, near Fashoda, took up his residence on the island of Abba, in the White Nile. There he gradually acquired a great reputation for sanctity, and in time assembled a considerable number of dervishes, or holy men, round him. He augmented his influence by marrying daughters of the leading chiefs of the Baggara Arabs,[2] and, by his power and tact, succeeded in uniting the various tribes.

Biography of the Mahdi.

In May 1881, when living at Marabieh, near the island of Abba, he first advanced his claims to being the Messiah, or Prophet foretold by Mahomed. By his followers he was styled "El-

[1] This document came down with the fourth Journal. It was compiled in the Intelligence Branch, Quartermaster-General's Department of the War Office.

[2] Powerful nomad tribes inhabiting the country west of the White Nile, and south-east of Kordofan and Darfur.

Mahdi," more usually, but incorrectly written "El-Mahdi." This is an Arabic word meaning simply a "Leader" or "Guide," and is not found in the Koran. In the early days of Islam, it was not unfrequently used as a name or title. The notion which prevails among Moslems generally, regarding the expected great "El-Mahdi," is, that he will be a descendant of the Prophet, and will appear towards the end of time to uproot wickedness, to avenge the blood of the Imams who were slain unjustly, and to establish a reign of righteousness on the earth.

The Ulema[3] of Kartoum did not hesitate to pronounce against Mahomed Achmet, and he was likewise discredited at Cairo and Constantinople, and soon became known as the "False Prophet." Among many reasons for disbelief, one was, that the Redeemer of the World, promised in the Koran, would come from the East, and not from the West.

The intentions of Mahomed Achmet, as set forth in various proclamations, were as follows :—

To gain over the whole of the Soudan to his cause, then march on Egypt and overthrow the false-believing Turks, and, finally, to establish the thousand years' kingdom in Mecca, and convert the whole world.

The principles of his teachings were universal equality, universal law and religion, and community of goods. All who opposed his mission were to be destroyed, whether Christian, Mahomedan, or Pagan.

Causes of rebellion.

The religious fanaticism of the native tribes of the Soudan was, however, only one of the many causes of the insurrection which broke out after the appearance of the Mahdi. The principal one appears to have been hatred of the Government, due to—

(1.) The venality of the Egyptian officials, and the oppressive and unjust manner of collecting the taxes, and especially to
(2.) The suppression of the slave trade. Most of the supporters of the Mahdi, more especially the Baggara tribes, owe all their wealth to the traffic in slaves, which the Egyptian Government has now for many years been taking measures to put an end to.

The time selected for the rising was after the garrisons of the Soudan had been diminished for reasons of economy. Lieut.-Colonel Stewart is, however, of opinion that the military weakness of Egypt was not any real cause of the rebellion, as he believes the troops in the Soudan would have been sufficient to quell it had they been properly handled.[4]

[3] A body corresponding to the Divines in Christendom, who are appealed to by the Sultan respecting the right application of precepts of the Moslem faith, and their decision is known as a *fetua*.

[4] This opinion hardly agrees with that of a military correspondent of the *Times*, who, writing from Kartoum, on the 24th July, 1883, states

In July, 1881, the attention of Raouf Pasha, the Governor-General of the Soudan, was drawn to the pretensions of the Mahdi; and he sent a commission of inquiry from Kartoum to interview him, and ascertain the true state of affairs. 1881. July.

On their return, it was determined to send a military expedition to Marabieh to bring the Mahdi to Kartoum. A force of 200 men left the latter place by steamer on the 11th August, reaching Djeziret Abba in 15 hours. There they disembarked, and advanced towards the residence of the Mahdi. When quite close to it, they suddenly found themselves in the presence of 4,000 to 5,000 of his followers, armed with swords and lances. The troops fired one volley, but were almost immediately overpowered, and forced to retire, leaving behind them 120 of their party dead, among whom were the two officers. 11th August. Military expedition sent to bring the Mahdi to Kartoum.

After this, the Mahdi sent emissaries to all the neighbouring chiefs, calling on them to join him.

The Governor-General, on hearing of the disaster, ordered all the available troops from Kartoum, Sennaar, Fashoda, Kordofan, and Berber to assemble near Kawa, on the White Nile. The garrisons were left so weak that hardly sufficient troops remained to carry on the ordinary duties. Concentration of troops at Kawa.

Great excitement prevailed in Kartoum, which had no defences of any kind; and the inhabitants commenced to agitate for the construction of earthworks. Fears were entertained that the insurrection would spread rapidly, and even that the slaves, who formed more than half of the population of the town, would rise. Many were of opinion that a large garrison of Egyptian troops was absolutely necessary to ensure safety.

By the end of August, 1881, 1400 troops were concentrated near Kawa. There they remained idle for more than a month, and then dispersed to their quarters without having made the slightest attempt to follow the Mahdi, who retreated into the mountainous district of Takalla.[5] It is probable that, had he been resolutely attacked, he would have been defeated, his followers would have deserted him, and the rebellion, with all its disastrous consequences, would have been crushed. August. Inactivity of the troops at Kawa.

Rashid Bey, the Mudir of Fashoda, twice asked to be allowed to march against the Mahdi, but on both occasions permission was refused. At length, acting on his own responsibility, he set out

---

that to preserve tranquillity, at ordinary times, 9,000 troops, exclusive of the Garrison at Kartoum, would be necessary, even supposing the provinces of Kordofan and Darfur to be abandoned, as has been recommended by several high authorities. He suggests that the 9,000 troops should be distributed as follows—viz., 4,000 between Kartoum and Jebel Ain on both sides of the White Nile, 1000 at Fashoda to keep the Denka tribes and Shilluks in order, and 4,000 on the Blue Nile between Kartoum and Karkoj.

[5] South of Kordofan. This district is principally inhabited by negro tribes, with a king of their own, nominally subject to Kordofan.

1881. with 400 regular soldiers, and 100 Shilluk negroes, led by their chief Kaikun, and after a four days' march reached the camp of the Mahdi, on the mountain of Gadir,[6] on the 8th December. In the fight which ensued, Rashid Bey and the greater part of his troops, including the Shilluk Chieftain, were cut down by the Baggara horsemen. But few escaped to carry the news of the defeat to Fashoda. A large quantity of rifles, ammunition, and stores fell into the hands of the Mahdi.

8th December. Defeat of Rashid Bey at Jebel Gadir.

Great fears for the safety of Fashoda were entertained at Kartoum, and 200 soldiers were immediately sent there by steamer.

It was becoming more evident every day that a regular campaign would be necessary to quell the rebellion, and that reinforcements of men and *matériel* were absolutely necessary. Large numbers of irregular troops from the Shaikiyeh,[7] Dongola and Berber districts were enrolled, and armed at Kartoum. Nubir Yussuf Pasha, who had formerly seen service under Gessi Pasha,[8] was put in command of them. On the 15th March he left Kartoum with a force 4000 strong to operate against the rebels in the Shilluk country; but by the time he reached Kawa, several hundreds of the irregular troops had already deserted, and gone over to the enemy, and he remained there with the rest of his force inactive for several weeks.

1882. 15th March.

4th March. Appointment of Abdel Kader Pasha as Governor-General of the Soudan.

Raouf Pasha, the Governor-General of the Soudan, was recalled to Egypt on the 4th March, and Abdel Kader Pasha was appointed to succeed him. Pending the arrival of the latter, Giegler Pasha assumed temporary charge of the Soudan.

Taking advantage of the concentration at Kawa, the rebels attempted to make themselves masters of the district of Sennaar, and had many minor successes.

6th April. Defeat of the garrison of Sennaar.

On the 6th April, the garrison of the town of Sennaar attacked a large force of Arabs, led by a nephew of the Mahdi, who were encamped in the neighbourhood, but the attack was repulsed, and the Egyptian troops, having suffered great loss, retreated to the town, and shut themselves up in the Government buildings, which they succeeded in defending.

They were followed by the rebels, and for three days the greater part of the town was given up to murder, plunder, and fire. Many of the inhabitants, as well as 14 foreign merchants, 9 officers, and more than 100 soldiers, were killed. The losses of the rebels were also very considerable. As soon as the news reached Kartoum, reinforcements were ordered to Sennaar from Kalabat,[9] Katarif,[10] and Kawa. On the arrival of a detachment from the last-mentioned place, the

[6] About 150 miles north-west of Kaka on the White Nile.

[7] A tribe above Korti, on the left bank of the Nile.

[8] An Italian of great force of character. He joined Colonel Gordon's Staff in the summer of 1874, and subsequently became Governor of the Bahr-el-Ghazāl province.

[9] A district on the Abyssinian frontier near the sources of the Atbara.

[10] Sometimes called Suk-abu-Sin.

rebels retired towards Karkoj,[11] which had already been some time in their hands. 1882.

About this time the Shilluks[12] were reported to be in revolt, and the news from Darfur was far from re-assuring. The insurrection appeared to be gaining ground in every direction, and the position of the Government was becoming most critical. Spread of the rebellion.

On the 15th April a detachment of 200 troops left Kartoum, and proceeded up the western bank of the Blue Nile. About the same time some Bashi-Bazuks, under Ali Kashef, arrived at Abou-Haraz (at the junction of the Blue Nile and the Rahad) from Katarif, to act on the eastern bank of the Blue Nile in conjunction with several thousand Shukuriyeh,[13] under the Sheikh Aud-el-Kerim Bey. By operating on both flanks, hopes were entertained of speedily restoring tranquillity in the Province of Sennaar. No engagement of importance took place till the end of the month, when 150 Egyptian troops were cut to pieces by the rebels near Mesalameh. 15th April.

During April the Mahdi with the bulk of his followers still remained on the mountain of Gadir.

News received from Kordofan stated that 15 soldiers at the frontier post of Abu Haraz (west of El-Obeyed[14] on the way to Shaka[15]) had been killed, and that 150 soldiers stationed in Nuba,[16] for the suppression of the slave trade had been recalled to El-Obeyed. The inhabitants of the last-mentioned place were arming themselves, and constructing entrenchments. 6000 rebels were reported to be encamped in the neighbourhood, and an attack was expected. State of affairs in Kordofan.

By the end of April a considerable force had been collected on the Blue Nile, and Giegler Pasha placed himself at the head of it. On the 3rd May he attacked the nephew of the Mahdi, Sherif Ahmed Taha, near Abou Haraz (on the Blue Nile). The fight was obstinate, and the troops made but little progress till Sheikh Aud-el-Kerim Bey came to his assistance with a large body of Shukuriyeh, 2000 of whom were mounted, and clad in armour. 3rd May. Defeat of the rebels at Abou Haraz by Giegler Pasha.

The rebels were at length overpowered. The Sherif was amongst the slain, and his head was sent to Kartoum, and publicly exposed. In the telegrams announcing the victory, Giegler Pasha made no mention of the assistance he had received from the Shukuriyeh, but spoke only of the bravery of the Khédivial troops.

On the 25th May Giegler Pasha appears to have gained another 25th May.

[11] Above Sennaar on the Blue Nile.

[12] A negro tribe, numbering nearly a million souls, inhabiting the banks of the White Nile for 200 miles northwards from the mouth of the Ghazal river.

[13] A powerful Arab tribe, living in the country between the Atbara and Kartoum.

[14] Capital of Kordofan.

[15] A large town in the south of Darfur.

[16] A district south of Kordofan.

1882. victory over the rebels in the neighbourhood of Sennaar, in which 800 of them, including their chief, were killed.

11th May. Arrival of Abdel Kader Pasha at Kartoum.

Abdel Kader Pasha reached Kartoum on the 11th May, and assumed the duties of Governor-General of the Soudan.

16th May. Revolt of the Hassaniyeh Arabs.

On the 16th May the tribe of Hassaniyeh Arabs, living along the road from Kartoum to Kordofan, having been reported to be in revolt, 200 soldiers were sent to Tur-el-Hadra, on the White Nile. They were to be followed by 600 more.

Communication with Darfur, Sennaar, and Fazokl was interrupted.

At Kartoum the formation of irregular regiments of Shaggyeh and Dongolese was being actively pushed forward. Reinforcements were coming in from Berber, and were mostly sent on to Kordofan, where great insecurity prevailed. Large quantities of warlike stores and some guns were reported to have reached Berber from Cairo.

27th May. Rashid Pasha appointed Governor of Kordofan.

On the 27th May Rashid Pasha, Chief of the Military Posts along the Abyssinian frontier, reached Kartoum, and left on the 3rd June for Kordofan, whither more than 1000 troops had already preceded him. It was supposed that he was to be appointed Hokmdar of Darfur, Kordofan, and Dongola.

3rd June.

Of the doings of the Mahdi, and the state of affairs in Darfur, there was no news.

9th June.

The Mudirieh of Sennaar was still far from being pacified, and, on the 9th June, a force of 20,000 rebels was reported to be a day's march from the town of that name. The insurrection was also reported to be spreading to the districts south of Karkoj.

Towards the end of May Yussuf Pasha, who had done little or nothing since March, was ordered to advance from Kawa against the Mahdi, still supposed to be somewhere near the mountain of Gadir. After great delays he set out with a large disorganized force of several thousand men and swarms of camp followers. The rains had begun, and progress was slow. On the 7th June he was face to face with the rebels in a densely wooded country. A seriba (or stockade of prickly shrubs) was commenced, and the troops were formed up inside it in a hollow square. The rebels, however, broke in upon them, and defeated and utterly routed the whole force. This crushing defeat gave a fresh impetus to the insurrection.

7th June. Defeat of Yussuf Pasha near Jebel Gadir.

13th June. Despatch of reinforcements to Fashada.

On the 13th June 400 men were sent by steamer to reinforce the garrison of Fashoda, and on the 29th a battalion, which had arrived at Kartoum from Senheit,[17] was also sent on there. These reinforcements were placed under the command of Rashid Pasha, whose orders had been altered, and who had only accompanied the troops for Kordofan as far as Tur-el-Hadra.

[17] A district called by the Abysrians Bogos, on the road between Kassala and Massowah.

News from Darfur was scant and unreliable. It was rumoured that an attack on Omohangah on the 17th June had been repulsed; but that towards Shaka an Egyptian force of 1000 men had been almost annihilated on the 20th July.

1882. Events in Darfur. 17th June. 20th July.

In Kordofan the rebels attacked Bara[18] on the 28th June, but were repulsed, it is said, with a loss of 32,000 men. At the same time large bands infested the neighbourhood of El Obeyed, and water, fuel, and grain were already reported to be scarce in that town.

28th June. Defeat of the rebels at Bara.

Early in July the insurrection was rumoured to have spread to the provinces of Bahr-el-Ghazel Shaka, and the Equator, but the reports turned out to be exaggerated, and the movement never obtained any hold in those parts.

July.

Towards the end of June the works of defence for the protection of Kartoum were commenced to the south of the town. It began to appear doubtful whether the irregular troops would be able to make head against the rebellion, and reinforcements from Cairo were not arriving. It was then resolved to form negro battalions, and every slave-owner in Kartoum was called upon to give up a certain number of slaves for the purpose. By this means it was estimated that 2000 troops could be obtained. The same system had been followed two years before, during the mobilization of the army for operations against Abyssinia. It had the double advantage of increasing the troops, and diminishing the number of slaves, who it was feared might revolt.

June and July.

Formation of slave battalions.

The foreign inhabitants, having no slaves, decided to give assistance in kind, and sent 525 ardebs[19] of dhoora,[20] worth 360 pounds sterling, towards the sustenance of these newly raised battalions.

In August a state of siege was proclaimed in Kartoum. Five forts had been constructed, each armed with one gun. The town was divided into four military sections, and pickets patrolled the streets both day and night. A rising in the town was expected, simultaneously with an attack from without.

August. Proclamation of a state of siege at Kartoum.

As a further protection, it was decided to cut a canal south of the town, joining the two branches of the Nile, but the commencement of this work appears to have been delayed till November.

The Kababish Arabs, an important tribe occupying a large tract of country between Kordofan and Dongola, were in revolt, and a large force of them were menacingly encamped within a day's march of Kartoum.

Revolt of the Kababish tribe.

During July and August many minor engagements were fought upon the lines of communication between the White Nile and Kordofan, which almost always resulted in favour of the rebels.

July and August.

[18] A pretty town, with a good supply of water, and surrounded by excellent gardens.

[19] One ardeb = $5\frac{3}{5}$ bushels.

[20] A kind of maize.

1882. The commercial town of Schatt, on the road from Duem, on the White Nile, to El Obeyed, was totally destroyed by them, the male population was put to the sword, and the women and children were carried off into captivity.

August. In the beginning of August the insurgent forces were divided into three principal groups :—

Distribution of the insurgent forces. The Mahdi, with the bulk of his forces, was still on the mountain of Gadir, in the Takalla district; a second army was wasting Kordofan, and a third stretched along the White Nile from Duem to Djezirit Abba, on the western bank, and from Kawa to Marabieh on the eastern.

19th August. On the 19th August the rebels were defeated near Bara, and El Obeyed was subsequently revictualled.

28th August. Defeat of the rebels near Duem. The rebels operating along the western bank of the White Nile, under Ahmed Woad-el-Makashef, were attacked by the Egyptian troops near Duem on the 28th of August, and routed, leaving 3,500 dead on the field of battle. This defeat frustrated the projected march on Kartoum.

Advance of the Mahdi into Kordofan. After this the Mahdi took the field in person, and advanced on El Obeyed, around which an earthen rampart, armed with a few guns, had been thrown up. The garrison consisted of 6,000 men, armed with Remington rifles. The rifles had been sent there in June by Abdel Kader Pasha, in anticipation of a siege.

The rebels were armed with spears and matchlocks.

8th, 11th, 14th September. Assaults of El Obeyed. On the 8th of September the Mahdi made a desperate assault on the town, but was repulsed with great slaughter, his losses being reported to be from 12,000 to 15,000 killed, while those of the garrison are put down at 288. Two brothers of the Mahdi and several insurgent chiefs were among the slain. The attack was repeated on the 11th and 14th September, but on both occasions without success. The rebels fought with the greatest fury, quite regardless of death. Their losses in the three assaults are said to have reached the enormous total of 40,000.[21]

Appeal to the loyalty of the Arabs, and promise of rewards. In presence of the disaffection of many of the regular troops, the Governor-General of the Soudan issued an appeal to the patriotism of those of the Shukuriyeh, Dabaina, and Kababish tribes who still remained loyal, urging them to take the field against the rebels, and promising the remission of one year's taxes. He further undertook to pay £2 for every dervish (as the followers of Mahdi were called) captured, dead or alive, and £18 for every chief.

[21] The information concerning the events of the rebellion up to the arrival of Lieut.-Colonel Stewart at Kartoum, is derived almost entirely from native sources, and it is consequently impossible to put much reliance on the statements as to the extent of the losses in the various engagements. It is even difficult to ascertain the correct dates of the principal events. Some accounts state that the assaults on El Obeyed took place on the 4th, 5th and 6th September.

All booty was to remain the property of the captors. The result was that shortly afterwards several thousand volunteers joined the troops at Kawa. 1882.

On the 3rd September, 300 negro recruits reached Kartoum from Lardo in the Equatorial provinces, and these were shortly followed by 1100 Bazingers (untrained soldiers from Dar-Fertit[22]), sent by the Mudir of the Bahr-el-Ghazel district. 3rd September.

A relief column of two battalions of regular troops and 850 Bashi Bazouks, altogether 3,000 strong, under Ali Bey Satfi, set out from Duem towards the end of September to attempt to raise the siege of Bara. It suffered terrible privations on the way, the rebels having filled in all the wells along the road between Abu Shoka and Bara (seven days' march). The troops had almost nothing but the juice of wild melons and dhoora stalks to quench their thirst. They were continually harassed by the enemy, but were not attacked in force till they approached El Kona, when Ali Satfi Bey and all the senior officers were killed. The losses of the Egyptians amounted to 1100, besides 1150 rifles and a large quantity of stores and ammunition. The remainder of the troops were at length rallied by a captain, and succeeded in driving off the enemy. They then continued the march to Bara, and were met some distance from the town by the garrison, which had come out to their assistance. The Mahdi was then encamped at a water station in the neighbourhood of Bara. On the 25th October the garrison made a sortie, and attacked and defeated him, but subsequently retired within the entrenchments. Defeat of a large relief column sent to Kordofan. 25th October. Defeat of the Mahdi near Bara.

After the repulses at El Obeyed and Bara the Mahdi was deserted by many of his followers, and his forces in Kordofan appear to have been quite shattered for the time. So much was the danger for Kordofan thought to be over, that, when the Mudir of Darfur appeared at Omchanga about the end of October with a considerable armed force, his proffered assistance was declined.

A report having reached Kartoum that the above-mentioned relief column had been totally destroyed, the Governor-General telegraphed to Cairo that he must have reinforcements of at least 10,000 men. He stated that without a large force at his disposal the insurrection would spread through all parts of the Soudan, and that then the pacification of the country would require an army of at least four times the strength of that for which he asked. Demand for reinforcements from Cairo.

During Arabi's short tenure of power, he had but little time to devote to the affairs of the Soudan, and no reinforcements were sent there; in fact, orders were actually given for some of the troops to be withdrawn from there to Egypt to assist in the war against the English.

[22] South of the country of the Baggara Arabs, and west of Bahr el-Ghazel.

1882. After the occupation of Cairo, the suppression of the rebellion in the Soudan was one of the first questions to occupy the attention of the Government of the Khedive. Various plans were suggested, and it was at length decided, after the receipt of the previously-mentioned telegram from Abdel Kader Pasha, to enlist about 10,000 officers and men who had fought under Arabi for service in the Soudan. At the request of the Khedive several English officers were appointed to the staff of this force.

November. Despatch of reinforcements to the Soudan.

By the beginning of November between two and three thousand troops had already been concentrated at the "Barrage" on the Nile near Cairo, and were being equipped for the expedition.

The first detachment, one thousand strong, left Suez for Suakin, whence they were to march to Berber, on the 14th November.

Desertions from the depôt at the "Barrage" were very frequent. They were due to a rumour among the soldiers that they were to be transported to the Soudan as prisoners. The arms and ammunition required for the expedition were forwarded to Suakin, separately from the troops, as a measure of precaution.

On the 12th December 1500 troops left Cairo for the Soudan, bringing up the total contingent already sent to 5,000.

Thanks to the energy of Al-ed-Deen Pasha, Governor of the Red Sea provinces, steps were taken at Suakin for the speedy despatch of the reinforcements as soon as they arrived from Suez. No delays occurred, the necessary supply of camels for the transport of baggage and stores having always been prepared beforehand. Throughout the revolt of Arabi, Al-ed-Deen Pasha had remained loyal, and had inspired such respect for the Khedive that even natives, who may have entertained sympathy with the rebellious movement, did not dare to commit any overt act of hostility, and thus public order and tranquillity were never for a moment disturbed in the provinces over which he was Governor.

By the 9th January, 1883, the arrivals of soldiers at the depôt at the "Barrage" had reached 9,500. The departures were already 7,700. They included 100 dismounted cavalry, 100 gunners, and nine battalions of infantry, formed into three regiments. The 1st Battalion of the 4th Regiment was on the point of leaving.

By the middle of February the last of these reinforcements for the Soudan had left Egypt.

12th November. About the 12th November, 1882, a rebel Sheikh attacked Duem, but he was defeated and captured, and subsequently hanged at Kartoum.

15th November. Construction of a canal south of Kartoum.

On the 15th November the long projected canal south of Kartoum was commenced, eight hundred to a thousand yards in front of the town. Its dimensions are as follow: length, when the rivers are in flood, 5,900 yards; when at low water, 6,700; depth of ditch, 8 feet; width at top, 17 feet; at bottom, 10 feet; slopes steep; width of parapet at bottom, 20 feet; at top, 14 feet; height, 7 feet. The principal defects of the parapet are its great length, and the absence of flanking defence. The idea of constructing a defensive canal, and turning Kartoum into an island, originated with Musa Pasha in 1864. 1882.

The garrison of El Obeyed was reported to be still fairly well supplied with food on the 12th December, and to be in good spirits. A few days previously it had sallied out and attacked Sheikh Mennoo, the leading rebel chief in the neighbourhood, killing about 70 of his people. December. State of the garrisons of El Obeyed and Bara.

At Bara,[23] the garrison was badly off for food, and in a depressed condition. Some of the irregular officers with their men had deserted to the rebels. The Mahdi, with the bulk of his forces, was encamped round the town. His ranks had been much thinned by desertion and sickness, but, on the other hand, he was gaining fresh adherents every day. For the moment he had ceased to take the offensive, and was contenting himself with blockading Bara and El Obeyed, while the Makashef operated with a large force on the Nile.

Darfur was so far quiet, though the Mahdi was reported to be doing his utmost to stir up the tribes.

On the 16th December, Lieut.-Colonel Stewart, of the 11th Hussars, arrived at Kartoum. 16th December. Arrival of Lieut.-Col. Stewart, 11th Hussars, at Kartoum.

Owing to the absence of any trustworthy information, he had been sent by the British Government to inquire into the true state of affairs in the Soudan.

Two battalions of reinforcements from Egypt (the 1st and 2nd Battalions, 1st Regiment) reached Kartoum early in December, and formed a camp at Omdurman on the left bank of the Nile, opposite Kartoum. December.

Almost immediately after their arrival there were rumours of fresh outbreak in the neighbourhood of Kawa, and later on, in those of Sennaar and Mesalamieh on the Blue Nile. Instead of forming a relief column for Kordofan, it was deemed necessary to employ these battalions first in restoring order on the banks of the Blue and White Niles. The 1st battalion was sent to Shawal on the White Nile, and on the evening of the 30th December the 2nd battalion left by steamer for Mesalamieh.

The Makashef, with a large force, was at Sibel threatening Sennaar, and was causing a great deal of trouble.

Abdel Kader Pasha gave orders for four companies at Sennaar and the garrison of irregulars at Abut (immediately north of Sibel) to make a combined attack on the last-mentioned place. It was to support this attack, which was ordered for the 4th January, that the 2nd Battalion 1st Regiment was sent to Mesalamieh.

The attack was, however, anticipated by the Makashef, who took the offensive, and attacked the detached post of Abut on the 31st December. He was repulsed, but succeeded in interrupting all communication between Mesalamieh and Sennaar. 31st December. Repulse of the rebels at Abut.

On the 1st January the four companies at Sennaar left for Sibel. 1883. 1st and 2nd January.

[23] Bara is due north of Obeyed.

1883. The following day they were attacked while on the march, and all but about eighty surrendered to the rebels after making but little, if any, resistance.

January. Reinforcements from Egypt.

By the beginning of January the under-mentioned reinforcements had arrived from Egypt, viz.: infantry, 5 battalions (4,170 men); artillery, 180 men, with 10 mountain guns and 10 rocket troughs; cavalry, 97 Circassians clad in chain armour. A few mules had accompanied the artillery, but there were no horses with the cavalry. With the exception of the two battalions, which had gone to Shawal and Mesalamieh, the whole of this force was encamped at Omdurman, near Kartoum. The troops were working at elementary drill and tactics, and making some progress, but the officers were, as a rule, ignorant, and incapable of grasping the meaning of the simplest movement, unwilling to assume any responsibility, and totally devoid of initiative.

Many of the troops had superstitious ideas regarding the power of the Mahdi, and others thought that the Khedive had only sent them to the Soudan to get rid of them.

They were dressed in long white cotton shirts and native cotton trousers. Most of them wore coarse leather sandals. Each man had a grey overcoat and hood. The infantry were all armed with Remington rifles.

The tactics of the Egyptians in the presence of the enemy were to form battalion or double company squares. The troops were formed in three ranks, to give them confidence. Each man was provided with four or five crow's feet (iron spikes with four points), which he was instructed to throw in front of him on the approach of the enemy. The rebels usually attacked in several masses.

January. Defeat of a detachment of troops near Jura Hadra.

Early in January news was received of a disaster on the eastern bank of the White Nile. A detachment of 190 men had been sent from the fort of Jura Hadra in a northerly direction to repair the line of telegraph to Kartoum. When a short distance from the fort, they were attacked by some rebels under Fakir Owde.[24] The troops formed square as usual, but after a short resistance commenced to give way, the square was broken, and many were killed. Half the party, however, managed to rally, and held out until a reinforcement came to their assistance from Jura Hadra.

2nd January.

On the 2nd January, Abdel Kader Pasha left Kartoum by steamer to take personal command of the troops operating between the Blue and White Niles. He did not reach Mesalamieh till the 7th, having stopped frequently on the journey to interview the chiefs of the villages on the banks of the river.

The town of Mesalamieh is six miles west of the river. On arrival, the Pasha proceeded immediately to inspect the battalion encamped there (2nd Battalion, 1st Regiment), and informed the officers that he intended to march with as small a baggage train as

[24] The Fakirs are learned pious men. The Dervishes are their satellites.

possible. They protested, and made all kinds of difficulties, but it was finally decided that each company should be accompanied by four camels only. 1883.

On the 8th January, the battalion, with some irregular troops under Saliha Bey, and some Shukuriyeh horsemen, started for Abut. The order of march was in company columns with scouts on both flanks, and advance and rear guards. The country traversed was a treeless but well-cultivated open plain, with many villages and plenty of water. The crops consisted chiefly of dhoora (maize) and cotton. There were also many large herds of cattle, and flocks of sheep. The inhabitants were very friendly, and freely supplied the troops with water, and even with bread. 8th January. Advance on Abut.

At 8 P.M., a halt was made at the Faulla (pond) of El-Sunga. The troops bivouacked, protected by a bank which had, on a previous occasion, been thrown up round the pond. Ten men per company were employed to patrol during the night some 500 yards from the camp.

On the 9th, the column started at 7 A.M. The order of march was the same as on the preceding day. Two miles from the bivouac, the village of Effena was passed. This was the last inhabited village met with on the road. Further on they were all deserted, the inhabitants having gone off willingly, or unwillingly, to join the rebels, leaving their crops standing, and ready for harvesting. 9th January.

At 1.30 P.M. the village of Abut was reached. It is a small military station, and had a garrison of 350 men, who were encamped in a zeriba with trench near the well. When attacked on the 31st December, only 150 of the garrison were present, 200 men under Osman Agha had arrived since then. Two new zeribas were at once constructed, one for the regular troops, and another for the irregulars. Reconnaissances were pushed in all directions, but especially along the roads leading to Kawa *viâ* Waliya, and to Manasra, south of Sibel.

Finding then that the quelling of the insurrection in the province of Sennaar would be a more difficult task than he had anticipated, the Pasha determined to call up the battalion from Shawal,[25] and to send for another from Kartoum.

The 3rd Battalion, 1st Regiment, left Kartoum accordingly on the afternoon of the 10th January, and proceeded up the Blue Nile in twelve sailing boats. 10th January.

On the 11th January, Abdel Kader was still at Abut. On that date his intention was to await the arrival of the 3rd Battalion, and then march on Sennaar. Reports had come in that that town was hard pressed by a large body of rebels, that Karkoj was again in their hands, that the tribe of Rufaa el Sherk,[26] under Sheikh Sherif 11th January.

[25] The junction between the 1st Battalion and Abdel Kader's force was to have taken place on the 15th January, but, for some reason or other, it did not take place till Abdel Kader's arrival at Kawa on the 1st February.

[26] An Arab tribe inhabiting the country between Sennaar and Fazokl.

1883. el Hindi, was in full revolt, and the last mentioned was doing his best to induce Aud el Kerim Bey, the powerful Sheikh of the Shukuriyeh, to join the movement.

12th January. On the 12th, however, it was reported that the Sheikh Wad el Kerif, at the head of a large force, was marching from Maatuk to attack Abdel Kader, that he was forcing all the men of the districts through which he passed to join him, and that Fakir Moosa, who was commanding the rebels in the neighbourhood of Kawa, would co-operate with him.

This news compelled the Pasha to reconsider his decision, and, instead of advancing on Sennaar, he resolved to await the approach of the Wad el Kerif.

On the White Nile, the Hassaniyeh nomads were again giving trouble. To pacify this tribe, and the villages in the neighbourhood of Karasah,[27] the 1st Battalion, 2nd Regiment, left Kartoum on the 16th January in two steamers, and proceeded up the White Nile. It was accompanied by the Vakeel[28] of the Mudiriyeh and some Ulemas. These officials were directed to enter into communication with the people, and to try to induce them to submit quietly. The orders given to the battalion were to disembark when still a little north of the village, and then advance in close order.

16th January. Despatch of troops to Karasah. Revolt of the Husseinyeh Arabs.

18th January. Defeat of the Egyptians at Karasah.

On the 18th, the steamers reached the neighbourhood of the village. Here one of the steamers ran aground in the middle of the river. The other, on board of which was the Bimbashi[29] with five companies, pushed up right abreast of the village. Three companies immediately disembarked, lined a low sand dyke parallel to and about 500 yards from the river, and opened fire on some rebels who were about 2,000 yards off. The latter advanced to the attack, but the severity of the fire forced them to incline away to the right and left as they approached.

Three or four horsemen of the right-hand party succeeded in penetrating between the dyke and the river, and fell upon the two companies which had disembarked last, and were not yet formed up. This was the signal for a regular panic, and the flight of all the Egyptians to the river. The rebels did not pursue. In the confusion the Bimbashi was killed, some account says by his own men, others by the enemy.

The other steamer, with the three remaining companies of the battalion having by this time come up, a council of war was held, when it was decided that the battalion was not strong enough to advance, and that reinforcements of men and guns from Kartoum were absolutely necessary. The rebel force did not in reality exceed 400 men.

26th January. During the next few days the battalion remained quietly on board the steamers off Karasah. On the 26th January, the Bimbashi of

[27] Sometimes written El Gerazeh or Qurassa. A village on the right bank of the White Nile.

[28] Deputy Governor.

[29] Major.

the 2nd battalion of the regiment arrived from Kartoum to replace the Bimbashi who had been killed. The steamers were then lying about two and a half hours' march from the village. An advance was ordered for 3 A.M. on the 27th, so as to attack the village at daybreak, and take the rebels by surprise. But, on the remonstrances of nearly all the officers, who said that they would certainly be killed if they marched in the dark through an unknown country, the order was cancelled, and that day nothing was done except a short reconnaissance inland. The Bimbashi, however, decided to attack on the 28th. After the orders were issued five of the senior officers proceeded to report themselves sick. 1883.

At 3.30 A.M. on the 28th the battalion marched off. It was formed up in a square, preceded by an advance guard and scouts, and at daybreak was within about 800 yards of the village, from which it was separated by a long, narrow strip of forest. 28th January.

Two companies were ordered into the forest to reconnoitre the path leading to the village, but the officers refused to advance, saying that they and their men would certainly be killed.

During the delay and discussion that followed, some soldiers, disobeying orders, fired at some cattle that were grazing near by. This gave the alarm to the rebels, and in a few minutes nine or ten horsemen appeared at the edge of the wood. By galloping about and waving their swords, these men engaged the attention of the troops, and gave time for the removal of the women and cattle from the village. When this was accomplished, the rebel foot advanced through the wood, and the troops immediately began to fall back. The rebels, who did not exceed 350, and had no firearms, followed them till within about half an hour's distance of the steamer, but generally keeping out of rifle range. It is estimated that about thirty of them were killed or wounded. A few hours after the return of the troops to the boats, the 2nd battalion of the 2nd regiment, as well as two guns and a rocket trough, arrived from Kartoum with the Kaimakan[30] of the regiment. These reinforcements had been sent on receipt of a direct order from the Khedive.

The rebels appear to have been subsequently attacked and defeated, but there does not appear to be any account of the engagement.

The 1st battalion, 3rd regiment, and 225 Bashi Bazouks, without horses, arrived at Kartoum from Egypt on the 24th January. 650 camels for transport purposes had already been collected at Kartoum, and 400 were expected in a few days from Dongola. According to the lowest estimate, 300 camels per battalion would be required for the Kordofan expedition, to be distributed as follows:—For rations, 115; water, 75; ammunition, 52; officers, 25; sick hospital, &c., 33. 24th January.

On the 23d January, Hussein Pasha Serri, the senior military officer at Kartoum, received a telegram from the Khedive ordering

[30] Lieutenant-Colonel.

1883. him to suspend all operations and to concentrate all the troops at Kartoum, pending the arrival of some English staff officers at Cairo. The fact of the Khedive communicating direct with this officer, instead of with Giegler Pasha, the representative of Abdel Kader, caused a great deal of unpleasantness. This order was communicated to Abdel Kader, then at Abut, who replied that, if he withdrew the troops to Kartoum the rebellion would unquestionably extend in the eastern provinces, and that, if the expedition did not soon leave for Kordofan, that province would be lost and with it Darfur.

24th January. To return to the operations of Abdel Kader. About the 24th January a party of rebels pillaged the village of Mangalla, which, together with some others of the south and south-west of Abut, had submitted to the Government of the Khedive.

Hearing of this, the Pasha, having been joined by the 3rd Battalion, 1st Regiment, determined to advance against a large body of rebels, reported to be about eight hours' march from his camp.

27th January. Defeat of the rebels near Maatuk. Early on the 27th he moved towards the village of Maatuk. When about three hours from it, the rebels were observed on a plain on the further side of a small wood. The troops were at once halted in the open, about 500 yards from the wood, and formed into square.

The rebels, after a short halt for prayer, advanced through the wood, but, contrary to expectation, halted again at the near edge, and Wad Eyoub, a revolted Benluk Bashi of irregulars, with some negroes, opened fire on the troops, killing one and wounding five. The square then fired, and after some minutes the rebels commenced to retire, pursued by the irregular cavalry. In this affair Faki Moosa was wounded. The losses of the rebels are estimated at 600 killed and wounded.

In the retreat the rebels broke up into two parties, one, under Sheikh Wad-el-Kerif, went in a south-westerly direction towards Göz Abu Djuma,[31] and the other, under Faki Moosa and Faki Mohammed Abu Shneb, retired to the village of Baatuk on the road to Kawa.

28th January. Against the latter, the Pasha directed the whole of his available cavalry and camel corps, altogether about 300 men. This force came up with the rebels at 3 A.M. on the 28th, and totally defeated them, killing Abu Shneb.

1st February. On the 1st February Abdel-Kader, with his two battalions, reached Kawa, where he met the 1st battalion, 1st regiment, from Shawal. On the 3rd February this force was increased by the arrival of the 1st and 2nd battalions 2nd regiment, which had marched along the river bank from Karasah, performing, according to their own account, prodigies of valour on the road.

3rd February. On the 3rd February Abdel-Kader left Kawa by the steamer for Kartoum leaving orders :—

[31] Sometimes written Goz Abou Goumeh.

(1.) That the three battalions of the 1st Regiment were to march at once to Wad el Medinet on the Blue Nile, where he would join them about the 15th for an advance on Sennaar; and 1883.

(2.) That the two battalions of the 2nd Regiment, under the Kaimakan, were to attack the rebels at Abu Djuma.

Disaffection among the Kababish Arabs.

Towards the end of January it was rumoured in Kartoum that the Kababish Arabs had gone over to the Mahdi, or rather to the Faki Manne, who commanded the rebels in Northern Kordofan. As the Kababish extend as far north as Dongola, fears were entertained that the rebellion might spread to that province, and early in February it was reported that the natives about Debbeh[32] were becoming very restless. Some Bashi Bazouks were sent there to maintain order.

10th February.

About the 10th February the troops in the camp at Omdurman comprised:—

4 battalions of Egyptian infantry (3,200 men).
420 Bashi Bazouks.
1,100 Negro recruits.
90 dismounted cavalry, and a few artillerymen.

Their health was very good.

Surrender of Bara, 5th January.

On the 11th February, a messenger arrived at Kartoum from the west confirming the rumours that Bara had fallen on the 5th January. The garrison were said to be fairly well treated by the Arabs, and only the officers were kept in confinement. By this surrender 2,000 troops, besides a considerable quantity of arms and ammunition, fell into the hands of the rebels.

Siege of El Obeyed.

Four days afterwards the news arrived that El Obeyed had capitulated on the 17th January, and that the whole of Kordofan was in the hands of the Mahdi.

After the repulse of the assaults on El Obeyed, in September, 1882, various plans were proposed for attacking the Mahdi, but the Council of War was always of opinion that the troops available were too few, and the garrison relapsed into a state of inactivity, which continued, so far as any operations of importance are concerned, till the end of the siege. Small sorties of two or three hundred men were, however, of frequent occurrence, generally resulting in the capture of some cattle and grain.

The besiegers, on their side, established themselves comfortably around the town, some availing themselves of the ruined houses, and others building straw huts, and patiently awaited the inevitable surrender.

Such was the attitude taken up by both sides till the 13th January, by which date the supply of food was almost exhausted, and everything eatable was being sold at fabulous prices.

[32] On the left bank of the Nile near Old Dongola.

1883. On the 14th, the Mahdi sent letters to Mahmoud Said, the Governor of the Western Soudan, and all the principal officers, telling them that they had held out long enough, and, if they would surrender, he would guarantee the safety of their lives. On the 16th, a party of rebels appeared outside the entrenchments to open negociations for a capitulation. Mahmoud Said Pasha was not present at the interview which followed, but the greater part of the garrison appear to have agreed to the terms that were proposed.

17th January. Surrender of El Obeyed.

During the night many of the garrison deserted. At daybreak on the 17th the insurgents advanced against the town in force. The Pasha ordered what remained of the garrison to fire, but the infantry refused to do so, and passed over to the enemy, while the artillery fired a few salvoes in a direction that could do no harm to the assailing force. The Pasha then understood that he was completely abandoned by his men, and consented to surrender and make submission to the Mahdi, who was then at an hour and a half's distance from the town.

On entering the town, the Mahdi proceeded immediately to the principal mosque.

Mahmoud Said Pasha, and Ali Sherif Bey, the Mudir of Kordofan, were at first treated with consideration, but, on their refusal to give up their money, they were seized and imprisoned. 8,000*l.* sterling in gold was found concealed in the house of the former, and 7,000*l.* in that of the latter.

Altogether, although little or no money was found in the public treasury, the Mahdi is said to have taken more than 100,000*l.* from the officials and notables. He kept all the booty for himself, and distributed none of it among his followers. This was a source of great dissatisfaction, and subsequently caused many to waver in their allegiance.

The garrison at the time of the surrender numbered about 3,500. They were made to swear fidelity to the Mahdi, enlisted in his service, and told off by companies to the various banners. About 6,000 Remington rifles, five guns, and one rocket trough passed into the hands of the rebels. As regards provisions, only 200 ardebs[33] of dhoora were found in the town. Towards the end of the siege famine had prevailed, and the inhabitants had kept themselves alive by chewing raw india-rubber, varied with a small ration of dhoora.

All the books and Government papers were destroyed and the town was completely looted.

The Mahdi took up his residence in the Government House, and appointed a Governor of the town, but did not make any attempt to form a regular administration. The following is a translation of a proclamation issued by him :—

Proclamation issued by the Mahdi.

"From the servant of his Lord Mohammed el Mahdi, son of Said Abdallah, to all the fervent proselytes.

[33] One ardeb = $5\frac{3}{5}$ bushels.

"We have appointed as your Prince our dear Sheikh Mansour, son of Abd el hakem. Execute his orders and commands, and follow him in the path of battle. 1883.

"He who submits to him submits to us; he who disobeys him disobey us, and disobeys God himself and His Prophet. Let all show penitence before God, and abandon all bad and forbidden habits, such as the degrading acts of the flesh, the use of wine and tobacco, lying, bearing false witness, disobedience to parents, brigandage, the non-restitution of goods to others, the clapping of hands, dancing, improper signs with the eyes, tears and lamentations at the bed of the dead, slanderous language, calumny, and the company of strange women. Clothe your women in a decent way, and let them be careful not to speak to unknown persons. All those who do not pay attention to these principles disobey God and His Prophet, and they shall be punished in accordance with the law.

"Say your prayers at the prescribed hours.

"Give the tenth part of your goods, handing it to our Prince, Sheikh Mansour, in order that he may forward it to the treasury of Islam.

"Adore God, and hate not each other, but assist each other to do good."

At the bottom of this, the seal of the Mahdi was affixed.

13th February. Advance of Abdel Kader towards Sennaar.

On the 13th February, Abdel Kader Pasha left Kartoum to rejoin the troops at Wad of Medinet, who had marched from Kawa. He proceeded thence towards Sennaar, his force consisting of the three battalions of the 1st Regiment, about 600 Bashi Bazouks, some Sakkeyer horsemen, and a few guns and rocket troughs.[34]

On the 22nd February he reached Meshoa-el-Dakhin, about eight hours' march from Sennaar. That evening, about 8 p.m., a large body of rebels under the Makashef, who had raised the siege of Sennaar, approached the camp. Some shots were exchanged, but the rebels, finding the soldiers on the alert, retired. The following day, Friday, a halt was made, and the neighbourhood was thoroughly reconnoitred. Abdel Kader received a letter from the Makashef, in which, after testifying to the divine mission and the invincibility of the Mahdi, he invited the Pasha to submit, saying that he had a regard for him, and was anxious to spare his life and spiritual hereafter.

24th February. Defeat of the rebels at Meshra-el-Dai.

Early on the 24th, the march was continued. On approaching Meshra-el-Dai, the Makashef was discovered with 10,000 or 12,000 followers in some bushy ground close to the river. The guns and rockets at once opened fire on them. After some time the rebels came out into the open and attacked the troops.

They advanced with great determination, but after a severe fight were dispersed and pursued by the cavalry; the engagement

[34] Number not stated.

1883. lasted from 10 a.m. till 1 p.m. Of the troops 27 were wounded. The rebel loss was estimated at 2,000 killed, including Sheikh Woad el Kerif, of Maatuk notoriety. Many of the rebels fled into the river, where they were cut down by the cavalry. The Makashef succeeded in escaping. Some of the rebels used firearms, and Abdel Kader had a narrow escape, his watch-chain being broken by a bullet.

25th February. Saturday night the troops remained halted, but on Sunday the 25th the march was continued to Sennaar. The inhabitants of the villages along the road came in, and tendered their submission.

The route between Sennaar and Kartoum, both by land and water, was reported to be safe. A regular postal service was immediately re-established, and steps were taken for repairing the line of telegraph.

After the defeat at Meshra-el-Dai on the 24th, the insurgents appear to have split themselves up into three bodies; one under Abdul Ghaffar retired to Karkoj and joined Faki Sherif, another under the Makashef took up a position at Jebel Sekhédy, about six hours west of Sennaar, and a third came into Sennaar and gave themselves up.

4th March. Defeat of the rebels at Sekhédy. Abdel Kader's scouts having brought in intelligence of the Makashef's whereabouts, a force of 1200 irregulars, made up of Shukuriyeh and Aburoff Arabs, under Saleh Agha, was directed against him. An engagement took place on the 4th March at Sekhédy, which resulted in the total defeat of the rebels, who lost 547 killed, among whom were Sheikhs Omr and Amr, brothers of the Makashef, and Sadyk, his nephew. The casualties among Saleh Agha's force were only two men wounded.

Abdel Kader then proposed marching south up the Blue Nile, and pacifying the country as far as Karkoj, after which he intended to cross the river, and advance eastward against the revolted Rufaa-el-Sherk and Kawakli tribes in the country between the rivers Dinder and Rahad. But, as will be seen further on, he was superseded before he had time to carry out these plans.

20th Feb. Arrival of Pashas Al-ed-din and Suleiman. On the 20th February, the Pashas Al-ed-Din and Suleiman Nyasi reached Kartoum. The latter was to take command of the troops, but the mission of the former was kept secret, though it was rumoured that he was to be appointed Governor-General of the Soudan.

Nyasi at Kartoum. 4th March. Arrival of Colonel Hicks at Kartoum. On the 4th March, Colonel Hicks[35] reached Kartoum, and with him the undermentioned English Officers, viz.:—Lieut.-Colonel Hon. J. Colborne,[36] Lieut.-Colonel de Coetlogon,[37] Major Martin,[38]

[35] Late Bombay Staff Corps.
[36] Late 11th Foot.
[37] Late 70th Foot.
[38] Late Captain of Baker's Horse in South Africa.

Major Farquhar,[39] Captain Warner, Captain Massey,[40] Captain Evans, Captain Walker,[41] and Surgeon-Major Rosenberg. 1883.

Colonel Hicks had been appointed Chief of the Staff of the Army of the Soudan, with local rank of Major-General, but it was intended that he should direct, and be responsible for, all preparations and operations—in fact, that he should in reality be the Commander-in-Chief, while nominally holding a subordinate post.

The Mahdi's movement being, at any rate ostensibly, a religious one, it was deemed inadvisable to place at the head of the Egyptian Army of the Soudan a foreigner and a non-Mussulman, lest the insurgent leader might make capital out of this to arouse still further the fanaticism of his followers.

Suleiman Nyasi, whose military career dates back to the days of Mahomet Ali and the Crimean War, was consequently named to the chief command, but on the understanding that he was to pay strict attention to, and carefully follow out General Hick's instructions and plans, but his indolence, apathy, ignorance, and in many instances apparent malignity and jealousy, caused him frequently to act in anything but the spirit of the instructions given him at Cairo.

8th March. Departure of Lieut.-Col. Stewart for Egypt.

On the 8th March, Lieut.-Colonel Stewart left Kartoum for Egypt, travelling by way of Sennaar, Katarif, Kassala, and Massowah.

18th March.

On the 18th March, Major Farquhar, who had been on a reconnaissance up the White Nile, returned to Kartoum. He reported the inhabitants along the western bank of the river to be hostile.

Four thousand five hundred rebels and 1800 Baggara Arab Cavalry were assembled about Marabieh and Abu Djuma, and at Jebel Ain there was a considerable body, which had lately been reinforced from Kordofan. The Baggaras had quarrelled with the Madhi regarding the booty taken at El Obeyed, and had seized and carried off some of it. The troops at the posts along the river were in rags, and from four to six months in arrears of pay.

News from Kordofan stated that the Mahdi's force was about one hundred thousand strong, that it had dispersed for the moment, but could be quickly reassembled. The chiefs met at El Obeyed every Friday for orders, but the Sheikhs of the Baggara did not attend.

Taking advantage of this discontent, General Hicks was trying to open communications with the last-mentioned, and hoped to arrange a meeting at Dem.

26th March. Proclamation of Al-ed-Deen Pasha as Governor-General of the Soudan.

On the 26th March Al-ed-Deen Pasha was publicly proclaimed at Kartoum as Governor-General of the Soudan, and, on the same day, Hussein Pasha left for Sennaar to inform Abdel Kader Pasha of his removal from office, and to relieve him of his military command.

[39] Late Guards, and subsequently 15th Foot.
[40] Late Duke of Cambridge's Own Middlesex Regiment.
[41] Late the Buffs, East Kent Regiment.

1883. General Hicks and his Staff left Kartoum on the 3rd April by steamer, and reached Kawa on the 6th. A force of about 5,000 men had been collected at the latter place, consisting of—

$5\frac{1}{2}$ battalions of regular infantry,[42]
$\frac{1}{2}$ battalion of negroes,
5 guns,
2 Nordenfeldts, and
some Bashi-Bazouks.

10th April. Reconnaissance up the White Nile.

On the 10th April General Hicks made a reconnaissance up the river. He started at 6 A.M. on the steamer *Bordeen*, taking with him one mountain gun, two Nordenfeldts, and 50 Bashi-Bazouks. After proceeding for about an hour and a-half, the steamer was fired on from the western bank. Higher up shots were fired from many places, especially opposite the island of Abba, where the rebels had constructed trenches along the banks. But a few shells, and some rounds from the Nordenfeldts and rifles, soon drove them inland. Owing to the failure of fuel, the reconnaissance could not be continued as far as the ford of Abu-Zed. The steamer returned to Kawa at 5.30 P.M.

On the 14th April, General Hicks telegraphed to Cairo that he was anxious to get to Jebel-Ain (eight marches distant), where the rebels were concentrating, as soon as possible, but that his supplies were insufficient, as he had only enough for from 15 to 20 days with him, and nothing was obtainable in the country. The administration of the army was most difficult, owing to the want of proper departments, and the troops were several months in arrears of pay. The steamers were out of repair, and too few in number to do all that was required of them—viz., to bring up supplies of ammunition and food, take possession of the ford at Abu-Zed, and patrol the river and stop communication between the banks. There was no store of fuel, all had to be cut as required.

23rd April. Seizure of the ford of Abu-zed.

It was not till the 23rd April that the main body, nearly 5,000 strong, set out from Kawa. Owing to the difficulty of obtaining reliable information, General Hicks himself with a small force had proceeded up the river on the 22nd to reconnoitre, and seize the ford of Abu-Zed. On arrival at the ford, it was found to be in possession of a small body of rebels, who were driven off without much difficulty. General Hicks remained there on the 23rd,

[42] Two of the battalions were those of the 2nd Regiment, which had been ordered by Abdel Kader Pasha to operate against the rebels at Abu-Djuma, but they had done absolutely nothing. It is not known to what regiments the other battalions belonged, and whether they had all been sent up from Kartoum, or if part of the 1st Regiment had been withdrawn from Sennaar. Owing to the hostility of the Hassanieh Arabs it had been necessary to reinforce the garrison of Duem by a battalion, and 2,000 troops remained in reserve at the camp of Omdurman.

placing boats containing Bashi Bazouks under the command of Jahier Bey, in échelon across the stream, in which position they could command a very considerable length of the ford (which extends about a mile), and support one another in case of any attempt to force the passage. 1883.

He left on the morning of the 24th to continue the reconnaissance up the river. The banks were found to be occupied by straggling groups of Arabs, with whom shots were exchanged.

On the 25th, the Chief of the Shilluk village of Musran reported that the rebels had left Jebel-Ain and were marching in force under the Makashef to attack the "Turks" on the march from Kawa.

Having ascertained that this information was correct, General Hicks steamed back to the ford, warned Jahier Bey, and, during the night, dropped down the river to join the army, which was then encamped opposite the northern end of the island of Abba.

29th April. Battle of Marabieh and death of the Makashef.

Being in a favourable position, it remained halted on the 26th and 27th in expectation of an attack. On the former date some rebel cavalry appeared, but were driven back with a few shells, and on the night of the 27th there were several false alarms. The march was resumed on the 28th. On the following day tents were struck as usual, at daybreak, and the order was given to march at seven A.M. About nine A.M.,[43] Colonel Farquhar, who had been reconnoitring in front, reported that the enemy was about two miles off, and advancing at a rapid pace. About a quarter of an hour afterwards they appeared in considerable numbers, both cavalry and infantry, and spread out towards the flanks with a view of attacking the angles of the square in which the Egyptian troops were formed.[44]

They then advanced quickly, led by chieftains on horseback with banners borne in front of them. There was considerable delay in getting the guns into action,[45] but the rebel cavalry broke as soon as the shells commenced falling among them, and moved off the field. The infantry still came on boldly, and, although shot down in numbers, succeeded in getting close enough to the square to throw some spears into it. But few of the enemy were armed with rifles.

[43] The column had then marched about five miles, and was close to the village of Marabiyeh.

[44] The troops both marched and fought, formed up in square, with camels and baggage in the centre, and a few mounted Bashi Bazouks and men on dromedaries in front to feel the way. In this formation the army could hardly accomplish eight miles a day, six being the usual march, and it could, consequently, only strike a blow when and where the enemy pleased.

[45] The Nordenfeldts were placed at the angles of the square, and the guns in the faces. Owing to obstacles thrown in the way by Suleiman Pasha, who was nominally in chief command, General Hicks had great difficulty in getting any of them to open fire.

1883. After half an hour's fighting, during which the Egyptian troops behaved steadily and well, though they appeared to have fired too high,[46] the rebel force was completely broken up, and fled in confusion. Owing to the absence of cavalry, the pursuit was not as vigorous as it would otherwise have been. The strength of the rebels exceeded 5000 men. Their losses in killed and wounded were about 500. The Makashef, his son, and several chiefs were among the slain.

The Khedival troops lost two killed and five wounded.[47]

After the action General Hicks, anticipating that an immediate attempt would be made by the rebels to cross to the western bank of the river at some point above the ford of Abu-Zed, embarked on board the steamer *Bordeen* at Gozabonne-Gomme, and proceeded up the river, taking with him two Nordenfeldt guns, a rifled howitzer, and 150 Bashi Bazouks. At the ford of Abu-Zed he picked up the steamer *Fascher*, with Jahier Bey and 90 Bashi Bazouks.

1st May. On the 1st of May, the rebels were found to be crossing in large numbers at a regular place of passage, about 10 miles below Jebel Ain. They were driven inland from both banks with some loss. Numbers had already crossed, but a large body with camels and baggage still remained on the eastern bank. In the hope of capturing these, General Hicks sent to Sulieman Pasha asking him to hurry on as fast as possible. But the Egyptians had no cavalry, and the infantry marched so slowly that it took them more than two days to accomplish the twelve miles between their camp and the place of passage.

General Hicks himself went towards Jebel Ain, landed, and sent a party up the mountain. On their return they stated that not a sign of a rebel was to be seen, and the Shilluks also reported that the district had been evacuated.

3rd May. On the 3rd May General Hicks rejoined the main body, then encamped near Jebel Ain. Suleiman Pasha was anxious to march through the district, as he was of opinion that there were several tribes in the neighbourhood to whom it was of importance to show the army. But it was finally decided to return to Duem at once, and prepare for an attack on Schatt, where the rebels were reported to be assembling in large numbers.

[46] At the battle of Marabiyeh, as the engagement of the 29th April is called, the Egyptians were formed in four ranks, but the front rank was never made to lie down, and the fourth or rear rank, not being able to reach over three men's shoulders, fired their rifles up into the air.

[47] Of the English officers, Colonels Colborne and de Coetlogon had marched with the army from Kawa, Colonel Farquhar, Captains Massey and Evans, and Dr. Rosenberg had accompanied General Hicks on his reconnaissance up the river.

The others were not present at the battle of Marabiyeh. Major Martin and Captain Walker had been invalided home, and Major Warner was with Hussein Pasha on the Blue Nile.

The victory of the 29th had a very great moral effect, and many of the Baggara and other chiefs subsequently surrendered. General Hicks, unaccompanied by any troops, received several of them on the western bank of the river, and thus gave confidence. Negotiations with the Kababish Arabs were also in progress. 1883. Moral effect of the victory at Marabiyeh.

Towards the end of May the rebels, who had been threatening Duem, dispersed, and it was reported that the western bank of the river was free from hostile bands. The main body of the army was then withdrawn to Kartoum, leaving garrisons at Kawa and Duem. On the Blue Nile, Sennaar and Wod-Medinet were garrisoned. Withdrawal of the army to Kartoum.

The expedition to Kordofan could not be undertaken till after the rains, when the wells in the desert would be full, and pools of water would have been formed.

On the 15th May, the Governor-General of the Soudan telegraphed to Cairo that he had only £40,000 in the treasury at Kartoum, and that he thought it inadvisable to enforce the taxes for fear of producing further disaffection among the natives. Estimate of the expenses of the war.

Arrears to the amount of £81,000 were still owing in the Mudiriyehs of Kartoum and Sennaar for pay, food, and transport.

He was anxious that in future all salaries should be paid punctually both to the officials and to the military, and that the Government should be able to meet its other expenses at the proper time. He requested that large sums of money might be forwarded to him, and estimated at £46,000 his monthly expenditure for the troops at Kartoum, Sennaar, the military posts on the White and Blue Niles, Fashoda, the Equatorial Provinces, and Bahr-Gazelle, but exclusive of those at Dongola, Berber, and in the Red Sea Provinces.

In reply to the above Cherif Pasha telegraphed on the 11th June, that the undermentioned amounts would be placed at the disposal of the Governor-General during the current year, viz. :— Amount of money to be forwarded from Cairo to meet the expenses entailed by the rebellion.

	£
Seven months' pay for the army actually engaged in the war	13,000
Rations for seven months	32,000
Forage (*Fourrage*)	37,500
Purchase of camels	25,000
Arrears	80,000
Total	187,500
But the amount actually in the Treasury at Kartoum was to be deducted from this	40,000
	£147,000

leaving £147,000 to be sent from Cairo.

Reinforcements to the number of 3,000 men were to be sent to the Soudan, but all the expenses connected with them, which were estimated at £40,000, would be defrayed by the Egyptian Government.

1883. For the expenses of the Civil Administration and the pay of soldiers not actually engaged in the war, the Governor-General was ordered to do the best he could with the revenues of the Soudan, as the Egyptian Government would not be able to furnish him with more than the sums already specified.

13th May. On the 13th May General Hicks telegraphed to Cairo requesting that he might be put in indisputable command of the army, as otherwise he could not be responsible for the success of the expedition to Kordofan. It was subsequently rumoured on several occasions that he had requested to be relieved of his post on account of the systematic obstructions he met with from native officials. These reports were always officially contradicted. However, on the 2nd August, Reuter's agent at Alexandria announced that the Governor-General of the Soudan had been appointed to command the troops in that province, and that Suleiman Pasha had been recalled, and appointed Governor of the Red Sea Provinces. By this means it was expected that General Hicks would regain complete liberty of action, though Al-ed-Deen Pasha was to accompany the expedition to Kordofan.

2nd August. Removal of Suleiman Pasha from the command of the army of the Soudan.

During the absence of the latter, Hussein Bey, Lieutenant-colonel of the 2nd Regiment, was to act as his deputy at Kartoum. Rashid Pasha, who was then Governor of the Red Sea Provinces, was to be given the command of one of the brigades of the Expeditionary Force.

Position of the Mahdi. The Mahdi only remained master of Kordofan. All reports from there tended to show that serious dissensions had broken out between him and his chiefs, and that the number of his adherents was daily diminishing. His position appeared to be getting critical. From the north he was threatened by the Egyptian army, and to the east the White Nile, which was constantly patrolled by Egyptian boats, would bar any attempt at escape in that direction. On the south King Adam of Takallé had sworn to kill the Mahdi if he attempted to pass through his country to Jebel Gedir, whither he had sent his family and most of the booty captured at El Obeyed. King Adam was also taking steps to arrange with Sheikh Asaker, chief of the Baggara Gimeh Arabs, inhabiting the desert from the island of Abba towards Takallé, a joint offensive movement against southern Kordofan. In the middle of July it was stated that the Mahdi had given up all hopes of resistance, and was only anxious about his personal safety; and that it was his intention to try to reach the copper mines in the south-west of Darfur, not far from Jebel Mara. In order to do this, however, he would have to make a long detour to avoid an encounter with the force under Slatin Bey, Governor of Darfur.

Operations in Darfur. Very little news has been received of the real state of affairs in that far-off province. It appears that, on receipt of orders from Cairo, a messenger was despatched from Kartoum to El Fascher in April of the present year with the following instructions for Slatin Bey—viz., to concentrate the garrisons of Darfur at El Fascher, attempt to organise a national Government under a descendant of one of the former kings, and then withdraw from the country, either to Dongola or Bahr el Ghazel. Report states that Slatin Bey subsequently evacuated El Fascher, defeated a tribe of hostile Hamr Arabs, and then intrenched himself at Omchanga, in an important strategical position on the road to El Obeyed, where he awaited the arrival of the garrison of Foga before undertaking any further operations. 1883.

Letter from Slatin Bey, Governor of Darfur.

The above-mentioned orders do not appear to have reached Slatin Bey, for on the 30th June he wrote as follows to the Governor-General of the Soudan from Dara, 200 miles south of El Fascher :—

"Up to this date I have fought 27 battles of more or less importance, and have been twice wounded. I am besides suffering from Guinea worm, and have consequently been obliged to retire on Dar Demittala, but not before killing in battle the Khalifa of Mohammed Ahmet, Bishari Wal-ud-Bakis.

"I have not only to fight external but internal enemies. Many of the Arab officers intrigue against me, and seek to undermine my authority. They spread rumours that Arabi has driven all the Europeans out of Egypt, and that I myself have been deprived of my functions."

* * * * *

"After the commencement of the rainy season, fighting will begin again with the Razagatt, Habanieh and Mali Arabs, and I am greatly in need of help, for my best officers and men have fallen, and ammunition is beginning to draw to an end."

* * * * *

"I ask your Excellency to send me a letter not in cipher, setting forth my absolute power, and I take upon myself, as long as I am alive, the responsibility of keeping the Province of Darfur for the Government."

* * * * *

The above letter reached Kartoum in August. It was in reply to one from Giegler Pasha, dated 14th March, 1883, which, Slatin Bey stated, was the first direct news he had received from Kartoum for more than a year.

20th August. Appointment of General Hicks as Commander-in-Chief of the Expedition to Kordofan. Plan of campaign.

On the 20th August, General Hicks received a telegram from the Khedive appointing him Commander-in-Chief of the expedition to Kordofan, with the rank of General of Division. His original plan was to leave Kartoum about the 8th of September, and march up the White Nile as far as Berair,[48] with 8,600 infantry, 1400 cavalry and Bashi-Bazouks, one battery of Krupp field guns, two batteries of mounted guns, and one battery of Nordenfeldts, and 5,000 camels.

[48] Sixteen miles below Duem.

1883. Leaving the river at Berair, he proposed to march first on Bara,[49] and then on El Obeyed, appearing before the last-mentioned place with 7,000 men, which it was considered would be sufficient to overcome the Mahdi. About 3,000 were to be employed in keeping open the line of communications. But the idea of establishing a line of fortified posts between the Nile and Kordofan was subsequently abandoned, and it was decided that the whole force should advance together, without attempting to keep up any communication with the rear. The reason for adopting this course was, that reports were brought in that large numbers of hostile Arabs were likely to reappear on the line of march after the passage of the army, and there would be great difficulty in inducing small bodies of Egyptian troops to escort convoys of stores between the posts.

The Egyptian officers attached to the force were inefficient, and, as a rule, apathetic; they carried little or no respect, and had but slight authority over their men. To bring the army into a state of efficiency, feed it, provide transport, and procure intelligence, taxed the energies of General Hicks and his small European Staff to the utmost. His greatest anxiety was regarding the water supply during the march, for Kordofan is the driest province in the whole Soudan. The wells along the roads across the desert contain but little water, except immediately after the rains, and it was feared that even then there would be insufficient for a large force accompanied by horses, mules, and several thousand camels.

On leaving the Nile, provisions for sixty days were to be carried with the army.

Rashid Pasha, who was to have commanded a brigade, telegraphed from Kassala that the Arabs in the neighbourhood were in a state of great excitement, and he thought it would be best for him to remain there till it had subsided.

9th September. Departure of the army from Kartoum.

On the 9th September the main body set out from Kartoum, and, passing Berair, reached Duem[50] on the 20th. No hostility was shown along the route, though many of the inhabitants fled on the approach of the troops. The heat was intense, and there was considerable loss of life among the camels during the march. The line of telegraph had been destroyed.

On the 23rd September, an advanced force, consisting of three battalions and six guns, seized the first water station, fifteen miles from Duem, without encountering any resistance.

General Hicks did not leave Kartoum till the 28th September, when he proceeded up the river by steamer to Duem, and then joined the main body.[51]

[49] Bara is nearer the Nile than El Obeyed, and in a fertile country, from which General Hicks hoped to be able to procure some supplies.

[50] The distance between Duem and Kartoum is about 110 miles.

[51] The other English officers with the Expeditionary Force are Colonel Farquhar, Chief of the Staff; Majors Warner, Massey, and Evans; Captains Heath and Walker, and Surgeon-Major Rosenburg. In addition to these,

On the 30th September the army encamped at a place 30 miles south-west of Duem. The heat was still intense, and the camels were dying in considerable numbers. 1883 30th September.

The square continued to be used as the fighting formation. Great precautions were taken on the line of march. The army marched in three columns prepared instantly to form square, with the camels and stores in the centre, the guns in the front faces, and the Nordenfeldts at the angles. Through constant practice, the men had become very perfect in this manœuvre. When camping square was formed, two tents per company were pitched behind piled arms. When possible a zeriba, or dense abattis of thorny bushes was formed round the square. In case of sudden attack on the march, each soldier carried four crows-feet, which he was to throw to a distance in his front to check the rush of the assailing forces. Tactics of the Egyptian army.

On the 7th October the army appears to have reached Sangi Hamferid, 45 miles south-west of Duem, where it remained halted for several days, owing to the uncertainty of the water supply in front. At the camp there was no water except on the surface in depressions of the ground. The camels were dropping, but the troops were in good health. 7th October.

On the 9th October Colonel Farquhar made a reconnaissance 30 miles forward, and ascertained that the pools were barely sufficient for a rapid march to Sarakna, at which village there are a few wells. 9th October.

The enemy was still retiring, and sweeping the country bare of cattle. The uncut harvest supplied ample forage.

In the beginning of August rumours reached Suakin that emissaries of the Mahdi were inciting the Arabs in the neighbourhood of Sinkat[52] and Erkowit[53] to revolt. On the 2nd Tewfik Bey, the Governor of Suakin, left for Sinkat, to inquire into the true state of affairs. He there learned that Osman Digna, a well-known slave-dealer, assisted by his nephews, Ahmed and Fagi Digna, had raised the Erkowit, Sherah, Mishab, Migadaff, and Bishirieh tribes in the name of the Mahdi. All these are small tribes, living in the Erkowit district; but the more important Langeb tribe, living in the neighbourhood of Toka, were said to be preparing to rise. Spread of the rebellion to the neighbourhood of Suakin. August.

Tewfik Bey immediately summoned Digna to come to him at Sinkat. He arrived on the 5th August, but accompanied by about 1500 armed followers, and demanded, in the name of the Mahdi, the surrender of Sinkat and Suakin, with all the arms and treasure 5th August. Defeat of the rebels at Sinkat.

there are several Austrians and Germans. Colonel de Coetlogon remains at Kartoum, and Colonel Colborne and Major Martin have been invalided home.

[52] On the road from Suakin to Berber, situated in a valley about three miles in breadth, enclosed by mountains. Many of the inhabitants of Suakin live there during the hot season.

[53] The lofty mountains of Erkowit lie 20 to 30 miles south-east of Sinkat, Erkowit is another summer retreat for the people of Suakin.

1883. they contain. These demands being, of course, refused, Digna attacked the barracks and the summer residences of the Suakis spread over the plain. The inhabitants defended themselves, and, with the assistance of the troops, drove off the rebels after an hour's fight. Digna was severely wounded, and his two nephews and sixty-three other rebels were killed. The number of their wounded is unknown. On the Government side, seven soldiers and Suakis were killed or died of their wounds.

The rebels retired to Erkowit, and it was reported that they were much discouraged by their defeat.

By the 13th August the garrison of Sinkat, which on the 5th was only 100 strong, had been increased to 200. On that date there were 100 soldiers, forty of whom were artillerymen, and six Krupp 9-pounders at Suakin. Some measures were being taken for the defence of the town.

Uneasiness at Berber.

Some uneasiness was also felt at Berber, and, in consequence, the Mudir of that place detained there two battalions of infantry, which arrived early in August, on their way to Kartoum.

It was reported that the last detachment of reinforcements for General Hicks, consisting of 200 infantry and 300 Bashi-Bazouks, had been abandoned by their camel-drivers and camels at a place called Kokreb, about half-way between Suakin and Berber. What became of the troops after the loss of their baggage and camels is not stated.

Although the attack on Sinkat had been repulsed with loss, the appearance of the enemy in the rear of General Hicks, and more or less commanding his line of communications, was sufficiently serious to cause much uneasiness at Cairo.

24th August. Despatch of reinforcements to Suakin.

300 troops were despatched from Egypt to Suakin about the 24th August, and they were to be followed by further large reinforcements.

The telegraph line between Suakin and Sinkat was cut on the 10th August. On the 8th October it was reported that communication between those places and Berber, which had been interrupted for some time, had been re-established.

Annihilation of a detachment of Egyptian troops between Suakin and Sinkat. 18th October.

On the 18th October, however, two officers and 156 Egyptian soldiers were killed by the Arabs in a mountain defile, about 20 miles from Suakin. They were on their way to support Tewfik Bey, who was said to be surrounded by rebels at Sinkat.

5th November. Destruction of a detachment of Egyptians at Tokar, and death of Commander Moncrieff, late R.N.

On the 5th November, a body of Egyptian troops, variously estimated at from 250 to 500 men, were attacked near Tokar[54] by a band of insurgents, and completely routed. They are said to have thrown their arms away and taken to flight, notwithstanding the efforts of their commander to rally them. The reports are not very clear as to whether the Egyptians were merely making a recon-

[54] Tokar is a small town in the centre of a great grain-producing district. It is a penal settlement for Suakin, from which it is about 45 miles distant.

naissance, or were attempting to reach Kartoum by way of Kassala. Commander Moncrieff,[55] late R.N., the British Consul at Suakin, who had accompanied them from that place, was among the killed. 1883.

The latest accounts state that Tokar is still held for the Egyptian Government by a small body of troops and some convicts. A panic had set in at Suakin, and the inhabitants were leaving for Jeddah.

9th September. Departure of General Hicks's Army from Kartoum.

On leaving the camp at Omdurman,[56] on the morning of the 9th September, the order of march was as follows, viz.—Two guides, mounted on camels, led the way. Behind them rode a detachment of men in armour, followed by the general staff. Then came a battalion of infantry in line, with several battalions in column in rear of each of its flanks. The artillery marched between the columns of infantry. Another battalion in line formed the fourth side of the infantry square.[57] A detachment of cavalry completed the fighting force. Behind it came a long train of pack animals, led and protected by Bashi-Bazouks. The rear was brought up by irregular cavalry.

Marching-out strength.

The marching-out strength was 10,000 men, 4 Krupp field guns, 10 mountain guns, 6 Nordenfeldts, 500 horses, and 5,500 camels.

Al-ed-Deen Pasha, the Governor-General of the Soudan, started at the same time, proceeding as far as Duem by steamer. He took in his suite several notables of great influence, who were to be considered as hostages, and answerable with their lives for any disturbances that might break out in Kartoum during their absence.

Precautions on the march.

On the march every precaution was taken to guard against surprise. The troops were always under arms, and lined the "zerebas" an hour before daybreak, the usual time for an Arab attack. The cavalry used to go out at dawn, and not till then were

[55] Commander Lynedoch Needham Moncrieff entered the Royal Navy in 1863, and in February 1865, while Sub-Lieutenant of the *Peloros*, was engaged in the destruction of piratical junks in Tungroa Bay. He became Lieutenant in July 1865, and retired with the rank of Commander in 1873. Proceeding to the Cape of Good Hope on the outbreak of the Zulu war, Commander Moncrieff served with the 2nd battalion of the Native Contingent from May 1879 till the close of the campaign, during which he was engaged in the battle of Ulundi, where he was slightly wounded, afterwards having Commissariat charge at Fort Cambridge. His services were officially commended at the close of the campaign. In January 1880, the deceased officer was nominated Consul at Cayenne, and, having passed the examination, was, on the 4th of March, 1880, appointed Consul for French Guiana, to reside at Cayenne, but did not proceed thither, being shortly afterwards sent as acting Consul to Jeddah. He was appointed Consul at Suakin on the 1st of April, 1882, the post being worth 750*l.* per annum, besides an annual allowance of 250*l.* for office expenses. Commander Moncrieff received the silver medal of the Royal Humane Society for saving life at sea in 1864.

[56] On the left bank of the White Nile, opposite Kartoum.

[57] After leaving Duem, the formation, with the camels in the centre of the square, appears to have been adopted.

1883. the tents allowed to be struck and the camels loaded. An hour later the whole force marched off. Owing to the enormous number of camels, progress was slow. After twelve days' marching, Duem, 110 miles from Omdurman, was reached, and the army rested for four days. The heat was intense, and both men and camels suffered considerably.

On quitting the Nile, General Hicks's original intention had been to retake Dara,[58] before marching on El Obeyed, but he altered his plans at the request of King Adam of Takallé, who promised assistance in the event of the army entering Kordofan from the south.

30th September. On the 30th September, General Hicks reached Zeraiga, about 30 miles from Duem. The following despatch was probably written at Sangi Hamferid,[59] some miles further on, though neither the date nor the name of the place is stated. It was sent by hand to Kartoum, and telegraphed thence to Cairo on the 17th October. It runs as follows, viz.: "The army has arrived within 28 miles of Sarakhna. We have depended upon pools of rain-water for supply, which we have fortunately found. A reconnaissance made to-day ensures us water as far as Sarakhna. Guide information is vague. I regret that I have to abandon my intention of establishing military posts, and line of communication with base at Duem. The Governor-General assures me that the Arabs will close in on my route after the army has passed in sufficient force to prevent posts forwarding supplies; besides, the pools of rain-water—the only supply—will dry up. Water not to be obtained by digging wells. I have no information regarding water between Sarakhna and Nurabi, nor reliable information of the supply there. This causes me great anxiety. I quite expected Sarakhna to be occupied by the enemy, but the reconnaissance to-day found the place evacuated. The Arabs had left this morning. The health of the troops is, on the whole, good, which is fortunate, as we have no sick carriage. The heat is intense."

3rd October. Camp near Sarakhna. Last despatch from General Hicks. Reasons for advancing without securing line of communications.

The following is the last dispatch received from General Hicks. It is dated "Camp, near Sarakhna, October 3rd, 1883":—

"On leaving Duem, on the White Nile, to march by the Khor-el-Nil to Melbeis and El Obeyed, I decided that my line of communication should be secured by posts of 200 men each, left in strongly fortified positions in the following places: Schatt, 16 miles distant; Zeraiga, 16 miles distant; Sarakhna, 32 miles distant; Nurabi, 16 miles distant; Agaila, 24 miles distant; Johan, 32 miles distant; Abli, 28 miles distant; Beliab, 22 miles distant; Um Sheikh, 12 miles distant; Rahad, 14 miles distant; Khashil (? Kazghil), 14 miles distant; Melbeis, 25 miles distant.[60]

58 An important town in Kordofan, north of El Obeyed.

59 From information received, the army appears to have arrived at Sangi Hamferid about the 1st October, and not on the date before mentioned—7th October.

60 Duem to Melbeis — total 251 miles. These distances are only approximate.

"At all these places I was informed water would be found. 1883.

"Large quantities of biscuits were to arrive at Duem, and as we were unable to leave a single camel at the base, 1000 were ordered to be purchased and forwarded to Duem.

"His Excellency Al-ed-Deen Pasha had already at Kartoum 300, and gave orders for the remaining 700 to be purchased and forwarded to Duem without delay.

"The biscuits would then, with ammunition and other stores, be pushed on to the front from post to post.

"Depôts would be formed at each post, and, in case of a reverse, a line of retreat secured, the troops falling back upon these depôts, where we should be certain of finding supplies of food, ammunition, and water.

"We marched to Schatt, and formed the first post and depôt there; but, before reaching Zeraiga, I was informed by the Governor-General of the Soudan that it was useless for me to expect any supplies to be pushed up from Duem, that the soldiers left at the posts would not guard the convoys; in fact, that they would be afraid to do so; that, to insure supplies being forwarded, an army would be required with each convoy; that the Arabs, although now absent from our line of route, would return after we had passed, and that they would be numerous, and the garrisons of the posts would not consider themselves strong enough to forward the supplies; that it would be dangerous; and I would find that they would not run the risk.

"The Governor-General requested me to abandon the idea of having this line of posts—to give up my line of communications and line of retreat, and to advance with the army *en l'air*, with 50 days' supply of food only, the Arabs closing in on our rear.

"I am naturally very averse to this, but if, as his Excellency assures me, it is a fact that the posts will not be supplied from the base at Duem, and supplies will not be forwarded through them, I should, in garrisoning these posts, be only weakening my fighting force without gaining any advantage. I have therefore called a Council, have had the matter explained, and requested the members to record their opinions."[61]

No news of the Expeditionary Force having been heard for several weeks, anxiety began to be felt as to its fate. Messengers were despatched from Duem along the various routes to Kordofan, but, for a long while, none of the few who returned brought any authentic information.

30th October. Rumoured defeat of the Mahdi.

On the 30th October, rumours were spread in Kartoum that the

[61] The existence of these two despatches was not known to Sir E. Baring till they appeared in the 'Egyptian Gazette' of the 27th November. Chérif Pasha had previously informed him that nothing had been heard of General Hicks since the 27th September, the date on which he started from Duem. Chérif Pasha subsequently admitted that he was mistaken in making that statement.

1883. Mahdi had been defeated in several important engagements, and that General Hicks was master of the whole of Kordofan. No official confirmation of the reported victories was, however, received, and after a few days the authenticity of the news began to be doubted.

5th November. Battle of Kazghil. Annihilation of General Hicks's army.

At length, on the 19th November, a messenger, who had failed to deliver his despatches to Al-ed-Deen Pasha, r. urned to Duem, bringing news of the total destruction of General Hicks's army. These sad tidings were soon confirmed by other persons arriving from Kordofan. Their accounts differ in detail, but most of them agree that the greater part, if not the whole, of the army was annihilated by the insurgent forces on the 4th or 5th November. The events which culminated in this terrible disaster are still shrouded in a certain amount of mystery. Nothing has been heard from any of the Europeans who accompanied the expedition, nor from any of the Egyptian Staff Officers, of a later date than General Hicks's despatch of the 3rd October. Probably the most trustworthy account of the fighting is that given by a camel-driver, who went as servant to a native officer. He states that the army, on leaving Duem, soon met the rebels, and engaged in skirmishes with them, the Mahdi's men being beaten, and the Egyptians losing a few Bashi-Bazouks and Shaggyehs. Thus the army arrived at Rahad, where there is a lake. There it filled up with water, and then marched towards Alouba. At the latter place there was an encounter with the rebels, in which General Hicks was victorious. On the 2nd November the army left Alouba, taking what water it could, and, while marching through a forest, was surprised by a large force of rebels. The Egyptians formed square, and, after fighting all day, finally defeated them and drove them off. On Saturday, the 3rd November, the march was resumed. Water was already becoming scarce. The rebels again appeared in force, and surrounded the army. A serious engagement ensued, in which heavy losses were suffered on both sides, but the rebels were once more beaten. That night was passed on the field of battle, and next day the army moved towards Kazghil. After proceeding for four hours, it suddenly came under a heavy fusillade from large numbers of the enemy. The troops were suffering great torments from thirst, but nevertheless fought throughout the whole day. On the 5th, when they were approaching the wells, which were only half an hour distant, the rebels, who had been concealed in the forest, again suddenly attacked the column on all sides. The Egyptians returned their fire, and a great battle raged. Towards midday the entire force of the rebels made a general charge with guns, swords, and spears, and General Hicks and his whole army perished, except 200 Egyptian soldiers and a few negro servants, most of whom were wounded.[62]

[62] The undermentioned European officers are believed to have perished, viz.—Lieut.-General Hicks, Colonel Farquhar, Majors Warner, Massey,

Of the whole of the Expeditionary Force, the only European supposed to be now alive is Adolf Klootz, formerly a sergeant of Prussian Uhlans, and recently servant to Major von Seckendorff. He is said to have deserted three days before the final struggle, to have commanded the insurgent artillery during the action, and to be at present an officer in the service of the Mahdi.[63]

NOTE.—The following is the Extract of a letter from the Mahdi's Emir at Berber to Zubair, by whom it was forwarded to Sir Henry Gordon.

Letter of the Emir Ali Mohammed Abou Saad Esshentrawi al Abadi (the Mahdi's Emir at Berber).

"Compliments,—After the arrival of Hussein Pasha Khalifat in the Soudan, it was found that all the inhabitants were aroused by the appearance of the Imam. Since this every week a disturbance took place among the Arabs and Jahleien and others. We tried to put down the disturbances. While we were trying to do so, news came that the influence of the Imam the Mahdi was established, and that all the districts of Darfur and Bahr el Ghezel, and Kordofan, Sennaar, and Jebel Khadir, and the Arabs, all of them, were under him. Why this was so was that they saw and heard what he has done to the backsliders at the battle of Jebel Khadir and in the slaughter of Yusuf Pasha Shelali and his army of 8,000 men, and in the destruction of Al-ed-Deen Pasha and his army of 36,000 men, which was altogether destroyed in a quarter of an hour. It was a fearful fight, in which you heard only the slashing of swords into the bodies. At that time we received letters from our lord the Imam strictly ordering us to fight the backsliders and to block the way against all mischief-makers whatever, which we prepared to do. Then came to us Mohammed El Kheir Ibu Abdullah, Governor-General of the district of Berber, bringing with

Evans, Alfred Freiherr von Seckendorff, Captains Arthur Herlth, and Alexander Matyuga, Lieut. Morris Brody, late Sergeant-Major R.H.A., Surgeon-General Georges Bey, and Surgeon-Major Rosenberg. And with them, Al-ed-Deen Pasha, Governor-General of the Soudan, and many Egyptian officers of high rank. Mr. O'Donovan and Mr. Vizetelly, newspaper correspondents who accompanied the expedition, have not since been heard of.

[63] The Paris *Temps* of 23rd November, 1883, states that the Mahdi's forces are organised and commanded by a Frenchman named Soulié, who has lived for many years in Egypt. He went there after having served in the French Army; and, after the bombardment of Alexandria, went to Kartoum, whence he proceeded to join the False Prophet, soon making his way into the latter's graces, and obtaining his confidence.

him standards of victory prepared for the siege of Berber. When he arrived at Metemma, he wrote letters to all the districts, calling for the aid of all the tribes and Arabs. It was only a short time after that he came to Berber with an army of 40,000 men, the youngest of whom were eager to die in the field for the sake of God. This was on the 1st Rejeb, 1301. Correspondence took place between the Governor and the Pasha for the space of eight days, and on Monday, the night of the 23rd Rejeb, the battle was fought; and before break of day we had won the victory and had killed all who opposed the Mahdi, and captured the Pasha. Then all the inhabitants of Bertou, of Berkou, of Islih, of Balalah, of Baskirmah, and of Salah came into the Imam, and then his reign was established in all the Soudan, east and west. This is what happened in these parts; and know, my friend, that the world is turned upside down, and henceforward there will be nothing but preparation for the holy war in the path of God, and spending of treasure and life in what pleases Him and His Prophet. Be on your guard against the covetousness of the world.

"As to your spy, Mohammed Abou Jibali, who was sent with your men, after they came to Berber, and had seen the Governor, and had permission to go to Kartoum, when they reached Shendy the Governor thought it better that they should return to Berber—which they did on the 1st Ramadan. They were imprisoned till the 20th. Then eight mounted men came from among your relatives, and had a conference with the Governor, who then released them, and they went to your friends living near Kartoum. After they left, the spy, Mohammed Abou Jibali, was detained, and imprisoned in Berber, as before, till the 3rd of Zu'l Kādih. For your sake and friendship, &c., we have done all we could, until we secretly released him and sent him away safely to you. I hope he will arrive in safety, and will tell you how honestly we have acted for you.

"Accept, &c.

"3rd Zu'l Kādih, 1301 [about 25th August, 1884]."

APPENDICES TO BOOK V.

APPENDIX Q.

From Saleh Bey, Governor at Galabat.

To his Excellency the Governor-General of all the Provinces of the Soudan.

SIR,

The two envelopes enclosed were sent to your servant from his Majesty the King of Kings of Abyssinia, with a special messenger from him, and a request that we would receive and forward them to your Excellency wherever you may be found. Therefore we now send these messengers with them. And we trust that after you have honoured them with your attention that your Excellency will quickly send back the answer to us, that we may send it to the King of Kings of Abyssinia by the two messengers who have come from his Majesty, and who are at present date with us at Kalabât (Galabât). Awaiting the said reply.

(Signed) SALEHH IBRAHIM,
District Inspector and Officer of Kalabât (Galabât).

Postscript.—SIR, The name of the bearer is Ali Othman.
In order not to increase expense (this) is written on ruled paper.

(Signed) SALEHH IBRAHIM.

1 Zu'l Hejjeh, 1301.
Sept. 22, 1884.

From Saleh Bey, Governor of Galabat.

To his Excellency the Honourable the Governor-General of the Soudan.

SIR,

Your servant, who stands in the attitude of service (to you), prays God with a sincere heart to grant his request and to extend His goodness towards me, in strengthening and preserving your Excellency under His shadow for the sake of the servants and subjects (of Government), and to change the condition of affairs from what they are, and to grant me the honour of seeing your Excellency, to kiss your bountiful hands, by which we have been covered with good and with blessings ;—(even you who are) the destroyer of the enemies of the Government, the wicked rebels who have lost their souls and their religion, and are deprived of the benefits of the Government, from which they had obtained glory and honour ; and turned, in spite of (all) that, from truth to error. May God preserve the glory of Government (so that) by presence of your Excellency you may destroy and utterly ruin the wretched Mohammed Ahhmed and his followers.

We have also to-day heard from the neighbourhood of Dukah of Abou Sitti and of Abou Haraz about what the energy of your Excellency has accomplished in beating the rebels and dispersing their people and troops, assembled for purposes of sedition.

And I beseech God most High, to whom be praise, to stretch out the sword of your Government more (and more)—(in order) to annihilate the false pretences of Mohammed Ahhmed, and to disperse his wicked hordes.

If your thoughts be directed towards your servant and the humble subject of the Government—(I have to say that) at present date I am well, under your protection, and am still continuing in the attitude of service to the Government. And oh ! what a Government ! (it is). How much compassion and benefit and kindness have you bestowed on us in goodness and bounty, which no man can deny ? I pray in the name of God and of His prophet that your servant may never depart from this path of duty (fidelity —being) obedient to the Government openly, without hindrance— under your protection.

With regard to the subjects of the Government under the care of your servant—they do not cease to remain as they were in respect of submission and obedience (loyalty), and will never follow the ways of rebellion—by the mercy of God most High and as a result of the advantage of being under your Government.

But, Excellency, we are surrounded by the enemy on all sides ; from the side of the Dukah, by the Shukryeh, by the Dhāniyeh, and by the Ja'alibiyeh : as on the side of the river, by the Rahbar ; also by the Bukadi, and those rebels who follow them.

But by the influence of your Excellency no harm will come to us from them. Nor do we take account of him (the Mahdi) ; our Lord will make us victorious over him through the strength of the Government and the reputation of its power and majesty, from which we derive glory and honour, through your Excellency and the favour of the Khedive.

As to what we have enclosed about ———, we trust and pray for the answer. Including this time we have now written to you four times.

The messenger takes them (the letters) from here, and when he gets to Katarif, or Dukah, he finds liers in wait, and the rebels torment him on meeting him in the road.

This prevented us from writing lately, but we are in constant communication with the Mudiriyeh ; and in that road we have lost two persons by (hands of) the rebels of Dhāniyeh and of Bukkād on the road of Tumruk.

This for the information of your Excellency.

(Signed) SALEHH IBRAHIM,
Ma'amoor and Nāzir, of Kalabât (Galabât)
(District Inspector and Officer.)

1 Zu'l Hejjeh, 1301.
Sept. 22, 1884.

From Saleh Bey, Governor of Kalakla.

To his Excellency the Honourable the Governor-General of the Soudan.

SIR,

I have the honour to lay before your Excellency that at the beginning of the month of Rajeb, from the time of the desertion and change of conduct of the Shukriyeh and the Dhāniyeh, and the Jaalāni, and the Bukkādi, in forsaking loyalty to Government and corrupting their ways when they joined the wretch (the Mahdi) and his followers : as soon as we received news of their having thrown off their allegiance we communicated with the Mudiriyeh in the month aforesaid. And these four tribes combined together against us and besieged us on the side of Dukah, having with them one called Hussein Abd el Wāhhad, and they wrote to us as to their intention that we should follow them into error, or they would fight and hem us in. When we perceived this, and that it was then the season of autumn and the time for sowing our seed for necessary provisions—and that their wicked intention was to prevent the inhabitants from sowing their grain, and that the soldiery we had were very few ; we tried by means of diplomacy and artifice with their chief Hussein, to get them to leave us during the autumn (seed time).

All that passed between us and them we have communicated in detail to the Mudiriyeh from time to time—so that there should be no misunderstanding from our silence—about what we wrote to them for putting them off by diplomacy, as it seemed best to us for bringing them to reason. And please God, after tranquillity is established, we will hasten to make copies of all the communications which have passed with them, as well as of what we wrote to the Mudiriyeh. On your seeing them, you will know the zeal of your servant in upholding his office ; and his exertions for honour of the Government, whose bounties overwhelm him, will appear.

And, Sir, now that autumn is over and these four tribes above mentioned are now in Katarif, and as there is great energy displayed in assembling them for the certain purpose of besieging Kalabât (Galabât), it became necessary to inform your Excellency, trusting and praying for issue of your Excellency's order, sanctioning all that we do for the purpose of impeding and destroying those wretches before named. And with the help of the most High God your servant will do nothing but what will lead to victory, and will increase the supremacy of the Government and the destruction of its enemies. It is not to be hidden from your Excellency about Mohammed Bey Zain, that when the Mudiriyeh sent orders to the Ma'amoor (district officer) of Katarif for payment of 6,000 dollars for payment of the salaries of the officials of Galabât, an officer and thirty-five soldiers were appointed to receive that amount from the officials of Katarif. And when they were coming to Galabât, Mahmood Bey, the above-named, took the money from them and left the officer to go his way. We wrote at the time to the Mudiriyeh about it, telling what Mahmood had done, and also to his Excellency, Mahmood Bey, and received his reply (denying) that the sum had been given to him at all, and refusing to have any more communication on the subject. And we made copy of what we received from him, and we wrote about him to the Mudiriyeh, and his answer is preserved by us in case of necessity.

(Signed) SALEHH IBRAHIM,
Nazir and Ma'amoor of Kalabat (District Inspector and Officer).

Date, 1 of Zu'l Hejjeh, 1301.
Sept. 22, 1884.

Postscript.—SIR, We learn from the Mudiriyeh of Saka (by letter) of this date of what the energy of your Excellency has done there to impede and repulse the rebels. They are joyful to-day at not being besieged as hitherto, and the neighbourhood is pretty clear at present. At this date there is perfect safety on account of the water from their being surrounded. After this month the crossing of the rivers will become possible, and (then) without doubt the rebels will be able to get at them. Your servant is constantly writing to the General of his troops to be always wide awake, and to look out for the preservation and the safety of the honour of the Government.

Always, Sir, at your order,
SALEHH IBRAHIM.

From the Greek Consul at Adowa to General Gordon.

Adowa (Abyssinia), 5/17 August, 1884.

MY DEAR GENERAL,

I arrived in Abyssinia on the 12/24 May, sent by my Government to aid the mission of Admiral Hewitt at the Court of His Majesty the Emperor John.

Thanks to the intelligence and the good feeling of His Majesty, aided by my counsels, the mission of the Admiral has completely succeeded.

In Egypt and in England we have been for four months without news from you, in spite of all the attempts which have been made to obtain news from you.

In England they have prepared an expedition of 15,000 men for the Nile, commanded by Lord Wolseley, besides which the Emperor John will put himself in the field after the Haref with a great army. Take courage, then. Give me news of you that I may send them to England.

The messenger is sent by the Emperor John, whom I have caused to understand the urgent need of news from you. You must not detain the messenger more than two days.

I wish you all honour and glory in your mission, and

I am your devoted friend,

MITZAKIS.

From Greek Consul Mitzakis, dated 24th August to Greek Consul, Kartoum, received 20th October, 1884.

Adowa (Abyssinia), 5/17 August, 1884.

SIR,

His Majesty's Government is much affected at the misfortunes of the Greeks in the Soudan, and has ordered me to come here, in order that by my relations with His Majesty the Emperor John, I may help the Greeks in the Soudan, and give them news.

His Majesty's Government is much distressed about its subjects, because there has been no news for four months of His Excellency Gordon Pasha, in spite of all the efforts of the Governments of England and of Egypt.

The Most Christian Emperor John, to whom I have spoken of the great interest of England and Greece in the Soudan, has promised me to send this letter by Metemma[1] (Galabat) by a trusty messenger, who will return, bringing your answer and a letter from His Excellency Gordon Pasha, to whom I also write. Therefore I beg you to be so good as to write to me all your news, that is to say, if the siege is very strict; if the Mahdi himself is at the head of the besiegers; if you have provisions and munitions, and for how many months; how many Greeks and Europeans there are in Kartoum, together with their names; how many soldiers have you, and what is the spirit of the soldiers and the inhabitants of the town, and all other important news.

It must be thoroughly understood that you are to send back the messenger at the earliest possible moment, and give him a letter in very small form, in order that he may conceal it in safety.

[1] Galabat, Kalabat and Metemma are the same place.

I am surprised that you have not sent any letter by Metemma or by Walkeit.

If you can send me letters by Metemma, you must address them to the Governour-General Gondar Axum-Gabroun; or by Walkeit, to the Governour Degias-Tessema.

Hoping that your siege will soon be raised,

I am, &c.,

THE CONSUL.

[NOTICE.]

The English Admiral Hewitt has come here, and has signed the Convention of the Emperor John with the Egyptian Government, by which Abyssinia takes Bogos,[2] Kassala, Katarif, and the right of importing and exporting merchandize and arms by the port of Massowa.

Even while I am writing, the Egyptians are giving up Bogos to Ras-Aloua (the Abyssinian Commander-in-Chief).

In England 15,000 soldiers are preparing to come to relieve Kartoum, and I trust that an expedition of from 100,000 to 200,000 brave men will start to save you.

If there is a messenger who can bring your letter to Metemma (or Galabat) or to Walkeit you can promise him whatever you wish, and we will pay him, because the English Government has a great interest in General Gordon.

I am yours, &c.

APPENDIX R.

From Slatin Bey.

His Excellency Gordon Pasha, Governor-General of the Soudan.

YOUR EXCELLENCY,

I have sent two letters, one by George Calamatino and the other by my servant, without having received an answer from your Excellency, neither has Consul Hansall answered me.

Your Excellency, I have fought twenty-seven times for the Government against the enemy, and they have beaten me twice, and I have done nothing dishonourable, nothing which should hinder your Excellency from writing me an answer, that I may know what to do.

They have taken the little steamer at Dar-Djumna, after it passed the Schelal of the Robatat, and they have brought the whole of the letters from Kartoum for Cairo here. In order to

[2] This territory is called Bogos by the Abyssinians, and Senheit by the Egyptians. Its capital is Keren.

assure you they have taken the steamer they have sent your Excellency some letters, and I have done all that I could to send your Military Journal,[3] because it may be, perhaps, of some value for your Excellency.

I hope that Consul Hansall has made a translation of my letter, in which I place all my feeble services to your Excellency's disposal, and I have been obliged to write in German, because they have burnt my French dictionary, believing that it was a prayer book.

His Excellency Stewart Pasha, with nine men, is dead. They have taken the others to Berber.

When you have a letter for Dongola I beg you to send it me, and I will find means of sending it on.

Your scribe has written a dispatch in cipher, half Arabic and half cipher, so badly, that they have been able to decipher it, and so they have found a key to your despatches, and have also deciphered your Excellency's despatch to his Excellency Towfik Pasha. If there are letters from Europe for me at the post I beg you to send them me, because it is almost three years since I have had any news of my family. I entreat your Excellency to honour me with an answer.

Your devoted and obedient servant,

SLATIN.

I and Seid Gjoma, Mudir of Fascher, are seeking occasion to enter Omdurman to remain with you. Pray, Excellency, do your best to give us permission, because we are always in fear of spies. I pray God that he may give you success in the siege.

P.S.—If your Excellency has perhaps understood that I have done anything contrary to the honour of an officer, and if that hinders you from writing to me, I pray you give me a chance of defending myself, and judge according to truth.

APPENDIX T.

From the Mudir of Sennaar.

To the Governor-General of the Soudan and its dependencies, to his Excellency the Honourable.

We stated to your Excellency that on Oct. 6, 1884, we had the honour to receive the order of your Excellency, dated September 24, announcing the arrival of nine regiments of the

[3] Evidently Colonel Stewart's journal.

braves of the English army and Moslems of India; artillery, cavalry, and infantry of the army, experienced in passing mountains, plains, and rough places, with new cannons and powerful horses. And our reading it to the public and publishing it in the country produced great rejoicing and happiness in all, and they augured all good and every benefit, and they are all praying for victory and success for you and for the army. And please God they are arrived at Berber and have taken possession of it, and have arrived at Kartoum. Everybody at Sennaar and the neighbourhood—Ulema, merchants, citizens, notables, officers, and soldiers—kiss the hands of your Excellency, and we proclaim about your Excellency, that by the power of God and His protection, and by the help of our prophet—on whom and on his people be the best of blessings and peace—the disturbances of the Soudan and the pretensions of the Mahdi are stopped, and nothing remains thereof but little trifles in some parts. And they will all submit to the sword of the Government.

To God belongs success, and help is in Him.

Mudir General of Sennaar,
(Signed) HASSIN SADAK.

Dated 18 Zu'l Hejje, 1301.
Oct. 9, 1884.

Postscript to his Excellency.—We beg your Excellency to give orders for the quick despatch of a steamer with what we asked for in our (letter) laid before you, No. 39/14.

APPENDIX U.

Letter from the Mahdi to General Gordon.

In the name of God the merciful and compassionate: praise be to God, the bountiful Ruler, and blessing on our lord Mahomed with peace.

From the servant who trusts in God—Mahomed the son of Abdallah.

To Gordon Pasha of Kartoum: may God guide him into the path of virtue, amen!

Know that your small steamer, named *Abbas*—which you sent with the intention of forwarding your news to Cairo, by the way of Dongola, the persons sent being your representative Stewart Pasha and the two Consuls, French and English, with other persons, has been captured by the will of God.

Those who believed in us as the Mahdi, and surrendered, have been delivered; and those who did not were destroyed—as your representative afore-named, with the Consuls and the rest—whose souls God has condemned to the fire and to eternal misery.

That steamer and all that was in it have fallen a prey to the Moslems, and we have taken knowledge of all the letters and telegrams which were in it, in Arabic and in Frankish (lauguages), and of the maps, which were opened to us (translated) by those on whom God has bestowed His gifts, and has enlightened their hearts with faith, and the benefits of willing submission. Also (we have found therein) the letters sent from you to the Mudir of Dongola, with the (letters, &c.) accompanying, to be forwarded to Egypt and to European countries. All has been seized, and the contents are known. It should all have been returned to you, not being wanted here; but as it was originally sent from you, and is known unto you, we prefer to send you part of the contents and mention the property therein, so that you may be certified; and in order that the truth may make a lasting impression on thy mind—in the hope that God may guide thee to the faith of Islam, and to surrender; that you and your followers may surrender to Him and to us, that so you and they may obtain everlasting good and happiness.

Now first (among the documents seized) is the cipher dated Sept. 22, 1884, sent to Mustafa Jāwer, Mudir of Dongola, in answer to his letter dated 30th August, 1884, European reckoning, (saying) that you have given him the rank of Liwa—on the back of which is your telegram to the Khedive of Egypt, asking that he will confirm the said appointment. We have also taken knowledge of (extract from) the Journal[4] (daily record) of the provision in the granary (as) seen by the Inspector Moosa Othmān, namely 3374 ardebs of dhoora; 4 ardebs and $\frac{1}{3}$ and $\frac{1}{4}$ of wheat, &c. Also (extract from) the Journal[4] (daily register) of the ammunition seized by the Inspector Mohamed, dated Aug. 18, 1884—the number (? of cartridges) in store being 581,395.

Also of the telegram sent to the Khedive of Egypt, and Nubar Pasha, and to the English Consul-General from nineteen persons who have put their seals to it, and who are presidents of the Court of Appeal, (namely) Hassan Abdul Munam, and the members and the merchants, who pray (therein) that the Soudan Railway, which the Egyptian Government find it difficult to make, (may be) exchanged for river steamers and military stations, with telegraphic lines between the stations.[5]

Further, (there is) the letter (found) with the French Consul, written by you to him on July 12, 1884, No. 512/38, in acknowledgment of the 100 francs distributed to the poor and needy.

(There is) also your letter dated Aug. 28, 1884, No. 35/144, sent to Nubar Pasha, and to the English Consul-General, and to the Chief of the Egyptian Treasury, with information about the 50,000

[4] Colonel Stewart's Journal.

[5] Suggests that, in place of the railway from Wady Halfa, the Cataracts be passed as suggested by General Gordon.

guineas sent from Egypt to Berber, and captured by the auxiliaries of the faith, and mentioning the advances (made) by the merchants at interest of one piastre per 100 piastres, with the hope of paying it back to the principals or their agents in that part.

(There is) also your communication dated Aug. 26, 1884, No. 34/144 sent to the President of the Council, with a list of sixteen persons, in which you ask for confirmation of the rank which you have bestowed on them.

Also your letter, No. 1/141, dated August 14, 1884, to the Mohurdâr (Keeper of the Seals) of the Khedive, as to disposal of the four decorations you have given, and of which you enclose a specimen.

Also (as to) the ranks of the officers named by you, and the note containing eleven names, like Nuehr Bey Mahomed, Commandant of the Army of Sennaar, whom you made Liwa (General).

Also your telegram, dated Sept. 3, 1884, No. 23, to the aforementioned Mohurdâr (Keeper of the Seals), to confirm the appointment of Ibrahim Foozi, and Mohammed Nefii, and Moosa Shoki as Liwas (Generals).

Also your letters, (written) in European (language), all about the siege of Kartoum, and all about the arranging of the steamers, with the number of the troops in them, and their arms, and the cannon, and about the movements of the troops, and the defeat of your people, and your request for reinforcements, even if only a single regiment, and all about how your agent Cuzzi turned Moslem.

Also many letters which had come to you from our lieutenants, and what they contained of advice; also stating the number of Europeans at Kartoum, 3 English, 2 Austrians, 1 Prussian, 1 Frenchman, 4 Italians, 40 Greeks.

Also the diary (registry) of the arms, ammunition, guns and soldiers sealed by Faraj (Ferratch) ez Zainy, Commander of the Army, which has 2 Krupp guns and 284 shells; 11 mountain field-pieces, and their ammunition (? cartridges), numbering 2303; 2 matchlock guns and their ammunition, 315; 5 mortars and their ammunition, 565; and 1 field piece, and 2 mitrailleuses without ammunition; and 8 howitzers (?) and their ammunition, 599; and 7064 Remington rifles, and 1205 percussion muskets; and 246 muskets (called) arshalik; and 127 rifles, old bore, and 19 pistols; and the ammunition (cartridges) for the Remingtons being 150,233 packets. And the number of the soldiers: 2 Liwas (Generals), 2 Colonels, 5 Lieut.-Colonels, and so on for other grades, and 2370 privates; the contingent of Bashi-Bazouk, and of the Shaggyeh and Khotriyeh and others, the amount of their strength (being) 26 divisions, numbering 4797 men. Also giving the number of the servants of the arsenal and on the steamers, ship by ship.

We have also taken knowledge of the two letters of Salehh, the Melek of the Sanjak (district) of Sanik, which he gave up to us (the Mahdi).

One of them, dated April 30, 1884, in which he threatens (this); and the second, dated May 1, in which he states that which he has already stated, and in which he asks for his reward.

We have also noted the telegram of the officials and of the presidents of courts, and of the Kadi and the Muftis and Ulema, numbering 34 sent to the Mohurdâr of the Khedive in Egypt, dated August 28, 1884, in which they ask for succour from the Egyptian Government; to which was attached your note to the Mudir of Dongola on account of his drafts. Also your cipher telegrams, one of which is dated August 8, 1884, to the Mohurdâr of the Khedive, in which you explain that on your arrival at Kartoum the impossibility had become clear to you of withdrawing the troops and the *employés*, and sending them to Egypt; on account of the disturbances (rebellions) in the country, and the cutting (closing) of the roads; for which reason you ask for reinforcements, which did not come until that happened which has happened to the Mudiriyeh of Berber.

Also about your coming to Kartoum with seven men after the annihilation of Hicks's army; and your requesting a telegram to be sent to you in Arabic, in plain language about the Soudan, to show to the people of Kartoum—as the telegrams in European cipher do not explain enough, except only certain news (matters), and their meaning is not intelligible, except only certain things (which are understood).

And also (you refer) to the useless waste of time, so much so, that from your repeated promises to the people of Kartoum about arrival of reinforcements, you have appeared to them as if you were a liar.

Also (about) your asking for Turkish troops and your promise to send your representative, Stewart, and Mr. Power to Dongola, both of whom the Most High God has destroyed.

And the second (telegram) with the same date and the same tenor, to the President of the Council and the English Minister in Cairo.

And the third (telegram) dated August 28, 1884, to the Mohurdâr (of the Khedive), in which you promise to send a detachment to attack Sheikh el Obeyed; which you sent, and the Most High God has destroyed.

Also your letter to the Khedive of Egypt, without date, in which you ask to have English soldiers sent, and appoint Zubair Pasha with reinforcements for withdrawal of the Egyptian troops to Egypt, and that you (will) give the Soudan to the Sultan on the arrival of the reinforcements of 200,000 men. And (you state that) if this be not done those in the Soudan will be killed, and their blood will be on their conscience (i.e. those to whom he writes will be responsible for their deaths). And the last you say in it (is) that Mahomed Ali Pasha is the only and single one in the Soudan on whom you (could) rely to take your place. But God has destroyed Mahomed Ali Pasha, on whom you rely.

The fourth telegram is dated August 28, to the Khedive of Egypt, and to Nubar Pasha and the English Consul in Egypt, in which you say that you were expecting the reinforcements before asked for—by way of Merowé—and also state the telegrams sent to the above-named at that date; in which you speak about fighting my auxiliaries, and about your having provisions for five months.

Also the telegram, dated August 25, 1884, to the above-mentioned, in which you pretend (suppose) that Ibrahim el Obeyed has been killed. And you say that you have the news of our arrival, which, however, was not confirmed.

And your letter to the President of the Council and the English Minister in Cairo, dated August 8, 1884, in which you speak of your appointing three steamers to go and inquire as to the state of Sennaar, and that you will send soldiers to Berber by the steamers to re-capture it, sending with them Stewart and the Consuls, whom the Most High God has destroyed.

And the telegram, dated August 8, 1884, sent to the President of the Council and the English Minister, in which you promise to send 2,000 soldiers to Berber for recovering it, and (say) that unless the reinforcements come to strengthen Berber, when the water of the Nile gets lower the same thing will happen again to Berber which had (already) happened.

Also your telegram to the Khedive of Egypt and Nubar Pasha, dated Sept. 8, 1884, in which you say it was your purpose to remove those (the garrison, &c.) at Sennaar, but that you saw that it would not be done; and (you mention) the sorrow of the inhabitants and of the *employés* at Kartoum and Sennaar at the non-arrival of succour.

Also the telegram, dated Sept. 9, to the Khedive of Egypt and Nubar Pasha and to the General, in which you speak of the sending of Stewart and those with him by the small steamer, and (with) the two large steamers escorting them for protection. And that you had so many times already asked for succour, and had deep anxiety for the state of the Soudan.

And (stating) that you had received no answer whatever, so that the people had become disgusted.

Also your telegram, dated August 28, 1884, stating that (as to) the Firmān emanating from the Khedive to all the nobles and notables and people of the Soudan, announcing the withdrawal of the troops of the Government from it, and their evacuation of the country, (and) leaving it to the Soudanese to appoint rulers of the country from among the natives,—you had not been able to communicate or to show it to anybody on account of what had taken place.

Also (we have seen) the two seals engraved with our name to imitate our seal.

We never miss any of your news, nor what is in your innermost thoughts, and about the strength and support—not of God—on which you rely. We have now understood it all.

Tricks in making ciphers, and using so many languages, are of no avail.

From the Most High God, to whom be praise, no secrets can be hidden.

As to your expecting reinforcements, reliance for succour on others than God, that will bring you nothing but destruction, and (cause you to) fall into utmost danger in this world and the next.

For God most High has dispersed sedition through our manifestation, and has vanquished the wicked and obstinate people, and has guided those who have understanding to the way of righteousness.

And there is no refuge but in God, and in obedience to His command, and that of His Prophet and of his Mahdi.

No doubt you have heard what has happened to your brethren, from whom you expected help, at Suakin and elsewhere, whom God has destroyed, and dispersed and abandoned.

Notwithstanding all this, as we have now arrived at Mushra' el Koweh', at a day's journey from Omdurman, and are coming, please God, to your place, if you return to the Most High God, and become a Moslem, and surrender to His order and that of His Prophet, and believe in us as the Mahdi, send us a message from thee, and from those with thee, after laying down your arms and giving up the thought of fighting, so that I may send you one with safe conduct, by which you will obtain (assurance of) benefit of the blessing in this world and the next. Otherwise, and if you do not act thus, you will have to encounter war from God and His Prophet. And know that the Most High God is mighty (able) for thy destruction, as He has destroyed (others) before thee, who were much stronger than thou, and more numerous.

And you, and your children and your property, will be for a prey to the Moslems, and you will repent when repentance will not avail. For, after the beginning of the battle were you to surrender, it would be from fear, and not willingly, and that will not be accepted.

And there is no succour or strength but in God, and peace be upon those who have followed the Guidance.[6]

Dated (Wednesday) 7th day 2nd of Moharram, 1302.
Oct. 22, 1884.

Postscript.—In one of your cipher telegrams sent to Bahhri and seized, you mention that the troops present in Bahr Gazelle and the Equator and elsewhere (number) 30,000 soldiers, whom you cannot leave behind, even though you should die.

And know that Bahr Gazelle and the Equator are both of them under our hand (power), and that both have followed us as Mahdi, and that they and their chief and all their officers are now among the auxiliaries of the Mahdi. And they have joined our lieutenant

[6] The word Mahdi signifies guide.

in that part, and letters from them are constantly coming and going without hindrance, or diminution of numbers.

And here inclosed are two letters of those which we have received from our agents (lieutenants) there. On seeing them thou wilt understand and know if Bahr Gazelle is (or not) in thy possession as thou thinkest, or whether it forms part and parcel of the Mahdi's dominions.

And for thy better information, and in our compassion for thee and the worshippers of God (with thee), we have thought of adding this postscript, and so that you should see clearly what to do, this postscript was necessary.

(Seal.) There is no God but (God) ALLAH.
Mahomed is the prophet of (God) ALLAH.
Mahomed the Mahdi (son of) ABD-ALLAH.
(Year) 1292.

[This Seal is square and very large. It is roughly engraved, and the inscription forms a triplet, each line ending with the name of God.

The letter is altogether written on one side of a very large sheet of paper.]

APPENDIX U *a*.

(ENCLOSURE IN U.)

Letter from Mohammed Sheikh Mohammed Kerkasâwi, to Achmet, Son of Suleiman.

In the name of God the Merciful and Compassionate. Praise be to God the Supreme Ruler, and blessing and peace upon our lord Mahomed and his successors with salutation.

From the Fakir of God, the humble and lowly, Mahomed Sheikh Mahomed Kerkasâwi to our brother and beloved in God, to

Achmed, son of Suleiman, Receiver General of the Treasury of the Moslems. May God preserve him. Amen!

After praying for the peace of God and His blessing and mercy upon you; if you inquire after me (I can say that) I am by God's help in possession of all the conditions of good health.

As to the information which we have to give you (it) is that on the arrival of the Emir Karm Illah Sheikh Mohammed in the parts of Bahr Gazelle and the neighbourhood of Sirkua, your servant had been appointed to the office of gathering in the crops; and we had not received news of his arrival, excepting from the letter which reached us from the Emir Abdullah,[7] surnamed Bilbitn, in which he asked my presence at the seat of the Mudiriyeh. On my arrival at the seat afore-named, I got to know positively about that, and after that I tried, with the Emir Abdullah, to obtain the consent and surrender (of the people there) without delay.

In the interval there came two dervishes from the Emir Karm Illah ; in their hands were several letters to us and to some of the brethren, and to the Emir Abdullah.

After these letters had been carefully read by us, the Emir Abdullah stopped the (carrying out of the) surrender to the Emir (Karm Illah), because no letter had been sent to him to his (own) address by his Highness.

So we and all the brethren used our utmost efforts with him, (urging) the desirableness of (his) sending a letter from him to the Emir Karm Illah, requesting him (the latter) to send (on) the letter of his Highness that it might be considered, and as to settling the mode of surrender And this was done. When the letter was written, I received it, and went with it in company of the two dervishes above-named, and with us went the Sheikh Wakîa' Allah Edrisi and Mahomed Sālim esh Shareef; and Haj Omar, all of them of the inhabitants of this seat (of the Mudiriyeh), they being appointed with me by order of the Emir Abdullah for bringing quickly the Proclamation written by H.E. the Mahdi.

On our arrival at (the place of) Karm Illah, and on his reading the letter of the said Emir (Abdullah), he ordered copy to be made of the Proclamation and gave it to me. Those appointed with me of the inhabitants of the seat (of the Mudiriyeh) also wrote a message as they remained with the Emir Karm Illah. On receiving the letter from the afore-named, I came back with it to the Emir Abdullah, who on reading it with intelligence, in the presence of the brethren, all of them became delighted and filled with happiness and joy which could not be exceeded.

Especially the Emir Abdullah obeyed and accepted (the terms of) the proclamation of his Highness; and so everything was settled with the help of God, the Lord to whom worship (is due).

All the brethren are longing to see his Highness, and so the letters were written from the Emir Abdullah and the brethren in the form of a deed (compact) of submission by them, and of obedience to the Emir Karm Illah, appointed by his Highness the Mahdi, which I took, and went to the town of Yānikah, the place where the afore-named Emir was encamped ; and I delivered it to him, and on his reading and understanding it, his countenance expressed joy thereat. And he wrote a letter to the Emir Abdullah, informing him of his being about to leave the town of Yānikah, and to come to the seat of the Mudiriyeh on Tuesday, the 25th of Jamād el Akhar, 1301, and he gave the safe conduct for

[7] Lupton Bey's assumed name.

all—for themselves, their families, and their property. And, praise be to God Most High, on the day named we and the Emir Karm Illah, and the troops with him, arrived at an hour's distance from the seat (of the Mudiriyeh). And the Emir Abdullah and all the notables and the brethren came to meet us outside of the wooden stockade surrounding the seat of the (Mudiriyeh). The meeting was like the meeting of dear friends with each other, and it was a memorable day for all that was accomplished therein, and for the filling up of (our joy).

On our entering the Mahhkameh (Court of Justice) of the Mudiriyeh, and on the friends and the Emirs being seated, the Emir Abdullah rose, and, standing upright, uttered the two declarations of testimony, saying, "I testify that there is no God but God; and I testify that our Lord Mohammed is the prophet of God, blessing be upon him, and that the (Seyyed[8]) Lord Mohammed, son of the Lord Abdullah, he (is) the Mahdi and Khalif of God and His prophet." Likewise (after this) the two Copts, Gabriel B'abal and Sālehh Shanooda, became Moslems, and uttered the two testimonies before the Emir Karm Illah (who received their profession of faith).

After which all (the property) which was in the stores of the Mudiriyeh, situated in the seat (thereof) and elsewhere, became the property of the Treasury of Islam, as stated in the letters of the Emir Karm Illah sent to his Highness.

And we pray God Most High, to whom be praise, that He may soon grant us the favour of a journey (Hejira) to the honoured place, that we may be blessed with sight of his Excellency the Mahdi, and that we may be included in the number of the warriors on the way (for the truth) of God.

I send from me to their Excellencies (the Hanifs) the nobles, and Emirs, and friends, and acquaintances who fight for God, thousands of salaams of God so long as I live.

(Signed) MOHAMMED SHAIKH MOHAMMED.

Written 17 Ramadan, 1301.
July 11, 1884.

[8] The term Seyyed (Lord) is given only to the reputed descendants (or a family) of Mohammed.

APPENDIX U *b*.

(ENCLOSURE IN U.)

In the name of God, the Merciful and Compassionate, &c.

From the servant of his Lord, the Fakir, Karam Illah, Sheikh Mohammed at Bahr el Gazelle to the relation of the Mahdi and Emir of the army of the Mahdi, the Khalif Abdallah Ben of the Seyyed Mohammed. May his glory be prolonged.

After paying our dutiful salutations and respectful compliments, if you enquire about us (we can say) all praise to the Most High, all is well, and I have the honour to announce to you we have captured a large number of (female) slaves as booty; and that about 1360 head of slaves have already been sent to Shakka,[9] including 200 slaves of Kanâwi (of) Alyoo, which family passes to the Moslem Treasury (*i.e.* their value); and this (was done) in three divisions the first time (under convoy of) the Fakir Ahhmed Mohammed, the Shakiyi; the second (party) which is considered the most numerous, (under convoy of) our brother Mohammed Sheikh Mohammed Karkasâwi, and the third under the convoy of the conductor Mohammed Salehh et Toom; (being) needed for buying (barter for) horses for use of our auxiliaries, with the knowledge of our brother Mohammed el Karkasâwi. And those which may be sent to your honour to the noble camp (*i.e.* the Mahdi's camp), will be also with his knowledge, as he has already been appointed from here for that purpose.

Also all the Fakirs, our auxiliaries, have been distributed in the different zerebas in order to collect the booty. And, please God, all that can be got will be sent to Shakka by degrees (as captured). And Mahomed Sheikh Mohammed Karkasâwi is my brother (son) of my father and mother—older than me, and he it is who helped us to take the town of Bahr Ghazel—and in consideration of his good management we have appointed him (to go) to Shakka to barter slaves for horses. And the slaves which may be sent to your Honour will be with his knowledge and by his instructions. And as the slaves taken as booty are exceedingly numerous in this part, and are continually arriving at the camp of the Mudir, we are much pressed in despatching them and in looking after them.

If it is agreeable to your Honour (please) to write to Sheikh Manzal Hamid, and the sons of Hamad Dodao, about their gratuitous assistance, and their surrendering the booty to our brother, Sheikh Mohammed Karkasâwi. We are at present awaiting the orders of your Excellency, (whether) to remain here or to come to

[9] Shakka is often pronounced Shagga.

you, or to wait for the drying up of the waters of the rain, out of compassion (in consideration for) the believers (the slaves) who have little infants.

And we pray the most high God, to whom be praise, to bring us soon together with your Excellency.

Salaam! (Signed) KARAM ILLAH MAHOMED.

Dated 22 Sha'abān, 1301.
June 17, 1884.

Postscript.—My Lord, after what I have stated to you, your servant awaits your orders; if your answer is that I should wait (here) or otherwise.

This is (all) that is needful (to write). Salaam.

APPENDIX U *d*.

(ENCLOSURE IN U.)

Copy of Telegram from his Excellency Gordon Pasha to his Excellency Ferratch Ullah Bey, Commandant of Omdurmān.

Sheikh Mahomed Achmed has sent us a letter to inform us that Lupton Bey, Mudir of Bahr Gazelle, has surrendered to him, and that the small steamer in which was Stewart Pasha has been captured by him, together with what was therein. And he demands that we should surrender to him.

But to me it is all one whether Lupton Bey has surrendered or has not surrendered. And whether he has captured twenty thousand steamers like the *Abbas*, or twenty thousand (officers) like Stewart Pasha (or not); it is all one to me.

I am here, like iron, and hope to see the newly arrived English; and if Mahomed Achmed says that the English die, it is all the same to me. And you must take a copy of this and give it to the messenger from Slātin, and send him out early in the morning, that he may go to him. It is impossible for me to have any more words with Mahomed Achmed, only lead; and if Mahomed Achmed is willing to fight he had better, instead of going to Omdurmān, go to the White Nile by the moat.

And after this the messengers whom he wants to send to us must not come by the Omdurmān; they had better come by the moat afore-mentioned. And send a literal copy of this, according to orders—when it has been sealed by you—by the emissary of Slātin Bey to be delivered, and explain to him that this is by our order.

At night.
3 of Moharram, 1302.
22nd October, 1884.

The forcible sentence: "I am here like iron, and I hope to see the newly-arrived English," runs as a rhymed couplet:—

"Wa ana mawjood hona zey el hhadeed
Wa ashoof el Ingleez el jadeed."

This *may* have been accidental on the part of the scribe, for the letter is written in Arabic, but it is worth notice. The phraseology, and even the words, are General Gordon's own—as he wrote in a former letter that he chose his own words by help of his dictionary, and did not suffer his scribes to write only as they pleased.

SUPPOSED ENCLOSURE IN MAHDI'S LETTER.

Intercepted communication from General Gordon to the Mudir of Dongola.

Note (in Arabic) from General Gordon to the Mudir of Dongola.

To His Excellency the Mudir of Dongola.

Wire the telegram enclosed herein to Cairo from the station at Dongola, and charge the expense to account of the Mudiriyeh (Government account).

(Signed) C. G. GORDON (*across the seal*).

Dated 7 Zu'l Hejjeh.
Sept. 28, 1884.
Gordon Pasha.

Written on a small piece of thin paper 4 by 4½ inches.

Au Consulat Général d'Autriche-Hongrie à Caire.

Kartoum, 21 September, 1884.

To-day was a joyful Sunday! The inhabitants of the city were stirred with joy when the salvoes of artillery announced from the fort the approach of the English relieving army.

Three express messengers brought to General Gordon an autograph letter from Lord Wolseley from Debbe. Rescue after all! Long live England!

Now at least the lives of (so many) these thousands will be saved, even though goods and chattels be lost.

Yesterday the news had been already orally spread of an army approaching from Dongola, but found no credence, any more than many other false rumours. It was also said that the first messenger who left on the 9th for Dongola had passed Berber without hindrance, and will probably reach Cairo in safety.

Further, I was able, on the 13th, to speak outside the city lines with Georgio Calamatino, the letter-carrier of the Mahdi. He was in dervish dress. I sent the missionaries 100 dollars by him. The Mahdi was then in Schatt, four hours from Duem, with all the European prisoners, and among them Slatin, who were enrolled as dervishes in the armoury. (*Secret:* the missionaries of both sexes have accepted [the religion of] Islam. The six sisters are married to Greeks; only the superior, Don Luigi Bonomi, remained steadfast, but he is condemned to martyrdom unless he also apostasizes).

It is to be hoped that soon after the arrival of the English we may or must remove (emigrate). No one knows whether they will permanently occupy the country or only effect the complete evacuation.

With respect and devotion,

(Signed) M. L. HANSALL,
Consulate General of Austro-Hungary, Cairo.

Also written on a small piece of thin paper.

Note (in Arabic) from General Gordon to the Mudir of Dongola.

To His Excellency the Mudir of Dongola.

Take from bearer Mohammed Achmet, on his safe arrival, the telegrams sent by him, and forward them to their destination, and give him fifty dollars; and if you have any telegrams for us send them by him that he may bring them here.

(Signed) GORDON.
C. G. GORDON (*written in pencil across the seal*).

Dated 15 Shawwāl, 1301.
Aug. 8, 1884.
Gordon Pasha in Kartoum.

Written on a small piece of thin paper 4 inches by 3.

APPENDIX V.

MANIFESTO OF THE MAHDI TO THE INHABITANTS OF KARTOUM.

In the year 1300.

In the name of God, the Merciful and Compassionate.

Praise be to God, the bountiful Ruler, and blessing on our Lord Mahomed and his successors, with peace.

From the servant of his Lord, Mahomed the Mahdi, son of the Seyyed Abdallah, to his beloved in God the believers in God, and in His Book (the Koran).

The changes (disturbances) of the times are not hidden from you, nor the forsaking of the Sunnas; and he who has the (true) faith and understanding will not be pleased thereat, but will leave all he needs and his native place (house and home) in defence of religion and the Sunnas; and therefore jealousy for Islam will not delay to possess in full strength (the heart of) the believer.

Now, O my beloved! as to what the Most High God, to whom be praise, has willed in His Eternity and in His decrees to grant to His servant, the humble and lowly, in (bestowing on him) the great Khalifate :—

The eminent Lord (Mahomed), on whom be blessing and peace, several times informed me that I am the Mahdi, the Expected One, and (appointed) me (as) successor [10] to himself, on whom be blessing and peace, to sit on his throne, and (as successors) to their Excellencies the four Khalifs and Princes [11] (of the Faith), and to El Khudr,[12] on whom be peace: And God gave as my helpers, the angels (who are), the Cherubim, and the saints from Adam to this our day, and also the believing Jinns; [13] and in the hour of battle the eminent Lord, the Bountiful One, on Whom be blessing and peace, will in person go with them before my hosts, as also the four Khalifs and the Princes (of the faith), and El Khudr, on whom be peace.

And He gave me the sword of victory of his Excellency (Mahomed), on whom be blessing and peace; and it was made known to me that none of either race, human or Jinn, can conquer him who has it.

Then said he, on whom be blessing and peace, "God has given to thee a sign that thou art the Mahdi"; which (sign) is the mole on my right cheek; and he likewise gave to me another sign (namely, that) there should go forth before me in the hour of battle a banner of light, borne by Azraïl,[14] on whom be peace, that by it God should convince my friends, and terror should fall upon the hearts of my enemies, and (that) God will destroy whoever should encounter me in hostility.

Then he, on whom be blessing and peace, said to me: "Thou are created out of the effulgence of my innermost heart," and he to whom happiness (is granted) will believe I am the Mahdi, the Expected One. But God has put hypocrisy (wickedness) into the

[10] The word here used is the one from which Khalif is derived.

[11] This word primarily means the pole or axis of the Universe, &c.

[12] The saint who is supposed to be immortal, and to have appeared first as Elijah and afterwards as St. George.

[13] The Mahommedans divide the Jinns (or demons) into believers in Mahommed and unbelievers.

[14] The Angel of Death.

heart of those who love vain pomp, and they will not believe being greedy of their vain pomps.

Then he, on whom be blessing and peace, said : Love of wealth and pomps cause hypocrisy to spring up in the heart as water causes the herb to spring up ; and it is found in the Athar (traditional sayings about Mahomed) : If you see worldlings loving this world, charge them with it. And it is found in some of the ancient books (saying) : Do not ask of me a world intoxicated with love of earthly things, for it will close against thee the way of my love. And these (are they who like brigands) stop the way of (true) service (of God).

And when there came to me, O my beloved, from God and His prophet the decree of the great Khalifate, He ordered me (to take my) Hegira[15] (flight) to Jebel Kadeer close by Masāt, and He commanded me to write thence to all entrusted with public offices. I wrote thus to the Emirs and Sheikhs of religion, and the wicked denied (my mission), but the righteous believed ; even those who do not mind any hardship they may encounter for God, nor what they fail to attain of their dearest wishes ; but steadfastly regard the promises of the most High God, to Whom be praise, in which He said that He will reserve that other world for those who do not desire exaltation in this world, nor (its) corruptions. Now since it is for God to decree, and since He was willed to bestow the office of Mahdi upon His humble and insignificant servant Mahomed the Mahdi, the son of the Seyyed Abdallah, it behoves us to submit to the will of God ; and, seeing that it is unanimously agreed by the present and past generations to attribute supreme knowledge to God, and as His knowledge, to Whom be praise, is not limited by control of rules nor by the knowledge of the malevolent, and since God will blot out (abrogate) or establish what He wills, and since He is the source of the Book (the Koran), of which none can understand anything save what He wills, and since with Him is the key of the unknown (future),—none knows it but He, nor is He to be questioned as to what He does,—He creates what He will,—He chooses and bestows His mercy on whom He will. Sheikh Mohi ed Deen Ibn el Arabi especially says in his commentary on the glorious Koran that knowledge of the Mahdi is like knowledge of the hour (of resurrection), and that hour none knoweth but God most High. And Sheikh Ahmed Ibn Edrees said, Fourteen generations of the generations of the people of God have denied the (coming of the) Mahdi. Then he said : He will come forth from a place that they do not know and in a condition which they will disown.

It is not hidden from your knowledge that the writings about the (coming of the) Mahdi are among others the Athar and the Keshef el Ulema and others ; and the conclusion of them all (is), and I understand from them, that God will blot out (abrogate) what

[15] This Hegira is an evident imitation of the Flight of Mahommed.

passages He will, and some of these are the Hadiths (traditional sayings), and among them Ed Dha'eef and El Maktooa' and El Mansookh and El Mowdhooa.' The Hadith Ed Dha'eef is superseded by the Hadith El Saheehh word for word. The Ayat also are replaced by other Ayat.[16] And the truth as to this is not known save to people of deep thought and insight.

Futher, this is what the eminent Lord (Mahomed), on whom be blessing and peace, said to me, "He who doubts that thou art the Mahdi has blasphemed God and His prophet." This he, blessing and peace be upon him, declared to me thrice.

All that I have told you about my succession to the office of Mahdi was told to me by the eminent Lord (Mahommed), on whom be blessing and peace, when I was awake and in perfect health, free from all transgressions of the law, not in sleep nor in (a state of) hallucination, or drunkenness or madness, but accounted to be of sound mind, following the traditions of the prophet, on whom be blessing and peace, in ordering what he ordered and forbidding what he forbade.

And my Hegira (flight) to the aforesaid places was necessary, according to the Book (the Koran) and to the Sunnas. The Most High God has said, "Those who have had to flee (make a Hegira) for the sake of God after having been persecuted; He will give them good things in this world, and the reward in the next will be greater. And He, on whom is blessing and peace, said, "One who has fled from land to land, even though it be but a handbreadth of land, has deserved Paradise, and has become (in so doing) a partaker with[17] Abraham, the friend of God and of Mahomed, on whom be blessing and peace."

Thus also in other passages of the Hadiths.

And the duty of listening to God and His prophet is binding. The Most High God has said, "Follow the way of those who are sincere to Me."

If you have understood this, we order all the chosen ones to flee (make their Hegira) unto us for the Jehād (holy war) in the cause of God, to the nearest town, because God Most High has said, "Slay the infidels who are nearest to you"; and he who holds back from this has come within the threat uttered by the Most High. Say if your fathers, your sons, your brethren, your wives, your tribes, the wealth you have gained, the merchandise you are in fear of losing, or the dwellings you delight in are dearer to you than God and His prophet and the Jehād (holy war) in His cause, then wait till God shall come with His sentence (against you). (So far) the Aya (verse).

The Most High has also said, "O you who have believed, why do you cleave to the earth when called upon to fly (to the war)

[16] Verses; usually applied to verses of the Koran.

[17] Inasmuch as Abraham, the Friend of God, was a pilgrim who left his land and his father's house by Divine command to escape the idolators.

for God? Do you love the life of this world better than that of the next? But the possessions of this world will be less than nothing in the other world."

The Most High has also said, "O you who have believed, why do you cleave to the earth when called upon to fly (to the war) for God? Do you love the life of this world better than that of the next? But the possessions of this world will be less than nothing in the other world."[18]

He has also said, "Seek not to fly." He will torment you with eternal torments, and will accept others in your place.

Now, if you have understood the foregoing, hasten to us, and fear none save God, for fear of the creature shows lack of trust and confidence in God, from which may God preserve (us).

The Most High has said, "Fear ye not man, but fear ye Me"; and the Most High has said, "Dread them not, but dread Me, if ye be believers."

The Most High has said, "God is worthy to be feared"; and especially because God has promised in his precious Book (the Koran) victory to him who contends for the faith.

The Most High has said, "If you fight for God, He will fight for you and establish your goings."

And the Most High has said, "If you do not fight for him (the Mahdi) God fighteth for him." Because you have known this, if you do not respond to him who calls (in the name) of God and hasten to fight for the faith, you must receive punishment from God, inasmuch as you are the light of creation, its strength, and its head.

Whoever among you is anxious about his faith and zealous for the command of his Lord will answer the call, and will join with those that fight for the religion of God.

Be it known unto you that I am of the family of the prophet of God, on whom be blessing and peace. My father is a Hhusni on his father's side; and his mother, and my mother likewise, on the side of both father and mother (are) Abbāssides, and God knows that I am of the blood of Hussein, and these excellent indications will suffice for him who has been touched by His grace and (by) the faith.

It will not be wonderful if some do see and do not believe it.

Fear God and join the righteous, and help one another in righteousness, and in the fear of God and in the Jehād (holy war) in the cause of God, and stand firm within the boundaries of God, for he who transgresses those boundaries will injure himself.

Know that all things are in the hand of God. Leave all to Him and rely on Him. He who makes God his support has been guided into the straight way.

Peace (be with you).

[18] This paragraph is thus repeated in the original.

In the year 1300.

In the name of God, the Merciful, the Compassionate. Praise be to God, the Bountiful Ruler, and blessing and blessing and peace on our Lord Mahomed and his successors.

From the slave of his Lord, the Imām Mahomed the Mahdi, the son of the Seyyed Abdallah, to all his beloved in God the believers, men and women, in God and in His Book.

What I have to inform you is that the world is the abode of him who has no (other) abode, and it is a prison to believers, and that the other (world) is better, and (is) enduring, and that is the abode of those who fear God.

Fear God and do . . . . .

This Manifesto is written on four sides of a two-leaved sheet of paper, and breaks off abruptly, "and do" being written at bottom as catch-word for the next page.

Specially to be noticed is the attempt made to forestall the objections of those who would see that this man contradicts well known passages in the writings which Moslems hold to be authoritative. Mahomed Achmet boldly declares all such passages to be either abrogated or superseded, or unintelligible save to those to whom deep thought and insight are given!

APPENDIX X.

Letter from Major Kitchener to General Gordon.

DEBBEH, 14th October, 1884.

MY DEAR GENERAL GORDON,

Please inform me by this present messenger, who is paid to return, who were on board the steamer that came down from Kartoum. I am sorry to say, whoever they were, they have fallen into the hands of Suleiman Wady Goun, Sheikh of the Minassir, and have, I am afraid, been killed. Lord Wolseley is now at Wady Halfa, and it is expected this expedition will definitely start from Dongola on or about the 1st November. Special boats are coming out from England for the passage up the Nile.

There are a considerable number of troops now at Dongola. I am instructed by Sir Evelyn Baring to send you the following telegram from the Austrian Consul-General :—

"Caire, 1er Oct.—Je vous remercie, de tout cœur, des nouvelles que vous avez bien voulu me donner. J'ai fait des démarches pour faciliter le voyage de notre consul de Berber jusqu'au Caire, mais on m'assure que les chemins de Berber à Debbeh ne sont pas libres ; en tous cas, je vous recommande chaudement la sécurité personnelle de notre consul et des sujets Austro-Hongrois et Allemands. Je serai très heureux d'avoir des nouvelles directes de Monsieur Hansall."

I also enclose two letters[1] that have arrived here for you.

I hope you have received some of my previous letters; I have received none from you in reply.

ENCLOSURE IN APPENDIX X.

GENERAL,

I hope you will excuse me such an intermezzo.

Notwithstanding they abandoned you, and they did not at all follow your instructions, I hope you will be victorious, and your name engraved in the history of the world.

I am, dear General,
Your most obedient servant,
TH. ROTH.

To his Excellency General Gordon, Kartoum.

Berlin, 4th May, 1884.

DEAR SIR,

I had the honour to write you on the 10th of April, &c.

Meantime I permitted me to do the following:

On the 22nd of April I wired to Earl Granville: "For Heaven's sake, help Gordon, Kartoum."

And confirmed this despatch with the following letter:—

To the Right Honourable Lord Granville, London.

Berlin, 22nd April, 1884.

"MY LORD,

"I have the honour to confirm my telegram of this afternoon: 'For Heaven's sake, help Gordon, Kartoum.'

"Your Lordship may be kind enough to excuse such a telegram.

"As I am an admirer of Gordon, and as he had the kindness to do his best to become liberated my brother Gottfried Roth, who is said prisoner of the Mahdi, and to whom your Lordship congratulated when he captured at Sint a band of slaveholders with several hundred slaves some years ago, I considered it a duty to do something too for Gordon. And so the idea to wire to your Lordship, who perhaps may be able in consequence of your powerful position to let have Gordon what he wants.

"I have the honour, &c., &c."

I had the pleasure to receive the following letter from the Secretary of State, Sir J. Pauncefote:—

[1] For one of these, see Roth's letter.

Foreign Office, 29th April, 1884.

"SIR,

"I am directed by Earl Granville to acknowledge the receipt of your telegram and letter of the 22nd instant, urging that assistance may be given to General Gordon at Khartoum.

"I am, Sir,
"Your most obedient humble servant,
(Signed) "J. PAUNCEFOTE."

Roth did not get much change out of his Lordship ! !
(C. G. GORDON).

APPENDIX X[1].

Arabic Cipher Telegram.

Above message from Lord Wolseley, dated 20 September forwarded by messenger for second time, 15/10/84, from Debbeh.

H. H. KITCHENER.
D.A.A.G.

This is the only paper received.

C. G. G.

APPENDICES TO BOOK VI.

APPENDIX Y.

From the Khedive of Egypt.

To His Excellency Gordon Pasha, the Honourable.

(Literally "to His Felicity ! . . .—the excellent," which is the usual formula.)

As it is known to you that the object of the coming of your Excellency to this part, and of your going to the Soudan, is only the evacuation of that neighbourhood and the withdrawal of our troops, now found there, with the Government officials of the realm, and the bringing hither of those inhabitants of that part who may desire to come together with their belongings, we trust that your Excellency will take every care in the fulfilment of this Commission by employing the best means and arrangements which may be necessary for the safety of those troops and *employés*, and inhabitants and merchants, both native and foreign, who may desire to come to this part.

Then, after completion of this (business), you will adopt the necessary means and arrangements indispensable for framing a firm government in the Soudan provinces, that there may be continuance of order in that part, and that there may be security from the misfortunes (which must befall) the ignorant populace (left) without a ruler. And I rely on your understanding and courage, to which is intrusted the carrying out of this commission in the manner desired.

(Sealed) MOHAMMED TEWFIK.

January 27, 1884.

(Seal of Mahomet Towfik).

From the Khedive of Egypt and its dependencies to all the Ulema, Judges, Notables, Sheikhs of Arabs of villages, Merchants, and all inhabitants, both Arabs and domesticated people in the Soudan countries, greeting.

It is known to all that when my grandfather JANTIMGAN MAHOMED ALI took the reigns of Government of the Lands of Egypt, he began to spread knowledge and education and enlarge the sphere of agriculture and commerce throughout the same, and increase the means of wealth of the inhabitants, until Egypt was considered a well-cultivated and civilised country. After that he saw the necessity of taking up (or opening up) the Soudan Region, to spread out the lights of civilisation therein—and God Almighty prospered him in that enterprise. From that time until now these regions have not ceased to grow in prosperity, until towns and market cities were established and enlarged, and commerce grew, and the inhabitants became enlightened by the means of commerce and agriculture. By a comparison of the condition of the Soudan Regions before these conquests, with their condition after it, it will clearly appear that they progressed and advanced greatly during the latter time. The minds of the people were enlightened by seeing their own interest and prosperity. This was the only purpose which moved our grandfather aforesaid to take these regions. But the great distance that lies between me and you caused a disintegration which had for its result the rising and rebelling of some disturbers against my Government. This rebellion caused great losses of money and men without any fruits at all; and the Land of Egypt sustained thereby very heavy burdens. Therefore I have concluded to give back again independence to the ancient families of the Kings of the Soudan Regions. And, as I know that His Excellency Gordon Pasha, during his stay among you, seeing that you witnessed the good results of his efforts for the quiet and prosperity of the country. Therefore, and also because he is deemed an able man of politics and of your judgment, and desirous of your welfare, We have appointed him to proceed to those regions as our representative, with full authority to agree with in establishing a peaceable and amicable way of withdrawing from those parts, and bringing away the officials of my Government and the troops with their belongings and the property of my Government, so that the departure from you may be brought about in perfect security. I therefore ask of all who bear arms to throw the same away, and to endeavour, with all diligence and quiet and peacefulness, to form their own Government of the future within my boundaries, and to work for the prosperity of their countries, and the security of the roads at all times; so that between us and them the bonds of communication shall continue to exist and so that commerce shall be rendered easy, which is conducive to wealth, and so that civilization and luxury may be furthered. And thus the bonds of friendship may be kept up, as is dictated by the laws of humanity.

Written on the 28th day of Rabia the First, 1301.
(January 26th, 1884).

NOTICE PUBLISHED BY GORDON.

Formerly the Government had decided to transport the Egyptians down to Cairo, and abandon the Soudan: and in fact some of them had been sent down during the time of Hussein Pasha Yusri, as you yourselves saw. On our arrival at Kartoum, we, on account of pity for you, and in order not to let your country be destroyed, we communicated with the Khedive of Egypt, our Effendi, concerning the importance and the inexpediency of abandoning it. Whereupon, the orders for abandoning the Soudan were cancelled ; and serious attention was turned, and all energy was directed towards smothering the disturbances and driving away the disturbers : therefore sufficient troops were appointed, both cavalry and infantry, some time ago ; and indeed they have reached Dongola and started in three divisions, one under the leader of the army and the Mudir of Dongola is coming on to Berber : the second division has the Sheikh of the Hawaweer, and is coming by way of Hobaji : the third division, with Sheikh Saleh, son of Salim, Sheikh of the Kababeesh, is coming to Metemma. Each one of these divisions is alone sufficient to oppose all the rebels. They will soon be in Kartoum. We shall increase in defence of the Soudan until the arrival of the troops here, as is the will of the Khedive's iradé issued to us on the 14th September, 1884. The Ulema and teachers of Kartoum had presented a telegram to the Khedive asking for reinforcements—now an iradé of the Khedive has been issued to them, a copy of which is given here above. Be therefore fully reassured as to yourselves and your families, and all your possessions in your houses, taking no heed of what has occurred in the past. If God will in the next few days the siege will be raised, and your alarm will pass away. Know also that if Mohammed Achmet should call upon me for three years to surrender Kartoum I will not listen to him, but will protect your lives and families and possessions with all energy and steadfastness.

(Signed) GORDON PASHA.

APPENDIX AB.

Translation of a letter addressed to General Gordon by the Khalifa Abdulla Mahommed, 10/12/84.

In the name of God the Merciful, the Compassionate. Praise be to the Bountiful God, and blessings be upon our Lord Mahomed and upon his family.

We, the servant of God ABDALLAH MOHAMMED JIFARAH, one of the governors of the Mahdi, on whom be peace, on the East, to Gordon, the Pasha of KARTOUM. You have paid no attention to the counsel and reasoning repeatedly sent to you, but have increased in folly ; and the numerous kindly admonitions have only made you more haughty and wayward ; because truth enlightens the breasts of believers and only increases the oppressors in their degenerations. Your letter has reached us, in which you deceived the population, saying that the British reinforcement is coming to you in three divisions, and that it will soon reach you and give you victory; thus your letter betrays the greatness of your fear, and anxiety, and alarm, as in your deceit you have caught hold of spider-web ropes and have feared to die at our hands; thou must inevitably die, O thou heathen! These promises you have been holding them out since last year to the inhabitants of KARTOUM, and have been promising them that the English will come soon. Your promise has only increased their sorrows; and now that you are in straits, and that evil is coming upon you, you are practising deceit from the interior of your den (*sic*) in which God has imprisoned you, upon him who is in the land of peace and crowned with exceeding much honour, and who is able to get the news of riders arriving from the remotest regions. I ask, do the sounds, winged and free, unfettered, need news from the like of thee in the sea of billows covered by waves upon wave, above which are clouds of darkness piled one over the other? Know thou, O thou enemy of God, that the true news is with us and not with you, and that the news which has reached us contains nothing to cheer thy eye or uphold thy power; on the contrary, there is no escape for thee from death at our hands, and from death by lack of food. But it is no wonder that you deny the Mahdiship, for you did not believe in the Apostleship of Mahomed; but the wonder is that the learned men of wickedness, who are raised to prominent positions by you, and whom God has left to go astray, and whose hearts He has closed, whose ears He has sealed, and over whose eyes He has put a veil, since they have been satisfied with you as a leader, and have taken you as a teacher, and have waged war against Believers, and seek victory to those who believe in more than one God, as though they had not heard the word of God. "If you wage war, war will come upon you, and if you end war it is better for you, and if you return He will return, and God is with the Believers." Do you not know, O you wicked learned men, that he who secedes from the Commonwealth has slipped away from the Faith, just as a hair is drawn out from the lump of dough? If you, by reason of your love of office and by reason of your association with darkness, are in doubt as to this Imàm, are you also in doubt as to the Apostleship of Mahommed, on whom be peace and blessings, that you followed his enemies the evil unbelievers, and have made your rulers in preference to the sons of Islam and desire them to be victorious? Have you not heard the word of God which says, "O ye who have believed, take not my enemy and your enemy to be rulers, nor bestow on them your affection, and I know what you have hidden and what you have made known; and he among you who does this has strayed away to the wrong path"? God also says, "O ye who have believed, do not take your fathers and your brothers to be your chiefs if they prefer unbelief to faith." God also says, "You will not find a people who believes in God and in the Last Day that will befriend those who stray from God and the Prophet, even though they be their fathers, brothers, or relations." But you,

you have taken the Christians to be your rulers when you have no doubt as to their heathenism. Look therefore to yourselves after these quotations; do you consider it to be counted of the company of Believers? (*sic*). It is strange how you frighten the people, saying the English are coming, and how you think that the Allies will be affected by your false rumours. No, by God! even though swarms of English and others should come, th. would only increase the faith of the Allies, and their steadfastness would grow in the labour of the siege until God shall make you taste confusion and destruction. Take warning by those who are like you if you are children of intelligence. Before you the people of Obeid were longing for reinforcements like the longing of the thirsty for water; and they too were writing deceitful and cheering letters, more than you have done; and, nevertheless, you have heard what befel them.

If you are content to remain as you are, then prepare for what shall come: but if you knock at the door of repentance, peradventure it may be opened unto you.

Peace be upon those who follow after the right way.

(Signed) ABDULLAH MAHOMMED.

19 S. 1302.
7th or 8th December, 1884.

APPENDIX CD.

Telegraphic Petition from the Ulema and officials of KARTOUM to the Khedive.

We make bold to present our humble thanks to our Sovereign the Khedive. The enemy drew near to KARTOUM and besieged it, and our lives were in our throats, and we had no more patience, and words cannot describe our miserable condition. Then the Governor-Generalship was conferred upon H. E. GORDON Pasha, and on his arrival he bestowed all kinds of favours and conceded all that had been demanded, and took all precautions and brought order out of chaos. And although KARTOUM was attacked on all four sides by musketry and cannon, the Governor-General watched day and night; and when the Nile rose he sent out the victorious soldiers who were victorious over the enemy, and we hope the victory will be soon complete. KARTOUM is fortified like an impregnable rock.

We pray God to give long life to H.H. the Khedive, and to remove our present disturbances.

Copy of the Khedive's Iradé sent in cipher to all the Ulema and Teachers, and to the Cadi and all military officers and civil officials in KARTOUM, dated September 21st, 1884.

Your telegram, dated 27th Shamal, 1301 (19th August, 1884), was received on the first day of Dhee-l-Hijjah, 1301 (September 20th, 1884). We regret the condition you are in by reason of the impossibility of sending you reinforcements, and help up till now on account of circumstances. But we are very glad because you are still safe, and the city is kept by your energy and bravery. If God will, reinforcements will soon reach you, and you shall be rewarded. We hope you will exercise all diligence in upholding the honour of Government. The difficulties are being overcome and the time of relief is at hand by the Grace of God.

APPENDIX EF.

ORGANISATION OF THE SOUDAN.

1. His Excellency, El Zubair Pasha, shall be the Governor (or Ruler) of the Soudan; he shall have the rank of Fareek and the Osmaniah decoration. His pay shall be £6000 per annum, *i.e.* £500 per month.

2. He shall be free to appoint and discharge the Mudirs and Wakeels, and all other officials and employés of his own motion, and make regulations for the employés necessary for the administrative and military work in every region in each mudirieh and in the central town, and for the finances and arsenal, etc.; and also regulations fixing the taxes and all the revenues and expenses needed yearly.

3. He is permitted to give military and civil grades up to the grade of Mir-Alâi, and shall refer to the Khedive's cabinet in Cairo asking for the brevets (or commissions), but above that grade he must refer to the Khedive of Egypt.

4. The boundaries of the Soudan on the north shall be at Handak, one of the Dongola regions: and the Soudan regions shall be by Mudirieh as follows: Dongola: whose boundary shall be Handak as aforesaid: and Berber and Kartoum: the extreme boundary of which shall be Donaim and Sennaar up to Faiz-Aghlon, Godareep, Gallabat, Kassala and Suakin. As for Massowa and Senheit, they shall not belong to the Soudan Government. The regions of Fashoda, the Equator and Bahr-Gazelle, shall be left (or abandoned) and the employés withdrawn from them.

5. The Egyptian Government now pays towards the Soudan expenses, £250,000; it shall further send a like sum for two more years.

6. The customs duties taken upon goods coming up and going down by way of Suakin shall be the same as before, and shall enter into the Soudan revenues. Also, goods coming to Suakin while passing Suez shall be paid at Suakin; but goods going from or

coming to the Soudan by Handak, the boundary of the Soudan, shall pay no duty and shall remain as formerly.

7. All warlike stores and all ammunition and arsenal stores, and baggage of soldiers that shall be needed, shall be asked for from the Egyptian Government, and shall be sent to the Soudan. The value of the same shall not be included in the sum of money fixed to be supplied by Egypt to the Soudan.

8. The military stores and soldiers' baggage, and apparatus for boats and steamers now in the Soudan, shall remain in it.

9. The boats and steamers which are in the Soudan and which are brought up with the English shall be left for the use of the Soudan.

10. Stations for steamers must be erected from Handak to Kartoum: each station shall have a fort and earthworks and that which is necessary for transport; but the stations from Handak northwards shall belong to the Egyptian Government.

11. The British troops must help in carrying on the war until the central town is passed and the siege raised from Kartoum and Sennaar: after which, under direction of the Ruler of the Soudan, that shall be done which will quell the disturbance.

12. His Excellency El Zubair Pasha shall undertake to capture Mohammed Achmed, the would-be Mahdi, and bring the captives that are with him, both Europeans and others, for the execution of which His said Excellency shall receive £30,000.

13. Trade in slaves shall be stopped, and the lines to be followed herein shall be the Convention of 1877 between England and Egypt.

14. The monopoly and contract of roads in the Soudan and the Atmoor (desert) shall be wholly denied to Hussein-Khalifa, his family, and relations.

15. The Soudan Government must pay the losses sustained by the family of Seyd Mahomet Osman during the disturbances.

INDEX

TO THE

JOURNAL AND APPENDICES.

A.

B.

C.

D.

E.

F.

G.

H.

I.

J.

K.

L.

M.

N.

O.

P.

T.